AF607858

Essays in Speech Processes

Essays in Speech Processes

Language Production and Perception

Edited by
Augustine Agwuele and Andrew Lotto

SHEFFIELD UK BRISTOL CT

Published by Equinox Publishing Ltd.

UK: Office 415, The Workstation, 15 Paternoster Row, Sheffield, South Yorkshire S1 2BX
USA: ISD, 70 Enterprise Drive, Bristol, CT 06010

www.equinoxpub.com

First published 2016

British Library Cataloguing-in-Publication Data

A catalogue record for this book is available from the British Library.

ISBN-13 978 1 78179 182 0 (hardback)

Library of Congress Cataloging-in-Publication Data
Essays in speech processes: language production and perception / edited by Augustine Agwuele and Andrew Lotto.
pages cm
Includes bibliographical references and index.
ISBN 978-1-78179-182-0 (hb)
1. Speech acts (Linguistics) 2. Oral communication. 3. Language awareness.
4. Biolinguistics. I. Agwuele, Augustine, editor. II. Lotto, Andrew, editor.
P95.55.E77 2015
306.44—dc23
2015010617

Typeset by S.J.I. Services, New Delhi
Printed and bound by Lightning Source Inc. (La Vergne, TN), Lightning Source UK Ltd. (Milton Keynes), Lightning Source AU Pty. (Scoresby, Victoria)

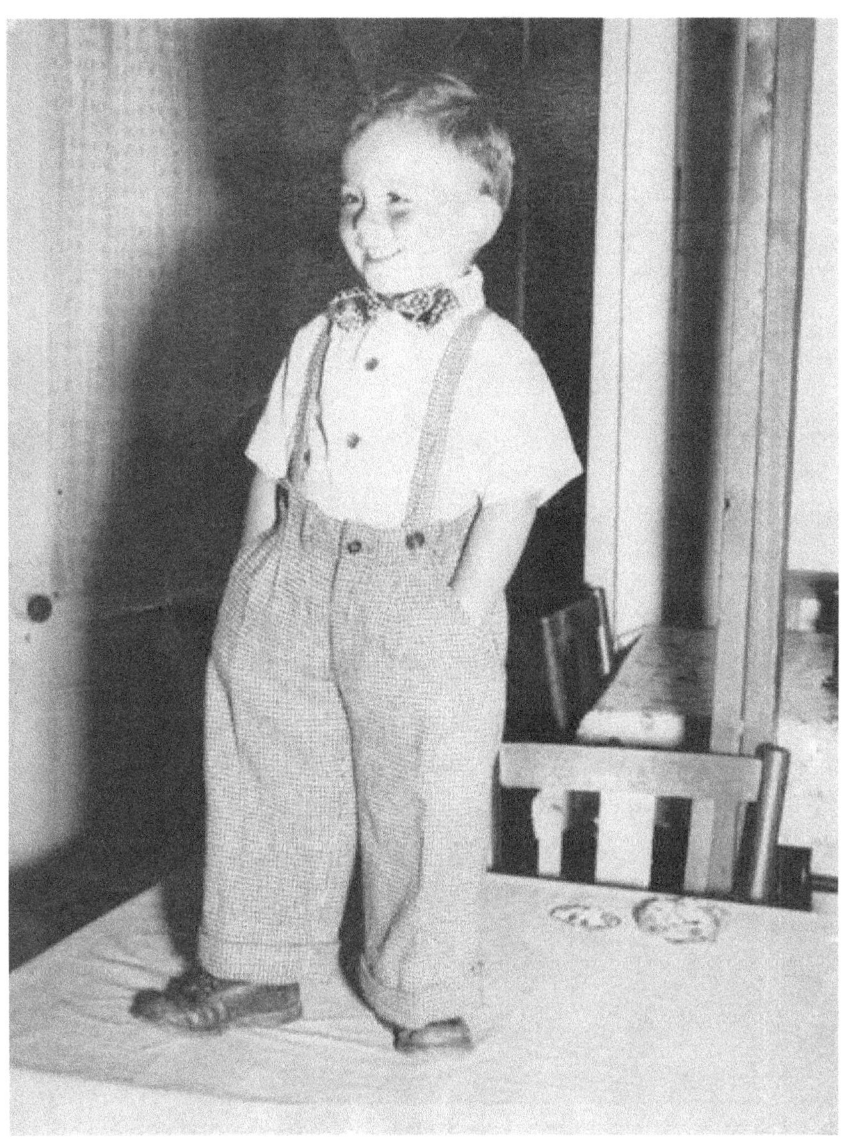

Harvey at the height of his cuteness, circa 1947.

Contents

Harvey M. Sussman: Curriculum Vitae

EDUCATION

University of Wisconsin (Madison), PhD, 1970
University of Wisconsin (Madison), MS, 1967
Queens College (CUNY), BA, 1965

ACADEMIC HONORS AND AWARDS

Phi Beta Kappa; Psi Chi Honorary Society
NSF Post-doctoral Fellowship (1970)
College of Liberal Arts Undergraduate Teaching Award, University of Texas, 1979
Journal of Speech and Hearing Research, Editors Award, Outstanding Article, 1981
President's Associates Teaching Excellence Award, University of Texas, 1987
College of Communication Research Award, University of Texas, 1986–7
College of Communication Research Award, University of Texas, 1989–90
College of Communication Research Award, University of Texas, 1999–2000
R.P. Doherty Sr. Centennial Professorship in Communication, September 1988
College of Communication Teaching Excellence Award, University of Texas, May 1997
Fellow, Acoustical Society of America, June 1998
The Academy of Distinguished Teachers, University of Texas, 2001
UT/NSSHLA "Professor of the Year" award, 2005; 2006

AREAS OF SPECIALIZATION

Cognitive Neuroscience:
Neurobiology of language representation in the brain; cerebral dominance; language neuropathology; neural representation of phonological categories

Speech Science/Experimental Phonetics:
Physiological, neuromuscular and acoustic aspects of speech production and speech perception; coarticulation; non-invariance dilemma; stuttering

RELEVANT WORK AND RESEARCH EXPERIENCE

University of Texas at Austin
R.P. Doherty Sr. Centennial Professorship, Fall 1988–present
Professor (Linguistics & Speech Communication), Fall 1980
Associate Professor, September 1975–August 1980
Assistant Professor, September 1971–August 1975

University of Wisconsin (Madison)
Research Assistant, Behavioral Cybernetics Lab, September 1965–June 1969
Department of Psychology

RESEARCH GRANTS

1. National Institute of Neurological Diseases & Stroke
   "Dynamic Properties of Speech Sensorimotor Systems," June 1974–June 1976, $60,455
2. Spencer Seed Grant
   September 1, 1974–August 31, 1975, $4900
3. Three-year continuation of NINDS (NIH) grant (#1 above)
   "Dynamic Properties of Speech Sensorimotor Systems," September 11, 1976–July 31, 1979, $170,635

4. National Institute of Health: Co-investigator with Dr MacNeilage and Dr Marquardt
   "Control of Movement in Speech Apraxia," July 1, 1979–June 30, 1982, $74,368 for 1st budgeted year
5. National Science Foundation, BNS–8919221
   "An Investigation of Locus Equations as a Source of Relational Invariance in Speech Perception," February 1, 1990–January 31, 1992, $62,463
6. National Institute of Health, R01 DC02014
   "A Locus Equation Approach to Relational Invariance," June 1994–May 1998, $271, 944
7. National Insitute of Health, R01 DC02014-07
   "Modeling coarticulation: An integrated phonetic approach," four years total costs amounting to $1,125,150

PROFESSIONAL ACTIVITIES

Editorial Reviewer

Journal of Speech and Hearing Research
Journal of Speech and Hearing Disorders
Journal of the Acoustical Society of America
Brain and Language
Behavioral and Brain Sciences
Journal of Phonetics
Phonetica

Editorial Advisory Board, *Brain and Language* (June 1987–June 2004)
Editorial Board, *International Journal of Language & Communication Disorders*
Consultant & Reviewer for NSF research grant proposals
Review, NIH: Program Development Awards, R01 research proposals

DEPARTMENTAL AND UNIVERSITY SERVICE

Undergraduate Adviser, Department of Linguistics, September 1975–August 1976; September 1991–June 1993; September 2009–present

Graduate Adviser, Department of Linguistics, September 1981–August 1983

Budget Council, Department of Communication Sciences & Disorders, 1980–present

Executive Committee (elected office): Department of Linguistics, September 1986–June 1987; September 1987–August 1988; September 1991–June 1992; 1993–4; 1997–8; 2001–2; 2008–9; 2010–11; 2012–13

Financial Aids Committee, Department of Linguistics, September 1983–June 1987; Chair, 2008

Chair, Course Committee, Department of Linguistics, September 1987–August 1989

Member, Senior Fellows Program Advisory Committee, Department of Speech Communication

College of Liberal Arts, Promotion and Tenure Committee, 1993–6

College of Communication, Promotion and Tenure Committee, 2000–1; 2011; 2012

University Calendar Committee; University of Texas Committee to select Career Research

UT: Award & Best Research Article Award, 1997

Reviewer: UT Research Grant Awards, Fall, 1998

Dean's Search Committee, College of Liberal Arts, 1999

UT Standing Committee, Research Policy, 2001, 2002, 2003

Chair, Financial Aids and Fellowship Committee, Department of Linguistics, 2008–9

PAPERS PRESENTED BEFORE LEARNED SOCIETIES AND INVITED COLLOQUIA

1. "Feature detectors in the perception of speech: a neurosensory theory of speech perception," presented at the American Speech and Hearing Association Convention, November 11–15, 1969
2. "Cerebral dominance and the laterality effect in lingual-auditory tracking," presented at the American Speech and Hearing Association Convention, New York, November 19–23, 1970
3. "Single motor unit potentials in speech musculature," presented at the VIIth International Congress of Phonetics Sciences, Montreal, August 22–28, 1971

4. "Labial and mandibular movement dynamics in speech," presented at the American Speech and Hearing Association Convention, Chicago, November 1971
5. "The role of sensory feedback in speech production," presented at a colloquium for the Department of Psychology, Hollins College, Roanoke, Virginia, November 8–9, 1972
6. "Opposite and overlapping coarticulatory effects in jaw opening and closing," presented at the American Speech and Hearing Association Convention, San Francisco, November 18–21, 1972
7. "Firing patterns of single motor units in speech musculature (with P. MacNeilage and R. Hanson)," American Association for Phonetic Sciences, Detroit, Michigan, October 11, 1973
8. "Sensorimotor dominance and the right ear advantage in mandibular-auditory tracking," presented at American Speech & Hearing Association Convention, Detroit, Michigan, October 12–15, 1973
9. "The assessment of speech-related sensorimotor laterality: Possible applications for disordered populations," invited presentation to the symposium sponsored by the University of Nebraska Medical School: Central Auditory Processing and Disorders, Omaha, Nebraska, May 23–24, 1974
10. "Motor unit training studies of speech musculature," presented at the 1975 annual convention of the American Speech and Hearing Association, Washington, DC, November 21–24, 1975
11. "Recruitment and discharge pattern of single motor units during speech gestures: Implications for speech motor control," presented at the annual convention of the American Speech and Hearing Association, Houston, Texas, November 20–23, 1976
12. "Single motor units: Why? How? So?" invited miniseminar presented at the annual convention of the American Speech and Hearing Association, Chicago, Illinois, November 1977
13. "Motor unit correlates of stress: Reorganization of motor programming," paper presented at Conference on Speech Motor Control, University of Wisconsin-Madison, June 2–3, 1978
14. "Motor unit correlates of stress: Preliminary observations," paper presented at meeting of the American Speech and Hearing Association, San Francisco, California, November 17–21, 1978
15. "The effects of antagonistic muscle contraction on anticipatory coarticulation of lip rounding," paper presented at the Conference on Speech Motor Control, University of Wisconsin-Madison, June 1–3, 1979

16. "Motor unit discharge patterns during speech: Temporal reorganization due to coarticulatory and prosodic events," paper presented at the Ninth International Congress of Phonetic Science, Copenhagen, Denmark, August 6–11, 1979
17. "Bilingual speech: Bilateral control?" presented at BABBLE, Niagara Falls, Ontario, Canada, March 1981
18. "Hemispheric lateralization in aphasic language recovery," invited lecture to the Clinical Neuroscience Conference, University of Texas-San Antonio, January 7, 1982
19. "Language lateralization in aphasia," paper presented at the Speech Motor Control Symposium, University of Wisconsin-Madison, May 2, 1982
20. "Lateralization in language disordered children," presented to the annual convention of the American Speech-Language-Hearing Association, Toronto, Canada, November 18, 1982
21. "Hemisphericity in aphasic language recovery," presented at the annual convention of the American Speech-Language-Hearing Association, Toronto, Canada, November 18, 1982
22. "The elusive lesion-apraxia link in Broca's aphasia," presented to the annual convention of American Speech-Language-Hearing Association, Cincinnati, Ohio, November 1983
23. "The relationship between lesion site/volume and apraxia in Broca's aphasia," presented at BABBLE, Niagara Falls, Ontario, Canada, March 24–25, 1984
24. "Compensatory articulation in Broca's aphasia," presented to the annual convention of American Speech-Language-Hearing Association, San Francisco, California, November 1984
25. "A neuronal model of vowel normalization & representation," paper presented to annual convention of BABBLE, Niagara Falls, Ontario, Canada, March 1985
26. "The neurogenesis of phonology," invited colloquium presented to Southwestern Medical School and Callier Speech & Hearing Center, University of Texas-Dallas, May 10, 1985
27. "Language and the brain," invited address to the Austin Independent School District Gifted & Talented Science Symposium, University of Texas-Austin, May 16, 1985
28. "A critical analysis of experimental techniques investigating stuttering," invited address at the Oxford Dysfluency Conference, Oxford University, UK, August 4–7, 1985

29. "The neurogenesis of phonology," paper presented at annual BABBLE conference on the Neuropsychology of Language, Niagara Falls, Ontario, March 21–22, 1986
30. "Developmental apraxia of speech," invited workshop, Office of Continuing Education, held at Our Lady of the Lake University, San Antonio, Texas, February 14, 1987
31. "Neurolinguistics," invited workshop/seminar presented to NWAV-XVI (New Ways to Analyze Variation) annual conference, held at University of Texas-Austin, October 23–25, 1987
32. "Time sharing task effects in spasmodic dysphonia: Cerebral motor disorganization" (with M. Cannito), paper presented at annual convention of the American Speech-Hearing-Language Association, New Orleans, November 1987
33. "The neurogenesis of phonology: Emergent properties," invited address to Cognitive Science Center, University of Texas-Austin, November 19, 1987
34. "The effects of gender, handedness, L1/L2, & baseline tapping rate on language lateralization: An assessment of the time-sharing paradigm," paper presented at annual convention of International Neuropsychological Society, New Orleans, January 26–30, 1988
35. "Anticipatory coarticulation in aphasia: Some data and methodological considerations," paper presented at BABBLE, Niagara Falls, New York, March 25–26, 1988
36. "The neural coding of relational invariance in speech: Human language analogs to the barn owl," paper presented at Acoustical Society of America, Honolulu, Hawaii, November 14–18, 1988
37. "An investigation of locus equations as a source of relational invariance in speech," paper presented at Phonetic Approaches to Linguistics international conference, held at University of Michigan, Ann Arbor, May 1–3, 1989
38. "The neural coding of relational invariance in speech: Human language analogs to the barn owl," invited paper presented to 5th annual meeting of the Language Origins Society, University of Texas-Austin, August 10–12, 1989
39. "An investigation of locus equations as a source of relational invariance for the stop place dimension," presented at American Speech and Hearing Association, Seattle, Washington, November 1990.
40. "A locus equation perspective on the invariance issue in speech perception," invited colloquium presented to the Department of Communication Sciences and Disorders, University of British Columbia, Canada, September 1990

41. "An investigation of locus equations as a source of relational invariance for stop place categorization," paper presented at Acoustical Society of America, Baltimore, Maryland, April 1991
42. "An investigation of locus equations as a source of relational invariance for stop place categorization," invited paper presented at Current Phonetic Research Paradigms: Implication for Speech Motor Control conference, Stockholm University, Sweden, August 13–16, 1991
43. "An investigation of locus equations as a source of relational invariance for the stop place dimension," paper presented at XIIth International Congress of Phonetic Sciences, Aix-en-Provence, France, August 19–24, 1991
44. "The phonological representation of stop place categories: A brain-based phonetic approach with implications for linguistic rules," paper presented at 21st Annual Linguistics Symposium – The Reality of Linguistic Rules, University of Wisconsin-Milwaukee, April 10–12, 1992
45. "A cross-linguistic validation of locus equations: Are there 'phonetic hot spots' in CV acoustic space?" paper presented at meeting of Acoustical Society of America, New Orleans, November 1–4, 1992
46. "Locus equations in the speech of hearing-impaired speakers" (with Marc Fagelson), paper presented at meeting of American Speech and Hearing Association, San Antonio, Texas, November 1992
47. "A neurolinguistic approach to the invariance issue," invited colloquium presented to Cognitive Science and Psychology departments, McGill University, Montreal, Canada, April 1993
48. "The phonological reality of locus equations across manner class distinctions," paper presented at Acoustical Society of America meeting, Denver, Colorado, October 4–8, 1993
49. "Locus equations during compensatory articulation," paper presented at Acoustical Society of America meeting, Cambridge, MA, June 6–10, 1994
50. "Comparison of CV and VC coarticulation using locus equations," paper presented at Acoustical Society of America meeting, Austin, Texas, November 1994
51. "The Orderly Output Constraint: A functional role for linear relationships in the signal," paper presented at Cognitive Neuroscience Society meeting, San Francisco, California, March 26–28, 1995
52. "Cross-language comparisons of consonant-vowel coarticulation: A locus equation-derived phonetic index for stop place of

articulation," paper presented at Alberta Conference on Linguistics, Banff, Alberta, October 28, 1995

53. "The acquisition of CV coarticulation," paper presented at 8th Biennial Conference on Motor Speech: Speech Motor Control, Amelia Island, Florida, February 22–25, 1996
54. "Locus equations as viewed from a neurobiological perspective: What may they be telling us?" keynote address presented at Focus on the Locus Symposium, Stockholm University, Sweden, May 28, 1996
55. "An acoustic study of the development of CV coarticulation: A case study," paper presented at annual meeting of American Speech and Hearing Association, Atlanta, Georgia, 1997
56 "CV coarticulation: a developmental case study," paper presented at Motor Control Conference, Tucson, Arizona, February 1, 1998
57. Invited address presented to Minifie Symposium, Department of Speech and Hearing Sciences, University of Washington, Seattle, June 27, 1998
58. "The effect of speaking style alterations on locus equation stability," presented at 135th meeting of the Acoustical Society of America, Seattle, Washington, June 1998
59. Invited address presented on panel: Early Speech & Language Development to International Society of Phonetic Sciences, Western Washington University, June 28–30, 1998
60. "The effect of speaking style alterations on locus equation stability," paper presented at 135th meeting of the Acoustical Society of America, Seattle, Washington, June 1998
61. Colloquia presented to Departments of Psychology, University of Sussex, University of Southampton and York University, UK, September 1999
62. "A neurobiological approach to speech categorization and representation," colloquium presented to Department of CSD, University of New Hampshire, October 6, 1999
63. "An acoustic analysis of phonemic integrity and contrastiveness in developmental apraxia of speech," paper presented at Conference on Motor Speech, San Antonio, February 6, 2000
64. "Phonemic integrity and contrastiveness in Developmental Apraxia of Speech," paper presented at VIIIth meeting of the International Clinical Phonetics and Linguistics Association, Edinburgh, Scotland, August 16–19, 2000
65. "The effect of syllabification and VOT on F2 onsets at the CV2 boundary" and "The effect of stress on F2 onsets in VCV utterances,"

two papers presented at 140th Meeting of the Acoustical Society of America, Newport Beach, California, December 3–8, 2000

66. "A neurobiological approach to the representation of phonological categories: A functional role for neural columns," invited lecture presented to Department of Psychology, University of Exeter, UK, June 14, 2001
67. "The brain and sensory plasticity: Basic science and clinical application to language acquisition and hearing," invited address presented at symposium, LSU Health Sciences Center, New Orleans, October 8, 2001
68. "How might the brain deal with linguistic variability: The development of phonologicaol categories," invited colloquium presented to Department of Linguistics, University of Oregon-Eugene, April 5, 2002
69. "A neurobiological approach to lingusitic variability," invited colloquium, Department of Linguistics, Rice University, Houston, Texas, February 20, 2003
70. Two refereed papers presented at 15th International Congress of Phonetic Sciences, Barcelona, August 3–9, 2003
71. Two refereed papers presented at 147th Meeting of Acoustical Society of America, New York, June 2004
72. Refereed paper presented at 149th Meeting of Acoustical Society of America, Vancouver, Canada, May 16–20, 2005
73. "The effect of stress on consonant vowel coarticulation: Decoupling of the CV bond," paper presented at Acoustical Society of America, Honolulu, Hawaii, November 28–December 2, 2006
74. "A neurobiological approach to phonetic categorization," invited colloquium, University of Vermont, June 2007
75. "Differentiating the effect of speech tempo on CV coarticulation," paper presented at 16th International Congress of Phonetic Sciences, Saarbrucken, Germany, August 6–10, 2007
76. "A neurobiological solution to a phonetic coding problem," invited talk to Texas Linguistic Series, University of Texas, November 9, 2007
77. "The assessment of speech motor skills in people who stutter," invited colloquium presented to Department of CSD, University of Vermont, Burlington, May 20, 2008
78. "A neurophonetic approach to stop place of articulation categories," invited colloquium presented to Department of Linguistics, University of Kansas, October 24, 2008

79. "A duration-dependent account of coarticulation for hyper- and hypoarticulation" (with B. Lindblom and A. Agwuele), paper presented at 157th meeting of Acoustical Society of America, Portland, Oregon, May 2009
80. "The emergence of phonological categories: A neurobiological perspective," invited colloquium, Department of Linguistics, University of Victoria, British Columbia, Canada, July 16, 2009
81. "The integrity of anticipatory coarticulation in fluent and non-fluent tokens of adults who stutter," paper presented at Motor Speech Conference, Savannah, Georgia, April 2010
82. "Phonetic aspects of locus equations: Practical applications to clinical research in speech and language disorders in children," invited colloquium, Department of Linguistics, University of Victoria, British Columbia, Canada, June 22, 2010
83. "CV coarticulation in Yoruba: A tonal language" (with A. Agwuele), paper presented at the XVII International Congress of Phonetic Sciences, Hong Kong, August 2011
84. "The non-invariance theory: A locus equation perspective and a possible solution," invited colloquium, Department of Speech and Hearing Sciences, University of Memphis, October 13, 2011
85. "Clinical applications of locus equations," invited colloquium, Department of CSD, University of Maine, Orono, July 14, 2011
86. "A neurobiological approach to resolving phonetic variability," invited colloquium, Department of Psychology, University of Maine, Orono, July 12, 2011
87. "Clinical applications of locus equations in stuttering and developmental apraxia of speech," invited colloquium presented to Department of Speech & Hearing Sciences, University of Memphis, October 13, 2012
88. "Neuroethology in the service of neurophonetics," invited colloquium, Departments of Linguistics and Psychology, University of Alberta, Edmonton, Canada, July 24, 2012
89. "Nonword repetition and phoneme elision in adults who stutter," poster presentation (with Byrd, Valley, Anderson), presented at American Speech and Hearing Association annual convention, Atlanta, Georgia, November 16, 2012

PUBLICATIONS

(* indicates refereed journal)

1. Smith, K.U., & H.M. Sussman. (1969). Cybernetic theory and analysis of motor learning and memory. In E. Bilodeau (ed.), *Principles of Skill Acquisition* (pp. 103–39). New York: Academic Press.
2. Sussman, H.M., & K.U. Smith. (1969). Analysis of memory as a feed-forward control mechanism. *Journal of Motor Behavior*, 1(2), 101–17. http://dx.doi.org/10.1080/00222895.1969.10734839
3. Mendel, M.I., H.M. Sussman, R.M. Merson, M.A. Naeser & F.D. Minifie. (1970). Loudness judgements of speech and non-speech stimuli. *Journal of the Acoustical Society of America*, 46, 1561–1667.
4. Sussman, H.M., & K.U. Smith. (1970). Sensory feedback persistence in determining memory. *Journal of Applied Psychology*, 54(6), 503–8. http://dx.doi.org/10.1037/h0029985
5. Sussman, H.M., & K.U. Smith. (1970). Sensory feedback modes as determinants of learning and memory. *Journal of Educational Research*, 64(2), 64–6. http://dx.doi.org/10.1080/00220671.1970.10884096
6. Smith, K.U., & H.M. Sussman. (1970). Delayed feedback in steering during learning and transfer of learning. *Journal of Applied Psychology*, 54(4), 334–42. http://dx.doi.org/10.1037/h0029523
7. Sussman, H.M., & K.U. Smith. (1970). A transducer for measuring mandibular movements during speech. *Journal of the Acoustical Society of America*, 48(4A), 857–8. http://dx.doi.org/10.1121/1.1912215
8. Sussman, H.M., & K.U. Smith. (1970). A transducer for measuring lip movements during speech. *Journal of the Acoustical Society of America*, 48(4A), 858–60. http://dx.doi.org/10.1121/1.1912216
9. Sussman, H.M. (1970). The role of sensory feedback in tongue movement control. *Journal of Auditory Research*, 10, 296–321.
10. Abbs, J.H., & Sussman, H.M. (1971). Neurophysiological feature detectors and speech perception: A discussion of theoretical implications. *Journal of Speech and Hearing Research*, 14(1), 23–36. http://dx.doi.org/10.1044/jshr.1401.23
11. Sussman, H.M. (1971). The laterality effect in lingual auditory tracking. *Journal of the Acoustical Society of America*, 49(6B), 1874–80. http://dx.doi.org/10.1121/1.1912594
12. Sussman, H.M., & Smith, K.U. (1971). Jaw movements under delayed auditory feedback. *Journal of the Acoustical Society of America*, 50(2B), 685–91. http://dx.doi.org/10.1121/1.1912684
13. Sussman, H.M. (1972). What the tongue tells the brain. *Psychological Bulletin*, 77(4), 262–72. http://dx.doi.org/10.1037/h0032374
14. Hanson, R.J., P.F. MacNeilage & H.M. Sussman. (1972). Single motor unit potentials in speech musculature. In A. Rigault and R. Charbonneau (eds.),

Proceedings of the Seventh International Congress of Phonetic Sciences, pp. 316 –31. The Hague: Mouton.

15. Sussman, H.M., P.F. MacNeilage & R.J. Hanson. (1972). Studies of single motor units in the speech musculature: Methodology and preliminary findings. *Journal of the Acoustical Society of America*, 51(4B), 1374–5. http://dx.doi.org/10.1121/1.1912987
16. Sussman, H.M., P.F. MacNeilage & R.J. Hanson. (1973). Labial and mandibular dynamics during the production of bilabial consonants: Preliminary observations. *Journal of Speech and Hearing Research*, 16(3), 397–420. http://dx.doi.org/10.1044/jshr.1603.397
17. Sussman, H.M. (1974). The assessment of speech-related sensorimotor laterality: Possible application for disordered populations. *Proceedings of a Symposium on Central Auditory Processing Disorders*, University of Nebraska Medical Center, pp. 128–47.
18. MacNeilage, P.F., R.J. Hanson & H.M. Sussman. (1974). Studies of single motor unit activity in speech musculature. *Speech Communication Seminar*, Stockholm, August 1–3, vol. 2, pp. 1–7.
19. Sussman, H.M., & P.F. MacNeilage. (1974). Some studies of hemispheric specialization for speech production. *Speech Communication Seminar*, Stockholm, Aug. 1–3, vol. 3, pp. 1–8.
20. Sussman, H.M., P.F. MacNeilage & J. Lumbley, J. (1974). Sensori-motor dominance and the right ear advantage in mandibular-auditory tracking. *Journal of the Acoustical Society of America*, 56(1), 214–16. http://dx.doi.org/10.1121/1.1903258
21. Sussman, H.M., & P.F. MacNeilage. (1975). Studies of hemispheric specialization for speech production. *Brain and Language*, 2, 131–51. http://dx.doi.org/10.1016/S0093-934X(75)80060-5
22. Sussman, H.M., & P.F. MacNeilage. (1975). Hemispheric specialization for speech production and perception in stuttering. *Neuropsychologia*, 13(1), 19–26. http://dx.doi.org/10.1016/0028-3932(75)90043-3
23. Sussman, H.M., P.F. MacNeilage & J. Lumbley. (1975). Pursuit auditory tracking of dichotically presented tonal amplitudes. *Journal of Speech and Hearing Research*, 18(1), 74–81. http://dx.doi.org/10.1044/jshr.1801.74
24. Sussman, H.M., & P.F. MacNeilage. (1975). Dichotic pursuit auditory tracking following anterior temporal lobectomy. *Archives of Otolaryngology*, 101(6), 389–91. http://dx.doi.org/10.1001/archotol.1975.00780350053014
25. MacNeilage, P.F., H.M. Sussman & W. Stolz. (1975). Incidence of laterality effects in mandibular and manual performance of dichoptic visual pursuit tracking. *Cortex*, 11(3), 251–8. http://dx.doi.org/10.1016/S0010-9452(75)80007-4
26. Sussman, H.M. (1975). Hemispheric specialization for processing movement produced stimuli. In W.W. Spriduso and J.D. King (eds.), *Proceedings: Motor Control Symposium* (pp. 57–69). Austin: The University of Texas Printing Division.

27. MacNeilage, P.F., H.M. Sussman & R.K. Powers. (1977). Discharge patterns accompanying sustained activation of motor units in human cranial musculature. *Journal of Phonetics*, 5, 135–47.
28. Sussman, H.M. (1977). Respiratory tracking of dichotically presented tonal amplitudes. *Journal of Speech and Hearing Research*, 20(3), 555–64. http://dx.doi.org/10.1044/jshr.2003.555
29. Sussman, H.M. (1977). Recruitment and discharge patterns of single motor units during speech production. *Journal of Speech and Hearing Research*, 21, 127–44.
30. Sussman, H.M., & J.R. Westbury. (1978). A laterality effect in isometric and isotonic labial tracking. *Journal of Speech and Hearing Research*, 21(3), 563–79. http://dx.doi.org/10.1044/jshr.2103.563
31. Sussman, H.M., & P.F. MacNeilage. (1978). Motor unit correlates of stress: Preliminary observations. *Journal of the Acoustical Society of America*, 64(1), 338–40. http://dx.doi.org/10.1121/1.381953
32. Sussman, H.M. (1979). Evidence for left hemisphere superiority in processing movement-related tonal signals. *Journal of Speech and Hearing Research*, 22(2), 224–35. http://dx.doi.org/10.1044/jshr.2202.224
33. Thibodeau, L.M., & H.M. Sussman. (1979). Performance on a test of categorical perception of speech in normal and communication disordered children. *Journal of Phonetics*, 7, 1–17.
34. MacNeilage, P.F., H.M. Sussman, J.R. Westbury & R.K. Powers. (1979). Mechanical properties of single motor units in speech musculature. *Journal of the Acoustical Society of America*, 65(4), 1047–52. http://dx.doi.org/10.1121/1.382573
35. Sussman, H.M., & M. Hernandez. (1979). A spectrographic analysis of the suprasegmental aspects of the speech of hearing impaired adolescents. *Audiology & Hearing Education*, 5, 12–16.
36. Sussman, H.M. (1979). Motor unit discharge patterns during speech: Temporal reorganization due to coarticulatory and prosodic events. In *Proceedings of the Ninth International Congress of Phonetic Sciences*, vol. 11 (pp. 365–71). Copenhagen: Institute of Phonetics, University of Copenhagen.
37.* Sussman, H.M. (1980). Motor equivalence and lip/jaw reciprocity: An artifact? *Journal of Speech and Hearing Research*, 23, 669–702.
38. Sussman, H.M., & J.R. Westbury. (1981). The effects of antagonistic gestures on temporal and amplitude parameters of anticipatory labial coarticulation. *Journal of Speech and Hearing Research*, 24, 21–9 (this article was chosen as "the article of highest merit published in 1981" in *JSHR*). http://dx.doi.org/10.1044/jshr.2401.16
39. Sussman, H.M. (1982). Contrastive patterns of intrahemispheric interference to verbal and spatial concurrent tasks in right handed, left handed, and stuttering populations. *Neuropsychologia*, 20(6), 675–84. http://dx.doi.org/10.1016/0028-3932(82)90067-7

40. Sussman, H.M., P. Franklin & T. Simon. (1982). Bilingual speech: Bilateral control? *Brain and Language*, 15(1), 125–42. http://dx.doi.org/10.1016/0093-934X(82)90052-9
41. Klingman, K., & H.M. Sussman. (1983). Hemisphericity in aphasic language recovery. *Journal of Speech and Hearing Research*, 26(2), 249–56. http://dx.doi.org/10.1044/jshr.2602.249
42. Hughes, M., & H.M. Sussman. (1983). An assessment of cerebral dominance in language-disordered children via a time-sharing paradigm. *Brain and Language*, 19(1), 48–64. http://dx.doi.org/10.1016/0093-934X(83)90055-X
43. Sussman, H.M. (1984). A reply to Kee's comments on Hughes and Sussman's time-sharing study of cerebral laterality in language-disordered and normal children. *Brain and Language*, 22(2), 357–8. http://dx.doi.org/10.1016/0093-934X(84)90101-9
44. Marquardt, T., & Sussman, H.M. (1984). The elusive lesion-apraxia link in Broca's aphasia. In J.C. Rosenbek, M.R. McNeil and A.E. Aronson (eds.), *Apraxia of Speech: Physiology-acoustics-linguistics-management.* San Diego, CA: College Hill Press.
45. Sussman, H.M. (1984). A neuronal model for syllable representation. *Brain and Language*, 22(1), 167–77. http://dx.doi.org/10.1016/0093-934X(84)90087-7
46. Sussman, H.M. (1985). Neuropsychology and political science: The time is not yet ripe for beneficial interaction. *Politics and the Life Sciences*, 4(1), 18–19.
47. Sussman, H.M., T. Marquardt, J. Hutchinson & P. MacNeilage. (1986). Compensatory articulation in Broca's aphasia. *Brain and Language*, 27(1), 56–74. http://dx.doi.org/10.1016/0093-934X(86)90005-2
48. Sussman, H.M. (1986). A neuronal model of vowel normalization and representation. *Brain and Language*, 28(1), 12–23. http://dx.doi.org/10.1016/0093-934X(86)90087-8
49. Sussman, H.M. (1987). Compensatory articulation in Broca's aphasia: Who said the facts are in? A reply to Katz and Baum. *Brain and Language*, 30(2), 374–80. http://dx.doi.org/10.1016/0093-934X(87)90111-8
50. Sussman, H.M. (1987). Psychomotor therapy for aphasia: A commentary. *Aphasiology*, 1(6), 503–6. http://dx.doi.org/10.1080/02687038708248876
51. Simon, T.J., & H.M. Sussman. (1987). The dual task paradigm: Speech dominance or manual dominance? *Neuropsychologia*, 25(3), 559–69. http://dx.doi.org/10.1016/0028-3932(87)90080-7
52.* Sussman, H.M. (1988). The neurogenesis of phonology. In H. Whitaker (ed.), *Phonological Processes and Brain Mechanism* (pp. 1–23). New York: Springer-Verlag Publishers. http://dx.doi.org/10.1007/978-1-4615-7581-8_1
53.* Sussman, H.M., T. Marquardt, P.F. MacNeilage and J. Hutchinson (1988). Anticipatory coarticulation in aphasia: some data and methodological considerations. *Brain and Language*, 35, 369–79. http://dx.doi.org/10.1016/0093-934X(88)90117-4
54. Marquardt, T.P., J. Stoll & H.M. Sussman. (1988). Disorders of communication in adults with brain trauma. *Journal of Learning Disabilities*, 21(6), 340–51. http://dx.doi.org/10.1177/002221948802100605

55. Sussman, H.M. (1989). The neural coding of relational invariance in speech: Human language analogs to the barn owl. *Psychological Review*, 96(4), 631–42. http://dx.doi.org/10.1037/0033-295X.96.4.631
56. Sussman, H.M. (1989). A reassessment of the time-sharing paradigm with ANCOVA. *Brain and Language*, 37(3), 514–20. http://dx.doi.org/10.1016/0093-934X(89)90033-3
57. Sussman, H.M. (1989). A bird brain approach to language. *ASHA* (May), 83–6.
58. Sussman, H.M. (1990). Acoustic correlates of the front/back vowel distinction: A comparison of transition onset values versus "steady state." *Journal of the Acoustical Society of America*, 88(1), 87–96. http://dx.doi.org/10.1121/1.399848
59. Sussman, H.M. (1991). The representation of stop consonants in three dimensional acoustic space. *Phonetica*, 48(1), 18–31. http://dx.doi.org/10.1159/000261869
60.* Sussman, H.M., H. McCaffrey & S. Matthews. (1991). An investigation of locus equations as a source of relational invariance for stop place categorization. *Journal of the Acoustical Society of America*, 90, 1309–25.
61. Sussman, H.M. (1991). An investigation of locus equations as a source of relational invariance for the stop place dimension. *Proceedings of the XIIth International Congress of Phonetic Sciences*, Vol. 2/5, 74–7.
62. Marquardt, T.P., & H.M. Sussman. (1991). Developmental apraxia of speech: Theory and practice. In D. Vogel & M. Cannito (eds.), *Treating Disordered Speech Motor Control* (pp. 341–90). Austin, Texas: Pro-Ed Publishers, Inc.
63. Sussman, H.M., K. Hoemeke & H. McCaffrey. (1992). Locus equations as an index of coarticulation for place of articulation distinctions in children. *Journal of Speech and Hearing Research*, 35(4), 769–81. http://dx.doi.org/10.1044/jshr.3504.769
64. Sussman, H.M., K. Hoemeke & F. Ahmed. (1993). A cross-linguistic investigation of locus equations as a phonetic descriptor for place of articulation. *Journal of the Acoustical Society of America*, 94(3), 1256–68. http://dx.doi.org/10.1121/1.408178
65. Marion, M.J., M.H. Sussman & T.P. Marquardt. (1993). The perception and production of rhyme in normal and developmentally apraxic children. *Journal of Communication Disorders*, 26(3), 129–60. http://dx.doi.org/10.1016/0021-9924(93)90005-U
66. Sussman, H.M. (1994). The phonological reality of locus equations across manner class distinctions: Preliminary observations. *Phonetica*, 51(1–3), 119–31. http://dx.doi.org/10.1159/000261964
67.* Sussman, H.M. (1994). Let's get down to the "wet stuff" and look at evolutionarily-motivated mechanisms. *Behavioral and Brain Sciences*, 17(1), 182–5.
68. McCaffrey, H.A., & H.M. Sussman. (1994). An investigation of vowel organization in speakers with severe and profound hearing impairment. *Journal of Speech and Hearing Research*, 37(4), 938–51. http://dx.doi.org/10.1044/jshr.3704.938

69. Sussman, H.M., D. Fruchter & A. Cable. (1995). Locus equations derived from compensatory articulation. *Journal of the Acoustical Society of America*, 97(5), 3112–24. http://dx.doi.org/10.1121/1.411873
70. Sussman, H.M., & J. Shore. (1996). Locus equations as phonetic descriptors of consonantal place of articulation. *Perception & Psychophysics*, 58(6), 936–46. http://dx.doi.org/10.3758/BF03205495
71. Sussman, H.M., F. Minifie, E. Buder, C. Stoel-Gammon & J. Smith. (1996). Consonant-vowel interdependencies in babbling and early words: A locus equation approach. *Journal of Speech and Hearing Research*, 39(2), 424–33. http://dx.doi.org/10.1044/jshr.3902.424
72.* Sussman, H.M., N. Bessell, E. Dalston & T. Majors. (1997). An investigation of stop place of articulation as a function of syllable position: A locus equation perspective. *Journal of the Acoustic Society of America*, 101, 2826–38.
73. Sussman, H.M. (1997). A neurobiological approach to the noninvariance problem in stop consonant categorization. In M. Gopnik (ed.), *The Inheritance and Innateness of Grammars* (pp. 209–32). Vancouver Studies in Cognitive Science.
74. Fruchter, D., & H.M. Sussman. (1997). The perceptual relevance of locus equations. *Journal of the Acoustical Society of America*, 102(5), 2997–3008. http://dx.doi.org/10.1121/1.421012
75. Cannito, M.P., G.V. Kondraske & H.M. Sussman. (1998). Influence of voicing on verbal/manual interference in normal speakers and speakers with spasmodic dysphonia. In M.P. Cannito, K.M. Yorkston & D.R. Beukelman (eds.), *Neuromotor Speech Disorders: Nature, Assessment and Treatment*. Baltimore: Brookes Publishers.
76. Sussman, H.M., D.D. Fruchter, J. Hilbert & J. Sirosh. (1998). Linear corrrelates in the speech signal: The orderly output constraint. Target article, *Behavioral and Brain Sciences*, 21, 241–99.
77. Marquardt, T., H.M. Sussman & B. Davis. (1998). Developmental apraxia of speech: Advances in theory and practice. In D. Vogel & M. Cannito (eds.), *Treating Disordered Speech Motor Control*. Austin, Texas: Pro-Ed.
78. Sussman, H.M., E. Dalston & S. Gumbert. (1998). The effect of speaking style on a locus equation characterization of stop place of articulation. *Phonetica*, 55(4), 204–25. http://dx.doi.org/10.1159/000028433
79. Sussman, H.M., C. Duder, E. Dalston & A. Cacciatore. (1999). An acoustic analysis of the development of CV coarticulation: A case study. *Journal of Speech, Language, and Hearing Research*, 42(5), 1080–96. http://dx.doi.org/10.1044/jslhr.4205.1080
80. Sussman, H.M. (1999). A neural mapping hypothesis to explain why velar stops have an allophonic split. *Brain and Language*, 70(2), 294–304. http://dx.doi.org/10.1006/brln.1999.2182
81.* Sussman, H.M. (2000). Phonemic representation: A 21st c challenge. *Brain and Language*, Special Millenium issue, 71, 237–40.

82. Sussman, H.M., T.P. Marquardt, H. Knapp & J. Doyle. (2000). An acoustic and perceptual analysis of phonemic integrity and contrastiveness in developmental apraxia of speech. *Journal of Medical Speech-Language Pathology*, 8, 301–14.
83. Marquardt, T., H.M. Sussman & A. Jacks. (2001). The integrity of the syllable in developmental apraxia of speech. *Journal of Communication Disorders*, 35, 1–19.
84. Sussman, H.M., T. Marquardt, J. Doyle & H. Knapp. (2002). Phonemic integrity and contrastiveness in developmental apraxia of speech. In F. Windsor, N. Hewlett & L. Kelly (eds.), *Themes in Clinical Linguistics and Phonetics* (pp. 311–26). New York: Lawrence Erlbaum.
85. Sussman, H.M. (2002). Representation of phonological categories: A functional role for auditory columns. *Brain and Language*, 80(1), 1–13. http://dx.doi.org/10.1006/brln.2001.2489
86. Lindblom, B., H.M. Sussman, G. Modarresi & E. Burlingame, E. (2002). The trough effect: Implications for speech motor programming. *Phonetica*, 59(4), 245–62. http://dx.doi.org/10.1159/000068349
87. Lindblom, B., & H.M. Sussman. (2002). Principal components analysis of tongue shapes in symmetrical VCV utterances. In *TMH-QPSR*, Vol. 44. Stockholm, Sweden: Fonetik.
88. Sussman, H.M. (2003). Neuroethology: Providing insights into human language representation. In C.I. Berlin & T.G. Weyand (eds.), *The Brain and Sensory Plasticity: Language Acquisition and Hearing* (pp. 25–56). Clifton Park, NY: Thomson Delmar Learning.
89. Modarresi, G., H.M. Sussman, B. Lindblom, & E. Burlingame. (2004). An acoustic analysis of the bidirectionality of coarticulation in VCV utterances. *Journal of Phonetics*, 32(3), 291–312. http://dx.doi.org/10.1016/j.wocn.2003.11.002
90. Modarresi, G., H.M. Sussman, B. Lindblom & E. Burlingame. (2004). Stop place coding: An acoustic study of CV, VC#, and C#V sequences. *Phonetica*, 61(1), 2–21. http://dx.doi.org/10.1159/000078660
91.* Modarresi, G., H.M. Sussman, B. Lindblom & E. Burlingame. (2005). Locus equation encoding of stop place: Revisiting the voicing/VOT issue. *Journal of Phonetics*, 33(1), 101–13. http://dx.doi.org/10.1016/j.wocn.2004.06.002
92.* Burlingame, E., H.M. Sussman, R.B. Gillam & J.F. Hay. (2005). An investigation of speech perception in children with SLI on a continuum of formant transition duration. *Journal of Speech, Hearing, and Language Research*, 48, 805–16.
93. Lindblom, B., A. Agwuele, H.M. Sussman & E.E. Cortes. (2007). The effect of emphatic stress on consonant vowel coarticulation. *Journal of the Acoustical Society of America*, 121(6), 3802–13. http://dx.doi.org/10.1121/1.2730622
94. Agwuele, A., H.M. Sussman, B. Lindblom & A. Miller. (2007). Differentiating the effect of speech tempo on CV coarticulation. *ICPhS XVI, Saarbrucken*, 6–10 (August), 617–20.
95. Agwuele, A., H.M. Sussman & B. Lindblom. (2008). The effect of speaking rate on consonant vowel coarticulation. *Phonetica*, 65(4), 194–209. http://dx.doi.org/10.1159/000192792

96. Lindblom, B., H.M. Sussman & A. Agwuele, A. (2009). A duration-dependent account of coarticulation for hyper- and hypoarticulation. *Phonetica*, 66(3), 188–95. http://dx.doi.org/10.1159/000235660
97. Lindblom, B., D. Krull & H.M. Sussman. (2010). Coarticulation as incomplete interpolation. In *Proceedings of FONETIK*, pp. 57–62. Lund, Sweden: Department of Phonetics, Centre for Languages and Literature, Lund University.
98. Sussman, H.M., C. Byrd & B. Guitar. (2011). The integrity of anticipatory coarticulation in fluent and non-fluent tokens of adults who stutter. *Clinical Linguistics & Phonetics*, 25(3), 169–86. http://dx.doi.org/10.3109/02699206.2010.517896
99. Lindblom, B., & H.M. Sussman. (2012). Dissecting coarticulation: How locus equations happen. *Journal of Phonetics*, 40(1), 1–19. http://dx.doi.org/10.1016/j.wocn.2011.09.005
100. Byrd, C.T., M. Vallely, J.D. Anderson & H. Sussman. (2012). Nonword repetition and phoneme elision in adults who do and do not stutter. *Journal of Fluency Disorders*, 37(3), 188–201. http://dx.doi.org/10.1016/j.jfludis.2012.03.003
101. Sussman, H.M. (2012). On the relation between linguistic categories and neural systems. *Talking Brains: News and Views on the Neural Organization of Language* (March 19). http://www.talkingbrains.org.
102. Sussman, H.M. (2013). Neuroethology in the service of neurophonetics. *Journal of Neurolinguistics*, 26(5), 511–25. http://dx.doi.org/10.1016/j.jneuroling.2013.02.004
103. Sussman, H.M. (2014). Why the left hemisphere is dominant for speech production: Connecting the dots. Under review, *Journal of Neurolinguistics.*

1
Introduction: The Animal-to-Human Speech Connection – Harvey Sussman's Conjectures

Augustine Agwuele and Celeste Domsch[1]

Harvey Sussman has literally pioneered a novel yet simple approach to study human speech processing – he pays close attention to what animal neural systems are telling us, especially in species biologically specialized for hearing (e.g., bats, barn owls). The field of neuroethology, or animal communication, uses the gold standard of investigating brain function, single neuron recording. The spatial and temporal resolutions of this methodology are far superior to fMRI, MEG or ERP, as none of these commonly employed techniques can measure neural events occurring across temporal spans measured in milliseconds and neural extents measured in microns. What is especially noteworthy in this endeavor is that Sussman was doing this line of research decades before our current brain imaging methodologies were even on the drawing board. Another advantage of the neuroethology-to-speech route is that the animal-based data relates to the "how" of speech processing, not the "where." This chapter will discuss several of Professor Sussman's published papers which have contributed to enhancing our understanding of how micro-level neural events enable macro-level processing to happen.

1 Augustine Agwuele is an Associate Professor of Linguistics in the Department of Anthropology at Texas State University, San Marcos.
Celeste Domsch is an Associate Professor in the Department of Communication Disorders at Texas State University, San Marcos.

1.1 Speech Perception: Auditory Feature Detectors

Harvey Sussman, then a psychology PhD student in Behavioral Cybernetics at the University of Wisconsin, enrolled in his first Communication Sciences and Disorders (CSD) course in 1969. It was a seminar in Speech Perception, taught by Dr Fred Minifie, who became one of his most influential and beloved mentors. The course material served as an "awakening" of sorts for Sussman, as he had no idea people were studying how the brain perceives speech. Upon initially learning of the perception experiments emanating from Haskins Labs, and the eventual formulation of the Motor Theory of Speech Perception, and never one to shy away from controversial issues, Sussman, and his colleague, James Abbs, realized they could, as graduate students, forever shape the discussion in this new emerging field of study. Being well versed in the neurophysiological research investigating feature detectors in animal visual and auditory systems, Abbs and Sussman formulated a novel, auditory-based position to account for the micro-level brain mechanisms underlying speech perception in humans. Their 1971 article in the *Journal of Speech and Hearing Research* was the first published account suggesting that human auditory feature detectors, similar to the various FM-sensitive neurons found in the auditory cortex of the cat (Evans & Whitfield 1964), could easily provide the necessary decoding for speech perception.

This seminal paper provided a summary of the newly emerging feature detector literature, from "bug detectors" in the frog, to horizontal edge detectors in the pigeon, to "mating calls" of bull frogs, to "meow" detectors in the cat. Their insights, however, extended well beyond the mere existence of these highly specialized neuronal populations, to other related processing mechanisms that were essential to fully account for speech perception in humans. One example was the concept of "tolerance limits" exhibited by pigeons (Maturana & Frenk 1963). Neuronal edge detectors in the pigeon exhibited various sensitivities to small (but limited) variations off the horizontal (= 0 degrees). For example, certain populations of neurons in the pigeon's visual system would show neural firings to specific ranges of horizontal-oriented lines of light – e.g., 0 to 10 degrees, 0 to15 degrees, etc. Thus, the concept of tolerance limits was neurally established as a brain-based means of absorbing normal variations within the input signal, a crucial mechanism for speech decoding.

A second operational principle, gleaned from the elegant work of Hartline & Ratliff (1958) in the horseshoe crab, illustrated how "lateral inhibition" could sharpen perception of competing nearby stimuli. The newly discovered paradigm of categorical perception was just then being explored, and the existence of neural mechanisms performing lateral inhibition could conveniently account for the sharpening of category boundaries in stop + vowel continua.

1.2 Speech Production: Muscle Spindles in the Tongue

The bridge from neuroethology to speech/language was also valuable for gaining new insights into production and kinesthetic feedback circuits. Sussman's PhD dissertation investigated the tongue's motor ability to perform pursuit tracking movements guided by visual, auditory and tactile stimuli serving as the target and cursor signals, providing feedback of the tongue's changing position in horizontal space. In learning about the tongue's unique sensory and motor abilities, he came across the intricate kinesthesia system in the tongue allowing for rapid and precise afferent signaling of the tongue's rapidly changing position/contours, and direction and speed of movement (Bowman & Combs 1968). His 1972 *Psychological Bulletin* paper was titled "What the tongue tells the brain," (honoring the classic 1959 paper by Lettvin et al., "What the frog's eye tells the frog's brain").

Typically, signaling of bodily limb position (flexion at elbow, wrist, fingers, jaw, knee etc.) is mediated by joint receptors. The muscle fibers moving these body structures are typically arranged in parallel. The intrinsic muscles of the tongue are oriented in three spatial directions (front-back, left-right, up-down), and moreover, they are superabundant with muscle spindles. Bowman & Combs (1968) demonstrated that the tongue muscle spindles of a rhesus monkey showed directional sensitivity to stretch stimuli. Afferent signaling from 1a sensory fibers arrived at motor cortex destinations with a 4–5 msec latency. Spindle firing rate also coded the velocity of the tongue stretch motion. Sussman concluded that, "The intricate muscle-spindle system of the tongue, which is a built-in spatial reference system, can provide the necessary information to keep the motor control centers aware of instantaneous muscle length, spatial position, and velocity" (1972: 269).

1.3 Speech Perception: The Non-invariance Issue and Locus Equations

Perhaps Sussman's most significant contribution to speech production/perception was his programmatic research on stop consonant production using the locus equation paradigm. This important work also provided the impetus to once again forge a theoretical bridge from neuroethology to neurophonetics, this time delving into the sound localization system of the barn owl (using the elegant studies of Mark Konishi and his colleagues).

But, first things first: what are locus equations? A long-time colleague of Dr Sussman, Bjorn Lindblom, is credited with the original discovery of locus equations (LEs), based on his dissertation work in Sweden. Sussman is credited with putting LEs on the phonetic map and with extending their applicability to several languages, and across several dimensions of phonetic structure (e.g., varying syllable position, stress, speaking rate/style, compensatory bite block speech). Sussman has defined and described LEs as follows:

> LEs are linear regressions of the frequency of the F2 transition sampled at its onset on the frequency of F2 when measured in the vowel nucleus. These frequency values are plotted for a single stop consonant produced with a wide range of following vowels. F2onsets are plotted along the y-axis and F2midpoints along the x-axis. For a given stop place category, for example [dV] as in deet, dit, debt, date, dot, dut, doot, daught, dote, data coordinates have been consistently shown to tightly cluster in a positively correlated distribution. This scatter plot is fit with a linear regression line, the locus equation, of the form F2onset = k × F2vowel + c, where k and c are constants, slope and y-intercept respectively. LEs are remarkable in that the category-level scatter plots are extremely linear, with very small scatter of coordinates about the trend line, and most importantly, the slopes of the functions statistically distinguish across stop place categories/bdg/ (Sussman et al. 1991).

What made LEs novel was that, for the first time, stop place tokens (CVs) were represented as a higher order phonetic/phonological category, showing all allophonic variants (different vowel contexts) of a given stop in one scatterplot. Thus, the infamous tokens used to support motor/gesture-oriented theories, showing divergent directions of F2 transitions – *di* versus *du* – were now simply just two more <*x*, *y*> coordinates tightly clustered around a linear regression line, just like all the other vowel contexts. Somehow the extreme variability of the various F2 transitions disappeared when plotted as a LE scatter plot. No explicit normalization algorithm was applied; the measured data coordinates (F2-onset and F2-vowel) were simply the way the speech sounds were produced.

Interestingly, the slopes for LEs across stop place (labial, alveolar, velar) were also statistically different. Since LE slopes were direct reflections of the extent of anticipatory coarticulation underlying their production (how much each vowel context affected the location of the stop occlusion), the LE paradigm clearly showed that degree of coarticulation is what actually creates the necessary acoustic distinctions across stop categories. This new concept contradicted the long-held view argued by the Haskins group, i.e., coarticulation is the reason why there is so much variability within a stop category and therefore why a motor (rather than auditory) route to perception is needed.

1.4 A Neural Example of Resolving Variability: ITD Coding in the Barn Owl

With the locus equation paradigm firmly established as an empirically based linguistic universal (it has been replicated in several languages), Professor Sussman embarked on another neuroethology search to turn the debate on LEs away from their simply being considered a curious epiphenomenon, to an acoustic patterning of speech sounds possessing a functional significance. Two crucial facts motivated this search: (1) the F2 transition is arguably the most important acoustic cue in stop place perception; and (2) the extremely high degree of statistical regularity in LE plots strongly suggests that F2-onset and F2-vowel can serve as "information-bearing elements" (Suga et al. 1978) to maximize learning and hence "mapability" in the neural representation of phonemic units. The goal was to find a neural coding system that deals with stimulus variability/ambiguity, and most importantly, successfully resolves it. When Sussman read the article: "Representation of interaural time difference in the central nucleus of the barn owl's inferior colliculus," by Wagner, Takahashi & Konishi (1987), a critical insight emerged.

A barn owl faces a similar coding problem in sound localization as an infant does in establishing equivalence classes for stop consonants – both have to normalize inherent variability of an input signal to arrive at an emergent property shaped by the laws of physics.

Interaural time difference (ITD) arrays in the barn owl's central nucleus of the inferior colliculus do not have access to a neural clock, but rather use combinatorial coding of both frequency and phase information to derive an emergent property, ITDs. The coding problem derives from the simple fact that phase information is non-informative for single frequency values, but can only be useful across numerous frequencies. The tonotopically organized delay lines in the barn owl's brain stem do a splendid job of coding for phase differences between the lead vs lag ear. An example will clarify where the ambiguity arises. Let's say that a sound approaches an owl from an azimuth source located 30 degrees to the right of the owl's head. This sound arrives at the right ear 50 μsec before it reaches the left ear. But the owl doesn't possess any neural clock. How does the 50 μsec value emerge? If one examines frequencies from a complex input sound, e.g., 2 kHz, 3 kHz, 4 kHz, 5 kHz, 6 kHz and 7 kHz, the period of these frequencies are 500 μsec, 333 μsec, 250 μsec, 200 μsec, 167μ and 143 μsec, respectively. These phase differences, expressed as a percentage of a cycle that would be completed as the sound traverses the owl's head, would be 10 per cent (50/500), 15 per cent (50/333), 20 per cent (50/250), 25 per cent (50/200), 30 per cent (50/167) and 35 per cent (50/143), respectively. Every frequency in the complex input sound possesses a different phase value. How is an owl expected to know which combination of frequency and phase is accurately coding time? Think of an infant thinking to himself – which F2 transition is the *real* /d/?

The central nucleus of the inferior colliculus, similar to all brain areas, both cortical and subcortical, is organized by a columnar architecture. The central nucleus columns span the wide frequency range of the owl's hearing spectrum. Each lamina (horizontal layer) of a column encodes a specific Hz-phase disparity % combination. Using retrograde transport techniques Wagner et al. then traced the connections from the upstream, unambiguous/ invariant coding areas of the external nucleus back down to these ITD columns of the central nucleus. What they discovered was that the *functional unit* of information transmission from the central-to-external nuclei was *the entire column*. So, if they were staining an area of the external nucleus that invariantly responded to a sound located 30 degrees to the right of midline, all axonal projections to that area originated in the single column that encoded the various Hz-phase disparity %s that *collectively* coded a 50 μsec leading to the right ear. Thus, the resolution of the variability conundrum is resolved by the collective lamina forming each column, as they all possess a common emergent property – the specific interaural time difference. The frequency-phase variability disappears when the entire column, encoding all possible combinations, functions as one information source. It is a clever way to absorb signal variability created by the laws of physics.

Sussman surmised that the ITD neural columnar structure, as mapped by Wagner et al., could very well represent an evolutionarily conserved neural architecture to resolve variability arising from any lawfully generated sensory input signal. Why not speech? He published a series of papers espousing this idea of neural columns encoding the various F2-onset + F2-vowel frequency combinations (as plotted in LE scatterplots) for each stop place category (Sussman et al. 1998; Sussman 1989a, 1989b, 2002, 2003, 2013). The parameterization of the diverse F2 transitions, per stop place category, was mapped as a columnar array. The neural correlate of the LE slope could now be conceptualized as a neural column. Various tolerance limits would be postulated to account for LE slope ranges for a given stop across speakers. There was one serious glitch, however. All the input frequencies in the complex sound the owl is listening to are present *at the same moment.* Speech sounds are processed by themselves, one hears the single word *deed,* not all [dV] contexts. Categorical identity is something that is learned, over time, across years of language acquisition.

This *coding over time* dilemma was soon rectified when Sussman came across the work of Tanaka (1997), investigating the neural basis of object recognition in the macaque monkey. Surely, object recognition is a longitudinal learning process, as an organism does not view all objects simultaneously. Tanaka's single neuron recording revealed the existence of columnar structures in the IT area of the macaque's temporal lobe that basically coded an assortment of critical visual features that, throughout a given column, captured all the lawful variations caused by different illuminations, viewing angles, articulations, that normally occur in vision. The findings of Tanaka were what the doctor ordered for Sussman's emerging story of how stimulus variability is handled in the brain. The visual column works like a buffer to absorb changes. Columns create as a collective and thereby establish "tolerance bandwidths" for acceptable images belonging to a given category of object. All visual features are lawfully related, similar to sound variations in human speech. The cross-sensory example of object recognition in the macaque provided a stronger neural legitimacy to Sussman's barn owl story.

1.5 Summary and Aim of this Anthology

It is apparent that since the 1970s, the work of Harvey M. Sussman has significantly shaped scholarship in speech processes, specifically in the areas of perception and production. From the concept of feature detectors in the human auditory system to the work on locus equations and their speculated neural correlates, Sussman has consistently sought out animal models of perception and production, and used those models to hypothesize on the biological foundations of human speech. Indeed, his argument that speech is processed in the brain on a auditory feature basis has found strong support in the recent studies of Chang and colleagues at UCSF (Chang et al. 2010; Mesgarani et al. 2014). The use of high-density direct cortical (STG) surface recordings in humans listening to a wide assortment of speech sounds has revealed distributed yet discrete population responses to stop place categories (/b, d, g/) and a wide variety of acoustic-based phonetic features.

This book was born out of the recognition of Harvey's exemplary contributions to the study of speech and communication processes that have significantly advanced the frontiers of knowledge in the field. The collected essays exemplify some of the subject matter touched by the works of Harvey. One of the reviewers of this anthology commented pertaining to chapter 11, a cross-cultural analysis of medical students' views on dementia patients, that it is not immediately connected to Harvey's work. Indeed, one can argue that Harvey has not been concerned with socio-cultural phenomena in his works; however, the rigor of his scholarship, the keenness of his mind, the clarity of his approach, the lucidity and accessibility of his writings ripple across disciplines to inspire many. A dominant paradigm, according Thomas Kuhn, will continue until it confronts a question it is unable to adequately answer. Harvey's locus equation perspective to coarticulation not only resolved the crisis that resulted at the point when an existing paradigm (e.g., motor theory) became ineffectual with respect to the non-invariance problem, but supplanted it to become the dominant paradigm that has been able to withstand all theoretical, conceptual and practical questions thus far thrown at it. Related to the rise and popularization of the locus equations are several thoughts, described above and artfully articulated in chapter 16 by Randy Diehl, that have attracted many collaborators and informed several other research questions and practical applications as exemplified by the different works and perspectives represented by the contributing authors. Harvey is also a distinguished teacher and mentor. His passion for teaching and his remarkable ability to inspire his students, colleagues and peers is in part also reflected by the diverse contributors to this work.

Finally, readers may be surprised to see that Harvey is also a contributor to this work. When we approached him with the idea for this book, Harvey resisted, saying he would be happy to get together with few friends and have dinner, but a "festschrift" was out of the question. He does not believe in celebratory works. Later when he learned that we were not interested in a festive or celebratory book that sings a personality's praise, but that we intended to honor him with a collection of previously unpublished and peer reviewed works of active scholars, he sent in an email with an abstract and the question: "Is it kosher to contribute to a work that will be dedicated to me?" We dedicate this collection of studies to Harvey Sussman for his unfaltering commitment to the intellectual enterprise, for his distinguished scholarship that has inspired many publications and informed important debates, for his inspirational teachings and exemplary mentorship, and for his collegiality and friendship.

References

Abbs, J.H., & H.M. Sussman. (1971). Neurophysiological feature detectors and speech perception: A discussion of theoretical implications. *Journal of Speech and Hearing Research*, 14(1), 23–36. http://dx.doi.org/10.1044/jshr.1401.23

Bowman, J.P., & C.M. Combs. (1968). Discharge patterns of lingual spindle afferent fibers in the hypoglossal nerve of the rhesus monkey. *Experimental Neurology*, 21(1), 105–19. http://dx.doi.org/10.1016/0014-4886(68)90037-X

Chang, E.F., J.W. Rieger, K. Johnson, M.S. Berger, N.M. Barbaro & R.T. Knight. (2010). Categorical speech representation in human superior temporal gyrus. *Nature Neuroscience*, 13(11), 1428–32. http://dx.doi.org/10.1038/nn.2641

Evans, E.F., & I.C. Whitfield. (1964). Classification of unit responses in the auditory cortex of the non-anaesthetized and unrestrained cat. *Journal of Physiology*, 171(3), 476–93. http://dx.doi.org/10.1113/jphysiol.1964.sp007391

Hartline, H.K., & F. Ratliff. (1958). Spatial summation of inhibitory influences in the eye of Limulus and the mutual interaction of receptor units. *Journal of General Physiology*, 41(5), 1049–66. http://dx.doi.org/10.1085/jgp.41.5.1049

Lettvin, J.Y., H.R. Maturana, W.S. McCulloch & W.H. Pitts. (1959). What the frog's eye tells the frog's brain. *Proceedings of the Institute of Radio Engineers*, 47, 1940–51.

Maturana, H.R., & S. Frenk. (1963). Directional movement and horizontal edge detectors in the pigeon retina. *Science*, 142(3594), 977–9. http://dx.doi.org/10.1126/science.142.3594.977

Mesgarani, M., C. Cheung, K. Johnson, & E.F. Chang. (2014). Phonetic feature encoding in human superior temporal gyrus. *Sciencexpress* /http://www.sciencemag.org/content/early/recent/January 30, 10.1126/science.1245994.

Suga, N., W.E. O'Neill & T. Manabe. (1978). Cortical neurons sensitive to combinations of information-bearing elements of biosonar signals in the mustached bat. *Science*, 200(4343), 778–81. http://dx.doi.org/10.1126/science.644320

Sussman, H.M. (1972). What the tongue tells the brain. *Psychological Bulletin*, 77(4), 262–72. http://dx.doi.org/10.1037/h0032374

Sussman, H.M. (1989a). Neural coding of relational invariance in speech: Human language analogs to the barn owl. *Psychological Review*, 96(4), 631–42. http://dx.doi.org/10.1037/0033-295X.96.4.631

Sussman, H.M. (1989b). A bird brain approach to language. *ASHA* (May), 83–6.

Sussman, H.M. (2002). Representation of phonological categories: A functional role for auditory columns. *Brain and Language*, 80(1), 1–13. http://dx.doi.org/10.1006/brln.2001.2489

Sussman, H.M. (2003). Neuroethology: Providing insights into human language representation. In C.I. Berlin & T.G. Weyand, eds., *The Brain and Sensory Plasticity: Language Acquisition and Hearing* (pp. 25–56). Clifton Park, NY: Thomson Delmar Learning.

Sussman, H.M. (2013). Neuroethology in the service of neurophonetics. *Journal of Neurolinguistics*, 26(5), 511–25. http://dx.doi.org/10.1016/j.jneuroling.2013.02.004

Sussman, H.M., H. McCaffrey & S. Matthews. (1991). An investigation of locus equations as a source of relational invariance for stop place categorization. *Journal of the Acoustical Society of America*, 90, 1309–25.

Sussman, H.M., D.D. Fruchter, J. Hilbert & J. Sirosh. (1998). Linear correlates in the speech signal: The orderly output constraint. Target article, *Behavioral and Brain Sciences*, 21, 241–99.

Tanaka, K. (1997). Mechanisms of visual object recognition: Monkey and human studies. *Current Opinion in Neurobiology*, 7, 523–9.

Wagner, H., T. Takahashi & M. Konishi. (1987). Representation of interaural time difference in the central nucleus of the barn owl's inferior colliculus. *Journal of Neuroscience*, 7, 3105–16.

2
Relativity in Speech Perception: From Locus Equations to Predictive Coding

Bob McMurray, Ariane E. Rhone and Kayleen Hannaway[1]

2.1 Introduction

One of the most vexing and persistent problems in the language sciences is solved by listeners hundreds of times a minute as they recognize speech: the problem of arriving at a somewhat abstract (though not necessarily discrete) encoding of speech despite pervasive variability in the acoustic signal. Such variability derives from factors like talker differences, speaking rate, coarticulation and the like. This so-called problem of lack of invariance motivates a great deal of work in phonetics and speech perception.

However, a somewhat parallel line of work in psycholinguistics suggests listeners must also solve a second, quite independent problem: the problem of time (Marslen-Wilson et al. 1981). Because speech arrives over time, and because words overlap with one another, even if phonemes can be identified unambiguously (the system has solved the problem of lack of invariance) there is still ambiguity, albeit of a more temporary nature. For example, during the early portion of the word *beetle,* once /b/ and /i/ have been identified, there is still ambiguity at the lexical about which word is intended – it could be *beet, beetle, beater* and so forth. The intended word won't be disambiguated until later, when the remainder of the input has

1 Bob McMurray is a professor and Collegiate Scholar in the Department of Psychological and Brain Sciences, the Department of Communication Sciences and Disorders and the Department of Linguistics at the University of Iowa.
Ariane E. Rhone is a research scientist in the Department of Neurosurgery at the University of Iowa.
Kayleen Hannaway is a doctoral candidtate in the Interdisciplinary Neuroscience Program at the University of Iowa.

been heard. This raises important questions about the memory processes involved in resolving this ambiguity (McClelland & Elman 1986) and about when during this process lexical decisions are made (Marslen-Wilson 1987).

As even this cursory framing makes clear, understanding how people process spoken language is inherently a multidisciplinary problem with important insights from phonetics and psycholinguistics (as just described), but also from neuroscience, computational work and clinical work (hearing science, speech pathology). Harvey Sussman's work on locus equations exemplifies this spirit by drawing fundamental insights from neuroscience, applying them to careful phonetic analysis, testing them with the behavioral methods of psychology and often exploring them in clinical populations. Because of his interdisciplinary strategy, he has provided hypotheses about how the system may solve the problem of lack invariance, how this solution may be instantiated neurally, and how it may impact the structure of language or languages.

However, locus equations represent one of a large number of theoretical approaches in speech perception. A partial list includes motor theory (Liberman et al. 1967), acoustic invariance (Blumstein & Stevens 1980), the Fuzzy Logical Model of Perception (FLMP: Oden & Massaro 1978), direct realism (Fowler 1986), the Normal A Posteriori Probability model (NAPP: Nearey 1990), auditory contrast (Kluender et al. 2003), statistical learning (Maye et al. 2003; Toscano & McMurray 2010), and Computing Cues Relative to Expectations (C-CuRE: McMurray & Jongman 2011). But perhaps there are more models than ideas. Perhaps under this sea of acronyms there are deeper principles that may help solve the problems of speech perception regardless of what theoretical wrapper we put them in. This volume is an opportunity to look back and examine one such idea, relativity, the idea that information in speech is not absolute; rather information in the acoustic signal must be interpreted relative to something. Starting from this nugget, which is exemplified by Harvey Sussman's seminal work on locus equations (Sussman, Fruchter et al. 1998; Sussman & Shore 1996), we trace how it appears (in importantly different guises) in three theoretical approaches: compound cues (including locus equations: Sussman, Fruchter et al. 1998), auditory contrast (Kluender et al. 2003), and expectation-relative (or predictive) coding schemes (McMurray & Jongman 2011).

Borrowing from the interdisciplinary line of argumentation exemplified by Harvey Sussman's work, we will build this case using phonetics, neuroscience and, of course, studies of perception. A critical point is that while *speech* has long been dominated by the debates about whether it is subserved by a specialized processing mechanism or not, and about whether speech perception relies on primarily articulatory representations (for both sides, see: Fowler 1991; Holt & Lotto 2008; Liberman & Whalen 2000; Lindblom 1996; Ohala 1996), *relativity* in its various forms has played an important role in showing how accounts based on general auditory, perceptual or information processing principles can account for the variability in the speech signal without the need for such mechanisms.

If this volume is an opportunity to synthesize and distill current theories, it is also an opportunity to challenge them. Relativity in all of its forms has been largely conceived as a solution to the problem of lack of invariance. However, as the field has come to realize a closer coupling between speech perception and word recognition (Andruski et al. 1994; Goldinger 1998; Gow 2001; McClelland & Elman 1986; McMurray et al. 2002, 2009; Port 2007; Utman et al. 2000), we must also confront the problem of time. And indeed, each approach to relativity interacts in interesting ways with this fundamental problem that listeners must solve. Thus, the second goal of this chapter is to understand how approaches to relativity may need to change or be reinterpreted given what we know about the problem of time.

We start with a brief overview of each problem and introduce a working definition of relativity. We then turn to each of our three theoretical approaches.

2.2 Relativity and the Problem of Lack of Invariance

Consider a phonetic cue (which we define as some simple, measurable property of the speech signal that may be involved in perception) like the spectral mean of a fricative (Figure 2.1A). Spectral mean can distinguish place of articulation among sibilants (Forrest et al. 1988; Jongman et al. 2000), discriminating alveolars like /s, z/ with high spectral means (M = 6814 Hz, in the Jongman et al. [2000] data set) from post-alveolars like /ʃ, ʒ/ with lower spectral means (M = 4632 Hz). While this is an apparently large difference, spectral mean is quite variable and differs as a function of talker gender (Strand 1999), the voicing of the consonant (McMurray & Jongman 2011), the neighboring vowel (Daniloff & Moll 1968) and dialect (Munson 2007). Consequently, there is substantial variance within a category which makes it difficult to find an invariant boundary for place of articulation on the basis of this cue (Figure 2.1B).

Intuitively one could imagine several solutions to this problem. First, perhaps we have the wrong cue. Indeed the field has spent many years sifting through possible cues that may be more invariant (Blumstein & Stevens

1979, 1980; Lahiri et al. 1984; Stevens & Keyser 2010). However, the difficulty in identifying such cues, coupled with demonstrations that speech perception could occur with fairly radical transformations of the signal (Remez et al. 1981; Shannon et al. 1995) – transformations that surely would have disrupted such cues – have led many to believe that such cues may not be forthcoming (Lindblom 1996; McMurray & Jongman 2011; Ohala, 1996; Remez 2005).

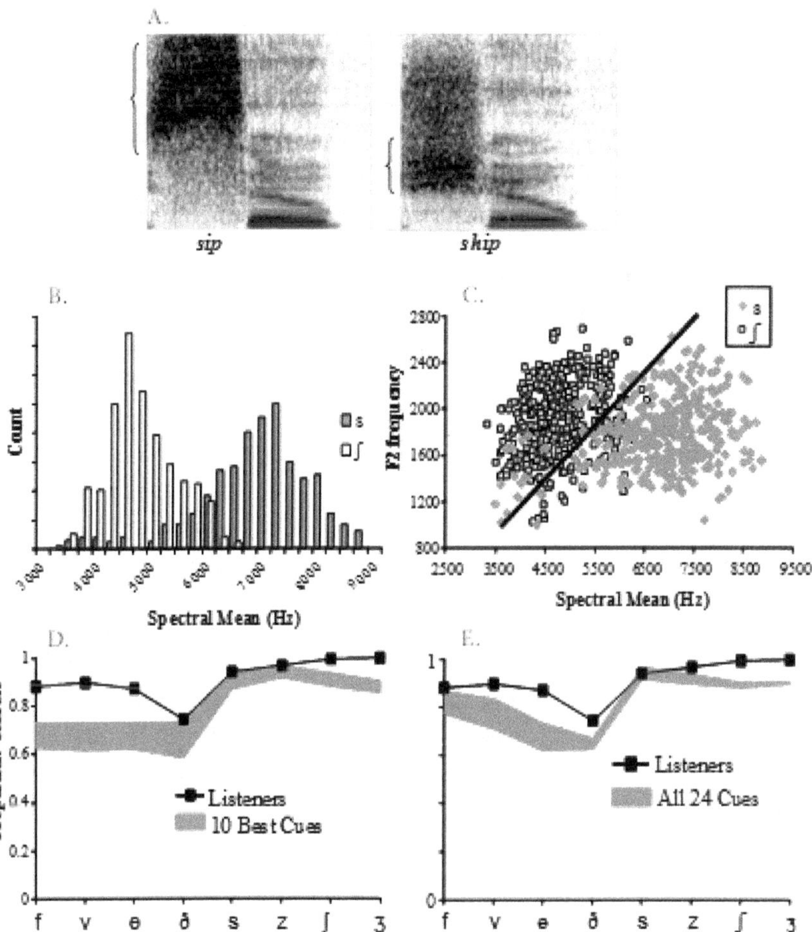

Figure 2.1. A: Spectrograms of two sibilant fricatives with the spectral mean marked. B: Histogram showing the number of tokens at each spectral mean in the Jongman et al. (2000) corpus of 2880 fricatives (20 talkers, 8 fricatives, 6 vowels).
C: The same tokens plotted by both spectral mean and F2-onset frequency.
D: When the 10 "best" cues are optimally combined with logistic regression, the model's performance (gray region) is well below listeners' performance on the same fricatives.
E: While using all available cues results in a substantially better fit, it is still well below listener levels of performance.

Second, if one cue won't do it, perhaps the system uses more? Phonological features leave their mark on many cues (Hillenbrand et al. 1995; Jongman et al. 2000; Lisker 1986) raising the possibility that integrating more information may solve the problem (Nearey 1997). This is illustrated in Figure 2.1C where we plot the same set of fricatives in a spectral mean × F2-onset frequency space – clearly a diagonal boundary making use of both cues would be more accurate. Such ideas are easily instantiated in mathematical models of cue integration like FLMP (Oden & Massaro 1978), NAPP (Nearey 1990) and Mixture of Gaussian frameworks (Toscano & McMurray 2010).

However, ultimately this too may be doomed to failure. In one of the most comprehensive measurement studies attempted, Jongman et al. (2000) measured 20 cues to 2880 fricatives. This included every cue identified in the literature; and a later study (McMurray & Jongman 2011) added four new ones to that same corpus. Thus, their corpus represents as complete a record of the acoustic cues of a large number of fricatives as we might have. These cues were used as input to a simple statistical classification model which was trained to predict the intended fricative on the basis of these cues (similar to FLMP and NAPP). It was clear that more cues were better than a few, but that performance was still about 10 per cent lower than listeners' accuracy in identifying those same fricatives (Figure 2.1D, E). Given that this corpus included virtually every cue for fricatives proposed to date, and used a powerful supervised learning technique, this suggests that simply adding cues may not be sufficient.

The explanation for this is readily apparent when we think about the source of the variability in these cues. Men, for example, have lower spectral means for /s/ (closer to /ʃ/) than women; this is partly because their tongue is placed further back in the mouth when making the /s/ as a socio-linguistic marker (see Strand 1999, for a discussion). One consequence is that their second and third formant frequencies are also lower. Thus, these secondary cues (the formant frequencies) may not do a good job of compensating for a poor primary cue (the spectral mean). Rather than counteracting the noise in the primary cues, many secondary cues reflect it as well, since they derive from the same source.

These issues with using raw cues in some form raise the possibility that a *relative* approach is needed. That is, interpreting cues relative to each other – or relative to abstract cognitive inferences – may yield better perception. An account of speech based on relative encoding could maintain or even enhance sensitivity to small differences in the input that can be highly meaningful, and as we show here, such an approach can be implemented at any level of speech processing, from basic auditory mechanisms to high-level cognitive expectations. Relativity embraces the notion that the variance in any one cue is not variance at all, but really *covariance.* Variance in cues like spectral mean are lawfully related to the causal factors coarticulation, talker, etc. – factors that also affect other cues.

For example, F0 is rather robustly related to talker, but is also a secondary cue for voicing. However, due to these overlapping sources of variance, it can be difficult to interpret in isolation – is an F0 of 150 Hz high for a man because it is a voiceless sound? Or low for a woman because the sound is voiced? However, by interpreting F0 relative to either the surrounding F0 (most of the surrounding F0s are 120 Hz, this F0 is higher than expected so it must mean the sound is voiceless) or relative to knowledge (this is high for a man), the value of this cue could increase markedly. This approach is at the heart of relativity, and though the three theories we review here differ on the implementation (in important ways), the broader notion represents a principled way to both harness variability in the speech signal, and overcome it.

The Problem of Time. In psycholinguistics, a substantial body of work has examined how listeners cope with the temporary ambiguity inherent in words. As we described, for a word like *beetle* the target word may not be identifiable for 150 ms or more (until the arrival of the /əl/).This raises a fundamental problem from the perspective of processing – when does the system start to make commitments at the lexical level (deciding which word was heard, accessing its meaning and so forth)?

The consensus in spoken word recognition clearly favors early and partial commitments at the lexical level – listeners activate multiple words (including their meanings) in parallel from the earliest moments of processing and these compete as the input unfolds until only one is remaining (Allopenna et al. 1998; Marslen-Wilson 1987; Marslen-Wilson & Zwitserlood 1989; McClelland & Elman 1986). If we assume word recognition starts from a phonemic level of representation, all of this would seem to be quite orthogonal to the issues of invariance that motivate relativity. However, a number of recent studies suggest that variability at the acoustic level within a phoneme is preserved throughout lexical processing (Andruski et al. 1994; Goldinger 1998; McMurray et al. 2002; McMurray, Aslin et al. 2008; Salverda et al. 2003; Utman et al. 2000) (see Figure 2.2A). That is, information that would seem to be category-irrelevant is preserved at late stages of language processing after phonemic analysis is complete. Consequently, processes that deal with acoustic variability may be occurring simultaneously to or interactively with those that deal with temporal ambiguity.

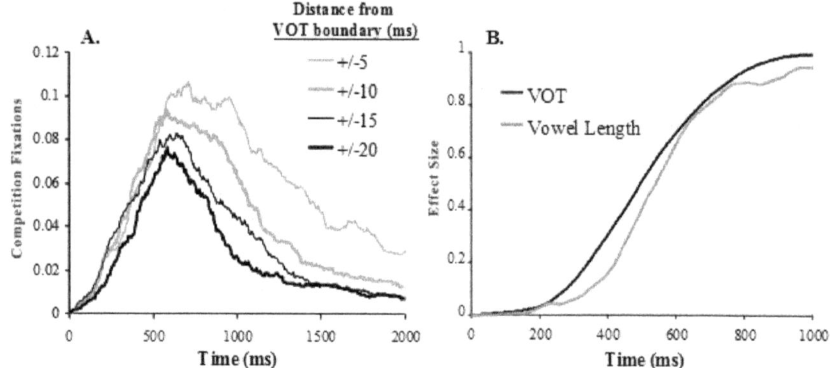

Figure 2.2. A: In McMurray et al. (2002) subjects heard tokens from a voice onset time (VOT) continuum (e.g., *beach* to *peach*) and clicked on the corresponding referent while their eye-movements to each object were monitored. Shown is the proportion of trials on which they fixated the competitor (*peach* when the target word was *beach*) as a function of time. This was treated relative to each participant's own boundary and excludes trials on which the competitor was selected, so the increase in fixations with VOT represents sensitivity to within-category differences.
B: In McMurray, Clayards et al. (2008) the differences between curves as in Panel A were computed as a function of VOT or vowel length every 4 ms to determine the effect size of that cue on real-time fixation behavior. The effect of VOT began *before* the effect of the subsequent vowel length suggesting that each cue is used as soon as it arrives, and the system does not wait for all of the cues to voicing before activating words in the lexicon.

This is well illustrated by several recent studies by McMurray and colleagues examining how asynchronous cues (e.g., voice onset time [VOT] and the length of the subsequent vowel) are integrated prior to lexical access. If there were some sort of pre-lexical integration stage, one might expect that the system would accumulate information and only access the lexicon once all of the cues to a particular phoneme have arrived. In contrast, a more integrated system might partially activate lexical items on the basis of one cue and then update as more cues arrive. Two studies by McMurray and colleagues (McMurray, Clayards et al. 2008; Toscano & McMurray 2012) addressed this question by examining when VOT and the length of the subsequent vowel affect decisions between minimal pair words at the lexical level. They showed that VOT affected fixations as soon as it was available, and prior to the availability of vowel length (Figure 2.2B). This has also been extended to manner of articulation (b/w: McMurray, Clayards et al. 2008), word-final fricative voicing (Galle 2014), and vowel quantity (Reinisch & Sjerps 2013) as well as to VOT stimuli constructed from natural speech and in sentence context (Toscano & McMurray 2012, 2015) and thus may represent a more general property of speech perception (though not universal: see Galle 2014).

This poses a particularly interesting problem for models that use relative cues. In almost all of the relativity approaches, the information that listeners need to relativize the input is not consistently simultaneous with the relevant cues. For example, the spectral mean of a fricative must be evaluated with respect to the preceding or subsequent vowel; or F0 must be evaluated against neighboring F0s, or against long-term representations of the talker. If the system must use later information as the basis for relativizing cues, then it may be forced to wait for them to arrive in order to make any decisions. Understanding how relative encoding processes may deal with the asynchrony in the signal and with the ongoing dynamics of lexical activation is thus a crucial avenue for further work.

Overview. In the next three sections, we review three theories based around relativity: compound cues (including locus equations), auditory contrast accounts, and expectation-relative encoding (or predictive coding). In each we have twin goals. First we seek to highlight the common principle that underlies these three theories, and we seek to identify the important differences in how this is carried out. Second, we wish to examine these specific accounts with respect to the problem of time, and to show some preliminary hints as to how this might be handled.

2.3 Locus Equations and Compound Cues

A seminal problem in speech is the identification of stop consonants. While it has long been clear that formant transitions are crucial for this (Delattre et al. 1955), at the moment of the stop closure there is by definition no sound. Thus the formant transitions into or out of the closure are at best a trace of where the formant would have been during closure, marking the movement between the unobservable formants at closure, and the audible formants during the vowel. Thus, the audible onset frequencies of the formants are heavily influenced by the formant frequencies of the vowel. Consequently there may be no single onset frequency that characterizes a given place of articulation.

Locus equations were meant to compensate for this variability. To obtain locus equations, the second formant (F2) transition is measured twice: at the onset and at a midpoint of the vocalic portion of a CV utterance (Figure 2.3A). This captures the difference between the onset formant

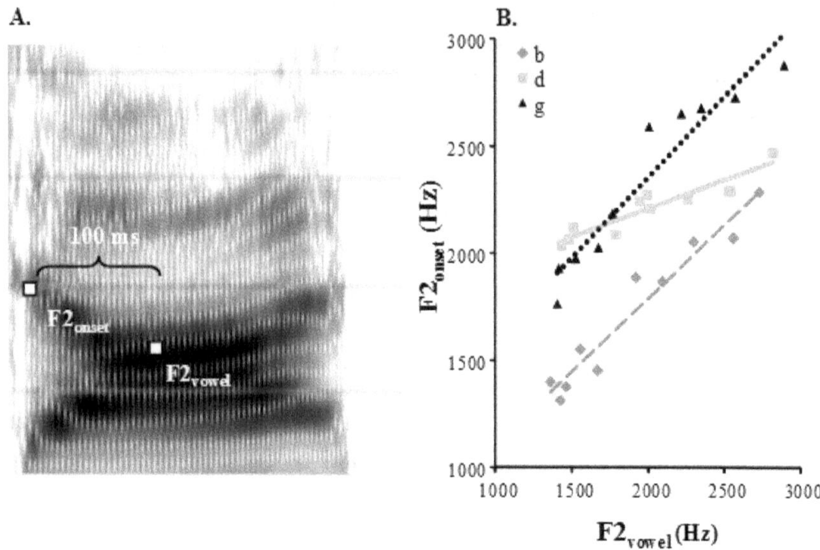

Figure 2.3. A: Spectrogram of *dot* spoken by a female. Locus equations are typically derived by measuring the second formant at vowel onset and near vowel midpoint. These measurement points can span more than one hundred milliseconds, depending on the length of the vowel and the shape of the formant transition (see Sussman et al. 1991).
B: Locus equation scatterplot derived from Rhone & Jongman (2012) showing average F2-vowel by F2-onset measurements for 10 female talkers. Each point represents one consonant + vowel token. Scatterplots show high linear relationships and cluster by consonant category.

frequency and the steady state, and simultaneously compensates for this coarticulatory influence and estimates it. Given the immense variability among individuals in vowel steady states (Hillenbrand et al. 1995; Peterson & Barney 1952), this measure also implicitly computes formant transitions relative to talker differences. Crucially, when F2-onset /F2-vowel measurements obtained from several vowel contexts are plotted, a higher-order relationship appears, and this linear relationship appears unique for different places of articulation (Figure 2.3B), and even for different allophones of the same phoneme (e.g., the palatal and velar /g/'s which appear as different clusters of points in Figure 2.3B). Thus, while F2-onset may be variable and/or context-dependent, as part of a locus equation with F2-vowel it may be more invariant, and hence more useful as a basis for categorization. It is this higher-order relationship (between F2-onsets and F2-vowels across multiple tokens) that is described by the locus equation, rather than any single relationship between one onset/vowel measurement pair.

When Sussman and colleagues revived and quantified the locus equation – a concept that dates back to the mid-20th century (Delattre et al. 1955; Lindblom 1963) – they brought compound cues back into the spotlight of phonetic analysis. Compound cues more broadly refer to cues constructed from multiple traditional measurements, typically with the same goals as locus equations. For example, formant ratios have been implicated in the identification of vowels: the messy, overlapping F2 by F1 vowel space becomes orderly and clustered by vowel quality when F2–F1 by F1 is used as the measure, and normalizing against F3 or F0 can result in more orderly clusters (Miller 1989; Monahan & Idsardi 2010; Peterson 1951). Similarly, the ratio of consonant and vowel durations may help compensate for the effect of speaking rate on temporal cues to voicing like VOT (Boucher 2002; Pind 1995; Port & Dalby 1982). In these cases, the primary cues (formant onset, formant steady-states, VOT) are related to some estimate of the surrounding variance (other formants, vowel length) as a form of compensation or relativization.

Locus equations (and other compound cues) do not in and of themselves *solve* the lack of invariance problem. That requires both specification of the information (e.g., the locus equation) and a metric for mapping that information onto phonological categories. Rather, locus equations offer a metric of relational invariance, demonstrating proof that this form of relativization yields a more invariant set of cues. The phonetic grounding and biological plausibility of this construct make it an attractive candidate cue for reconciling the difficulty of finding a single place of articulation cue with the apparent ease of human speech perception. Indeed, in place of articulation – long the seminal test-bed of theories of coping with the lack of invariance – Sussman's extensive work on locus equations has shown consistently the vast potential for using locus equations as the basis of categorization.

Compound cues do not avoid or limit variability, but instead take advantage of it, thus taming the beast that had seemed so impossible to overcome in prior search for acoustic cues signaling stop place.

> [Locus Equations] demonstrate that the variable F2 transitions, that led Motor Theorists to abandon the auditory signal in favor of motor gestures, have been normalized in a self-organized fashion, at the level of the stop place category. (Sussman 2009)

Importantly, the locus equation itself can only be estimated by taking measurements from a variety of vowel contexts (Figure 2.3B). This suggests a profoundly developmental origin in which children must learn the statistical distribution of these cues in their own input. While this has not been extensively examined, it is clearly consistent with recent statistical learning accounts (McMurray & Farris-Trimble 2012; Werker & Curtin 2005). Without this variability in the steady-state of the formants across utterances (which provide the *x*-axis measurements for typical locus equation scatterplots), the higher-order invariants cannot be discovered by the phonetician, or presumably by the developing child (cf. Rost & McMurray 2010, for an analogous problem in development). The locus equation absorbs this variability, and from relativized F2-onset/F2-vowel measurements emerges a higher-order feature for categorization.

Locus equations are correlated with intelligibility at the broadest level. People with developmental apraxia, young children and people who stutter have all been shown to have less invariant locus equations (Mccaffrey Morrison 2012; Sussman et al. 1999, 2002, 2011), suggesting a relationship between this measure and intelligibility. More direct tests of perception are promising but limited. Fruchter and Sussman (1997) used synthetic F2-onset/F2-vowel pairs to test listeners' categorization of tokens within a locus equation space derived from Sussman et al. (1991). They found overlap between the perceptual space and locus equation values, suggesting perceptual space is organized in a way that does not conflict with the locus equation notion. However, Brancazio and Fowler (1998) argue that the direct perceptual support has yet to be shown. Parametric evaluation of perceptual space is quite difficult, as the compound nature of the cue makes it likely that just about any manipulation of F2-onset/F2-vowel will be necessarily confounded with other metrics (e.g., the raw F2-onset, spectral shape etc.)

However, Figure 2.3B suggests that such investigations are clearly necessary. If we assume that listeners compute the place of articulation of any given token by comparing its position in F2-onset/F2-vowel space to the nearest line, there are points that will clearly be attributable to multiple places of articulation (e.g., the cluster of overlapping squares and triangles at the left, and the cluster of overlapping squares and diamonds on the right). Thus, there is a clear need to investigate this framing in a way more sensitive to categorization.

Despite the limitations discussed above, the basic finding of linear separability in F2-onset/F2-vowel space has been shown for stop consonants of English (Sussman et al. 1991), as well as a variety of other languages (Celdran & Villalba 1995; Eek & Meister 1995; Krull 1989; Sussman et al. 1993), in children (Sussman et al. 1992), and across speaking styles (Sussman, Dalston & Gumpert 1998). Similarly, CV ratios for voicing have been shown to be largely rate invariant for a number of languages across variable speaking rates (Pind 1995; Port & Dalby 1982), and across dramatic shifts in register (e.g., infant vs adult directed speech, McMurray et al. 2013).

An essential aspect of locus equations – and one that sets them apart from other compound cues – is their grounding in neurobiology. Sussman extended his primarily phonetic and articulatory work on the locus equation by using comparative neuro-ethology to show how such compound cues could be calculated in the brain. For simple cues like formant frequencies or spectral moments, presumed tonotopic maps in sub-cortical and cortical regions offered a loose justification for how such cues could be computed. However, a compound, relativistic cue like the locus equation requires a slightly more advanced receptor, challenging the validity of this approach. Something in the brain has to be able to compare the two values to compute the relative cue.

Sussman built the neurobiological case for locus equations on auditory neurophysiology in non-human animals that demonstrates *combination*-sensitive neurons in early auditory areas (Sussman, Fruchter et al. 1998). Such neurons respond only weakly to individual auditory events, but instead preferentially respond to combinations of events. These events must be bound across both time and frequency to result in a meaningful percept. For example, in the mustached bat, combination sensitive neurons in the inferior colliculus preferentially respond to pulse-echo pairs used in echolocation (the sent and received FM sweep). Such neurons require sensitivity across a large frequency range (because the pulses are frequency modulated) and across a (relatively) large timespan, but must be selective to particular combinations in order to compute location (Suga et al. 1978, 1983). Similarly, in the barn owl, frequency and phase information, which are inherently non-informative in isolation, are combined via combination sensitive neurons to compute interaural time and intensity differences (Knudsen & Konishi 1978) and provide spatial localization information along the lines suggested by Jeffress (1948). In both cases, highly species-specific functions like echolocation are ultimately achieved by general neural structures. Sussman and colleagues proposed a similar model for human speech in which the encoding of F2 transition (which occurs over time and frequency) might rely on similar processes, and could be organized in some sort of neural column (Lindblom & Sussman 2012; Sussman 2002). While this has not been extended to other compound cues, the neurophysiological approach proposed for locus equations clearly offers a strong framework for thinking about these issues.

Thus far compound cues have largely been applied to the problem of lack of invariance and not to the problem of time. The practical timing of the measurements necessary to derive locus equations has long been considered a shortcoming of this approach on phonetic grounds (Blumstein 1998; Jongman 1998) as the time point at which the F2-vowel measurement is made can appear arbitrary (Sussman, Fruchter et al. 1998). But this is more than an issue of measurement that phoneticians must confront; the auditory system must also confront the problem of time.

To estimate F2-vowel at approximately vowel midpoint or steady state, the listener may have to wait for over a hundred milliseconds to decide whether the word was *bill, dill* or *gill.* This appears to fly in the face of work using offline measures showing that that listeners can identify/categorize word initial stop consonants with as little as 10–20 ms of second formant transition (Blumstein & Stevens 1980; Tekieli & Cullinan 1979). Similarly, CV ratios would require listeners to wait until the end of the syllable before they could make any judgments about voicing. Both approaches would appear to force listeners to wait for the appropriate cues before they could compute relative cues. Both types of approaches are challenged by the aforementioned studies showing that listeners do not appear to wait for asynchronous cues in order to access lexical candidates (McMurray, Clayards et al. 2008; Reinisch & Sjerps 2013). While these studies clearly show that listeners do not need to compute a CV ratio to recognize voicing, they have not addressed place of articulation. However, the fairly widespread finding of immediate integration would seem to pose a challenge to locus equations.

To address this issue, Rhone & Jongman (2012) investigated whether locus equations could be calculated in a more perceptually realistic time frame. They measured the first several pitch pulses of the CV transition, using these measurements in place of F2-vowel to compute the locus equation. Here, less than 30 ms of absolute time had elapsed between F2-onset and F2-vowel (though many of these F2-vowels were during the transition) and yet this modified version of locus equations showed linear separability and discriminability of English word initial voiced stops. This suggests that the locus equation approach is potentially not incompatible with the time course of auditory processing.

2.4 Auditory Contrast

Compound cues offer highly specific relationships between particular cues to cope with the variability of speech. Auditory contrast accounts (Holt & Lotto 2008; Kluender et al. 2003) argue that similar results can be achieved by more general perceptual mechanisms. It is well known that continuous perceptual values like hue, brightness and frequency are perceived in terms of their contrast to neighboring perceptual events – a gray patch on a black background will look lighter than that same patch on a white background. This principle, a form of relative encoding, seems to characterize perception in many domains, and work by Kluender, Lotto, Holt and colleagues has demonstrated how contrast may do the work of compensating for different forms of variance in speech perception (even though the mechanism is not geared specifically for processes like talker compensation).

For example, coarticulation exerts an influence between neighboring consonants that listeners must take into account. A /g/ after an /l/ is pronounced with the tongue slightly further back in the mouth than after an /r/. Listeners must "undo" this in order to recover the intended phoneme. In a series of seminal studies by Mann and Repp (Mann 1980; see also Mann & Repp 1980, 1981), listeners were presented with tokens from a /ga/ to /da/ continuum preceded by either /al/ or /ar/. Listeners identified the second consonant, and shifted their boundaries such that they perceived more tokens as /ga/ when preceded by /al/, and more as /da/ when preceded with /ar/. Thus listeners appear to "undo" the coarticulation.

Lotto & Kluender (1998) point out that *spectral contrast* may offer a simple explanation. They note that /l/ has a higher F3 than /r/. Consequently, when the F3 of the subsequent /d/ or /g/ is heard, it may be perceived as lower than it is (after /l/), biasing listeners toward more /g/ responses. Similarly, since /r/ has a low F3, this could lead the following F3 to be perceived as higher (resulting in a /d/). This suggests that simple auditory contrast mechanisms could do the work of a more explicit compensatory mechanism tuned to coarticulation. To test this, Lotto & Kluender (1998) replaced the preceding /al/ or /ar/ with a low or high tone, and tested the consequence of this for listeners' identification of the subsequent /d/ to /g/ continuum. Results mirrored the effects using the preceding speech sound, suggesting that explicit compensation-type effects can be accomplished with general auditory mechanisms.

One concern about this effect, however, is whether it can only derive from local contrast, or if longer-term representations of the auditory properties of the signal can play a role. This is important because if the effect is purely local, such mechanisms could not handle long-distance coarticulatory effects (Magen 1997) or talker effects which are often distributed throughout the preceding material. To examine this, Holt (2006) created acoustic histories made from a series of sine waves; these series always ended on the same mid-frequency tone, but differed in the statistical distribution of tones leading up to it (either centered at a high or low frequency).

Despite the fact that the adjacent tones were identical in both conditions, the distribution of tones affected d/g categorization much as in Lotto & Kluender (1998). Thus, even when the contrastive context is presented seconds before the target stimulus and with an intervening neutral tone, contrast continues to play a role. It is clear that not only local acoustic context can affect categorization, but that longer-term statistical properties of the auditory signal can as well.

These general contrastive mechanisms extend well beyond coarticulation. Diehl et al. (1978) asked listeners to categorize synthetic ambiguous /b/ and /p/ initial syllables when preceded by clear /b/ or /p/ initial syllables. Listeners' categorization was influenced by the preceding sound so that they categorized more target stimuli as the opposite phoneme from what the target was proceeded by. This may offer a rapid way to adapt to talker-specific differences in how phonemes are produced – hearing one idiosyncratic sound can set up contrasts that will cascade to other sounds. Similarly, Laing et al. (2012) suggest that general contrast mechanisms may also be involved in talker compensation. They manipulated the long-term average spectrum (LTAS) of the context that preceded a speech target (a consonant-vowel pair between /ga/ and /da/). This made the context sound like different talkers, but this manipulation did not influence the specific formant frequencies. LTAS differences only influenced categorization of a speech target when the changes were near the frequencies of relevant acoustic cues, but LTAS changes were influential both when embedded in synthesized sentences and as part of non-speech tone sequences.

The influence of pure tones on speech perception provides powerful evidence that these speech-like effects can derive from general processes, and animal work confirms this conclusion. Lotto et al. (1997) trained Japanese quail to categorize clear /g/ and /d/ exemplars. After mastering this task, the quail were tested on ambiguous /g/ and /d/ exemplars in the context of /ɑr/ and /ɑl/ and they showed a shift in their categorization similar to humans. As quail are unlikely to have much experience with coarticulation, and it certainly has no functional relevance to them, this provides converging evidence that compensation for coarticulation can be implemented with general auditory processes.

Similarly, classic studies have shown that while VOT is perhaps the most important cue to voicing for English listeners, first formant onset frequency serves as an important secondary cue (Summerfield & Haggard 1977). When F1 onset frequency is lowered, listeners require longer VOT in order to categorize a sound as voiceless. Importantly, the mechanisms with which this adjustment occurs are not unique to human speech but stem from more general processes. Kluender & Lotto (1994) demonstrated that Japanese quail trained to categorize voicing show a similar pattern, without any experience with the relevant covariation. This finding provides stronger support for general auditory mechanisms as a component of the perception of context dependent information.

The presence of such covariation effects raises the possibility that contrast effects are learned from the statistical properties of auditory events in the environment. Holt et al. (2001) addressed this by training quail to detect long or short VOTs. During training, the quail were exposed to natural (low F0 correlated with shorter VOTs), reverse (low F0 correlated with longer VOTs) or no covariation. They were then tested on a similar voicing task as Kluender & Lotto (1994), and their responses matched the pattern they had been trained on: quail who received uncorrelated cues showed no effect of F0; quail trained in one of the covarying conditions used F0 in the predicted direction. Therefore, these general auditory mechanisms are not hard-wired but can be shaped by experience.

There are still a number of open questions with the auditory contrast account – in particular, how we can generalize from experiments with non-speech stimuli to speech. Viswanathan et al. (2009) argue that sufficient spectral information may not be present in the speech signal in order for such mechanisms to influence categorization. Although pure tones that match the frequency offset of speech that provides context effects do influence perception in the same way as the speech sounds, they showed that tones that were matched to the trajectories and intensities of speech formants do not. In fact, natural speech that had been filtered to only contain the critical F3 spectral information also had no influence on categorization. Thus, the pure tone studies may produce an effect that does not account for the compensation for coarticulation in typical circumstances.

Similarly, auditory contrast mechanisms have yet to be applied in a systematic way to the problem of lack of invariance. As we've described, many of the compound cues have been validated by phonetic analysis of large numbers of speech tokens. Although contrast mechanisms have been shown to produce behavioral results that mimic listeners, they have not had the same amount of phonetic scrutiny to establish how and if they can account for the known sources of variance in the acoustic signal. Contrast mechanisms alone may not be able to deal with the full spectrum of variability in speech and if so contrast may be one of multiple mechanisms recruited during normal speech perception.

Finally, the problem of time is significant. Cues that set up contrast mechanisms, like a low F3 offset, happen before the target phoneme. During perception do individuals commit to a /ga/ when they hear the low F3 offset, or do they wait for /g/ in order to make their decision? Critically, is the low F3 associated with the preceding /r/ a direct (but partial) cue for distinguishing /d/ and /g/ (a phonetic cue for place)? Or does it only serve to modify how the cues for /d/ and /g/ are interpreted later (a context cue, cf. Repp 1982)? Reinisch & Sjerps (2013) addressed this in the domain of speaking rate variation. Here, a contrast account (durational contrast) would seem to suggest that vowel length and surrounding estimates of rate are contrasted. They presented listeners with minimal pair words in which the vowels differed in spectral and temporal information. They varied F2 frequencies and vowel duration of the target words and the context sentence preceding the target, using these manipulations of context to set up a context. As in McMurray, Clayards et al. (2008) they used eye-tracking to investigate when context influenced perception. They showed that changes in the cues during the context sentence did not have an immediate effect, but rather exerted their influence at approximately the same time as the target cue. This supports the idea that context serves to set up the contrast (with target cues), but does not activate phonemes or words directly, supporting an auditory account. However, as yet there have been no studies of situations in which the context *follows* the target segment – this could be critical in understanding if phonetic cues can be interpreted in the absence of such contrastive mechanisms, or if listeners must wait.

2.5 Expectation-Relative Coding

Both compound cue and auditory contrast mechanisms implement relativity in terms of the relationship between properties of the signal. Formant frequencies, for example, are computed relative to other formant frequencies, or relative to the more general surrounding auditory material. As we've described, such relationships appear to capture and compensate for the acoustic variability associated with speech.

At the same time, they may also be inflexible. Could one relativize F2-onset if there were not a vowel center (Strange et al. 1983)? Can auditory contrast work across cues that do not bear superficial resemblance, for example, contrasting the duration of aspiration against the duration of a vowel for rate normalization of VOT (Toscano & McMurray 2012)? There also may be opportunities that live beyond the signal – for example, if one knew that an /i/ was coming up (e.g. because semantics had indicated the word was *maybe*) one could relativize the formant transitions in /b/ against the *expectation* that F2 will be high, before it was heard.

Expectation-relative (ER) encoding, exemplified by the C-CuRE model (Cole et al. 2010; McMurray & Jongman 2011), appears to deal with some of these issues. The idea is that, just like in compound cue and auditory contrast approaches, speech perception is not based on raw cues like formant frequencies or VOTs, it is based on a difference. But, this difference is between the observed cues and the *listener's expectations*, expectations that can derive from more abstract knowledge about the signal.

For example, for a /g/, F2 falls when preceding a vowel like /u/ with a low F2, but rises before a vowel like /i/. The locus equation treats the relationship between the F2-onset and the F2 at steady state as information. In contrast, an ER approach uses the listener's identification of the vowel to predict the F2, rather than using the observed F2 at steady state (e.g., I heard an /i/ therefore this F2 is lower than expected). Comparison is based on expectations, not the actual cue. Crucially, these expectations may come from anywhere – knowledge of the talker (this F2 is higher than is typical for this talker), dialect, words (e.g., the word is likely *maybe* so an /i/ must be coming up), and of course, neighboring sounds.

This approach builds on a long debate over contingent categorization (Mermelstein 1978; Nearey 1990; Sawusch & Pisoni 1974; Smits 2001a; Whalen 1992). This work typically used large sets of stimuli in which the same cue could contribute to multiple decisions (e.g., vowel length as a cue both to word final voicing and to vowel identity) to ask if listeners' decisions about one sound influence the other. That is, if they decided the final consonant was voiced, would they then attribute the longer vowel to voicing and not apply it to vowel identity? In a sense, this work asked if listeners would interpret cues relative to other decisions they had made about the input. The conclusions from this were somewhat inconclusive and depended on what sort of statistical model one applied to the data and to the covariances latent in the stimuli.

However, a series of recent phonetic analyses and experimental studies shed crucial light on this issue. Cole et al. (2010) investigated vowel-to-vowel coarticulation; in particular, they asked whether one could use fine-grained coarticulatory modification in one vowel to predict an upcoming sound. For example, in the phrase *wet eagle*, the /ɛ/ in *wet* will be raised and fronted toward the /i/ in *eagle* (Ohman 1966) creating an opportunity for the listener to anticipate the following vowel. However, at the same time, this vowel will also have a higher F1 due to the voiceless /t/ and a higher F2 due to the coronal. Talker gender or other factors may impose yet additional noise, with the consequence that it may be quite difficult even to identify the target vowel as /ɛ/ or /ʌ/ from absolute measurements alone (Figure 2.4A), much less the upcoming vowel (Figure 2.4B).

However, Cole and colleagues point out that these factors were lawful, and in fact a simple regression analysis predicting F1 or F2 from the target vowel, the place and voicing of the intervening consonant, and the talker and context vowel could account for upwards of 90 per cent of the variance in the measurements. These same regressions could be used to partial these factors out of the cues. That is, cues could be calculated relative to the predicted cue values based on factors like talker, and these residuals (rather

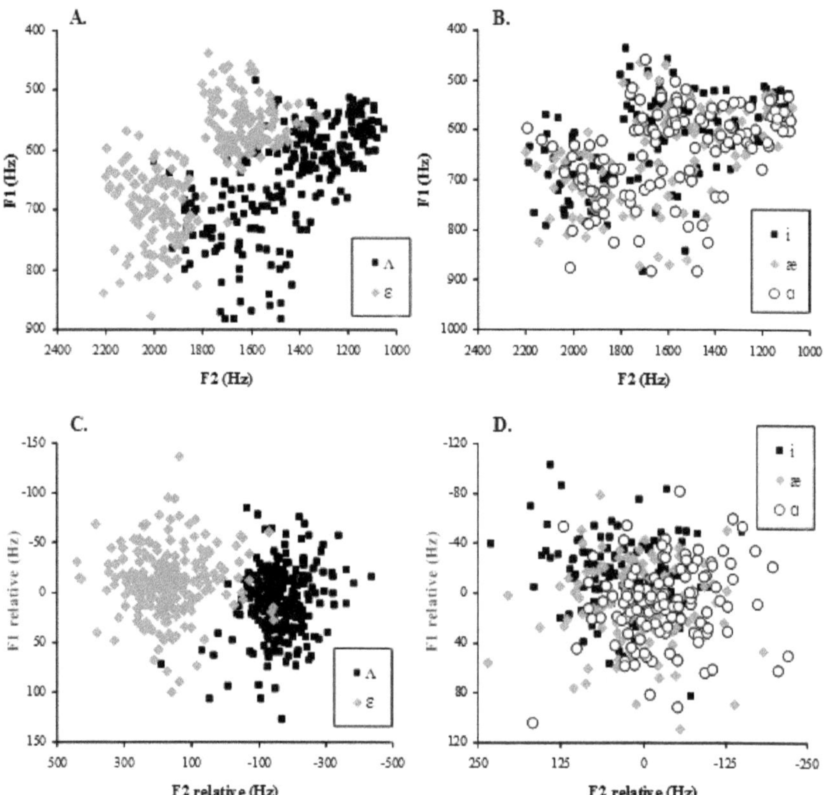

Figure 2.4. F1 and F2 measurements from the corpus of vowels studied by Cole et al. (2010). The first vowel of two word sequences (e.g., *wet eagle*) were measured and across tokens there was variability in talker, intervening consonant and context vowel. A: Raw cue values as a function of the target (first vowel) showing substantial overlap between the two categories.
B: Raw cue values as a function of the context vowel showing almost complete overlap.
C: F1 and F2 as a function of the target vowel after partialing out talker, intervening consonant and upcoming vowel – the categories are now much more clearly separated.
D: F1 and F2 as a function of the context vowel after partialing out known sources of variance. Now, vowels before /i/ appear in the top left, and vowels before /ɑ/ in the bottom right.

than the actual cue values) could serve as information for subsequent categorization. This consequently led to a much clearer distribution of cue values relative to both target vowel and the upcoming vowel (Figure 2.4C, D). This also suggested a theoretical model: if listeners make predictions about cue value (e.g., the talker is a male, so I should expect lower formant frequencies) and simply recode incoming cues relative to those predictions, accurate speech perception may be possible.

McMurray & Jongman (2011) offered a more conclusive test of this. They started with Jongman's seminal corpus of fricatives (Jongman et al. 2000), to achieve a fairly complete description of the acoustics of this corpus. This corpus encompassed substantial variability spanning 20 different talkers and six vowel contexts. Then, a small subset of these tokens was presented to listeners in an identification experiment.

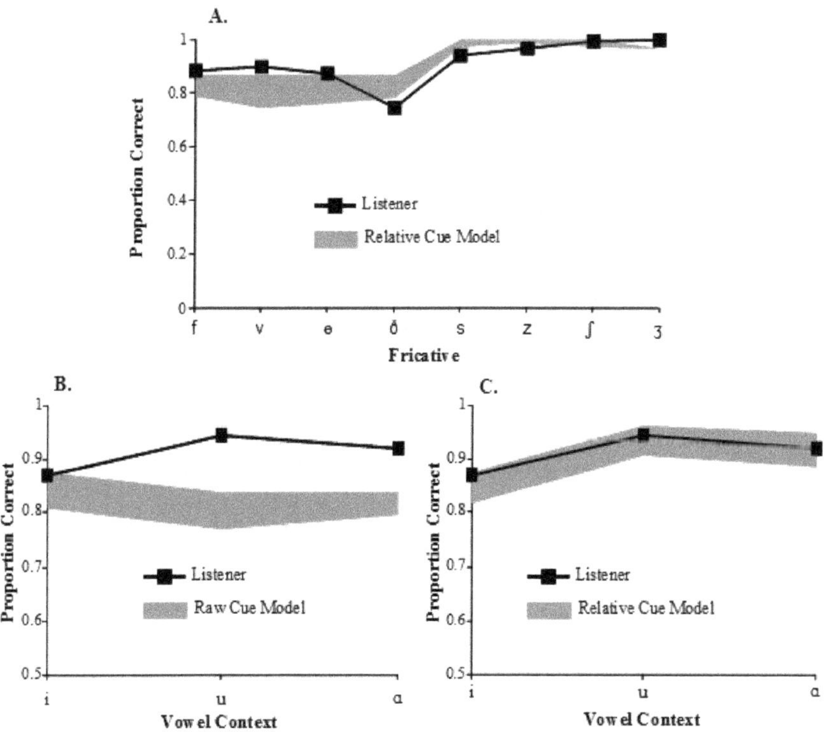

Figure 2.5. A: Performance of listeners on an 8AFC fricative identification task compared to a logistic regression trained on relative cues to predict the fricative. B: Both listeners' and the model's performance on fricative identification as a function of the vowel context. In this panel the model was trained on raw cues as in Figure 2.1E. C: Same as B, but trained on relative cue values.

With this data set, they trained a logistic regression model to predict the intended fricative from the cue values, and compared its results to listener performance. Here, logistic regression simply weights and combines the cues to achieve the best fit to the training data, and work in a way that is conceptually quite similar to prototype models like FLMP (Oden & Massaro 1978) and NAPP (Nearey 1997). As we illustrated in Figure 2.1, even with all 24 cues, the model's performance was still about 10 per cent lower than listeners'; however, when cues were treated relative to expectations, model performance matched listeners' (Figure 2.5A). Perhaps more intriguingly, this approach also best fit the pattern of errors, listeners were best when the fricatives preceded the vowel /u/, and worse at fricatives before /ɑ/ and /i/. Similarly, the model trained on raw cue values (Figure 2.5B) showed the opposite pattern, while that trained on relative cues showed the correct one (Figure 2.5C). Finally, when the models were compared to humans who had heard only the fricative in isolation (so they could not know the vowel or the talker), the raw cue model performed best.

So how does this process work mechanistically during perception? The basic idea is that as listeners hear speech they make inferences about aspects of it – who the talker is, or what phonemes/words they have heard. These can be used to form perceptual-level expectations about what they are going to hear (e.g., I should expect pitches in the 130 Hz range since the talker was Bob). New information is then evaluated against these expectations. For example, pitch in the McMurray and Jongman corpus was a moderately useful cue for voicing with a mean of 148 Hz for voiced sounds and 160 Hz for voiceless; however the variance was large (SD-voiced = 43 Hz; SD-voiceless = 49 Hz). Consequently, a token in the middle of this range (e.g., 154 Hz) would not be informative for voicing. However, if one knows that the talker has an average pitch of 130 Hz, this 154 Hz pitch is now 24 Hz *higher than expected* and clear evidence for a voiceless sound. The critical factor is that rather than comparing F0 to other aspects of the signal (e.g., the F0 in an adjacent segment), it is compared to expectations based on higher-level inferences.

This account is consistent with a number of behavioral studies that are difficult to account for in auditory contrast or compound cue approaches. These studies show that listeners' category boundaries can be shifted by manipulating participants' expectations in various ways. For example, seeing a still photograph of a face can create gender expectations and alter participants' categorizations of fricatives and vowels (Johnson et al. 1999; Strand 1999); even telling listeners to imagine that a talker is from a particular dialect group can do the same (Niedzielski 1999). Winn et al. (2013) have also shown that individuals who use cochlear implants show vowel- and talker-sensitive boundary shifts in categorization of /s/ to /ʃ/ continua. Given their reduced spectral sensitivity some version of an expectation-based account would appear to make more sense in this case. These studies provide powerful evidence that high-level expectations can shape speech perception. However, they do not demonstrate that such expectations can improve perceptual analysis and lead to greater accuracy.

Apfelbaum et al. (2014) investigated this by noting that in fricative-vowel pairs, the talker and/or vowel is likely to be quite difficult to identify from the fricative alone; consequently participants may have to reanalyze the fricative when the vocoid is heard. They manipulated this by constructing stimuli in which the fricative was taken from one context (e.g., before an /i/ spoken by a man) but the vocoid came from a different context (e.g., an /u/ spoken by woman). Critically, the bottom up cues in both portions matched the correct fricative. Thus, when listeners are presented with such stimuli, when they hear the vocoid, they will generate the wrong expectations about what the fricative should have sounded like and this should impair accuracy. This is indeed what was found: listeners were both less accurate and slower when they were misled on either the talker or the vowel.

Similar to the other relativistic approaches, this model also is grounded in neuroscience. In particular, in recent years, predictive coding (Rao & Ballard 1999) has become an important theory in the neuroscience of both vision and motor control, and extended as an account of cognition more generally (Clark 2013). For example, in motor control, researchers have long been concerned about transmission delays – when monitoring an ongoing a movement it may take too long to convert visual or somatosensory feedback into motor coordinates to effectively alter the movement. The solution is a forward model: when the movement is planned, the system simultaneously generates perceptual expectations about what the motion should look and feel like, expectations which can then be compared more rapidly with the incoming sensory signal (Flanagan et al. 2003; Wolpert & Flanagan 2001). Again, it is this comparison which is the critical source of information in motor control; when the perceived trajectory deviates from the expected, a correction is needed. Here, we see a similar process in speech, though driven purely by perception – expectations about what will be heard shape ongoing perception.

Speech perception both benefits from and contributes to the broader literature on predictive coding. The forward model approach points out that translating expectations to perceptual codes offers a great deal of efficiency gains, something which is likely to be important given the rapidity of speech. At the same time, the application of this model to speech offers new insight about predictive coding. While predictive coding usually frames expectations as the outcome of a *prospective* (forward in time) process, the approach offered by C-CuRE and the Apfelbaum et al. (2014) study also suggests that expectations can operate *retrospectively,* making predictions about what should have been heard in the past.

While the evidence for predictive coding in the neuroscience of vision and motor control is fairly extensive (see Clark 2013, for a review), there is much less in speech. In speech *production,* there is evidence for motor suppression, that early sensory areas show reduced activity in response to one's own speech (relative to externally heard speech) (Houde et al. 2002). This is consistent with predictive coding – if listeners are generating auditory expectations for what their own speech should sound like, less neural processing should be required when it is heard. There is evidence for a reduction in neural activity when lexical context enables better prediction (Gagnepain et al. 2012), though there is also evidence that predictability can enhance activity overall, somewhat counteracting these claims (Wild et al. 2012). Moreover there is as yet no evidence that factors like talker or neighboring phonemes modulate neural activity in this way, though a study by von Kriegstein et al. (2010) does suggest parallel interactive streams for talker and word identification. Thus, while there is neural support for expectation-relative processing or predictive coding in speech, much remains to be done.

As with the preceding approaches, though, the problem of time must be more effectively addressed in expectation-relative encoding. On the one hand, predictive coding offers some advantages with its emphasis on prediction. This is consistent with a number of studies showing that listeners can make use of fine-grained coarticulatory information to predict upcoming phonemes (Gow 2001; Martin & Bunnell 1981; Salverda et al. 2014; Yeni-Komshian & Soli 1981). However, this is not unambiguous evidence for predictive coding. In most of these cases, the information being used for prediction is direct, bottom-up support for the next phoneme (e.g., coarticulation), and it is not clear that these predictions are used as the basis of comparison. However in some cases, predictions must be based on contextual, rather than phonetic information. Here, *contextual information* refers to factors that affect the speech signal lawfully but that do not serve as information about a particular segment (Repp 1982). For example, knowing the talker doesn't tell the listener if an upcoming sound is voiced or voiceless – it helps the listener interpret the cues for voicing. This suggests a rather complex form of prediction that has not been investigated either empirically or theoretically.

However, prediction alone cannot be the whole story with respect to time. Just as with the other two approaches we have discussed, there is the issue of what listeners do when the relevant contextual information is delayed. On the one hand, McMurray & Jongman (2011)'s results suggest that listeners can behave flexibly, using raw cues when no contextual information (e.g., the fricative alone) is available but relativizing when context is available (when the vowel arrives). However, the mechanisms by which such flexibility is achieved are uncertain. Moreover, the evidence for the continuous integration of asynchronous cues comes almost entirely from studies of phonetic cue integration, with very little on the integration of contextual cues (though see Reinisch & Sjerps 2013; Toscano & McMurray 2015) and none on contextual factors that arrive *after* the segment of interest. The exception to this is a recent dissertation on fricative/vowel coarticulation by Galle (2014) that raises the possibility that listeners wait for context before committing to segmental interpretations. However, it is clear that much more work needs to be done on the temporal integration of such factors, before predictive coding or expectation-relative accounts can be truly fleshed out.

2.6 General Discussion

We have discussed three general approaches to the problem(s) of speech perception starting from different background and assumptions. Locus equations and compound cues build from largely phonetic considerations; auditory contrast has developed from a more general auditory processing basis; and expectation-relative coding has roots in information processing and computational modeling. Yet all three have converged on a similar principle, the idea that the information in the speech signal must be encoded relative to something. A diagram sketching out (and oversimplifying) the processing pathways of each approach is shown in Figure 2.6. While it is clear that the detailed processing in each theory differs quite a bit, there are also deep similarities. In compound cue approaches (Figure 2.6A), speech cues like formant frequencies or VOT are interpreted relative to other speech cues on the basis of a set of highly specific relationships. Thus, cue↔cue relationships are central and evaluated before categorization. Similarly, for auditory contrast accounts (Figure 2.6B), auditory principles like contrast or sensitivity to covariation learning shape the fundamental encoding of the signal, but the consequence of this is that information is always treated relatively. Again, cue↔cue relationships are stressed. Finally ER encoding or predictive coding schemes (Figure 2.6C) posit a quite different form of relativity in which higher-level knowledge (e.g., the talker,

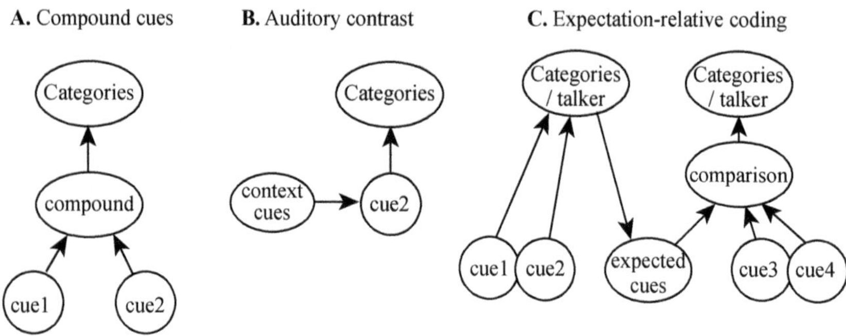

Figure 2.6. The rough processing pathways of each of the three approaches discussed here.

the preceding phoneme) generates expectations about what should be heard, and perception is based on the comparison of actual cue values and expected, fundamentally relativizing cue values against expectations. This stresses cue↔*expected* cue relationships, and places a prominent role for feedback in generating these expectations.

Beyond the deeper principle of relativity, however, there are several additional similarities between the approaches. First, both compound cues and contrast theories suggest primary cue↔cue relationships, a sort of lateral encoding. It is difficult, for example, to distinguish a CV ratio for voicing from durational contrast. In that sense, compound cues may offer a more precise phonetic and computational framing, while auditory contrast offers a more general theoretical framework in which to conceptualize compound cues. Could the combination-sensitive neurons posited by Sussman, Fruchter et al. (1998) be how contrast is realized?

Although expectation-relative coding appears different from these because of its emphasis on feedback, it is not this simple. While McMurray & Jongman (2011) emphasize the top-down nature of these predictions, auditory contrast accounts have pushed the notion that longer-term statistics such as the mean of a series of tones (Holt 2006) or the covariation between cues (Holt et al. 2001) can be the basis of contrast. In this way it is not so different from ER encoding and raises the valuable point that expectations may derive from complex analyses of the signal that do not necessarily involve a cognitive inference about the talker or phoneme.

Is one of these approaches clearly "right"? The overly simplistic answer is no – they can all clearly work together as part of a general auditory account. However, that suggests sort of a conglomerate theory rather than a unifying one. Although the fundamental insights of each approach are not incompatible, there is a clear need for a unifying theoretical approach, not just a blanket statement that everyone is right. In this way, work combining phonetic measurements with computational analysis and modeling – work exemplified by Sussman's approach (Sussman, Fruchter et al., 1998) and continued by others (Cole et al. 2010; McMurray & Jongman 2011; Nearey 1997; Smits 2001a, 2001b) may hold the key to such an integration.

However, at the same time, such work has identified redundancies. The locus equation approach, for example, compares F2-onset with F2-vowel, while C-CuRE compares it with expected F2-vowel. Do we need both? In fact, adding a locus equation approach to standard expectation relative processing showed very little benefit for fricatives (see McMurray & Jongman 2011, online supplement). Similarly, in the debates over compensation for coarticulation, auditory contrast had a difficult time capturing the results of Viswanathan et al. (2009) which suggested that formants in isolation are not enough to drive compensation for coarticulation. This led the authors to favor a gestural account. However, C-CuRE may offer a more parsimonious account, as the third formant alone would be insufficient to allow listeners to identify the /l/ or /r/ and generate expectations, but the complete set of cues (e.g., the fundamental, the other formants) in an unaltered /l/ or /r/ would be sufficient. Thus, expectation-relative encoding may do some of the work of both accounts.

Given results showing that high-level expectations like a still picture of a face can shape speech perception (Hay & Drager 2010; Johnson et al. 1999; Niedzielski 1999; Strand 1999), this would seem to favor a purely expectation-relative approach leaving no room for contrast or compound cues. We suspect, however, that this is not viable. There are a vast number of transformations that can be applied to the signal without rendering it unintelligible (Remez et al. 1981; Shannon et al. 1995; Smith et al. 2002); this speaks to the possibility that speech processing needs redundant and flexible mechanisms. Thus, even if locus equations (for example) don't add anything over and above expectation-relative encoding for unambiguous fricatives, they may offer useful redundancy in other circumstances.

All three approaches are also unified in that all have been developed in part to make the point that domain-general (or even species-general) mechanisms are sufficient to accommodate the variability in speech perception. This serves as a strong and robust counterpoint to the argument that only some form of motoric representation can deal with this variability (Fowler 1991; Liberman & Mattingly 1985). The consistency of these accounts with data from neuroscience only enhances both the domain generality of these accounts and the empirical basis of support for them. It is clear that the auditory system is specialized for processing rapid changes in (spectral/acoustic) information over time. This makes general accounts (like compound cues and auditory contrast) that can take advantage of such processing quite attractive. It is also quite consistent with expectation-relative encoding, as the fundamental operation is still a difference. It seems quite reasonable that the kind of combination-sensitive neurons proposed for locus equations could also compare expected cue values to the input.

As we move from locus equations, to contrast, to predictive coding, it becomes clear that time is an integral aspect of speech perception that cannot be ignored any more. The clear body of evidence from spoken word recognition suggests that inferences about speech are made continuously in time (Allopenna et al. 1998; Marslen-Wilson 1987; McClelland & Elman 1986; McMurray, Clayards et al. 2008; Miller & Dexter 1988), and our understanding of the phonetics of speech perception must begin to account for this. The theoretical models presented here use time in different ways, from locus equations and contrast accounts that combine two cues that happen sequentially in time, to predictive coding that must do this, but also generate longer-term expectations and make predictions. Here, as we've presented it, the asynchrony of the information is the major problem – what does each theory do while it waits for the information needed to relativize cues?

As we have described across theories there are three broad ways this can be accounted for. First, as Rhone & Jongman (2012) have shown, some of these conceptualizations like locus equations can be reconfigured to use smaller time windows. This eliminates the need to wait. However, this is unlikely to be a uniform solution – one simply cannot measure the vowel length (for a CV ratio) until the end of the vowel, while clearly listeners can make inferences about voicing before this (Toscano & McMurray 2012).

Second, relative encoding may be optional. While this does not appear to be possible for compound cues (or if so it has not been discussed), auditory contrast accounts clearly admit that you don't need contrasting information to perceive speech, and McMurray & Jongman (2011) show that when no context is available (e.g., a fricative in isolation) a raw cue model is a better fit to the data. This would seem to make a lot of sense when we're talking about integrating contextual cues – cues that do not directly cue phoneme representations, but do shape how other cues should be interpreted – one simply doesn't relativize. However, when two phonetic cues are asynchronous, things get a bit tricky as one must invoke memory mechanisms of some kind to either maintain cue values or maintain partial interpretations as the information arrives. Here, a tighter integration with spoken word recognition could be helpful – as words accumulate partial activation they could implicitly store partial inferences about the initial cues (as a degree of relative activation for /b/ versus /p/ words) (e.g., McMurray, Clayards et al., 2008; Toscano & McMurray 2012).

Third, ER encoding approaches, with their neural basis in predictive coding, also suggest another possibility – that prediction may help. There is a rich history of literature showing that listeners can use fine-grained coarticulatory cues to predict upcoming material (Gow 2001; Gow & McMurray, 2007; Martin & Bunnell 1981; Yeni-Komshian & Soli 1981). While this literature can largely be consistent with simply building activation for higher-level units (e.g., phonemes, words) on the basis of fine-grained detail in the signal, it is not inconsistent with predictive coding and it may help listeners form partial inferences that can then shape further processing. As with the prior point, a tighter integration of lexical processing is necessary, and a recent study by Salverda et al. (2014) suggests that these predictions do affect lexical activation. What is needed now is evidence that these lexical inferences can cascade back to affect sensory encoding, which would provide the crucial evidence for predictive coding.

Finally, all of these relativistic accounts are implicitly but deeply developmental. Locus equations require the child to accumulate a large body of "data" on the relationship between formant frequencies; auditory contrast accounts are embracing covariation – again, a product of the statistics of many inputs; and expectation-relative processing requires substantial learning to learn what to expect. All three are consistent with recent statistical learning accounts of development (Benders 2013; de Boer & Kuhl 2003; Maye et al. 2003; McMurray et al. 2009; Werker & Curtin 2005). However, at the same time, these accounts have largely focused on how children acquire the bottom-up statistics and use them to identify categories. All three relativistic approaches suggest something much more sophisticated in which such statistics must be *used* in complex ways to recognize speech. To understand development, we must understand more than just how children identify the categories of their language; we must understand how they use these statistics to shape real-time processing (McMurray & Farris-Trimble 2012). That is, we must understand speech development as an ability, not in terms of abstract knowledge of phoneme categories.

While speech perception is riddled with competing models, the foregoing review suggests that these models don't simply compete but, rather, serve as part of an incremental science. The form of relative cue encoding first posited by Sussman in the form of locus equations, when considered in light of apparently competing models featuring auditory contrast or predictive coding has led to deeper insight into the role of relativity in speech encoding. This in turn has led to new questions about time and development that set the stage for the next decades of research. In this spirit of an incremental science, and of predictive coding, we ask "what's next?"

References

Allopenna, P., J.S. Magnuson & M.K. Tanenhaus. (1998). Tracking the time course of spoken word recognition using eye-movements: Evidence for continuous mapping models. *Journal of Memory and Language*, 38(4), 419–39. http://dx.doi.org/10.1006/jmla.1997.2558

Andruski, J.E., S.E. Blumstein & W. Burton. (1994). The effect of subphonetic differences on lexical access. *Cognition*, 52(3), 163–87. http://dx.doi.org/10.1016/0010-0277(94)90042-6

Apfelbaum, K.S., N. Bullock-Rest, A. Rhone, A. Jongman & B. McMurray. (2014). Contingent categorization in speech perception. *Language, Cognition and Neuroscience*, 29(9), 1070–82. http://dx.doi.org/10.1080/01690965.2013.824995

Benders, T. (2013). Nature's distributional-learning experiment (PhD thesis). University of Amsterdam, The Netherlands.

Blumstein, S.E. (1998). The mapping from acoustic structure to the phonetic categories of speech: The invariance problem. *Behavioral and Brain Sciences*, 21(02), 260.260.http://dx.doi.org/10.1017/S0140525X98221170

Blumstein, S.E., & K.N. Stevens. (1979). Acoustic invariance in speech production: Evidence from measurements of the spectral characteristics of stop consonants. *Journal of the Acoustical Society of America*, 66(4), 1001–17. http://dx.doi.org/10.1121/1.383319

Blumstein, S.E., & K..N. Stevens. (1980). Perceptual invariance and onset spectra for stop consonants in different vowel environments. *Journal of the Acoustical Society of America*, 67(2), 648–62. http://dx.doi.org/10.1121/1.383890

Boucher, V.J. (2002). Timing relations in speech and the identification of voice-onset times: A stable perceptual boundary for voicing categories across speaking rates. *Perception & Psychophysics*, 64(1), 121–30. http://dx.doi.org/10.3758/BF03194561

Brancazio, L., & C.A. Fowler. (1998). On the relevance of locus equations for production and perception of stop consonants. *Perception & Psychophysics*, 60(1), 24–50. http://dx.doi.org/10.3758/BF03211916

Celdran, E., & X. Villalba. (1995). Locus equations as a metric for place of articulation in automatic speech recognition. Paper presented at the Proceedings of the XIIIth International Congress of Phonetic Sciences (Sweden).

Clark, A. (2013). Whatever next? Predictive brains, situated agents, and the future of cognitive science. *Behavioral and Brain Sciences*, 36(3), 181–204.

Cole, J.S., G. Linebaugh, C. Munson, & B. McMurray. (2010). Unmasking the acoustic effects of vowel-to-vowel coarticulation: A statistical modeling approach. *Journal of Phonetics*, 38(2), 167–84. http://dx.doi.org/10.1016/j.wocn.2009.08.004

Daniloff, R., and K. Moll. (1968). Coarticulation of lip rounding. *Journal of Speech, Language, and Hearing Research (JSLHR)*, 11, 707–21

de Boer, B., & P.K. Kuhl. (2003). Investigating the role of infant-directed speech with a computer model. *Auditory Research Letters On-Line (ARLO)*, 4, 129–34.

Delattre, P., A.M. Liberman & F.S. Cooper. (1955). Acoustic loci and transitional cues for consonants. *Journal of the Acoustical Society of America*, 27(4), 769–73. http://dx.doi.org/10.1121/1.1908024

Diehl, R.L., J.L. Elman & S.B. McCusker. (1978). Contrast effects on stop consonant identification. *Journal of Experimental Psychology: Human Perception and Performance*, 4(4), 599–609. http://dx.doi.org/10.1037/0096-1523.4.4.599

Eek, A., & E. Meister. (1995). The perception of stop consonants: Locus equations and spectral integration. Paper presented at the XIIIth International Congress of Phonetic Sciences (ICPhS XIII), Stockholm, Sweden.

Flanagan, J.R., P. Vetter, R.S. Johansson & D.M. Wolpert. (2003). Prediction precedes control in motor learning. *Current Biology*, 13(2), 146–50. http://dx.doi.org/10.1016/S0960-9822(03)00007-1

Forrest, K., G. Weismer, P. Milenkovic & R.N. Dougall. (1988). Statistical analysis of word-initial voiceless obstruents: Preliminary data. *Journal of the Acoustical Society of America*, 84(1), 115–24. http://dx.doi.org/10.1121/1.396977

Fowler, C.A. (1986). An event approach to the study of speech perception from a direct-realist perspective. *Journal of Phonetics*, 14(1), 3–28.

Fowler, C.A. (1991). Auditory perception is not special: We see the world, we feel the world, we hear the world. *Journal of the Acoustical Society of America*, 89(6), 2910–15. http://dx.doi.org/10.1121/1.400729

Fruchter, D., & H.M. Sussman. (1997). The perceptual relevance of locus equations. *Journal of the Acoustical Society of America*, 102(5), 2997–3008. http://dx.doi.org/10.1121/1.421012

Gagnepain, P., R.N. Henson & M.H. Davis. (2012). Temporal predictive codes for spoken words in auditory cortex. *Current Biology*, 22(7), 615–21. http://dx.doi.org/10.1016/j.cub.2012.02.015

Galle, M. (2014). Integration of asynchronous cues in fricative perception in real-time and developmental-time: Evidence for sublexical memory/integration systems. PhD thesis, University of Iowa.

Goldinger, S.D. (1998). Echoes of echos? An episodic theory of lexical access. *Psychological Review*, 105(2), 251–79. http://dx.doi.org/10.1037/0033-295X.105.2.251

Gow, D.W., Jr. (2001). Assimilation and anticipation in continuous spoken word recognition. *Journal of Memory and Language*, 45(1), 133–59. http://dx.doi.org/10.1006/jmla.2000.2764

Gow, D.W., & B. McMurray. (2007). Word recognition and phonology: The case of English coronal place assimilation. In J.S. Cole & J. Hualdo (eds.), *Papers in Laboratory Phonology 9* (pp. 173–200). New York, NY: Mouton de Gruyter.

Hay, J., & K. Drager. (2010). Stuffed toys and speech perception. *Linguistics*, 48(4), 865–92. http://dx.doi.org/10.1515/ling.2010.027

Hillenbrand, J.M., L. Getty, M.J. Clark, & K. Wheeler. (1995). Acoustic characteristics of American English vowels. *Journal of the Acoustical Society of America*, 97(5), 3099–111. http://dx.doi.org/10.1121/1.411872

Holt, L.L. (2006). The mean matters: Effects of statistically-defined non-speech spectral distributions on speech categorization. *Journal of the Acoustical Society of America*, 120(5), 2801–17. http://dx.doi.org/10.1121/1.2354071

Holt, L.L., & A.J. Lotto. (2008). Speech perception within an auditory cognitive science framework. *Current Directions in Psychological Science*, 17(1), 42–6. http://dx.doi.org/10.1111/j.1467-8721.2008.00545.x

Holt, L.L., A.J. Lotto & K.R. Kluender. (2001). Influence of fundamental frequency on stop-consonant voicing perception: A case of learned covariation or auditory enhancement? *Journal of the Acoustical Society of America*, 109(2), 764–74. http://dx.doi.org/10.1121/1.1339825

Houde, J.F., S.S. Nagarajan, K. Sekihara & M.M. Merzenich. (2002). Modulation of the auditory cortex during speech: An MEG study. *Journal of Cognitive Neuroscience*, 14(8), 1125–38. http://dx.doi.org/10.1162/089892902760807140

Jeffress, L.A. (1948). A place theory of sound localization. *Journal of Comparative and Physiological Psychology*, 41(1), 35–9. http://dx.doi.org/10.1037/h0061495

Johnson, K.C., E.A. Strand & M. D'Imperio. (1999). Auditory-visual integration of talker gender in vowel perception. *Journal of Phonetics*, 27(4), 359–84. http://dx.doi.org/10.1006/jpho.1999.0100

Jongman, A. (1998). Are locus equations sufficient or necessary for obstruent perception? *Behavioral and Brain Sciences*, 21(2), 271–2. http://dx.doi.org/10.1017/S0140525X98351171

Jongman, A., R. Wayland & S. Wong. (2000). Acoustic characteristics of English fricatives. *Journal of the Acoustical Society of America*, 108(3), 1252–63. http://dx.doi.org/10.1121/1.1288413

Kluender, K.R., J. Coady & M. Kiefte. (2003). Sensitivity to change in perception of speech. *Speech Communication*, 41(1), 59–69. http://dx.doi.org/10.1016/S0167-6393(02)00093-6

Kluender, K.R., & A.J. Lotto. (1994). Effects of first formant onset frequency on [-voice] judgments result from auditory processes not specific to humans. *Journal of the Acoustical Society of America*, 95(2), 1044–52. http://dx.doi.org/10.1121/1.408466

Knudsen, E.I., & M. Konishi. (1978). Space and frequency are represented separately in auditory midbrain of the owl. *Journal of Neurophysiology*, 41(4), 870–84.

Krull, D. (1989). Second formant locus patterns and consonant-vowel coarticulation in spontaneous speech. *Phonetic Experimental Research at the Institute of Linguistics at the University of Stockholm (PERILUS)*, X, 87–108.

Lahiri, A., L. Gewirth & S.E. Blumstein. (1984). A reconsideration of acoustic invariance for place of articulation in diffuse stop consonants: Evidence from a cross-language study. *Journal of the Acoustical Society of America*, 76(2), 391–404. http://dx.doi.org/10.1121/1.391580

Laing, E.J., R. Liu, A.J. Lotto & L.L. Holt. (2012). Tuned with a tune: Talker normalization via general auditory processes. *Frontiers in Psychology*, 3, 1–9. http://dx.doi.org/10.3389/fpsyg.2012.00203

Liberman, A.M., F.S. Cooper, D.P. Shankweiler & M. Studdert-Kennedy. (1967). Perception of the speech code. *Psychological Review*, 74(6), 431–61. http://dx.doi.org/10.1037/h0020279

Liberman, A.M., & I. Mattingly. (1985). The motor theory of speech perception revised. *Cognition*, 21(1), 1–36. http://dx.doi.org/10.1016/0010-0277(85)90021-6

Liberman, A.M., & D. Whalen. (2000). On the relation of speech to language. *Trends in Cognitive Sciences*, 4(5), 187–96. http://dx.doi.org/10.1016/S1364-6613(00)01471-6

Lindblom, B. (1963). On vowel reduction. *Report No. 29, The Royal Institute of Technology*. Stockholm: Speech Transmission Laboratory.

Lindblom, B. (1996). Role of articulation in speech perception: Clues from production. *Journal of the Acoustical Society of America*, 99(3), 1683–92. http://dx.doi.org/10.1121/1.414691

Lindblom, B., & H.M. Sussman. (2012). Dissecting coarticulation: How locus equations happen. *Journal of Phonetics*, 40(1), 1–19. http://dx.doi.org/10.1016/j.wocn.2011.09.005

Lisker, L. (1986). "Voicing" in English: A catalogue of acoustic features signaling /b/ versus /p/ in trochees. *Language and Speech*, 29(1), 3–11.

Lotto, A.J., & K.R. Kluender. (1998). General contrast effects in speech perception: Effect of preceding liquid on stop consonant identification. *Perception & Psychophysics*, 60(4), 602–19. http://dx.doi.org/10.3758/BF03206049

Lotto, A.J., K.R. Kluender & L.L. Holt (1997). Perceptual compensation for coarticulation by Japanese quail (*Coturnixcoturnix japonica*). *Journal of the Acoustical Society of America*, 102(2), 1134–40. http://dx.doi.org/10.1121/1.419865

Magen, H.S. (1997). The extent of vowel-to-vowel coarticulation in English. *Journal of Phonetics*, 25(2), 187–205. http://dx.doi.org/10.1006/jpho.1996.0041

Mann, V.A. (1980). Influence of preceding liquid on stop-consonant perception. *Perception & Psychophysics*, 28(5), 407–12. http://dx.doi.org/10.3758/BF03204884

Mann, V.A., & B. Repp. (1980). Influence of the vocalic context on perception of the [ʃ]-[s] distinction. *Perception & Psychophysics*, 28(3), 213–28. http://dx.doi.org/10.3758/BF03204377

Mann, V.A., & B. Repp. (1981). Influence of preceding fricative on stop consonant perception. *Journal of the Acoustical Society of America*, 69(2), 548–58. http://dx.doi.org/10.1121/1.385483

Marslen-Wilson, W.D. (1987). Functional parallelism in spoken word recognition. *Cognition*, 25(1–2), 71–102. http://dx.doi.org/10.1016/0010-0277(87)90005-9

Marslen-Wilson, W.D., L.K. Tyler & R.B.L. Page. (1981). Central processes in speech understanding [and discussion]. *Philosophical Transactions of the Royal*

Society of London. Series B, Biological Sciences, 295(1077), 317–32. http://dx.doi.org/10.1098/rstb.1981.0143

Marslen-Wilson, W.D., & P. Zwitserlood. (1989). Accessing spoken words: The importance of word onsets. *Journal of Experimental Psychology: Human Perception and Performance,* 15(3), 576–85. http://dx.doi.org/10.1037/0096-1523.15.3.576

Martin, J.G., & H.T. Bunnell. (1981). Perception of anticipatory coarticulation effects. *Journal of the Acoustical Society of America,* 69(2), 559–67. http://dx.doi.org/10.1121/1.385484

Maye, J., J.F. Werker & L. Gerken. (2003). Infant sensitivity to distributional information can affect phonetic discrimination. *Cognition,* 82(3), B101–11. http://dx.doi.org/10.1016/S0010-0277(01)00157-3

Mccaffrey Morrison, H. (2012). Coarticulation in early vocalizations by children with hearing loss: A locus perspective. *Clinical Linguistics & Phonetics,* 26(3), 288–309. http://dx.doi.org/10.3109/02699206.2011.614718

McClelland, J.L., & J.L. Elman. (1986). The TRACE model of speech perception. *Cognitive Psychology,* 18(1), 1–86. http://dx.doi.org/10.1016/0010-0285(86)90015-0

McMurray, B., R.N. Aslin, M.K. Tanenhaus, M.J. Spivey & D. Subik. (2008). Gradient sensitivity to within-category variation in words and syllables. *Journal of Experimental Psychology: Human Perception and Performance,* 34(6), 1609–31. http://dx.doi.org/10.1037/a0011747

McMurray, B., R.N. Aslin & J.C. Toscano. (2009). Statistical learning of phonetic categories: Insights from a computational approach. *Developmental Science,* 12(3), 369–378. http://dx.doi.org/10.1111/j.1467-7687.2009.00822.x

McMurray, B., M. Clayards, M.K. Tanenhaus & R.N. Aslin. (2008). Tracking the time course of phonetic cue integration during spoken word recognition. *Psychonomic Bulletin & Review,* 15(6), 1064–71. http://dx.doi.org/10.3758/PBR.15.6.1064

McMurray, B., & A. Farris-Trimble. (2012). Emergent information-level coupling between perception and production. In A. Cohn, C. Fougeron & M. Huffman (eds.), *The Oxford Handbook of Laboratory Phonology* (pp. 369–95). Oxford: Oxford University Press.

McMurray, B., & A. Jongman. (2011). What information is necessary for speech categorization? Harnessing variability in the speech signal by integrating cues computed relative to expectations. *Psychological Review,* 118(2), 219–46. http://dx.doi.org/10.1037/a0022325

McMurray, B., K. Kovack-Lesh, D. Goodwin & W.D. McEchron. (2013). Infant directed speech and the development of speech perception: Enhancing development or an unintended consequence? *Cognition,* 129(2), 362–78. http://dx.doi.org/10.1016/j.cognition.2013.07.015

McMurray, B., M.K. Tanenhaus & R.N. Aslin. (2002). Gradient effects of within-category phonetic variation on lexical access. *Cognition,* 86(2), B33–42. http://dx.doi.org/10.1016/S0010-0277(02)00157-9

McMurray, B., M.K. Tanenhaus & R.N. Aslin. (2009). Within-category VOT affects recovery from "lexical" garden paths: Evidence against phoneme-level inhibition. *Journal of Memory and Language*, 60(1), 65–91. http://dx.doi.org/10.1016/j.jml.2008.07.002

Mermelstein, P. (1978). On the relationship between vowel and consonant identification when cued by the same acoustic information. *Perception & Psychophysics*, 23(4), 331–6. http://dx.doi.org/10.3758/BF03199717

Miller, J.D. (1989). Auditory-perceptual interpretation of the vowel. *The Journal of the Acoustical Society of America*, 85(5), 2114–34. http://dx.doi.org/10.1121/1.397862

Miller, J.L., & E.R. Dexter. (1988). Effects of speaking rate and lexical status on phonetic perception. *Journal of Experimental Psychology: Human Perception and Performance*, 14(3), 369–78. http://dx.doi.org/10.1037/0096-1523.14.3.369

Monahan, P.J., & W.J. Idsardi. (2010). Auditory sensitivity to formant ratios: Toward an account of vowel normalisation. *Language and Cognitive Processes*, 25(6), 808–39. http://dx.doi.org/10.1080/01690965.2010.490047

Munson, B. (2007). The acoustic correlates of perceived masculinity, perceived femininity, and perceived sexual orientation. *Language and Speech*, 50(1), 125–42. http://dx.doi.org/10.1177/00238309070500010601

Nearey, T.M. (1990). The segment as a unit of speech perception. *Journal of Phonetics*, 18, 347–73.

Nearey, T.M. (1997). Speech perception as pattern recognition. *Journal of the Acoustical Society of America*, 101(6), 3241–54. http://dx.doi.org/10.1121/1.418290

Niedzielski, N. (1999). The effect of social information on the perception of sociolinguistic variables. *Journal of Language and Social Psychology*, 18(1), 62–85. http://dx.doi.org/10.1177/0261927X99018001005

Oden, G., & D.W. Massaro. (1978). Integration of featural information in speech perception. *Psychological Review*, 85(3), 172–91. http://dx.doi.org/10.1037/0033-295X.85.3.172

Ohala, J. (1996). Speech perception is hearing sounds, not tongues. *Journal of the Acoustical Society of America*, 99(3), 1718–25. http://dx.doi.org/10.1121/1.414696

Ohman, S.E.G. (1966). Coarticulation in VCV utterances: Spectrographic measurements. *Journal of the Acoustical Society of America*, 39(1), 151–68. http://dx.doi.org/10.1121/1.1909864

Peterson, G.E. (1951). The phonetic value of vowels. *Language*, 27(4), 541–53. http://dx.doi.org/10.2307/410041

Peterson, G.E., & H.L. Barney. (1952). Control methods used in a study of the vowels. *Journal of the Acoustical Society of America*, 24(2), 175–84. http://dx.doi.org/10.1121/1.1906875

Pind, J. (1995). Speaking rate, voice-onset time, and quantity: The search for higher order invariants for two Icelandic speech cues. *Perception & Psychophysics*, 57(3), 291–304. http://dx.doi.org/10.3758/BF03213055

Port, R.F. (2007). How are words stored in memory? Beyond phones and phonemes. *New Ideas in Psychology*, 25(2), 143–70. http://dx.doi.org/10.1016/j.newideapsych.2007.02.001

Port, R.F., & J. Dalby. (1982). Consonant/vowel ratio as a cue for voicing in English. *Perception & Psychophysics*, 32(2), 141–52. http://dx.doi.org/10.3758/BF03204273

Rao, R.P., & D.H. Ballard. (1999). Predictive coding in the visual cortex: A functional interpretation of some extra-classical receptive-field effects. *Nature Neuroscience*, 2(1), 79–87. http://dx.doi.org/10.1038/4580

Reinisch, E., & M.J. Sjerps. (2013). The uptake of spectral and temporal cues in vowel perception is rapidly influenced by context. *Journal of Phonetics*, 41(2), 101–16. http://dx.doi.org/10.1016/j.wocn.2013.01.002

Remez, R. (2005). Perceptual organization of speech. In D.B. Pisoni & R. Remez (eds.), *The Handbook of Speech Perception* (pp. 28–50). Oxford: Blackwell Publishing. http://dx.doi.org/10.1002/9780470757024.ch2

Remez, R., P. Rubin, D.B. Pisoni & T. Carrell. (1981). Speech perception without traditional speech cues. *Science*, 212(4497), 947–9. http://dx.doi.org/10.1126/science.7233191

Repp, B.H. (1982). Phonetic trading relations and context effects: New experimental evidence for a speech mode of perception. *Psychological Bulletin*, 92(1), 81–110. http://dx.doi.org/10.1037/0033-2909.92.1.81

Rhone, A.E., & A. Jongman. (2012). Modified locus equations categorize stop place in a perceptually realistic time frame. *Journal of the Acoustical Society of America*, 131(6), EL487–91. http://dx.doi.org/10.1121/1.4722169

Rost, G.C., & B. McMurray. (2010). Finding the signal by adding noise: The role of non-contrastive phonetic variability in early word learning. *Infancy*, 15(6), 608–35. http://dx.doi.org/10.1111/j.1532-7078.2010.00033.x

Salverda, A.P., D. Dahan & J. McQueen. (2003). The role of prosodic boundaries in the resolution of lexical embedding in speech comprehension. *Cognition*, 90(1), 51–89. http://dx.doi.org/10.1016/S0010-0277(03)00139-2

Salverda, A.P., D. Kleinschmidt & M.K. Tanenhaus. (2014). Immediate effects of anticipatory coarticulation in spoken-word recognition. *Journal of Memory and Language*, 71(1), 145–63. http://dx.doi.org/10.1016/j.jml.2013.11.002

Sawusch, J.R., & D.B. Pisoni. (1974). On the identification of place and voicing features in synthetic stop consonants. *Journal of Phonetics*, 2, 181–94.

Shannon, R., F. Zeng, V. Kamath, J. Wygonski & M. Ekelid. (1995). Speech recognition with primarily temporal cues. *Science*, 270(5234), 303–4. http://dx.doi.org/10.1126/science.270.5234.303

Smith, Z.M., B. Delgutte & A. Oxenham. (2002). Chimaeric sounds reveal dichotomies in auditory perception. *Nature*, 416(6876), 87–90. http://dx.doi.org/10.1038/416087a

Smits, R. (2001a). Evidence for hierarchical categorization of coarticulated phonemes. *Journal of Experimental Psychology: Human Perception and Performance*, 27(5), 1145–62. http://dx.doi.org/10.1037/0096-1523.27.5.1145

Smits, R. (2001b). Hierarchical categorization of coarticulated phonemes: A theoretical analysis. *Perception & Psychophysics*, 63(7), 1109–39. http://dx.doi.org/10.3758/BF03194529

Stevens, K.N., & S.J. Keyser. (2010). Quantal theory, enhancement and overlap. *Journal of Phonetics*, 38(1), 10–19. http://dx.doi.org/10.1016/j.wocn.2008.10.004

Strand, E. (1999). Uncovering the role of gender stereotypes in speech perception. *Journal of Language and Social Psychology*, 18(1), 86–100. http://dx.doi.org/10.1177/0261927X99018001006

Strange, W., J.J. Jenkins & T.L. Johnson. (1983). Dynamic specification of coarticulated vowels. *The Journal of the Acoustical Society of America*, 74(3), 695–705. http://dx.doi.org/10.1121/1.389855

Suga, N., W.E. O'Neill, K. Kujirai & T. Manabe. (1983). Specificity of combination-sensitive neurons for processing of complex biosonar signals in auditory cortex of the mustached bat. *Journal of Neurophysiology*, 49(6), 1573–626.

Suga, N., W.E. O'Neill & T. Manabe. (1978). Cortical neurons sensitive to combinations of information-bearing elements of biosonar signals in the mustached bat. *Science*, 200(4343), 778–81. http://dx.doi.org/10.1126/science.644320

Summerfield, Q., & M. Haggard. (1977). On the dissociation of spectral and temporal cues to the voicing distinction in initial stop consonants. *Journal of the Acoustical Society of America*, 62(2), 435–48. http://dx.doi.org/10.1121/1.381544

Sussman, H.M. (2002). Representation of phonological categories: A functional role for auditory columns. *Brain and Language*, 80(1), 1–13. http://dx.doi.org/10.1006/brln.2001.2489

Sussman, H.M. (2009). Motor influence of speech perception: The view from Grenoble. Retrieved from http://www.talkingbrains.org/2009/04/motor-influence-of-speech-perception.html?showComment=1241118960000#c8348248398128898600

Sussman, H.M., C.T. Byrd, & B. Guitar. (2011). The integrity of anticipatory coarticulation in fluent and non-fluent tokens of adults who stutter. *Clinical Linguistics & Phonetics*, 25(3), 169–86. http://dx.doi.org/10.3109/02699206.2010.517896

Sussman, H.M., E. Dalston & S. Gumpert. (1998). The effect of speaking style alterations on locus equation stability. *Journal of the Acoustical Society of America*, 103(5), 2984.

Sussman, H.M., C. Duder, E. Dalston & A. Cacciatore. (1999). An acoustic analysis of the development of CV coarticulation: A case study. *Journal of Speech, Language, and Hearing Research (JSLHR)*, 42(5), 1080–96. http://dx.doi.org/10.1044/jslhr.4205.1080

Sussman, H.M., D. Fruchter, J. Hilbert & J. Sirosh. (1998). Linear correlates in the speech signal: The orderly output constraint. *Behavioral and Brain Sciences*, 21(2), 241–99. http://dx.doi.org/10.1017/S0140525X98001174

Sussman, H.M., K.A. Hoemeke & F.S. Ahmed. (1993). A cross-linguistic investigation of locus equations as a phonetic descriptor for place of articulation. *The Journal of the Acoustical Society of America*, 94(3), 1256–68. http://dx.doi.org/10.1121/1.408178

Sussman, H.M., K.A. Hoemeke & H.A. McCaffrey. (1992). Locus equations as an index of coarticulation for place of articulation distinctions in children. *Journal of Speech and Hearing Research*, 35(4), 769. http://dx.doi.org/10.1044/jshr.3504.769

Sussman, H.M., T.P. Marquardt, J. Doyle & H. Knapp. (2002). Phonemic integrity and contrastiveness in developmental apraxia of speech. In F. Windsor, N. Hewlett and M. Kelly (eds.), *Themes in Clinical Phonetics and Linguistics* (pp. 311–26), New York: Lawrence Erlbaum.

Sussman, H.M., H.A. McCaffrey & S.A. Matthews. (1991). An investigation of locus equations as a source of relational invariance for stop place categorization. *Journal of the Acoustical Society of America*, 90(3), 1309–25. http://dx.doi.org/10.1121/1.401923

Sussman, H.M., & J. Shore. (1996). Locus equations as phonetic descriptors of consonantal place of articulation. *Perception & Psychophysics*, 58(6), 936–46. http://dx.doi.org/10.3758/BF03205495

Tekieli, M.E., & W.L. Cullinan. (1979). The perception of temporally segmented vowels and consonant-vowel syllables. *Journal of Speech, Language, and Hearing Research (JSLHR)*, 22(1), 103–21. http://dx.doi.org/10.1044/jshr.2201.103

Toscano, J.C., & B. McMurray. (2010). Cue integration with categories: Weighting acoustic cues in speech using unsupervised learning and distributional statistics. *Cognitive Science*, 34(3), 436–64. http://dx.doi.org/10.1111/j.1551-6709.2009.01077.x

Toscano, J.C., & B. McMurray. (2012). Cue-integration and context effects in speech: Evidence against speaking-rate normalization. *Attention, Perception & Psychophysics*, 74(6), 1284–301. http://dx.doi.org/10.3758/s13414-012-0306-z

Toscano, J.C., & B. McMurray. (2015). Speaking rate compensation revealed by the time-course of spoken word recognition: Effects of sentential rate and vowel length on voicing judgments. *Language, Cognition and Neuroscience* 30(5), 529–43.

Utman, J.A., S.E. Blumstein & M.W. Burton. (2000). Effects of subphonetic and syllable structure variation on word recognition. *Perception & Psychophysics*, 62(6), 1297–311. http://dx.doi.org/10.3758/BF03212131

Viswanathan, N., C.A. Fowler & J.S. Magnuson. (2009). A critical examination of the spectral contrast account of compensation for coarticulation. *Psychonomic Bulletin & Review*, 16(1), 74–9. http://dx.doi.org/10.3758/PBR.16.1.74

von Kriegstein, K., D.R.R. Smith, R.D. Patterson, S.J. Kiebel & T.D. Griffiths. (2010). How the human brain recognizes speech in the context of changing speakers. *Journal of Neuroscience*, 30(2), 629–38. http://dx.doi.org/10.1523/JNEUROSCI.2742-09.2010

Werker, J.F., & S. Curtin. (2005). PRIMIR: A developmental framework of infant speech processing. *Language Learning and Development*, 1(2), 197–234. http://dx.doi.org/10.1080/15475441.2005.9684216

Whalen, D.H. (1992). Perception of overlapping segments: Thoughts on Nearey's model. *Journal of Phonetics*, 20, 493–96.

Wild, C.J., M.H. Davis & I.S. Johnsrude. (2012). Human auditory cortex is sensitive to the perceived clarity of speech. *NeuroImage*, 60(2), 1490–502. http://dx.doi.org/10.1016/j.neuroimage.2012.01.035

Winn, M.B., A.E. Rhone, M. Chatterjee & W.J. Idsardi. (2013). The use of auditory and visual context in speech perception by listeners with normal hearing and listeners with cochlear implants. *Frontiers in Psychology*, 4, 824.

Wolpert, D.M., & J.R. Flanagan. (2001). Motor prediction. *Current Biology*, 11(18), R729–32. http://dx.doi.org/10.1016/S0960-9822(01)00432-8

Yeni–Komshian, G.H., & S.D. Soli. (1981). Recognition of vowels from information in fricatives: Perceptual evidence of fricative–vowel coarticulation. *Journal of the Acoustical Society of America*, 70(4), 966. http://dx.doi.org/10.1121/1.387031

3

The Frame Problem in Speech Communication: Defining the Dimensional Space for Phonetic Categorization

Andrew J. Lotto and Lori L. Holt[1]

3.1 Phonetic Perception as Categorization

In the last several decades in the field of speech perception there has been a move away from discussions of detection of invariant features and simple match-to-sample approaches toward modeling phonemic acquisition and perception as a complex categorization task occurring over a multidimensional perceptual space (Oden & Massaro 1978; Nearey 1997; Goldinger 1998; Lotto 2000; Holt & Lotto 2010; McMurray & Jongman 2011). It is typical in the categorization approach to presume that language learners parse perceptual spaces littered with exemplars of particular speech sounds into phonemic bins based on the distributions of these experienced exemplars. Subsequent phoneme perception then occurs with the target exemplar being mapped into this space and the most likely phoneme category chosen. An example of such a hypothesized space is presented in Figure 3.1.

Each point in this graph represents the measurement of the starting frequencies for the second and third formants (F2 and F3, respectively) from native English productions of /l/ and /r/ from a number of speakers producing two-syllable words in isolation, from Lotto et al. (2004). If one takes

1 Andrew Lotto is an Associate Professor in Speech, Language and Hearing Sciences at the University of Arizona.
Lori L. Holt is Professor of Psychology at Carnegie Mellon University.

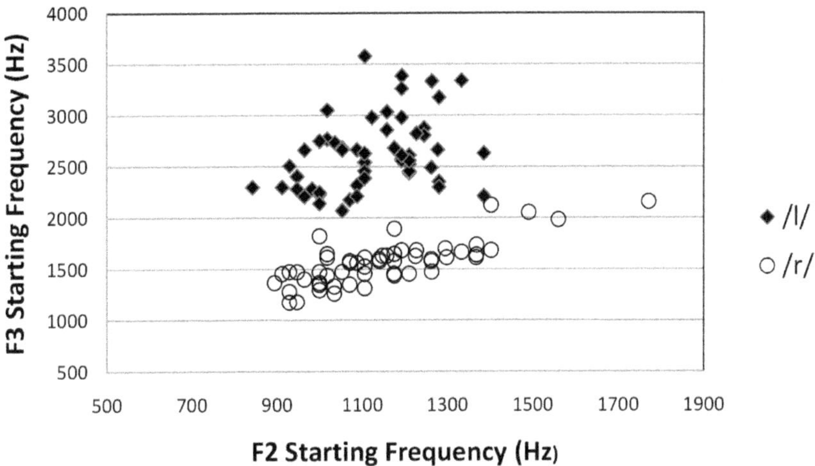

Figure 3.1. Map of English productions of /l/ and/r/ (syllable initial) in a space based on the starting frequencies of the second and third formant (modified from Lotto et al. 2004).

this as an estimate of the typical distribution of these two measures for this English contrast, then one can see that the two categories are fairly well distinguished by the value of the F3 starting frequency. But, the starting frequency of the second formant would need to be considered in order to perform optimally. In fact, one could readily determine the optimal boundary for separating these two categories of sounds in this space (the line would be nearly perpendicular to the F3 axis with a slight shallow positive slope). The categorization approach that is now in vogue in speech perception research presumes that native language learners form some representation of these distributional characteristics across this space and then determine the best category boundary in this space for subsequent categorization. The distributions in Figure 3.1 should result in native speakers making categorization decisions primarily based on the more informative dimension – the starting frequency of F3 – which is exactly what adult English speakers do (Yamada & Tohkura 1990).

Modeling phonemic acquisition and perception in terms of parsing multidimensional spaces has been quite successful in providing explanations and predictions in a wide variety of speech perception phenomena in children (see Kuhl 2000), native-speaking adults and adult second language (L2) learners. As an example of how this sort of approach can further understanding of (and/or contribute to practical applications for) L2 acquisition, Lotto et al. (2004) showed that native Japanese speakers make more of a distinction in F2-onset frequency than native English speakers when producing the English /l/-/r/ contrast. This heavier reliance on F2 is reflected in their perception of the contrast, resulting in non-native categorization patterns. Subsequently, Lim & Holt (2011) used a categorization approach, varying the distribution of stimuli on the F2 and F3 dimensions, as the basis for a training regimen that improved the perceptual categorization of /l/ and /r/ by native Japanese-speaking learners of English.

One of the appeals of this approach is that the proposed categorization processes are quite general and not specific to speech. In fact, much of the research on auditory categorization has been co-opted from the better developed categorization work in vision (Ashby & Maddox 2005) and the models of speech categorization are applicable to a wide variety of perceptual tasks (e.g., Massaro 1987; McMurray et al. 2009). Recently, Chandrasekaran et al. (2014) began applying a dual-systems approach to categorization that has been well-validated for vision to auditory categorization tasks including speech perception. In this newer model, perceptual spaces such as the one in Figure 3.1 are still parsed based on experienced distributions, but the neural mechanisms depend (at least partly) on how these distributions align in the dimensional space. For example, the distributions in Figure 3.1 are most compatible with the "reflective" system that involves the prefrontal cortex and anterior caudate nucleus. If one were to rotate the distributions in space so that the optimal boundary lies more along the dimensional diagonal (as one sees in the distributions from Japanese speakers) then the "reflexive" striatum-based learning system would be more appropriate.

Early in our work, we tried to take seriously the claim that speech perception was the result of general processes of auditory categorization (Holt et al. 1998; Lotto 2000). We reasoned that the best way to understand speech sound categorization was to understand auditory categorization. We undertook a large number of experiments using sounds varying in non-speech dimensions. The benefits of using novel non-speech sounds is that it allowed us precise control over the distributional properties of the sounds and over the listeners' exposure history. In order to tackle the questions we felt were most compelling, we developed a number of stimulus sets with a variety of relevant stimulus dimensions. Examples of relatively straightforward dimensions included the center frequency of a narrow noise band (Sullivan et al. 2011; Kittleson et al. 2012), the center frequency of a tone, the frequency modulation rate of a tone (Holt & Lotto 2006), the duration of amplitude ramps on noise bursts (Mirman et al. 2004) and the onset asynchrony of two tones at different frequencies (Holt et al. 2004). Other dimensions were a little less obvious. In several sets of studies we varied the center frequencies of two stop-band filters applied to white noise. That is, we created two independently positioned troughs in the spectrum of the noise (Janega & Lotto 2000; Mirman et al. 2004). Wade and Holt (2005) created a complicated set of stimuli that included an invariant square-wave portion and a simultaneous sawtooth wave that had an initial frequency sweep followed by a steady-state frequency (these sounds were designed to have characteristics similar to those seen in consonant-vowel syllables varying in place of articulation and vowel). The relevant perceptual space for these sound distributions was the frequency of the steady-state portion and the difference between the steady-state frequency and the starting frequency. This is a subset of the dimensions we have used and does not include dimensions developed by other researchers interested in auditory categorization (e.g., the variation of the center frequency and frequency modulation of some frication noise along with the duration of a silent gap in Christensen & Humes 1997; or the frequency of spectral prominences on inharmonic complexes in Smits et al. 2006).

The most easily summarized finding from all of this non-speech work is that categories defined in these dimensional spaces are readily learned by listeners. We also learned a lot about the *process* of auditory category formation that appears to be quite applicable to speech perception. For example, the non-speech work on cue weighting by Holt & Lotto (2006) was the inspiration for the successful L2 training work of Lim & Holt (2011). Similarly, the results using two-tone asynchrony by Holt et al. (2004) provide some basis for explaining the use of the voice-onset time dimension across languages.

However, in the midst of all this success is a lingering question with no clear answer. We have good models of how listeners parse the perceptual space given a set of distributions, but ... how can we be sure what the perceptual space is?

3.2 From Whence Come Thy Dimensions?

The question of whether the perceptual space that listeners are using is the same as that presumed by the researcher is important for modeling categorization and phonetic perception. As mentioned above, the relevant system for categorization according to a dual-systems approach, a la Ashby & Maddox (2005), depends on the relationship of the distributional structure to the dimensional axes of the perceptual space. The predictions of this model have been made presuming that the perceptual space maps onto the stimulus space being manipulated by the experimenter. If the listener/

learner is using a different "space" to represent the experienced exemplars, then these predictions would be difficult to make.

This is not just a concern about psychophysically scaling the dimensions to barks or mels or sones, it is a question of whether the listener is actually representing the exemplars using the same aspects of the signal that the researcher is manipulating. The presumption, of course, is that the stimulus space and perceptual spaces are similar. If this is the case (and given the effectiveness of auditory modeling efforts it appears to be so), then one is left to wonder how it is that listeners manage to so readily determine the relevant dimensions for a task. This is really a fundamental question for understanding auditory learning/categorization. In these laboratory tasks, listeners often hear one sound on each trial and then make a response often followed by feedback. From this coarse sampling, they must determine which aspects of the sound are relevant. Does this mean that listeners are monitoring all possible relevant dimensions of a stimulus – duration, onset amplitude slope, frequency and rate of change of resonances, fundamental frequency, etc. etc. – and determining which are most useful for the current task?

A typical explanation would be that listeners choose dimensions initially based on where the greatest variance lies (as a sign of potential information) and then parse these dimensions down to the working space on the basis of whether the variance in them is predictive of the feedback. That seems reasonable enough except that it still requires listeners to calculate relative variance across a large number of potential dimensions. The list of dimensions used in the non-speech tasks above provides some sense of the potential size of this set. For example, the categorization task of Wade and Holt (2005) was solvable on a space with the dimensions – (1) steady-state frequency of the resonance on the higher frequency square wave and (2) that steady-state frequency minus the onset frequency of that resonance. Why would these be readily available dimensions for listeners? To make matters more complicated, Wade and Holt (2005) did not provide explicit feedback for auditory categorization nor were participants instructed to categorize the sounds. The learning – apparently based on something like these dimensions – was implicit, arising in playing an action video game.

The above argument is not to say that it is a miracle that listeners come up with the relevant dimensions; it is a call for a theoretical investigation of how listeners come up with these dimensions. This basic first step is in many ways more interesting than the modeling of how listeners parse this space once they have it. Considering the importance of dimensions leads to a number of interesting questions. Is there a constrained set of possible dimensions? What would constrain the set? Are the constraints more interesting than the variance in that dimension not being robustly encoded in the auditory periphery or falling beyond a temporal window of possible integration? That is, are there categories that cannot be learned even if they could be potentially linearly separated in a perceptual space? If the set is not constrained, then is there a cost to adding novel dimensions? How does a listener monitor the dimensions at all?

In addition to these theoretically interesting questions that arise when we focus on the dimensions, there are also some troubling concerns that emerge for those who investigate auditory categorization. Above, we described non-speech dimensions based on the center frequency of troughs of energy in the spectrum of white noise. Of course, it is unlikely that listeners are in fact using that center frequency. It is more likely that they are using the higher or lower cutoff frequencies (which will be released from inhibition by the trough of energy). A listener may also use a center of spectral gravity dimension or some other aspect of the shape of the spectral envelope. Listeners may differ in which one of these dimensions they use to perform the task. In the case of these laboratory experiments, this lack of precision in defining the dimensions is not too detrimental because these dimensions would be highly correlated and would all provide sufficient resolving power to show categorization. However, it is easy to construct scenarios in which these differences *will* matter and, in particular, the importance of properly defining dimensions becomes much more obvious for speech categories.

3.3 A Case of Dimensional Imprecision: Voice Onset Time

One of the most common variables in speech acoustics and phoneme categorization research has been voice onset time (VOT: Lisker & Abramson 1968). In essence VOT is the time between the release of the occlusion for a stop consonant and the onset of vocal fold vibration (we will focus here on the classic word-initial stop consonant voicing contrast). The first obvious problem with the use of VOT as a perceptual dimension is that it is an articulatory definition and not an auditory one. With due respect to the Motor Theory of Speech Perception (Liberman et al. 1967) or the direct realism of Fowler (1986), it would be far more satisfactory to have perceptual dimensions that cohere to our current understanding of what is encoded by the auditory system. The problem is that the articulatory definition provided above corresponds to a large number of acoustic changes that could serve as perceptual dimensions (Lisker 1986). (We understand that it is this many-to-one mapping that provides some of the motivation for the theories mentioned above but we choose to ignore this debate here as we have engaged in it in other places, see Diehl et al. 2004).

When VOT is discussed in terms of an acoustic dimension, it appears to usually stand-in for the duration of the aspiration noise prior to the onset of periodic energy. Figure 3.2 presents a pseudo-spectrogram of a consonant-vowel. The dashed lines represent formants being excited by aspiration energy and solid lines represent formants excited by periodic energy. The duration of the aspirated portion could be a dimension that listeners use to categorize a voicing contrast (e.g., /b/ versus /p/). Of course, one can quickly come up with other acoustic measures that would serve the same purpose – e.g., the duration of the periodic portion or the duration of formant transitions that are excited by periodic energy. One could also rely on the loudness of the aspiration noise given that loudness is a function of the amplitude of the energy *and* the duration of the energy (Bloch's Law).

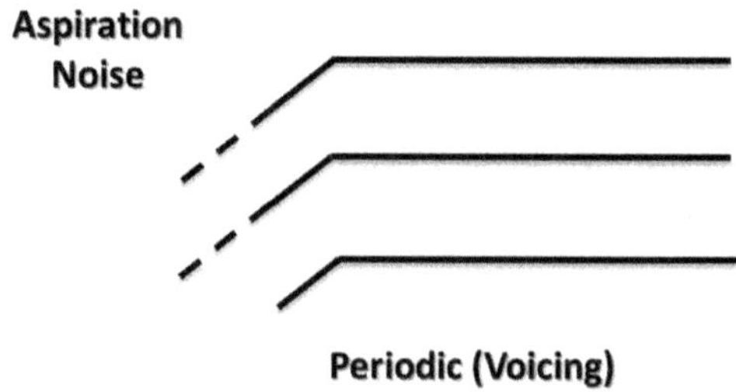

Figure 3.2. Pseudo-spectrogram of a consonant-vowel.

One might also note that there is little aspiration energy in the region of the first formant (no dashed lines in the figure). This lack of energy is due to an anti-resonance caused primarily by tracheal coupling with the vocal tract. This feature results in several other potential acoustic dimensions that relate to voicing categorizations. For instance, the starting frequency of the first formant would be higher for voiceless stops (since the formant transitions for these stops are always increasing in frequency and one would be delaying the onset; see Kluender & Lotto 1994). In addition, instead of measuring the time of aspiration noise, one could measure the time from stimulus onset to F1-onset. F1-onset delay or F1-onset frequency may seem like unlikely perceptual dimensions in this case but Lotto & Kluender (2002) demonstrated that reasonable voicing categorizations can be made even for stimuli varying only in the "cutback" of F1 with no aspirated portion. That is, a good exemplar of /pa/ can be created by filtering energy near F1 even when the entire stimulus is excited by a periodic source (equivalent to Figure 3.2 with no dashed lines; see also Lisker 1975).

The above discussion of the many acoustic dimensions related to voicing is nothing new. The use of multiple cues to arrive at a phonemic decision is the basis of the work on trading relations (see Repp 1984, for a review). In fact, the effectiveness of so many dimensions for phonemic perception was not considered a problem for the listener because all of these cues arise from the same articulatory actions. If listeners were perceiving speech in terms of these articulatory actions (or the planning of those actions) in accordance with Motor Theory, then the problems of unconstrained sets of dimensions go away. What is important is the perception of the voicing gesture and not the individual acoustic dimensions.

For those of us who are not satisfied with such an explanation, the problem of being explicit about the dimensional space for phonetic categorization remains. Despite its ubiquity, VOT is not an adequate dimension for models of auditory categorization. Even after decades of empirical and theoretical work in speech perception, there is a lack of theory on how listeners uncover the dimensions underlying speech sound categorization. However, there is at least one attempt to provide such an explanation that provides a template for future endeavors and that comes from the work of Harvey Sussman.

3.4 Harvey Sussman: Solving the Frame Problem

One of the best examples of the need to get the perceptual dimensions "right" when trying to understand auditory categorization comes from the categorization of stop consonants by place of articulation. If one looks at the acoustics of /ba/, /da/ and /ga/ spoken by a typical speaker, there is a salient difference in the onset frequency of the second formant. F2-onset frequency appears to be a good dimension for categorizing these stops. However, the distinctiveness of these stops on F2-onset disappears as one varies the following vowel. The extreme context-dependence of the acoustics of these stops has been one of the principal/classic demonstrations of the lack of invariance in speech (Liberman et al. 1967; Stevens & Blumstein 1978; Blumstein & Stevens 1979). However, as Sussman and colleagues have shown (Sussman et al. 1991), a tremendous amount of orderly structure can be witnessed by plotting exemplars in an F2-onset frequency by F2-vowel-midpoint frequency space. What appears to be a nearly impossible categorization problem becomes less mystical when one sees the structure inherent in a different acoustic space.

The stimulus distributions in the non-speech experiment by Wade & Holt (2005) had a similar structure to what one sees for place of articulation in speech – the categories were separable in an acoustic space defined by the onset and steady-state frequencies of the second resonance filter applied to the stimulus. In fact, this stimulus space was inspired by Sussman's work in categorization of speech. As discussed above, the problem that arises with these complex stimulus spaces is the lack of an explanation of how listeners determine the relevant space. The question is analogous to the Frame Problem in artificial intelligence (AI) and philosophy (McCarthy & Hayes 1969). In AI, the problem comes from determining which aspects of representation of the environment are relevant for any action – this is very difficult to determine a priori. In the case of auditory categorization research, the problem is determining which acoustic dimensions are relevant for a task – again, very difficult to do a priori. How does a listener come to appreciate that the key to the categorization of place of articulation is the linear relations between F2-onset and -mid-vowel frequencies, if that is in fact the correct dimension?

Sussman (e.g., Sussman et al. 1998; Sussman 2013) has provided one of the only attempts to answer the frame problem for audition. He has taken a neuro-ethological approach and pointed out that the type of relational processing required for place of articulation categorization is seen in auditory processing across a number of species (with well-described neural models of this processing). Based on this cross-species work, he proposes that humans are biologically endowed with neural processes that would favor the perception of relational cues in audition. Further, the importance of these types of cues for processing speech sounds is not a happy coincidence but is the result of evolving a communication system that takes advantage of these biases in perceptual processing.

The most beneficial aspect of Sussman's work is not that it provides a basis for understanding how humans distinguish /b/, /d/ and /g/, but that it offers some guidelines and hope for theories about the possible set of auditory dimensions and the development of perceptual spaces. The key is first to admit that there are important unanswered questions about perceptual spaces and then to go back to first principles and think about auditory representation and what kinds of processing the auditory system does well.

3.5 A Thought-Experiment: Formants

Probably the most popular stimulus/perceptual space in speech research is the F1-frequency x F2-frequency space for plotting vowel exemplars. Since the classic plot from Peterson & Barney (1952), the F1 x F2 space has been used to explain acquisition of vowel categories in native language (e.g., Kuhl 1991), in a second language (e.g., Bosch et al. 2000) and as the basis for computational modeling of speech categorization (e.g., Kluender et al. 1998; Maddox et al. 2002). It is widely accepted that vowel perception is strongly related to, if not strictly dependent on, the frequency of the first two formants.

Despite the centrality of formant frequencies to the science of speech perception, it is difficult to derive these as basic perceptual dimensions if one goes back to first principles. Formants are resonances of the vocal tract. They often result in spectral peaks, but not always – especially for higher fundamental frequencies. It is often difficult to measure the frequencies of these measures from spectra (as anyone who has done extensive acoustic analyses knows) and we often use methods such as linear predictive coding to estimate what the resonant frequencies are, based on a model of speech production/acoustics. We are again left with dimensions that are inherently related to speech production but may be acoustically obscure. To make matters more confusing, we treat the formant frequencies as if they vary independently, but they do not.

It is not clear that the frequencies of resonances of the vocal tract are salient features of the auditory input of vowels. Here is a quick thought experiment: if you consider the encoding of vowel stimuli in the auditory periphery, what is the likelihood that the dimensions that will be considered most relevant will be F1-F2 frequencies (presuming one does not have a special module or innate knowledge of vocal tracts and the physics of speech production)? We can even start with simplifying obviously wrong starting assumptions, such as – we only receive steady-state vowels and the auditory system provides something like a spectral envelope of the incoming stimulus. One may imagine that during vowel learning, the initial dimensions arise from tracking the spectral variance and coming up with dimensions that account for most of that variance. This would be similar to computing a principal components analysis (PCA) across the experienced exemplars. Figure 3.3 shows what the first two components of such an analysis would look like. In this case, we simply took the spectral envelopes (log-scaled in amplitude) for 10 English vowels and performed a PCA.

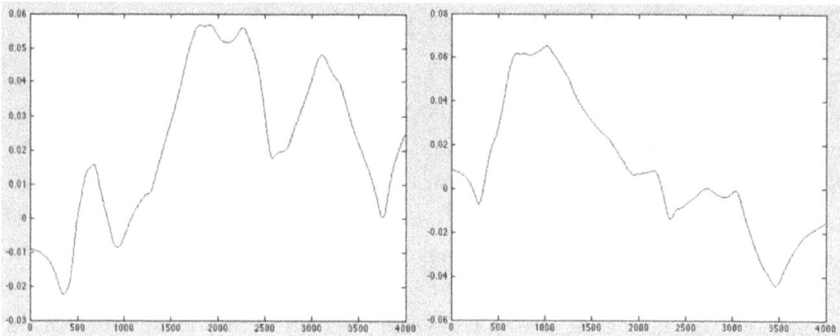

Figure 3.3. First two components of principal component analysis from spectral envelopes of 10 English vowels.

These two components are independent spectral shapes and one can reconstruct the 10 vowels by weighting each of these spectral shapes in a combination (this accounts for 78 per cent of the variance in the original vowel spectra). In essence the weights represent dimensions for a perceptual space that is related to peripheral auditory encoding. Note that there is no reference here to formants or tube models of speech production.

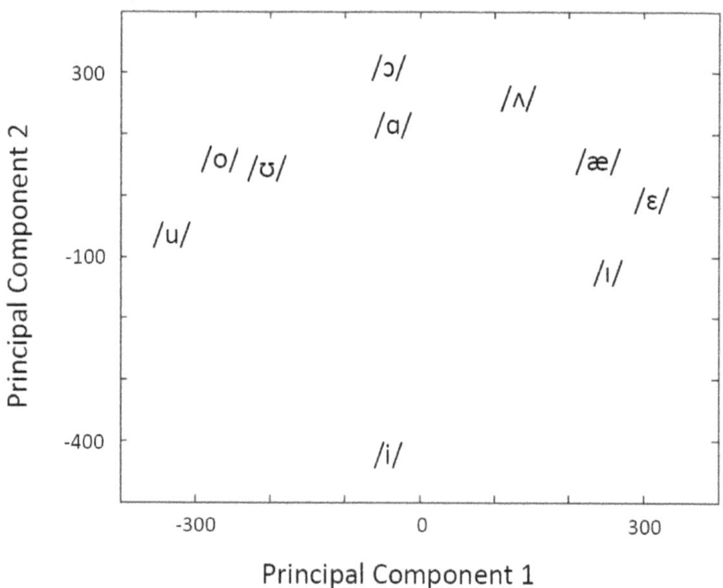

Figure 3.4. Vowel space across first two components.

Figure 3.4 is a plot of the original 10 vowels represented within this new space. This simple exercise is NOT intended as a model of how vowels are perceptually represented. To start with, one would want to scale the spectra either psychophysically or using a model of the auditory periphery. Also, one needs to determine whether the strict requirements of orthogonal dimensions for PCA are necessary. The real purpose of this thought experiment is to provoke the idea that we may want to derive our auditory dimensions for speech categorization instead of accepting those that were developed mainly in research on the acoustics of speech production. It is this sort of analysis from the auditory perspective that is inspired by the successful example provided by Harvey Sussman. The end result may be a solution to the dimensional Frame Problem and could lead to a better understanding of how humans acquire and use auditory categories for communication.

Acknowledgments

We wish to thank Nico Carbonell and Jessamyn Schertz for assistance with editing, proofreading and graph construction. Also, we want to express our gratitude to Harvey Sussman, who has been a supportive of us for our entire careers starting in graduate school. We are honored to call him a friend. This work is supported by NIH- R01 DC004674–09 to AJL and LLH.

References

Ashby, F.G., & T.W. Maddox. (2005). Human category learning. *Annual Review of Psychology*, 56(1), 149–78.http://dx.doi.org/10.1146/annurev.psych.56.091103.070217

Blumstein, S.E., & K.N. Stevens. (1979).Acoustic invariance in speech production: Evidence from measurements of the spectral characteristics of stop consonants. *Journal of the Acoustical Society of America*, 66(4), 1001. http://dx.doi.org/10.1121/1.383319

Bosch, L., A. Costa & N. Sebastian-Galles. (2000). First and second language vowel perception in early bilinguals. *European Journal of Cognitive Psychology*, 12(2), 189–221. http://dx.doi.org/10.1080/09541446.2000.10590222

Chandrasekaran, B., H.G. Yi & W.T. Maddox. (2014). Dual-learning systems during speech category learning. *Psychonomic Bulletin & Review*, 21(2), 488–95. http://dx.doi.org/10.3758/s13423-013-0501-5

Christensen, L.A., & L.E. Humes. (1997). Identification of multidimensional stimuli containing speech cues and the effects of training. *Journal of the Acoustical Society of America*, 102(4), 2297–310. http://dx.doi.org/10.1121/1.419639

Diehl, R.L., A.J. Lotto & L.L. Holt. (2004). Speech perception. *Annual Review of Psychology*, 55(1), 149–79. http://dx.doi.org/10.1146/annurev.psych.55.090902.142028

Fowler, C.A. (1986). An event approach to the study of speech perception from a direct-realist perspective. *Journal of Phonetics*, 14(1), 3–28.

Goldinger, S.D. (1998). Echoes of echoes? An episodic theory of lexical access. *Psychological Review*, 105(2), 251–79. http://dx.doi.org/10.1037/0033-295X.105.2.251

Holt, L.L. & A.J. Lotto. (2006). Cue weighting in auditory categorization: Implications for first and second language acquisition. *Journal of the Acoustical Society of America*, 119(5), 3059–71. http://dx.doi.org/10.1121/1.2188377

Holt, L.L., & A.J. Lotto. (2010). Speech perception as categorization. *Attention, Perception & Psychophysics*, 72(5), 1218–27. http://dx.doi.org/10.3758/APP.72.5.1218

Holt, L.L., A.J. Lotto & R.L. Diehl. (2004). Auditory discontinuities interact with categorization: Implications for speech perception. *Journal of the Acoustical Society of America*, 116(3), 1763–73. http://dx.doi.org/10.1121/1.1778838

Holt, L.L., A.J. Lotto & K. R. Kluender. (1998). Incorporating principles of general learning in theories of language acquisition. In M.C. Gruber, D. Higgins, K.S. Olson & T. Wysocki (eds.), *Chicago Linguistic Society—Vol. 34: The Panels* (pp. 253–68). Chicago: Chicago Linguistic Society.

Janega, J., & A.J. Lotto. (2000). Explicit training of complex auditory categories. Presentation at the 72nd Meeting of the Midwestern Psychological Association, Chicago, IL.

Kittleson, M., R.L. Diehl & A.J. Lotto. (2012). Optimal categorization of sounds varying on a single dimension. *Journal of the Acoustical Society of America*, 132(3), 2051. http://dx.doi.org/10.1121/1.4755546

Kluender, K.R., & A.J. Lotto. (1994). Effects of first formant onset frequency on [-voice] judgments result from auditory processes not specific to humans. *Journal of the Acoustical Society of America*, 95(2), 1044–52. http://dx.doi.org/10.1121/1.408466

Kluender, K.R., A.J. Lotto, L.L. Holt & S.L. Bloedel. (1998). Role of experience for language-specific functional mappings of vowel sounds. *Journal of the Acoustical Society of America*, 104(6), 3568–82. http://dx.doi.org/10.1121/1.423939

Kuhl, P.K. (1991). Human adults and human infants show a "perceptual magnet effect" for the prototype of speech categories, monkeys do not. *Perception & Psychophysics*, 50(2), 93–107. http://dx.doi.org/10.3758/BF03212211

Kuhl, P.K. (2000). Language, mind, and brain: Experience alters perception. In M.S. Gazzaniga (ed.), *The New Cognitive Neurosciences* (2nd ed., pp. 99–115). Cambridge, MA: MIT Press.

Liberman, A.M., F.S. Cooper, D.P. Shankweiler & M. Studdert-Kennedy. (1967). Perception of the speech code. *Psychological Review*, 74(6), 431–61. http://dx.doi.org/10.1037/h0020279

Lim, S.-J., & L.L. Holt. (2011). Learning foreign sounds in an alien world: Videogame training improves non-native speech categorization. *Cognitive Science*, 35(7), 1390–405. http://dx.doi.org/10.1111/j.1551-6709.2011.01192.x

Lisker, L. (1975). Is it VOT or a first-formant transition detector? *Journal of the Acoustical Society of America*, 57, 1547–51.

Lisker, L. (1986). "Voicing" in English: A catalogue of acoustic features signaling /b/ versus /p/ in trochees. *Language and Speech*, 29, 3–11.

Lisker, L. & A.S. Abramson. (1968). The voicing dimension: Some experiments in comparative phonetics. *Proceedings of the 6th International Congress on Phonetic Sciences, Prague.*

Lotto, A.J. (2000). Language acquisition as complex category formation. *Phonetica*, 57(2–4), 189–96. http://dx.doi.org/10.1159/000028472

Lotto, A.J., & K.R. Kluender. (2002). Synchrony capture hypothesis fails to account for effects of amplitude on voicing perception. *Journal of the Acoustical Society of America*, 111(2), 1056–62. http://dx.doi.org/10.1121/1.1433809

Lotto, A.J., M. Sato & R.L. Diehl. (2004). Mapping the task for the second language learner: The case of Japanese acquisition of /r/ and /l/. In J. Slifka, S. Manuel & M. Matthies (eds.), *From Sound to Sense: 50+ Years of Discoveries in Speech Communication*. Cambridge, MA: MIT.

Maddox, W.T., M.R. Molis & R.L. Diehl. (2002). Generalizing a neuropsychological model of visual categorization to auditory categorization of vowels. *Perception & Psychophysics*, 64(4), 584–97. http://dx.doi.org/10.3758/BF03194728

Massaro, D.W. (1987). *Speech Perception by Ear and Eye: A Paradigm for Psychological Inquiry*. Hillsdale, NJ: Lawrence Erlbaum Associates.

McCarthy, J. and P.J. Hayes. (1969). Some philosophical problems from the standpoint of artificial intelligence. In D. Michie (ed.), *Machine Intelligence 4*. New York, NY: American Elsevier.

McMurray, B., R.N. Aslin & J.C. Toscano. (2009). Statistical learning of phonetic categories: Insights from a computational approach. *Developmental Science*, 12(3), 369–78. http://dx.doi.org/10.1111/j.1467-7687.2009.00822.x

McMurray, B., & A. Jongman. (2011). What information is necessary for speech categorization? Harnessing variability in the speech signal by integrating cues computed relative to expectations. *Psychological Review*, 118(2), 219–46. http://dx.doi.org/10.1037/a0022325

Mirman, D., L.L. Holt & J.L. McClelland. (2004). Categorization and discrimination of nonspeech sounds: Differences between steady-state and rapidly-changing acoustic cues. *Journal of the Acoustical Society of America*, 116(2), 1198. http://dx.doi.org/10.1121/1.1766020

Nearey, T.M. (1997). Speech perception as pattern recognition. *Journal of the Acoustical Society of America*, 101(6), 3241–54. http://dx.doi.org/10.1121/1.418290

Oden, G.C., & D.W. Massaro. (1978). Integration of featural information in speech perception. *Psychological Review,* 85(3), 172–91. http://dx.doi.org/10.1037/0033-295X.85.3.172

Peterson, G.E. & H.L. Barney (1952). Control methods used in a study of the vowels. *Journal of the Acoustical Society of America,* 24, 175–84.

Repp, B. (1984).Closure duration and release burst amplitude cues to stop consonant manner and place of articulation. *Language and Speech,* 27, 245–54.

Smits, R., J. Sereno & A. Jongman. (2006). Categorization of sounds. *Journal of Experimental Psychology: Human Perception and Performance,* 32(3), 733–54. http://dx.doi.org/10.1037/0096-1523.32.3.733

Stevens, K.N., & S.E. Blumstein. (1978). Invariant cues for place of articulation in stop consonants. *Journal of the Acoustical Society of America,* 64(5), 1358. http://dx.doi.org/10.1121/1.382102

Sullivan, S.C., J.A. Tanji, A.J. Lotto & R.L. Diehl. (2011). Sensitivity to changing characteristics of Gaussian-shaped stimulus distributions in auditory categorization. *Journal of the Acoustical Society of America,* 130(4), 2516. http://dx.doi.org/10.1121/1.3655030

Sussman, H.M. (2013). Neuroethology in the service of neurophonetics. *Journal of Neurolinguistics,* 26(5), 511–25. http://dx.doi.org/10.1016/j.jneuroling.2013.02.004

Sussman, H.M., D. Fruchter, J. Hilbert & J. Sirosh. (1998). Linear correlates in the speech signal: The orderly output constraint. *Behavioral and Brain Sciences,* 21(02), 241–99. http://dx.doi.org/10.1017/S0140525X98001174

Sussman, H.M., H.A. McCaffrey & S.A. Matthews. (1991). An investigation of locus equations as a source of relational invariance for stop place categorization. *Journal of the Acoustical Society of America,* 90(3), 1309. http://dx.doi.org/10.1121/1.401923

Wade, T., & L.L. Holt. (2005). Incidental categorization of spectrally complex non-invariant auditory stimuli in a computer game task. *Journal of the Acoustical Society of America,* 118(4), 2618–33. http://dx.doi.org/10.1121/1.2011156

Yamada, R.A., & Y. Tohkura (1990). Perception and production of syllable-initial English /r/ and /l/ by native speakers of Japanese. In *Proceedings of International Conference on Spoken Language Processing* (pp. 757–60), Kobe, Japan: ICSLP.

4
Perceptual Cues in Korean Fricatives

Goun Lee and Allard Jongman[1]

4.1 Introduction

Harvey Sussman has made important contributions to speech science in an impressive range of areas, ranging from motor planning to hemispheric organization to coarticulation. Most recently, Sussman has provided new insights into the mapping between acoustic cues and perceived phonological categories. Specifically, he has proposed the concept of the "locus equation" as a relational invariant (Sussman et al. 1991 and many more), arguing that there is, in fact, an invariant relationship between (derived) acoustic properties and perceived phonemes that is not affected by typical sources of variability such as speaker and vowel context.

In the present contribution, we also study the relationship between acoustic properties and perception, and the potential role of vowel context, with focus on a unique phonemic distinction in Korean that has received relatively little attention. Korean has two types of alveolar fricatives that are distinguished not by a voicing contrast but by a difference in phonation type. It is widely accepted that these alveolar fricatives – the fortis /s'/ and the non-fortis or plain /s/ – are fully contrastive: both can be produced in all vowel contexts. The precise articulatory and acoustic characteristics that differentiate the two fricatives are not fully understood, however, and are a topic of interest among phoneticians. There is also some debate regarding the perceptual cues that Korean listeners use to distinguish between the two fricatives: previous studies indicate that the acoustic cues of the two fricatives vary across different vowel contexts, but it is unclear

1 Goun Lee is a doctoral student in the Phonetics and Psycholinguistics Laboratory at the University of Kansas.
Allard Jongman is a professor in the Department of Linguistics, Phonetics and Psycholinguistics Laboratory, at the University of Kansas.

whether this variation triggers changes in perception, as well. The overall purpose of the current study, then, is to contribute new information to the debate by determining the perceptual cues that distinguish Korean fricatives, the extent to which they differ depending on vowel context, and the relative importance of consonantal and vocalic cues in the perception of the distinction.

We will start with a review of the acoustic, articulatory and perceptual properties of Korean fricatives. We will then present two perception experiments as well as an acoustic analysis of the stimuli used in these experiments, and end with a discussion of the results and conclusions that can be drawn. In general, our results indicate that the strength of different perceptual cues varies with vowel context, suggesting that listeners might use different perceptual strategies depending on the vowel context.

4.2 Acoustic and Articulatory Studies of Korean Fricatives

A number of studies have examined the articulatory and acoustic characteristics of the two Korean fricatives in an attempt to determine the properties which distinguish them. Articulatory studies suggest that the plain fricative is produced with a wider glottal opening than the fortis fricative (Iverson 1983; Jun et al. 1998; Kagaya 1974; Kim, Maeda & Honda 2011). During production of the plain fricative, the glottis gradually widens until it reaches a degree of opening comparable to that used for respiration. This stands in contrast to the glottal adduction observed during production of the fortis fricative (Kagaya 1974). Additional articulatory evidence comes from lingual gesture comparisons, which suggest that the plain fricative is produced with less constriction than the fortis fricative. Furthermore, when compared to the fortis fricative, the plain fricative is produced with a greater groove width (Baik 1998), a smaller area of linguopalatal contact (Kim 2001) and lower airflow resistance (Kim, Maeda & Honda 2010).

In terms of acoustics, an interval of aspiration toward the end of the frication noise has been reported as a key component of the plain fricative in low vowel contexts (Ahn 1999; Chang 2007, 2013; Cho et al. 2002; Holliday 2010, 2011; Kagaya 1974; Kim, Maeda et al. 2010; Lee 2011; Yoon 1999). Figure 4.1 represents the plain (left) and fortis (right) fricatives in the low vowel context /a/. In the spectrogram of the plain fricative which appears in the lower left-hand corner, aspiration is visible as a shift in spectral

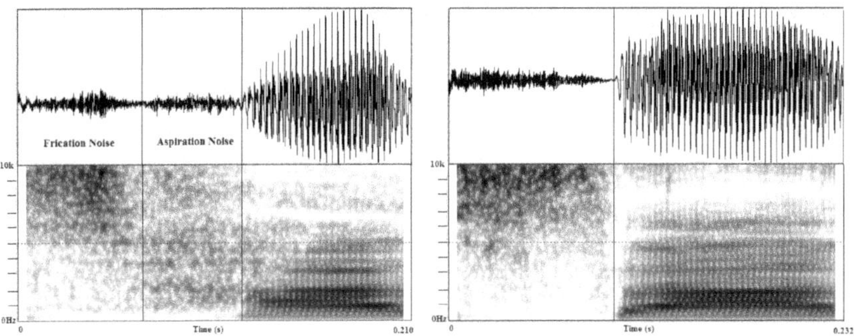

Figure 4.1. Waveform and spectrogram of the plain /sʰa/ (left) and fortis /s'a/ (right) fricatives in the /a/ vowel context. The interval of aspiration in the plain fricative is marked.

energy from higher to lower frequencies. However, no aspiration is visible in the fortis fricative which appears on the right.

A number of studies have also pointed to the overall spectral differences between the two fricatives as a distinguishing acoustic factor, with results indicating that the plain fricative has a significantly lower center of gravity (COG) value than the fortis fricative (Cho et al. 2002; Chang, 2013; Hwang 2004; Holliday 2010; Kang et al. 2009; Lee 2011). One of the ways that previous researchers have interpreted this finding is by noting the fact that the spectral energy of the fortis fricative remains in the high frequency ranges precisely because it is not aspirated (Cho et al. 2002; Hwang 2004; Kang 2000; Kang et al. 2009; Lee 2011; Park 1999; Yoon 1999). In this sense, COG and aspiration results may be seen as being related. The plain fricative has a lower COG, particularly in low vowel contexts, presumably because aspiration introduces low-frequency energy. Thus, the COG results seem to support the claim that the plain fricative in the low vowel context is produced with aspiration, while the fortis fricative is not.

In addition to the spectral differences, other acoustic parameters such as H1-H2, the difference between the amplitudes of the first and second harmonic of the FFT spectrum, can also indicate whether the fricative is produced with aspiration. Previous studies have consistently found that the plain fricative yields greater H1-H2 values than the fortis fricative (Cho et al. 2002; Kang et al. 2009; Lee 2011; Park 1999), indicating that the plain fricative is produced with a breathier voice quality than the fortis fricative.

Beyond measurements of aspiration in the plain fricative, the most widely examined cues related to phonation type in the two fricatives are fundamental frequency (F0) of the following vowel and fricative duration. For both of these parameters, previous studies have failed to produce consistent results. Some researchers have found that the fortis fricative has a higher F0 value (Ahn 1999; Yoon 1999) and a longer duration than the plain fricative (Chang 2008, 2013; Cho et al. 2002; Kim, Maeda et al. 2010; Yoon 1999). Other studies have not found a significant difference in either F0 values (Chang 2007; Cho et al. 2002; Holliday 2012; Lee 2011) or in duration (Kang 2000; Lee 2011; Park 2002). Accordingly, questions regarding the extent to which F0 and fricative duration differ between the two fricatives remain open.

Several of the acoustic cues distinguishing the fricatives discussed above pattern differently in different vowel contexts. One of the most salient vowel context effects that has been observed is that the visually apparent aspiration portion (low-frequency energy) of the plain fricative seen in Figure 4.1 disappears in the high vowel context. Figure 4.2 represents a waveform and spectrogram of two fricatives in the high vowel context /i/. Note that the spectral energy remains in the high frequency range regardless of the fricative type when the following vowel is /i/ (Figure 4.2), whereas a shift in spectral energy from the higher to the lower frequencies was observed for the plain fricative before /a/ (Figure 4.1).

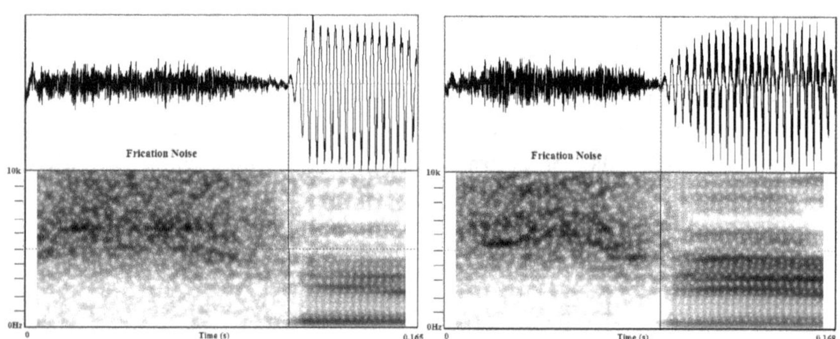

Figure 4.2. Waveform and spectrogram of the plain /si/ (left) and fortis /s'i/ (right) fricatives in the /i/ vowel context.

That a spectral shift is visible in the plain fricative in only one of the two vowel contexts might indicate that aspiration weakens or disappears in the high vowel context. In fact, this is exactly what has been reported in previous studies which examined the aspiration duration of the plain fricative. These studies found a shorter aspiration interval in the high vowel contexts (/i/ and /u/) than in the low vowel context /a/ (Chang 2007, 2008, 2013; Kagaya 1974; Kim, Maeda et al. 2010; Yoon 2002). Figure 4.3 represents differences in the aspiration duration reported for the two fricatives in three

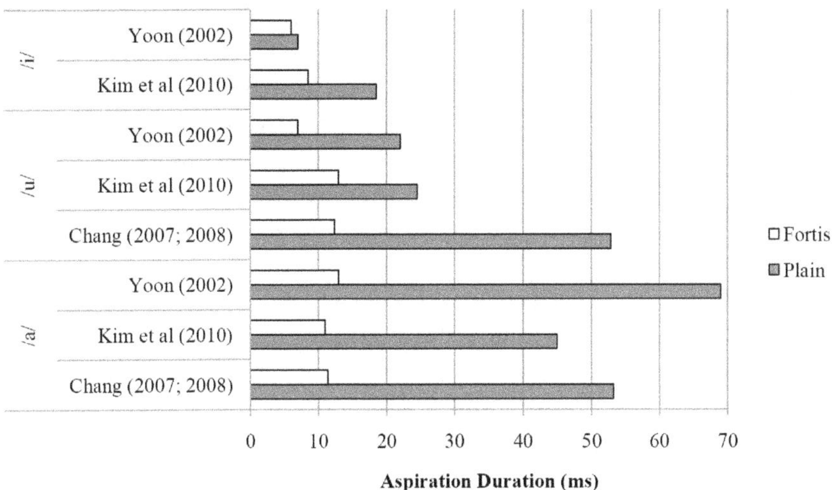

Figure 4.3. Previously reported differences in aspiration duration for the two fricatives in three vowel contexts (adapted from Chang 2007, 2008; Kim, Maeda et al. 2010; Yoon 2002).

distinct vowel contexts (/i/, /u/ and /a/) as reported in previous studies (Chang 2007, 2008; Kim, Maeda et al. 2010; Yoon 2002). All of these measurements were taken from fricatives in word-initial position.

We should note, though, that the techniques used for measuring aspiration in these previous studies were neither precise nor consistent. Since no studies have reported a clear criterion which should be used to measure the aspiration interval in the plain fricative, the absence of such a criterion may have led to different results regarding whether aspiration completely disappears or gradually reduces in different vowel contexts. Moreover, there are reasons to question the presence of aspiration in the fortis fricative that has been reported in previous papers (Chang 2007, 2008; Kim, Maeda et al. 2010; Yoon 2002). Cho et al. (2002) reported glottalization associated with the fortis fricative, which was described as a short silent gap between the frication noise and the vowel portion. This very interval was used for measuring aspiration in other studies, however (Chang 2007, 2008; Kim, Maeda et al. 2010; Yoon 2002), which means what was reported as aspiration may in fact have been glottalization. Since aspiration and glottalization are identified with reference to the degree of glottal opening, glottalization and aspiration by definition cannot co-occur (Holliday 2011). Kagaya (1974) found that the vocal folds are completely abducted when producing the fortis fricative, and therefore concluded that the fortis fricative is not aspirated regardless of the vowel context (/i/, /e/, /a/). Furthermore, Lee (2011) reports that the sudden decline in frequency values that is associated with the aspiration interval is only present for the plain fricative in three vowel contexts (/ɛ/, /ʌ/, /a/), indicating that the fortis fricative is not aspirated. Based on both articulatory and acoustic evidence, then, it seems improbable that the fortis fricative is aspirated. Regardless of that issue, however, the most important point is that different vowel contexts affect the characteristics of the plain fricative, and therefore the acoustic cues that distinguish the two fricatives differ depending on the vowel context.

For example, the COG and H1-H2 differences between the two fricatives are greater in the low vowel context than in the high vowel context (Chang 2013; Kang et al. 2009). Also, the intensity build-up and the mean intensity value of the following vowel vary across vowel contexts. The intensity build-up differs significantly between the two fricatives in high and mid vowel contexts (/i, ʌ, u/) but not in the low vowel context (/a/), whereas the mean intensity value difference between the two fricatives is significant in the low vowel context /a/ but not in the other vowel contexts (/i, ʌ, u/) (Chang 2013).

With respect to the findings related to COG values, however, there is also a possibility that the drop in COG values which has been reported for fricatives in the high vowel context is due to palatalization. It has been claimed that Korean fricatives become palatalized in certain vowel environments like /i/ and /j/ (Cheon 2005; Sohn 1994; Yoon 1999), but very few studies have supported this claim with articulatory or acoustic evidence. Baik (1998) examined palatalization of Korean fricatives in an EPG study, and found that only the fortis fricative is palatalized in casual speech. However, it should be noted that Baik (1998) had only one subject – he used his own speech production for the study.

Taken together, it seems that both the consonant (aspiration, COG) and the subsequent vowel (H1-H2, F1 and intensity) contain cues to signal the plain-fortis distinction. The studies reviewed above also tell us that acoustic cues differ by vowel context. We may wonder, then, whether the perceptual cues vary across vowel contexts as well. If aspiration is a strong perceptual cue, for instance, we may predict that identification of the plain fricative in the high vowel context – where aspiration is reduced or absent – may suffer. We turn now to a review of results related to the perception of Korean fricatives.

4.3 Perception of Korean Fricatives

A limited number of studies have examined the perceptual cues associated with Korean fricatives. Among these studies, some have found that aspiration plays an important role in distinguishing the laryngeal contrast between Korean fricatives (Chang 2007, 2013; Park 1999; Yoon 1999, 2002). For example, there is some evidence that artificially shortening the aspiration portion of a plain fricative causes listeners to perceive the fricative as fortis (Yoon 1999, 2002). Yoon tested 20 native Korean listeners using two types of manipulated stimuli: naturally produced tokens such as /s^{h}ata/, in which the aspiration was incrementally decreased, and a pair of artificially created stimuli with or without aspiration (/s^{h}a/ and /s'a/). When the aspiration interval was less than 37 ms, the listeners started to shift their identification from plain to fortis responses. When identifying the artificially created stimuli, Korean listeners predominantly perceived the tokens containing aspiration as plain. These results highlight the importance of aspiration as a perceptual cue for Korean fricatives, but did not account for other acoustic cues – especially vocalic cues like H1-H2, F1 and intensity values – which also signal the distinction between the fricatives.

Park (1999) focused on the perceptual importance of the vocalic cues in identifying the fricatives and conducted two perception experiments with 12 Korean native listeners. In the first experiment, the consonantal and vocalic segments of the plain fricative [s^{h}ata] and the fortis fricative [s'ata] were cross-spliced and presented for identification. The results showed that the listeners' responses were strongly associated with the vowel rather than the consonant. In the second experiment, the listeners were presented with manipulated stimuli for the identification task. Starting with a plain fricative-vowel syllable, a 15-step continuum was created by starting at a point 50 ms into the vowel and removing 10 ms increments moving back toward fricative onset. When both aspiration and the earlier portion of the vowel were removed, listeners started to classify the stimuli as fortis.

However, the results of the two experiments do not support each other. Whereas the first experiment indicates that the vocalic cues are the only perceptual cues crucial to distinguishing the fricatives, the second experiment indicates that both consonantal (aspiration) and vocalic cues are necessary to identify the fricatives. This conflict might be because excision of the segments could have changed the temporal cues or compromised other perceptual cues related to fricative identification. Still, Park's results emphasize the importance of the vocalic cues in identifying the fricatives.

However, the question of whether the importance of the vocalic cues remains consistent in other vowel contexts is still open.

Chang (2007, 2013) conducted perception experiments in which he manipulated a number of acoustic cues in different vowel contexts. Specifically, Chang (2013) manipulated frication duration, aspiration duration and F0 in the context of the vowels /i, ɯ, u, a/. Results showed that listeners tended to identify the stimuli that have longer frication duration, longer aspiration duration and higher F0 values as plain rather than fortis. However, the coherence of the phonation type between the vowel and consonant (i.e., whether the stimuli were cross-spliced or not) was the strongest predictor of accurate fricative perception in the /a/ vowel context. While the listeners predominantly followed the phonation type of the cross-spliced vowel in the /a/ vowel context, the effect was not as strong in the high vowel contexts (/i, ɯ, u/). Furthermore, among the different high vowel contexts the response pattern varied. For /ɯ/, listeners showed a response bias toward fortis regardless of the vowel phonation type, whereas they were more likely to follow the phonation type of the vowels for the stimuli with /i/ and /u/. Based on these results, Chang concluded that perception is most accurate when the vocalic cues are consistent with consonantal cues. However, in the high vowel context the effect of coherence between the consonant and vowel is not as strong as in the /a/ vowel context. This is because the vocalic cues are not strong enough for accurate fricative distinction in high vowel contexts.

The work by Chang (2008, 2013) is an important contribution to the research regarding the relative impact of consonantal and vocalic cues in Korean fricative perception in different vowel contexts, but it is hard to tease apart the overall effect of each type of cue on perception. Since Chang (2013) only used CV tokens, it remains unclear whether a single class of cues, either consonantal or vocalic, could provide sufficient information to distinguish the fricatives. In addition, his results may have been affected by the great number of manipulations performed on the stimuli. Chang (2013) manipulated fricative duration (100 ms, 170 ms, 240 ms), aspiration duration (0 ms, 50 ms, 100 ms) and F0 (low, mid, high) before he cross-spliced the vowels. Therefore, his stimuli did not contain any natural tokens.

Furthermore, none of the previous studies used tokens that were naturally produced by multiple talkers. The auditory stimuli were recorded by a single talker in word-isolation in careful speech, and sometimes were explicitly chosen as the ones with the maximal centroid differences and with the minimal vowel duration differences. Therefore, we might wonder whether the choice of tokens could have facilitated listeners' perception.

With these facts in mind, in the current study we try to investigate the individual effect of consonantal and vocalic cues on fricative perception using two perception experiments. Ten female speakers were recorded producing a set of target words in a carrier sentence (see Table 4.1). The targets were then excised for the purpose of the experiment. Experiment 1 investigates the identification of fricatives using isolated consonant or vowel segments excised from syllables. The main purpose of Experiment 1 is to examine how well participants can identify the fricatives with only one set of cues. Considering that consonantal and vocalic cues signaling the fricative distinction vary across different vowel contexts, Korean listeners' perceptual accuracy might vary across both the type of portion (consonantal or vocalic) and the vowel context (/i/ versus /a/). In the low vowel context, both aspiration noise in the consonant segment and voice quality in the vowel segment will be strong cues for correctly distinguishing the fricatives (Chang 2013). Thus, listeners are predicted to be able to distinguish the two fricatives from both the consonantal and the vocalic segments. However, when voice quality is not as strong a cue to phonation type, as in high vowel contexts, listeners might not be able to discriminate the fricatives based on the vowel portion.

Experiment 2 investigates identification of fricatives using cross-spliced stimuli in which the consonantal and vocalic information conflict. This will help us to better understand the relative contribution of each set of cues as well as the importance of coherence of cues between the fricative and the following vowel in perception. Experiment 2 is a partial replication of Chang (2013), but no manipulation is conducted except for cross-splicing the vowels. There are two reasons why no additional manipulations should be performed, and both arise from the fact that the debate regarding the acoustic characteristics of the Korean fricatives is still ongoing.

First, it is difficult to completely tease apart the effect of aspiration on fricative perception from other perceptual cues. Previous studies have not clearly shown which portion should be measured as aspiration duration in the plain fricative (see Holliday 2011).[2] Aspiration onset has generally been described as the point where frication noise turns into aspiration noise. But this is a vague and circular criterion. For example, as illustrated in Figure 4.2, due to the lack of a spectral shift from high energy to low energy in the /i/ vowel context, designation of the precise aspiration onset point based on the spectrogram is almost impossible. Different researchers may not agree on the exact point of aspiration onset. In addition, if even a

2 See Lee (2011) for a more detailed description of the criteria used for measuring aspiration.

very brief interval of the preceding frication noise is included in the aspiration portion of the auditory stimuli, the listeners could be influenced by the perceptual information carried in the frication portion. Thus, until a precise and replicable method for measurement of aspiration is broadly agreed upon among phoneticians, it is hard to discuss the independent effect of aspiration on fricative perception. Furthermore, manipulating the temporal cues of fricatives is complicated because multiple cues co-vary. Since aspiration noise has lower-frequency spectral energy than the frication noise (Lee 2011), manipulating aspiration duration will also cause a decrease in the overall COG value of the fricative. Considering that acoustic research indicates the importance of COG in differentiating the fricatives (Chang 2013; Cho et al. 2002; Holliday 2010; Hwang 2004; Kang et al. 2009; Lee 2011), the data obtained from manipulated aspiration duration will be hard to interpret because the listeners could have been affected by both cues, instead of a single cue.

Second, categorization of the plain fricative remains controversial, with researchers disagreeing about whether it should be considered "aspirated" or "lenis" (Chang 2008, 2013; Cho et al. 2002; Hwang 2004; Kang 2000; Kang et al. 2009; Kim, Maeda et al. 2010; Lee 2011; Park 2002). Since disagreement about the status of the plain fricative abounds, manipulating a parameter that is more strongly correlated with one category than the other might make the result somewhat hard to interpret. For example, Chang (2008, 2013) found that listeners gave more plain responses when presented with tokens that had artificially raised F0 values. Considering that F0 has not been found to consistently distinguish the two fricatives (Ahn 1999; Chang 2007, 2013; Cho et al. 2002; Holliday 2012; Lee 2011; Yoon 1999), it is questionable whether the listeners' perceptual responses are truly based on the manipulated F0.

Thus, the purpose of Experiment 2 is to investigate which cues the listeners privilege in perceiving the fricatives when the consonantal and vocalic cues conflict. We also examine whether listeners change their perceptual strategy when the breathiness of the plain fricative becomes weaker, as in the /i/ vowel context. As Chang (2008, 2013) found, if voice quality differences provide the strongest cue for distinguishing the fricatives, listeners should follow the vowel cues in the /a/ vowel context. In the /i/ context, however, where the effect of aspiration becomes weaker, if listeners use the same strategy as they did in the /a/ vowel context, then they will not able to distinguish the fricatives easily. Thus, we expect that listeners will use a different strategy in fricative identification in the high-vowel context. Since we do not manipulate the stimuli in any way other than cross-splicing the consonant and vowel, we will be able to directly compare the perceptual cues that the listeners follow in both vowel contexts.

4.4 Recording and Analysis of Auditory Stimuli

The auditory stimuli were recorded using 10 female speakers of Seoul Korean. The mean age of the speakers was 26.9 years (range 21–32), and no one reported any articulatory or auditory impairment. The speakers were asked to read 4 target words in a carrier sentence. The stimuli and carrier sentence are presented in Table 4.1.

Table 4.1. Stimuli and carrier sentence that were used for the recording.

	/i/ vowel context	**/a/ vowel context**
Plain fricative	[silɨm] "worry"	[sʰata] "to buy"
Fortis fricative	[s'ilɨm] "wrestling"	[s'ata] "cheap"
Carrier sentence	[nega rago malhamnida] "I say"	

Thus, a total of 40 tokens were recorded for this study. The recording was conducted in the multimedia room of Yonsei University in Seoul. A Sony Vaio Notebook with an external sound card and a Shure SM58 microphone were used for the recording. Recorded materials were digitized at a sampling rate of 44,100 Hz. The target CV syllables were then excised from the carrier sentence for use in the perception experiment.

Prior to the perception experiments, *acoustic analysis of the auditory stimuli* was conducted using Praat (version 5.2.21) and VoiceSauce (version 1.11, 2011) to examine the acoustic characteristics of the fricatives in the two vowel contexts. A total of 15 measurements (7 measurements for the fricative segment, 8 measurements for the vowel) were analyzed, yielding a total of 600 measurements (15 measurements × 40 tokens). A list of all acoustic parameters investigated is provided in Table 4.2.

Table 4.2. Measurements that were analyzed for the auditory stimuli.

Measurements for the fricative segment	**Measurements for the vowel segment**
1) Fricative duration	1) Vowel duration
2) Aspiration duration	2) F0 values (at onset of the vowel)
3) Rise time	3) F0 values (at midpoint of the vowel)
4) Normalized RMS energy	4) H1-H2* (at onset of the vowel)
5) COG (initial 60% portion of the fricative)	5) H1-H2* (at midpoint of the vowel)
6) COG (final 40% portion of the fricative)	6) Cepstral Peak Prominence (CPP) (at onset of the vowel)
7) COG (total fricative duration)	7) CPP (at midpoint of the vowel)
	8) F1 (at onset of the vowel)

Frication duration was measured from the onset of aperiodic noise to the onset of periodic voicing for the following vowel using the waveform of each token.

Aspiration duration was measured from the onset of the aspiration to the onset of the following vowel. Visual evidence from FFT spectra and spectrograms, and COG values were used to designate and confirm the onset of aspiration. Aspiration onset was defined as the point in the fricative at which energy in the high-frequency band disappeared while strong energy in the lower-frequency band started to emerge on the spectrogram. In addition, this shift in energy was reflected in a substantial lowering in COG values. (See Lee 2011 for more detail.)

Rise Time was calculated by measuring the duration from the minimum to the maximum point of intensity in the frication noise. All stimuli were high-pass filtered at 3.6 kHz (48 dB per octave, implemented in Matlab) to exclude any effects of coarticulation (Howell & Rosen 1983).

Vowel duration was measured from the onset of regular periodicity in the waveform subsequent to the turbulent noise of the fricative to the offset of periodicity associated with the vowel, which coincided with the onset of the subsequent consonant.

Normalized Root Mean Square (RMS) energy (in dB) was calculated by subtracting the vowel amplitude from the fricative noise amplitude, following Jongman et al. (2000). Vowel amplitude (maximum vowel amplitude) value was measured by averaging the amplitude values over 3 pulse periods at the maximum vowel amplitude point (Behrens & Blumstein 1988).

Center of Gravity (COG) values of three types were examined. First, the COG value of the total consonantal segment was analyzed. Second, the consonantal segment was divided into two portions to compare the aspirated portion with the unaspirated portion of the frication. For the plain fricative, mean COG of the portion of the fricative before onset of aspiration (BOA) was compared with mean COG of the portion after onset of aspiration (AOA). For the fortis fricative, the mean COG of the initial 60 per cent of the fricative was compared with the mean value of the final 40 per cent of the fricative. The proportions used to segment the fortis fricative (initial 60 and final 40 per cent of the consonantal segment) were based on the mean aspiration portion of the fricatives and affricates measured in Lee (2011), which analyzed a total of 300 tokens [(2 fricatives + 3 affricates) × 3 vowels × 20 speakers (10 females)]. Data from that study indicated that aspiration accounted for 40 per cent of the total duration of the plain fricative, on average, motivating segmentation of the fortis fricative into intervals composed of the initial 60 and the final 40 per cent.

F0 values were measured using a 25 ms window *at the onset and the midpoint of the vowel.* Measurements were obtained using VoiceSauce (version 1.11, 2011).

Voice quality was measured by assessing the relative increase between the first and second harmonic (H1-H2*) and by assessing the additive noise (Cepstral Peak Prominence, CPP). In cases where H1-H2* is rendered less reliable by low vowel formants in high vowel contexts, CPP can compensate by providing information about the presence of noise in the signal and the periodicity of the noise in the higher frequency ranges

Since H1-H2 values are affected by vowel height (Keating & Esposito 2007), VoiceSauce was used to measure corrected H1-H2 values (referred to as H1-H2*) from 25 ms windows at the onset and midpoint of the following vowel. VoiceSauce calculates H1-H2* values by using an algorithm that estimates the spectral magnitudes before vocal fold filtering to remove the effect of F1 (Iseli & Alwan 2004).

Both H1-H2 and CPP are widely used to capture differences in voice quality, but while H1-H2 assesses the amplitude of the first and second harmonics, CPP is calculated by using harmonic-to-noise ratio. CPP is obtained from the normalized amplitude of Fourier spectra by measuring the peak prominence of the harmonic structure. VoiceSauce follows Hillenbrand et al. (1994)'s method, which calculates the distance from the linear regression line relating quefrency to cepstral magnitude. If the voice is clear and modal, the periodic signal from the vocal fold vibration will show a prominent cepstral peak, and consequently a higher CPP value is observed. When speech is produced with a breathy voice quality, where the speech signal is less periodic, a smaller CPP value is obtained (Hillenbrand et al. 1994). CPP was also analyzed using VoiceSauce. Like H1-H2* values, CPP was calculated by VoiceSauce from a 25 ms window at the onset and midpoint of the vowel.

The value of the *first formant (F1)* at the onset of the following vowel was measured using VoiceSauce. VoiceSauce uses the algorithm from the Snack sound toolkit (Sjölander 2004) for formant estimation, averaging over a 25 ms window length with a 1 ms frame shift.

4.4.1 Acoustic Characteristics of the Auditory Stimuli

Repeated-measures two-way ANOVAs were conducted with fricative (plain, fortis) and vowel (i, a) as independent variables and the following 15 measurements as dependent variables: Fricative duration, Rise time,

RMS energy (fricative), COG (initial 60 per cent), COG (final 40 per cent), COG (total), Vowel duration, F0 (onset), F0 (midpoint), H1-H2* (onset), H1-H2* (midpoint), CPP (onset), CPP(midpoint), RMS energy (vowel) and F1 (onset). Statistical analysis for aspiration duration was not conducted due to the absence of a visible aspiration interval in the /i/ vowel context. When the ANOVAs showed a significant interaction between fricative and vowel, paired-samples *t*-tests were conducted for the post-hoc comparisons (e.g. /si/-/s'i/ versus /sʰa/-/s'a/).

Table 4.3 presents the means and standard deviations of the seven measures taken in the fricative portion of the CV sequence.

Table 4.3. Mean values and standard deviation (in parentheses) of 7 measurements analyzed in the fricative segment of the CV sequence.

	Plain /si/	Fortis /s'i/	Plain /sʰa/	Fortis /s'a/
Fricative duration (ms)	130(26)	123(33)	98(33)	106(28)
Aspiration duration (ms)			42(19)	
Rise time (ms)	63(31)	66(31)	46(31)	24(7)
RMS energy (db)	−10.06(2.94)	12.67(2.81)	−17.64(3.62)	−18.00(2.93)
COG (Hz) (initial 60%)	6543(540)	7052(492)	7368(900)	7930(589)
COG (Hz) (final 40%)	5888(461)	6846(685)	3567(506)	7891(880)
COG (Hz) (total)	6456(506)	7127(623)	6084(1242)	8140(560)

Table 4.4 presents the ANOVA results conducted for the measurements taken in the consonant segments. Statistical significance is marked with asterisks and *p* values are noted in parentheses.

Table 4.4. Statistical results of repeated-measures ANOVAs and paired-samples *t*-tests for the consonantal measurements analyzed.

Dependant variable	Factor fricative F(1, 36)	Vowel F(1, 36)	Interaction fricative × vowel	*t*-test /si/-/s'i/	/sʰa/-/s'a/
Fricative duration		***($p = .013$)			
Rise time		***($p = .002$)			
RMS energy		***($p < .001$)			
COG (initial 60%)	***($p = .013$)	***($p < .001$)			
COG (final 40%)	***($p < .001$)	***($p = .004$)	***($p < .001$)	***($p < .001$)	***($p < .001$)
COG (total)	***($p < .001$)		***($p = .009$)	***($p < .001$)	***($p < .001$)

Regarding the measurements of the consonantal segment, repeated-measures two-way ANOVAs found main effects of fricative for COG (final 40 per cent) [$F(1, 36) = 162.967$, $p < .001$] and COG (total) [$F(1, 36) = 29.736$, $p < .001$]. The main effects of fricative indicated that the COG values of the fortis fricative (final 40 per cent: 7368 Hz; total: 7631 Hz) are significantly higher than those for the plain fricative (final 40 per cent: 4727 Hz; total: 6270 Hz).

The main effects of vowel were found for fricative duration [$F(1, 36) = 6.827$, $p = .013$], Rise Time [$F(1, 36) = 11.793$, $p = .002$], COG (initial 60 per cent) [$F(1, 36) = 17.148$, $p < .001$] and COG (final 40 per cent) [$F(1, 36) = 9.496$, $p = .004$]. The main effect of vowel indicated that the fricatives in the /i/ vowel context were longer (127 ms), and had a longer rise time (65 ms), higher RMS energy (−11.49 dB), and higher COG (final 40 per cent) values (6798 Hz) than the fricatives in the /a/ vowel context (fricative duration: 102 ms; rise time: 35ms; RMS energy: −17.82 dB; COG [final 40 per cent]: 5729 Hz). However, fricatives in the /a/ vowel context had significantly higher COG (initial 60 per cent) values (7946 Hz) than those in the /i/ vowel context (6367 Hz).

Statistically significant interactions between fricative and vowel were found for COG (total) [$F(1, 36) = 7.662$, $p = .009$], and COG (final 40 per cent) [$F(1, 36) = 66.194$, $p < .001$]. The paired samples *t*-test comparing /si/-/s'i/ also found significant differences in COG (final 40 per cent) [$t(9) = -6.776$, $p < .001$] and COG (total) [$t(9) = -8.696$, $p < .001$]. Both COG (total) and COG (final 40 per cent) values of the fortis fricative /s'i/ were significantly higher (final 40 per cent: 6845 Hz; total: 7123 Hz) than the plain fricative /si/ (COG final 40 per cent: 5888 Hz; COG total: 6455 Hz). The paired samples *t*-test comparing /s^ha/-/s'a/ also found significant differences in COG (final 40 per cent) [$t(9) = 11.821$, $p < .001$] and in COG (total) [$t(9) = -6.276$, $p < .001$]. The fortis fricative /s'a/ had greater COG (final 40 per cent: 7891 Hz; and total: 8140 Hz) than the plain fricative /s^ha/ (COG final 40 per cent: 3567 Hz; COG total: 6084 Hz).

Table 4.5 presents the means and standard deviations of the 10 measurements that were analyzed in the vowel segment.

Table 4.5. Means and standard deviations (in parentheses) of eight measurements analyzed from vowel segments.

	Plain /si/	Fortis /s'i/	Plain /sʰa/	Fortis /s'a/
Vowel duration (ms)	76 (22)	108 (29)	104 (21)	136 (21)
F0-onset (Hz)	333 (31)	302 (33)	299 (32)	300 (18)
F0-midpoint (Hz)	334 (32)	315 (29)	309 (27)	298 (17)
H1-H2 onset (dB)	−6.1 (2.9)	−4.6 (2.9)	−12.9 (3.12)	2.7 (8.5)
H1-H2 midpoint (dB)	−6.3 (3.8)	−2.6 (6.0)	6.1 (4.3)	1.7 (8.0)
CPP-onset (dB)	20.3 (3.3)	21.3 (5.1)	15.3 (2.5)	20.1 (2.9)
CPP-midpoint (dB)	26.1 (2.9)	26.8 (3.4)	26.5 (3.2)	28.3 (1.7)
F1-onset (Hz)	343 (33)	331 (38)	550 (280)	555 (131)

Table 4.6 presents the results of the ANOVAs conducted for the measurements taken in the vowel segments.

Table 4.6. Statistical results of repeated-measures ANOVAs and paired-samples *t*-tests for the measurements analyzed from the vowel segment.

Dependant variable	**Factor fricative F(1, 36)**	**Vowel F(1, 36)**	**Interaction fricative × Vowel**	***t*-test /si/-/s'i/**	**/sʰa/-/s'a/**
Vowel duration	***(p< .001)	***(p = .001)			
F0-onset					
F0-midpoint		***(p = .025)			
H1-H2* onset	***(p = .013)	***(p < .001)	***(p = .001)		***(p = .005)
H1-H2* midpoint		***(p < .001)	***(p = .001)	***(p = .010)	
CPP-onset	***(p = .023)	***(p < .014)			
CPP-midpoint					
F1-onset		***(p < .001)			

Regarding the measurements of the vowel segment, two-way repeated-measures ANOVAs found the main effects of fricative for vowel duration [F(1, 36) = 16.552, $p < .001$], H1-H2* (onset) [F(1, 36) = 6.838, $p = .013$] and CPP (onset) [F(1, 36) = 5.671, $p = .023$]. The main effects of fricative indicated that the vowels after the fortis fricative were significantly longer (122 ms) and had higher CPP (onset) values (20.5 dB) than those after the plain fricative (vowel duration: 90 ms; CPP (onset): 17.5 dB). However, H1-H2* (onset) values of the vowel following the plain fricative were significantly higher (10.2 dB) than those following the fortis fricative (−1.5 dB). The higher H1-H2* (onset) and lower CPP (onset) values after plain as compared with fortis fricatives indicate that vowels following plain fricatives have a breathier voice quality than vowels after fortis fricatives.

A main effect of vowel was found for vowel duration [$F(1, 36) = 13.154$, $p < .001$], F0 (midpoint) [$F(1, 36) = 5.505$, $p < .025$], H1-H2* (onset) [$F(1, 36) = 62.070$, $p < .001$], H1-H2* (midpoint) [$F(1, 36) = 18.218$, $p < .001$], CPP (onset) [$F(1, 36) = 6.612$, $p = .014$] and F1 (onset) [$F(1, 36) = 58.614$, $p < .001$]. The main effect of vowel indicates that /a/ had a longer (120 ms) duration, higher F0 at midpoint (325 Hz), higher H1-H2* (onset) values (7.8 dB), higher H1-H2* (midpoint) values (3.9 dB), lower CPP (onset) values (17.5 dB) and higher F1-onset values (552 Hz) than /i/ [vowel duration: 92 ms; F0 (midpoint): 304 Hz; H1-H2* (onset): –5.35 dB; H1-H2* (midpoint): –4.45; CPP (onset): 20.5 dB; F1 (onset): 337 Hz; intensity (midpoint): 71 dB).

Statistically significant interactions between fricative and vowel were found for H1-H2* (onset) [$F(1, 36) = 12.451$, $p = .001$], and H1-H2* (midpoint) [$F(1, 36) = 4.283$, $p = .046$]. A paired samples *t*-test comparing mean values in /si/ and /s'i/ also found a significant difference in H1-H2* (midpoint) [$t(9) = -3.224$, $p = .010$]. In /s'i/, the vowel following the fortis fricative had higher H1-H2* (midpoint) (–2.6 dB) than the vowel following the plain fricative in /si/ [H1-H2* (midpoint): –6.3 dB]. H1-H2* (onset) [$t(9) = 3.631$, $p = .005$] was found to be significantly different between /s^{h}a/ and /s'a/, as well. The vowel following the plain fricative in /s^{h}a/ had higher H1-H2* (onset) (12.9 dB) than the vowel following the fortis fricative in /s'a/ [H1-H2 (onset): 2.7 dB].

Altogether, the acoustic analysis of the auditory stimuli found that the acoustic cues which distinguish the two fricatives differed depending on the vowel context. For the consonantal segment, three cues – COG (initial 60 per cent), COG (final 40 per cent) and COG (total) – were found to distinguish the Korean fricatives in both vowel contexts, which is consistent with previous studies (Cho et al. 2002; Hwang 2004; Kang et al. 2009; Holliday 2010; Chang 2013). Even though the lower-frequency energy illustrated in Figure 4.1 only appears in /s^{h}a/, and not in /si/, the COG values of the final 40 per cent portion of the fricative still distinguish between the plain /s/ in /si/ and the fortis /s'/ in /s'i/ – but, the mean difference in COG (final 40 per cent) was substantially greater in the /a/ vowel context (4324 Hz) than the /i/ vowel context (958 Hz).

For the vowel segment, vowel duration, CPP (onset), H1-H2* (onset) and H1-H2* (midpoint) distinguish the Korean fricatives. The vowel after the plain fricative (/i/: 76 ms; /a/: 104 ms) was shorter than the vowel after the fortis fricative (/i/: 108 ms; /a/: 136 ms) in both vowel contexts. With regard to voice quality, H1-H2* values showed a greater difference between the two fricatives in the /a/ vowel context (10.2 dB difference at onset, 4.4 dB at midpoint) than in the /i/ vowel context (1.5 dB difference at onset, 3.7

dB at midpoint). CPP (onset) values patterned with H1-H2* values, in that differences were greater in the low vowel context (/i/: –1 dB difference; /a/: –1.8 dB difference)

Table 4.7 summarizes the consonantal and vocalic cues distinguishing the fricatives in the two vowel contexts.

Table 4.7. Summary of consonantal and vocalic cues distinguishing the two fricatives in /i/ and /a/ vowel contexts.

	/si/-/s'i/	**/s^{h}a/-/s'a/**
Consonantal cues	COG (initial 60%, final 40%, total)	COG (initial 60%, final 40%, total)
Vowel cues	Vowel duration, voice quality (H1-H2*-midpoint, CPP-onset)	Vowel duration, voice quality (H1-H2*-onset, CPP-onset)

For consonantal cues, the three types of COG values (initial 60 per cent, final 40 per cent, total) distinguish the fricatives in both vowel contexts. Although mean COG values for the fricatives were found to be significantly different in both contexts, how they distinguish the fricatives might vary by vowel context. A huge drop in COG between the initial 60 and final 40 per cent of the fricative in /s^{h}a/ (3801 Hz) but not in /si/ (655 Hz) might suggest that the aspiration in the plain fricative is weaker or disappears in the /i/ vowel context.

For vocalic cues, we found that the same vocalic cues distinguish the fricatives in both vowel contexts (vowel duration and voice quality). However, the pattern for the parameters measuring voice quality (H1-H2* and CPP) varied by vowel context as well as by measurement position (onset vs midpoint of the vowel). In the /a/ vowel context, mean H1-H2* and CPP at vowel onset distinguish the fricatives. Only mean CPP at vowel onset distinguishes the fricative in the /i/ vowel context, however. Again, the lack of a difference in mean H1-H2* at the onset of the /i/ vowel might suggest that aspiration is not as strongly produced as in the /a/ vowel context.

The results reported above establish the acoustic characteristics of the tokens used in this study. Next we will investigate how the acoustic cues distinguishing the fricatives influence perception.

4.4.2 Experiment 1: Identification with Non-Conflicting Cues

In this experiment, we investigate whether Korean listeners are able to distinguish between the two fricatives when they hear only the consonant or only the vowel portion of the syllable. In order to establish baseline performance, we also included a condition in which participants heard the whole

CV syllable. Participants listened to tokens of either a full syllable, only a consonant (with the vowel excised; consonant-only condition), or only a vowel (with the consonant excised; vowel-only condition).

Our prediction is that identification will be most accurate when both segments are provided (syllable condition). Since Korean has minimal pairs in both vowel contexts, [/si/ "poetry" and /s'i/ "seed", /sʰa/ "to buy (imperative)" and /s'a/ "cheap"], we expect that Korean listeners will be able to distinguish them without difficulty.

For the consonant-only condition, fricative identification performance will be equally good in both vowel contexts, considering that the same number of acoustic cues were found in both vowel contexts [COG (initial 60 per cent), COG (final 40 per cent), and COG (total)]. However, as previous literature has suggested (Holliday 2012; Yoon 1999), if the drastic COG change caused by the aspiration in /sʰa/ is a highly salient perceptual cue, then fricative identification will be more accurate in the /a/ vowel context than the /i/ vowel context.

For the vowel-only condition, accurate identification of the fricative types will be possible in both vowel contexts, since the same number of acoustic cues was found in both contexts (vowel duration and voice quality).

Between the types of segments, more accurate identification is expected in the vowel-only condition than the consonant-only condition, considering that we found more acoustic cues in the vowel than in the consonant.

Three types of stimuli were used for Experiment 1: (1) whole CV syllable stimuli, (2) consonant-only stimuli and (3) vowel-only stimuli. Each condition consisted of two blocks divided by the different vowel contexts – in other words, an [i] block and an [a] block. Consonant-only and vowel-only stimuli were created by removing the vowel or consonant portions from the natural syllables. The target portions were excised from the original sound files of two sets of minimal pairs: (1) /silɨm/ (worry) and /s'ilɨm' (traditional wrestling) and (2) /sata/ (to buy) and /s'ata/ (cheap). These tokens had been recorded in a carrier sentence (see Table 4.1). Table 4.8 shows the stimuli that were used in Experiment 1.

Table 4.8. Stimuli and block order for Experiment 1 (the portions removed from the stimuli are in parentheses).

		Plain fricative	Fortis fricative
Whole-syllable	Block 1	/si/	/s'i/
	Block 2	/sʰa/	/s'a/
Consonant-only	Block 1	s(i)/	/s'(i)/
	Block 2	/sʰ(a)/	/s'(a)/
Vowel-only	Block 1	/(s)i/	/(s')i/
	Block 2	/(sɨ)a/	/(s')a/

4.4.3 Experiment 2: Identification with Conflicting Cues (Cross-Spliced Syllables)

We also examined which cues Korean listeners follow when they hear stimuli containing conflicting consonantal and vocalic cues. In Experiment 2, participants heard cross-spliced syllables in which the fricative and the vowel contained mismatched cues, and we examined which set of cues participants were more likely to follow when making a forced choice.

For Experiment 2, four types of cross-spliced stimuli were constructed by manipulating the natural tokens: (1) frication excised from /si/ and vowel excised from /s'i/, (2) frication excised from /s'i/ and vowel excised from /si/, (3) frication excised from /sʰa/ and vowel excised from /s'a/ and (4) frication excised from /s'a/ and vowel excised from /sʰa/. Experiment 2 also consisted of two blocks divided by the different vowel contexts. Table 4.9 presents the types of stimuli that were used for Experiment 2. The consonant segment was cross-spliced with the vowel segment of the counterpart fricative while matching the vowel height.

Table 4.9. Stimuli and block order for Experiment 2. The portions removed from the stimuli are in parentheses.

	Plain fricative + Post-fortis vowel	Fortis fricative + Post-plain vowel
Block 1	(1) Plain fricative + fortis vowel = [/s(i)/ + /(s')i/]	(2) Fortis fricative + plain vowel = [/s'(i)/ + /(s)i/]
Block 2	(3) Plain fricative + fortis vowel = [/sʰ(a)/ + /(s')a/]	(4) Fortis fricative + plain vowel = [/s' (a)/ + /(s)a/]

Our prediction is that perception will differ depending on the vowel context. In both vowel contexts, the listeners are expected to rely primarily on the vocalic cues (vowel duration, voice quality, RMS energy), as more acoustic cues are found in the vowel than in the fricative. However, the results presented in Chang (2013) indicate that the effect of the vocalic cues might be stronger in the /a/ vowel context than the /i/ vowel context. Chang (2013) showed that the listeners' reliance on the vowel segment in the high vowel context (/i, ɯ, u/) was not as strong as in the /a/ vowel context. Based on this, we expect that the perceptual pattern will vary by the vowel context, showing a strong dependency on the vocalic cues only in the /a/ vowel context.

4.4.4 Participants and Procedure

A total of 60 native listeners of Korean (30 female, 30 male) participated in the perception study. The mean age of the participants was 27.8 (range 19–36), and none of them reported any articulatory or auditory impairment. Participants received 7,000 KRW (equivalent to $6.00 USD) each.

Experiment 1 had a 3 (portion: consonant-only, vowel-only, whole-syllable) × 2 (vowel: /a/, /i/) × 2 (fricative: plain, fortis) design, forming 12 conditions. Experiment 2 had a 2 (plain vs fortis segment) × 2 (vowel: /a/, /i/) design, forming four conditions. The perception test was conducted in quiet rooms at Yonsei University, Sunkyunkwan University and Joong-ang University, all in Seoul. The experiment was conducted with the Paradigm software package (Perception Research Systems, Inc.; version 1.2.0). A Sony Vaio Notebook with an external sound card and Sennheiser HD600 headphones were used. On each trial, the participant heard an auditory stimulus and was asked to use a mouse to indicate which syllable s/he thought s/he heard by clicking one of two options presented in Korean orthography on the screen. The response options were either plain or fortis across all the experiment blocks.

Experiments 1 and 2 were conducted together in one session, which took approximately 40 minutes to complete. Based on the comments of subjects who participated in a pilot version of this study, the stimuli were blocked in order of decreasing familiarity and increasing task complexity. Thus in the first part, two blocks of whole CV syllable stimuli were presented, followed by two blocks of cross-spliced syllable stimuli (Experiment 2).

In part two, a pair of consonant-only blocks was presented, followed by a pair of vowel-only blocks. Considering that all participants were naïve listeners who had not heard excised segments before, stimuli in vowel-only blocks were the least familiar to the participants. Also, vowel-only blocks were considered to be the most complicated because the subjects were asked to identify the consonant preceding the sound that they heard instead of identifying the sound they heard. For each condition, a block of stimuli in the /a/ vowel context always preceded a block of /i/ vowel stimuli. This decision was made based on Chang (2007), who found a higher error rate for fricative identification in the high vowel context (/u/). As such, we expected that the high vowel stimuli would be more difficult.

Within blocks, fortis and plain tokens were presented in a fully randomized order. Prior to the experiment, a practice session consisting of 8 practice trials (4 stimuli × 2 repetitions) was presented. The trial stimuli were chosen from the two speakers whose values were most similar to the average value for the production data. In the main session, 60 tokens were played per block (10 speakers × 3 repetitions × 2 phonation types). As a result, each participant heard a total of 360 tokens for this experiment.

4.4.5 Data Analysis

Experiment 1. A series of mixed effects logistic regression models was constructed to examine the effects of the predictors' fricative type, portion and vowel context on participants' response accuracy (whether the participant correctly selected "fortis" or "plain" as their response; "fortis" was chosen as the reference category by the alphabetical order of the two factors). Fricative type was a categorical predictor with two levels, representing whether the stimuli were originally "fortis" (the reference category) or "plain." Portion was a categorical predictor with three levels (representing whether the participant heard the consonant portion of the syllable, the vowel portion of the syllable or the whole syllable). Consonant was chosen as the reference category. Vowel context was a categorical predictor with two levels, representing whether the vowel following the fricative was /a/ (the reference category) or /i/.

Random intercepts were included for participants and for speakers (since the productions from different speakers were effectively different items). The effects of the predictors were assessed using log-likelihood tests comparing models with and without each predictor. Analysis was performed using the lme4 package (Bates 2005) in the R statistical environment (R Development Core Team 2012).

To investigate which acoustic cue is the single biggest predictor accounting for fricative perception, we built three separate mixed effects binomial regressions with a probit link to standardize the independent variables. We chose a probit link function because the acoustic parameters that were entered as fixed effects were measured on greatly varying metrics which the probit link standardizes before estimating the model (Agresti 2007).

Fricative type (two levels: "fortis" and "plain"; fortis was chosen as the reference category), portion (three levels "consonant," "vowel," "both"), and vowel context (two levels: "/a/" and /i/") were entered as main effects. Thus, "choice" was used as the dependent variable with "fortis" as the reference category, rather than correctness. This analysis was conducted only for Experiment 1 when no manipulation was included.

Beyond the three predictors – fricative type, portion and vowel context – that were used for mixed effect logistic regressions (see above), six parameters were chosen as continuous predictors to examine their effect on participants' response accuracy. This was done using the results gained from the acoustic analysis of the auditory stimuli. The parameters included COG (initial 60 per cent), COG (final 40 per cent), H1-H2* (onset), H1-H2* (midpoint), CPP (onset) and vowel duration. The parameters included in the analysis depended on the experiment block under investigation. Thus, the intercepts for the acoustic cues were included as fixed effects with random intercepts estimated for subject and speaker. For the consonant model (when the participants heard the consonant portion only), two parameters associated with the consonantal portion [COG (initial 60 per cent) and COG (final 40 per cent)] were entered as fixed variables. For the vowel model (when the participants heard the vowel portion only), the four parameters associated with the vowel portion [H1-H2* (onset), H1-H2* (midpoint), CPP (onset) and vowel duration] were included as fixed variables. For the syllable model (when the participants heard both the consonant and vowel portions), all six parameters were included as fixed effects. Random intercepts were included on subjects and speakers as well.

The effects of the predictors were assessed using log-likelihood tests comparing models with and without each predictor. Analysis was performed using the lme4 package (Bates 2005) in the R statistical environment (R Development Core Team 2012).

Experiment 2. The data analysis for Experiment 2 was the same as that for Experiment 1, except that the outcome variable was "choice" (meaning whether the participant selected "fortis" or "plain" as their response; "fortis" was the reference category) rather than correctness, and a different set of fixed predictors was used. Mixed effects logistic regression models were constructed to examine the effects of plain segment and vowel context on the outcome variable choice. The predictor plain segment represents whether it was the consonant or the vowel that was plain; "consonant" was chosen as the reference category.

4.4.6 Results

Experiment 1, Logistic Regression. There were statistically significant main effects of portion ($X^2(2) = 757.13, p < .001$), vowel context ($X^2(1) = 2549.35$, $p < .001$), and fricative type ($X^2(1) = 71.22, p < .001$). The finding of a main effect for portion can be interpreted as follows: perception is most accurate in the whole-syllable condition (99 per cent), followed by the vowel-only condition (86 per cent) and the consonant-only condition (85 per cent). Overall, participants responded more accurately when the vowel context was /a/ (90 per cent) than /i/ (63 per cent) ($B = -1.38, z = -19.840, p < .001$)

and when the stimuli were originally from the plain context (79 per cent) than the fortis context (74 per cent) ($B = 0.734$, $z = 9.078$, $p < .001$).

There was a statistically significant two-way interaction between portion and vowel context ($X^2(2) = 275$, $p < .001$). When vowel-only stimuli were provided, the participants responded more accurately when the vowel context was /a/ (86 per cent) than /i/ (51 per cent) ($B = -0.70$, $z = -8.01$, $p < .001$). When whole-syllable segment was provided, the participants responded more accurately when the vowel context was /a/ (99 per cent) than /i/ (74 per cent) ($B = -2.35$, $z = -12.98$, $p < .001$).

A statistically significant two-way interaction was also found between portion and fricative type ($X^2(2) = 457.54$, $p < .001$). When the participant heard only the vowel (vowel-only stimuli), the response accuracy was higher when the stimuli were originally from fortis (73 per cent) rather than plain tokens (64 per cent) ($B = -1.55$, $z = 0.08$, $p < .001$).

A statistically significant interaction was also found between fricative type and vowel context ($X^2(1) = 7.3687$, $p = .007$). When the vowel height was /i/, the participants responded more accurately when the stimuli were originally from plain (68 per cent) rather than fortis tokens (58 per cent) ($B = 0.23$, $z = 2.72$, $p < .007$).

Figure 4.4 illustrates the results of Experiment 1.

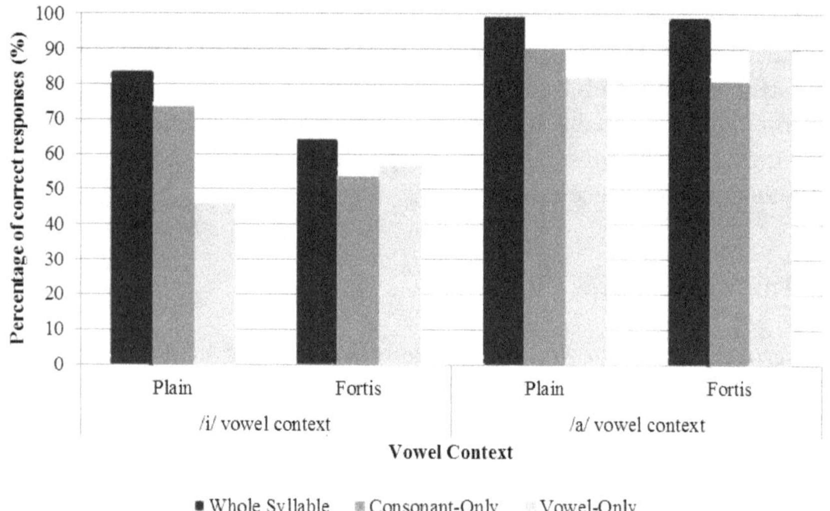

Figure 4.4. Results of Experiment 1: Correct fricative identification scores as a function of fricative type (plain, fortis), vowel context (/i/ and /a/), and portion (whole-syllable, consonant-only and vowel-only).

Experiment 1, Perceptual Cue Weighting. In this section, the results of the *p*-values, estimates (*B*), and *z*-values of each acoustic parameter for consonant-only, vowel-only, and syllable condition in Experiment 1 will be reported. The statistical results for each condition are presented in Tables 4.10, 4.11 and 4.12, respectively. The magnitude of the effect for each acoustic cue is discussed based on the absolute *z*-values.

Table 4.10 presents the results of the consonant-only model of Experiment 1. Perception of the fortis fricative was predicted by COG (final 40 per cent) in both vowel contexts. However, the perception of the plain fricative in the /a/ vowel context was predicted by both COG (initial 60 per cent) and COG (final 40 per cent). COG (final 40 per cent) was a stronger cue to identify the plain fricative /s^{h}a/ than COG (initial 60 per cent), as indicated by the greater *z*-values.

Table 4.10. Results of perceptual weighting for consonant-only condition in Experiment 1.

Variable	Estimate (SE)	*z*	*p*
Consonant by /i/ by Fortis by COG (final 40%)	−0.0006 (0.0001)	−5.111	< .01
Consonant by /a/ by Plain by COG (final 40%)	−0.0007	−6.724	< .01
Consonant by /a/ by Plain by COG (final 60%)	0.0004	5.465	< .01
Consonant by /i/ by Fortis by COG (final 60%)	−0.0001	−2.072	0.04

Table 4.11 presents the results of the vowel-only condition. Here, H1-H2 (onset) is found to be an important perceptual cue for identification of the two fricatives in both vowel contexts.

Table 4.11. Results of perceptual weighting for vowel-only condition in Experiment 1.

Variable	Estimate (SE)	*z*	*p*
Vowel by /i/ by Plain by CPP (onset)	0.059(0.016)	3.676	< .01
Vowel by /i/ by Plain by H1-H2* (onset)	−0.364(0.012)	−2.927	< .01
Vowel by /i/ by Plain by H1-H2* (midpoint)	0.074(0.017)	4.495	< .01
Vowel by /i/ by Fortis by Vowel duration	0.006(0.002)	3.044	< .01
Vowel by /i/ by Fortis by CPP (onset)	0.027(0.008)	3.5	< .01
Vowel by /i/ by Fortis by H1-H2* (onset)	0.075(0.014)	5.238	< .01
Vowel by /a/ by Fortis by Vowel duration	0.013(0.003)	4.254	< .01
Vowel by /a/ by Fortis by H1-H2* (onset)	−0.025(0.006)	−4.312	< .01

In the /i/ vowel context, perception of the plain fricative is predicted by three vocalic cues [H1-H2* (onset), H1-H2* (midpoint) and CPP (onset)]; the fortis fricative is also predicted by three vocalic cues [CPP (onset), H1-H2* (onset) and vowel duration]. H1-H2* (onset) is the strongest perceptual cue for identifying the fortis fricative /s'i/, and H1-H2* (midpoint) is the strongest cue for identifying the plain fricative /si/, as indicated by the largest absolute *z*-values.

In the /a/ vowel context, the fortis fricative is predicted by two vocalic cues [H1-H2* (onset), and vowel duration]. None of the vocalic cues predicts the identification of the plain fricative. H1-H2* (onset) is the strongest perceptual cue for perception of the fortis fricatives in the /a/ vowel context, as indicated by the largest absolute *z*-values.

Table 4.12 presents the results of the whole-syllable condition in Experiment 1.

Table 4.12. Results of perceptual weighting for whole-syllable condition in Experiment 1.

Variable	Estimate (SE)	*z*	*p*
/i/ by Plain by COG (initial 60%)	−0.001(0.0002)	−3.310	< .01
/i/ by Plain by H1-H2* (onset)	0.069(0.028)	2.495	= .013
/i/ by Fortis by COG (final 40%)	−0.001(0.0002)	−5.289	< .01
/i/ by Fortis by H1-H2* (onset)	−0.065(0.021)	−3.130	< .01
/i/ by Fortis by CPP (onset)	−0.045(0.015)	−3.007	< .01
/i/ by Fortis by Vowel duration	0.008(0.003)	2.608	< .01
/a/ by Plain by COG (final 40%)	−0.001(0.0003)	−2.343	= .019
/a/ by Plain by H1-H2* (mid)	0.084(0.039)	2.161	= .031
/a/ by Plain by Vowel duration	0.019(0.009)	2.044	= 0.41
/a/ by Fortis by Vowel duration	−0.020(0.010)	−2.111	.035

In the /i/ vowel context, the plain fricative is predicted by two cues [COG (initial 60 per cent) and H1-H2* (onset)], whereas the fortis fricative is predicted by four cues [COG (final 40 per cent), H1-H2* (onset), CPP (onset) and vowel duration]. In perceiving the plain fricative /si/, COG (initial 60 per cent) is the strongest cue in perceiving the plain fricative, as indicated by the largest absolute *z*-values. In perceiving the fortis fricative /s'i/, however, COG (final 40 per cent) is the strongest perceptual cue. In the /a/ vowel context, the plain fricative is predicted by only three cues [COG (final 40 per cent), H1-H2* (midpoint), vowel duration], whereas the fortis fricative is predicted by only one cue [vowel duration]. In perceiving the plain fricative /sʰa/, COG (final 40 per cent) was the strongest cue, as indicated by the largest absolute *z*-values.

Experiment 2. Figure 4.5 illustrates the results of Experiment 2 with cross-spliced syllables.

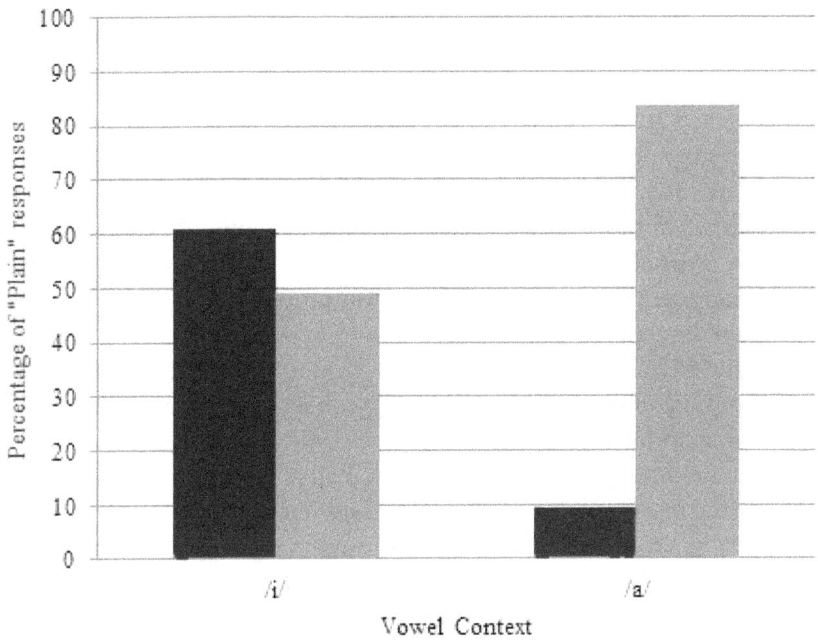

Figure 4.5. Results of Experiment 2.

The model found statistically significant main effects of plain segment [$X^2(1) = 807.67$, $p < .001$] as well as vowel [$X^2(1) = 63.264$, $p < .001$]. The finding that there is a main effect of plain segment indicated that the listeners' "plain" response rate was higher when the vowel segment was plain (66 per cent) than fortis (35 per cent). The main effect of vowel indicated that the listeners' plain response was higher in the /i/ vowel context (55 per cent) than in the /a/ vowel context (47 per cent).

An interaction between plain segment and vowel [$X^2(1) = 1839.26$, $p < .001$] was also found. When the vowel was /a/, participants were more likely to respond "plain" when the vowel was plain (84 per cent) ($B = 4.67$, $z = 39.28$, $p < .001$). On the other hand, when the vowel was /i/, participants were more likely to respond "plain" when the consonant was plain (61 per cent) ($B = 3.24$, $z = 30.43$, $p < .001$). In short, Korean listeners seem to follow vocalic cues to distinguish the Korean fricatives in the low vowel context, while using consonantal cues in the high vowel context.

4.5 Discussion and Conclusion

The results from Experiment 1 showed that three predictors – the type of segment that the listeners heard (portion), the vowel context, and the phonation type of the fricative (fricative type) – influenced the listeners' perception of fricatives. Participants performed best in identifying the two fricatives when both segments were provided (whole-syllable), but identification of whole-syllable stimuli was not as good in the /i/ context as in the /a/ context. When a single segment was provided (consonant-only and vowel-only), identification accuracy varied depending on the phonation type of the fricative and the vowel context. As in the whole-syllable condition, identification performance in the /i/ context was less accurate than in the /a/ context for both consonant-only and vowel-only segments.

In the /a/ vowel context, both consonantal and vocalic cues are strong enough on their own to trigger high rates of accuracy in perception. However, in the /i/ vowel context only consonant segments which were taken from plain fricative tokens triggered a moderately higher rate of identification. In other words, for the /i/ context the listeners showed a response bias toward one type of fricative when they heard consonant-only segments. When listeners heard vowel-only segments in the /i/ context, fricative identification was at chance level, indicating that vocalic cues are insufficient by themselves to trigger accurate identification in the /i/ context. When paired with congruent consonantal cues in the whole-syllable stimuli, however, vocalic cues can improve perception in both /i/ and /a/ contexts.

We also found that the type of stimuli presented changes the perceptual cue weighting. When the listeners were presented with the consonant-only segment, COG (final 40 per cent) was the strongest perceptual cue to identify the fricative type. When the listeners were presented with the vowel-only segment, H1-H2* (onset) and H1-H2* (midpoint) are the strongest perceptual cues for identifying the fricative type in the /i/ and /a/ vowel context, respectively. However, when both cues are presented (whole-syllable), the effect of the vocalic cues in perceiving the fricative diminished, while COG (initial 60 per cent) and (final 40 per cent) remained the strongest perceptual cues for fricative identification.

Experiment 2 results showed that listeners' perceptual patterns vary based on vowel context. Listeners followed the vocalic cues in distinguishing the fricatives in the /a/ vowel context, but followed the consonantal cues in the /i/ vowel context. This result is compatible with Chang (2013), as it is consistent with the prediction that the voice quality of the following vowel strongly influences the perception of fricative phonation-type distinctions in the /a/ vowel context. It seems that when consonantal and vocalic cues conflict in the /a/ vowel context, the vocalic cues override the consonantal cues. In the /i/ vowel context, on the other hand, consonantal cues in the plain fricative trigger perception of the distinction in the /i/ vowel context. That said, they are not strong enough to completely override conflicting vocalic cues.

Both experiments provide evidence that the consonantal cues are slightly stronger than the vocalic cues in the context of /i/. Even though we found a greater number of acoustic cues associated with the vowel segment than with the consonantal segment in the acoustic study (Table 4.7), the consonantal cues seem to outweigh the vocalic cues in terms of influencing fricative perception. The listeners were unable to distinguish the fricatives when provided with the vocalic segment alone (Experiment 1, vowel-only condition), and they followed the consonantal cues when the cues conflicted in cross-spliced stimuli (Experiment 2). These facts taken together seem to indicate that, in the high vowel context, the consonantal cues are stronger perceptual cues than the vocalic cues.

In the low vowel /a/ context, however, it is surprising that the listeners mainly followed the vocalic cues in cross-spliced stimuli, considering that both types of segments yielded successful distinction of the fricative types in Experiment 1. This result indicates that the vocalic cues are more salient in the low vowel context, while the consonantal cues are more salient in the high vowel context.

One point that should be made is that since the order of blocks was fixed across all participants, vowel context in both experiments and portion (whole-syllable, consonant-only or vowel-only) in Experiment 1 were confounded with block order. If the results collected were due to familiarity or fatigue effects, we might expect a monotonic increase or decrease in accuracy across the three portion conditions of Experiment 1 (e.g., from whole-syllable blocks, to consonant-only blocks, to vowel-only blocks). However, the results of Experiment 1 are not consistent with such a prediction. Neither improvement nor a decrease in accuracy was found in the /i/ vowel context. This indicates that the result of the current study was not because of the fixed block order, but because of the vowel context effect in the stimuli with which the participants were presented.

Taken together, the two experiments indicate that listeners rely on acoustic cues that vary by vowel context in order to perceive the contrast between the two fricatives. In the /a/ vowel context, both types of cues provided enough perceptual information to distinguish between the two fricatives (Experiment 1), but the vocalic cues were more salient perceptually than the consonantal cues (Experiment 2). In the /i/ vowel context, although listeners seem to rely on the consonantal cues to make the fricative distinction (Experiment 1), they are not salient enough to override the vocalic cues (Experiment 2).

When considering the facts outlined above, two questions remain:

(1) Why does listener identification performance vary by vowel context?
(2) How do listeners weight the perceptual cues in different vowel contexts?

First, the vowel effect in fricative identification suggests that the perceptual cues in the fricative might be altered by the following vowel. A vowel effect on fricative identification has also been found in English: listeners showed a poorer identification performance in the /i/ vowel context than in the /u/ or /a/ contexts (Yeni-Komshian & Soli 1981; McMurray & Jongman 2011; but see also Jongman 1989). Differences in listener performance might be due to the spectral differences that emerge based on the following vowel. Soli (1981) explained that the spectral characteristics of the fricatives [s, z, ʃ, ʒ] in the /a/ vowel context are the most similar to the cues present when the fricatives were produced in isolation. McMurray & Jongman (2011) explained that particular vowels either facilitate or hinder listeners in categorizing the sound, since certain features of the vowel change the perceptual cues available in the vocalic portion. For example, the roundness feature of /u/ provides additional cues in the vocalic portion, guiding the listeners to process the consonantal portion differently than in other vowel contexts.

The facilitation and inhibition effects of different vowel contexts on the perception of the Korean fricatives can be explained by the presence of perceptual cues related to phonation type. In previous studies, two cues that are crucial to the perception of breathy phonation have emerged: aspiration noise and increased H1 amplitude (Klatt & Klatt 1990). These cues, which are associated with the plain fricative in Korean, are available only in the /a/ context. While both aspiration noise and the higher H1-H2* values of the plain fricative in the /a/ vowel context facilitate listeners' identification performance, the alternation associated with the weakened aspiration in the /i/ vowel context hinders listeners' ability to distinguish the fricatives. As seen from the results of the acoustic measurements, the characteristics of the perceptual cues (e.g. COG, H1-H2*, CPP and vowel duration) are drastically affected by the following vowel (see section 4.4). Since the perceptual cues indicating a breathy phonation type are lacking in the /i/ vowel context, listeners' perception would have been impeded, contributing to the poorer identification in the /i/ vowel context.

One other acoustic characteristic that might have contributed to the degraded identification performance in the /i/ vowel context is the reduction in spectral difference between the two fricatives in that context due to palatalization. As mentioned earlier, Korean fricatives are described as being palatalized in certain vowel contexts. Baik (1998) has claimed that only the fortis fricative is palatalized in certain vowel environments, while Lee & Ramsey (2000) have claimed that younger Koreans are palatalizing both fricatives while losing the contrast between the two. The COG values of the fricatives reported in the current study, however, do not seem to support either of these claims. If the fortis fricative is palatalized in the /i/ vowel context, the COG values of the two fricatives should be very similar. However, the acoustic results reported here showed that the speakers still make a distinction between the two fricatives, as indicated by a significant difference in COG values between the fricatives in both vowel contexts (see Table 4.4 for the statistical results; for the COG values of the total fricative duration, refer to Table 4.13).

Table 4.13. COG values (Hz) of the plain and fortis fricatives in two vowel contexts as produced by 10 female speakers.

Speaker	**/si/**	**/s'i/**	**/s^{h}a/**	**/s'a/**
1	6322	6844	7200	8043
2	5834	6224	5156	7702
3	6864	7468	5720	8503
4	6317	7001	5406	7245
5	5655	6539	6044	7580
6	6588	7543	6630	8935
7	7453	8375	8140	8879
8	6699	7520	6441	8494
9	6434	6640	6535	8134
10	6389	7114	3568	7880
Mean	6456	7127	6084	8140
Standard Deviation	480	591	1179	531

These results suggest that it is not the case that both fricatives are palatalized, nor is the contrast between the fricatives fading away among Koreans. However, one might still argue that even if all tokens are not palatalized, the presence of some palatalized tokens in the stimulus set may still have influenced listener perception. Since the listeners were forced to choose the fricative type in an experimental setting where all tokens of both fricatives were randomly presented, it might be the case that the listeners responded to the tokens with high COG values as fortis and low COG values as plain. If this were the case, it would explain why we found a plain response bias when the consonant-only segments were presented. Since the palatalized plain fricative does not affect classification of the plain fricative, listeners could have incorrectly responded to the palatalized fortis tokens as plain.

Second, the different identification performances in the two vowel contexts make us wonder whether the listeners integrate the perceptual cues differently in the different contexts. One possibility that we may entertain is that the listeners might strategically choose a different perceptual mechanism depending on the vowel context. For example, when information about aspiration is available, the listeners might use the perceptual cues selectively, whereas they may try to access all possible information when aspiration is not available. Previous work on speech recognition has found that listeners access their mental lexicon as soon as relevant phonetic cues are available (McMurray et al. 2008; Toscano & McMurray 2012). McMurray et al. (2008) have found that listeners activate their mental lexicon as soon as the relative cues – in the case of their experiment, VOT – are available in order to perceive voicing (/b/ versus /p/) and manner (/b/ versus /w/) distinctions between labial sounds in the vowel contexts of /i/ and /ɛ/. However, a recent study by Galle & McMurray (2012) has found that when the following vowel is /u/ and additional acoustic information about lip rounding is available, the listeners hold their perceptual judgment until the vocalic cues are provided. These findings may suggest that the listeners use two different speech recognition modes interchangeably, depending on the nature of the speech sound they are trying to distinguish.

If something similar is happening here, the differing performances in identifying Korean fricatives is to be expected. Recall that the participants perform much better in the /a/ context than in the /i/ context. In the /a/ vowel context, listener performance is facilitated by the acoustic cues that are related to the phonation type of the plain fricative – namely strong aspiration noise and increased H1 amplitude. Thus, the listeners can identify the fricative type as soon as they hear the aspiration noise in the consonant segment. This is also true for the vowel segment; as soon as the listeners hear breathiness in the vocalic segment, they recognize which fricative they heard. However, in the /i/ vowel context, since characteristics related to the phonation type of the plain fricative differ and the aspiration noise and H1 amplitude cues are diminished or absent, listeners must wait to make their identification judgment until all accessible perceptual information is available. In other words, when hearing the fricatives in the /i/ vowel context, the listeners choose to wait until they have access to both consonantal and vocalic information in order to make more accurate identification.

Ultimately, we can think of the two factors that most strongly influence perception of the plain fricative – aspiration and high H1 amplitude – as either facilitating or hindering fricative identification. As a consequence, listeners change their perceptual strategy in different vowel contexts. However, we do not yet know how and when the perceptual cues are integrated in perceiving the fricatives. As a follow-up study, it might be worthwhile to examine where the listeners start to perceive the fricatives in syllables by using a visual world eye-tracking paradigm. The latency at which looks begin to converge on the target might be able to inform us about when listeners begin to reliably distinguish the fricatives and whether differences arise due to the differences between the perceptual cues available in the two vowel contexts.

This study set out to answer open questions related to the perception of the plain and fortis fricatives in Korean. We began by reviewing the existing articulatory, acoustic, and perceptual data, and then presented a series of experiments. We investigated the independent effect of each type of cue in two vowel contexts – both the consonantal cues and the vocalic cues – and the results establish that the perceptual cues for the Korean fricatives differ depending on vowel context. Experiment 1 showed that the identification performance of Korean listeners varies by vowel context. While identification was successful regardless of the type of cues presented (consonant-only, vowel-only, whole-syllable) in the /a/ vowel context, successful identification was only possible when both consonantal and vocalic cues were presented (whole-syllable) in the /i/ vowel context. In Experiment 2, we found that the vowel carries stronger perceptual cues for identifying the fricatives in the /a/ vowel context, whereas consonantal cues are stronger in the /i/ vowel context. The overall findings suggest that the alternation of acoustic cues by vowel context influences the identification performance. The listeners were facilitated by the perceptual cues associated with aspiration in the /a/ vowel context, whereas the lack of such cues in the /i/ vowel context hindered identification.

Although we found that the presence of aspiration information in the speech signal can facilitate fricative identification, an important next step is to examine whether having more perceptual information – such as roundness of the subsequent vowel – may also facilitate fricative identification. We also suggested that the listeners might use different perceptual processing mechanisms depending on the type of signal with which they are presented. More investigation is needed in order to examine when and in which condition the perceptual facilitation begins. Overall, however, these findings strongly suggest that listeners might weight the perceptual cues differently depending on the vowel context. This underscores the importance of including multiple vowel contexts when designing future perception-based research studies.

References

Agresti, A. (2007). *An Introduction to Categorical Data Analysis* (Vol. 423). New Jersey: Wiley-Interscience. http://dx.doi.org/10.1002/0470114754

Ahn, H. (1999). An acoustic investigation of the phonation types of post-fricative vowels in Korean. In S. Kuno (ed.), *Harvard Studies in Korean Linguistics VIII* (pp. 57–72). Cambridge, MA: Harvard University.

Baik, W. (1998). On tensity of Korean fricatives (Electropalatographic study). *Korean Journal of Speech Sciences*, 4, 135–45.

Bates, D. (2005). Fitting linear mixed models in R. *R News*, 5, 27–30.

Behrens, S.J., & S.E. Blumstein. (1988). On the role of the amplitude of the fricative noise in the perception of place of articulation in voiceless fricative consonants. *Journal of the Acoustical Society of America*, 84(3), 861–7. http://dx.doi.org/10.1121/1.396655

Chang, B.C. (2007). Korean fricatives: Production, perception, and laryngeal typology. *UC Berkeley Phonology Lab Annual Report, 2007*, 20–70.

Chang, B.C. (2008). The acoustics of Korean fricatives revisited. In S. Kuno, I.-H. Lee, J. Whitman, J. Maling, Y.-S. Kang, P. Sells, H.-S. Sohn & Y. Jang (eds.), *Harvard Studies in Korean Linguistics VIII* (pp. 137–50). Seoul: Hanshin Publishing Co.

Chang, B.C. (2013). The production and perception of coronal fricatives in Seoul Korean: The case for a fourth laryngeal category. *Korean Linguistics*, 15, 7–49.

Cheon, S.Y. (2005). "Production and perception of phonological contrasts in second language acquisition: Korean and English fricatives." PhD dissertation. University of Hawaii.

Cho, T., S.-A. Jun & P. Ladefoged. (2002). Acoustic and aerodynamic correlates of Korean stops and fricatives. *Journal of Phonetics*, 30(2), 193–228. http://dx.doi.org/10.1006/jpho.2001.0153

Galle, M., & B. McMurray. (2012, October). The waiting is the hardest part: How asynchronous acoustic cues are integrated for fricative place of articulation. Poster presented at the 164th Meeting of the Acoustical Society of America, Kansas City, Missouri. http://dx.doi.org/10.1121/1.4755244

Hillenbrand, J.M., R.A. Cleveland & R.L. Erickson. (1994). Acoustic correlates of breathy vocal quality. *Journal of Speech, Language, and Hearing Research (JSLHR)*, 37(4), 769–78. http://dx.doi.org/10.1044/jshr.3704.769

Holliday, J.J. (2010). An acoustic study of L2 perceptual acquisition of Korean fricatives. In I.-H. Lee (ed.), *Harvard Studies in Korean Linguistics, XIII* (pp. 17–32). Cambridge, MA: Harvard University.

Holliday, J.J. (2011). The emergence of L2 phonological contrast in perception: The case of Korean sibilant fricatives. PhD dissertation. Ohio State University.

Holliday, J.J. (2012). The acoustic realization of the Korean sibilant fricative contrast in Seoul and Daegu. *Journal of the Korean Society of Speech Sciences*, 4(1), 67–74. http://dx.doi.org/10.13064/KSSS.2012.4.1.067

Howell, P., & S. Rosen. (1983). Production and perception of rise time in the voiceless affricate/fricative distinction. *Journal of the Acoustical Society of America*, 73(3), 976–84. http://dx.doi.org/10.1121/1.389023

Hwang, H. (2004). Spectral characteristics of frication noise in Korean sibilants. *Malsori*, 49, 31–50.

Iseli, M., & A. Alwan. (2004). An improved correction formula for the estimation of harmonic magnitudes and its application to open quotient estimation. In *Proceedings ICASSP '04* (pp. 669–72). Montreal, Canada, May 2004. http://dx.doi.org/10.1109/ICASSP.2004.1326074

Iverson, G.K. (1983). *Korean Journal of Phonetics*, 11, 191–200.

Jongman, A. (1989). Duration of frication noise required for identification of English fricatives. *Journal of the Acoustical Society of America*, 85(4), 1718–25. http://dx.doi.org/10.1121/1.397961

Jongman, A., R. Wayland & S. Wong. (2000). Acoustic characteristics of English fricatives. *Journal of the Acoustical Society of America*, 108(3), 1252–63. http://dx.doi.org/10.1121/1.1288413

Jun, S., M. Beckman & H.-J. Lee. (1998). Fiberscopic evidence for the influence on vowel devoicing of the glottal configurations for Korean obstruents. *UCLA Working Papers in Phonetics*, 96, 43–68.

Kagaya, R. (1974). A fiberscopic and acoustic study of the Korean stops, affricates and fricatives. *Journal of Phonetics*, 2, 161–80.

Kang, K.-S. (2000). On Korean fricatives. *Eumseonggwahag*, 7, 53–68.

Kang, Y., A. Kochetov & D. Go. (2009). The acoustics of Korean fricatives. Paper presented at the CRC-Sponsored Summer Phonetics/Phonology Workshop, University of Toronto.

Keating, P., & C. Esposito. (2007). Linguistic voice quality. *UCLA Working Papers in Phonetics*, 105, 85–91.

Kim, S. (2001). The interaction between prosodic domain and segmental properties: Domain initial strengthening of fricatives and post obstruent tensing rule in Korean. MA thesis, UCLA.

Kim, H., S. Maeda & K. Honda. (2010). Invariant articulatory bases of the features [tense] and [spread glottis] in Korean plosives: New stroboscopic Cine-MRI data. *Journal of Phonetics*, 38(1), 90–108. http://dx.doi.org/10.1016/j.wocn.2009.03.003

Kim, H., S. Maeda & K. Honda. (2011). The laryngeal characterization of Korean fricatives: Stroboscopic cine-MRI data. *Journal of Phonetics*, 39(4), 626–41. http://dx.doi.org/10.1016/j.wocn.2011.06.001

Kim, H., S. Maeda, K. Honda & S. Hans. (2010). The laryngeal characterization of Korean fricatives: Acoustic and aerodynamic data. In S. Fuchs, M. Toda & M. Zygis (eds.), *Turbulent Sounds: An Interdisciplinary Guide* (pp. 143–66). Berlin: Mouton de Gruyter. http://dx.doi.org/10.1515/9783110226584.143

Klatt, D.H., & Klatt, L.C. (1990). Analysis, synthesis and perception of voice quality variations among male and female talkers. *Journal of the Acoustical Society of America*, 87(2), 820–56. http://dx.doi.org/10.1121/1.398894

Lee, G. (2011). Acoustic characteristics of Korean fricatives and affricates. MA thesis, University of Kansas.

Lee, I., & S.R. Ramsey. (2000). *The Korean Language*. Albany, NY: State University of New York Press.

McMurray, B., M. Clayards, M. Tanenhaus & R. Aslin. (2008). Tracking the time-course of phonetic cue integration during spoken word recognition. *Psychonomic Bulletin & Review*, 15(6), 1064–71. http://dx.doi.org/10.3758/PBR.15.6.1064

McMurray, B., & A. Jongman. (2011). What information is necessary for speech categorization? Harnessing variability in the speech signal by integrating cues computed relative to expectations. *Psychological Review*, 118(2), 219–46. http://dx.doi.org/10.1037/a0022325

Park, H. (1999). The phonetic nature of the phonological contrast between the lenis and fortis fricatives in Korean. In *Proceedings of the 14th International Congress of Phonetic Sciences* (Vol. 1, pp. 424–7). San Francisco: University of California.

Park, H. (2002). Temporal and spectral characteristics of Korean phonation types. PhD dissertation, University of Texas at Austin.

R Development Core Team (2012). R: A language and environment for statistical computing. Vienna: R Foundation for Statistical Computing. http://www.R-project.org

Sjölander, K. (2004). *Snack Sound Toolkit*. Stockholm: KTH. http://www.speech.kth.se/snack

Sohn, H.-M. (1994). *Korean*. New York: Routledge.

Soli, S.D. (1981). Second formants in fricatives: Acoustic consequences of fricative-vowel coarticulation. *Journal of the Acoustical Society of America*, 70(4), 976–84. http://dx.doi.org/10.1121/1.387032

Sussman, H.M., H.A. McCaffrey & S.A. Matthews. (1991). An investigation of locus equations as a source of relational invariance for stop place categorization. *Journal of the Acoustical Society of America*, 90(3), 1309–25. http://dx.doi.org/10.1121/1.401923

Toscano, J.C., & B. McMurray. (2012). Cue integration and context effects in speech: Evidence against speaking rate normalization. *Attention, Perception & Psychophysics*, 74(6), 1284–1301. http://dx.doi.org/10.3758/s13414-012-0306-z

VoiceSauce (2011). Version 1.11, June 23, 2011. http://www.seas.ucla.edu/spapl/voicesauce/

Yeni-Komshian, B., & S.D. Soli. (1981). Recognition of vowels from information in fricatives: Perceptual evidence of fricative-vowel coarticulation. *Journal of the Acoustical Society of America*, 70(4), 966–75. http://dx.doi.org/10.1121/1.387031

Yoon, K. (1999). A study of Korean alveolar fricatives: An acoustic analysis, synthesis, and perception experiment. MA thesis, University of Kansas.

Yoon, K. (2002). A production and perception experiment of Korean alveolar fricatives. *Speech Sciences*, 9(3), 169–84.

5
Context Effects in Speech: Talker Normalization or Relative Auditory Perception

Antonia "Davi" Vitela and Andrew J. Lotto[1]

5.1 Introduction: The LTAS Approach to Talker Normalization

Traditional theories of extrinsic talker normalization posit that the listener is extracting speaker-specific characteristics from the acoustics and that this information is used to "tune" perception to provide optimal categorization of speech sounds for that particular speaker. The classic experiments of Ladefoged & Broadbent (1957; hereafter L&B) have been interpreted as evidence for the existence of such speaker-specific tuning processes in perception. L&B presented listeners with several carrier phrases (these were actually the same phrase manipulated to sound like different talkers by lowering/raising the formants within the phrase) followed by an ambiguous target vowel sound in a /b-vowel-t/ (bVt) context. They found that listeners' perception of the target vowel sound changed as a function of the carrier phrase that preceded it. This was taken as evidence of talker normalization – a shift in talker led to a shift in perception. The interpretation offered by L&B and by many other researchers subsequently claimed that the listener was learning about the acoustic-phonetic mapping for the speaker using the available lexical information. Subsequent ambiguous vowel tokens are then identified by their relative position in this space. Despite its intuitive appeal, this theory of phonetic/acoustic mapping has been challenged by

1 Antonia "Davi" Vitela is a postdoctoral scholar in the Department of Psychology at the University of Nevada, Las Vegas.
Andrew Lotto is an associate professor in Speech, Language and Hearing Sciences at the University of Arizona.

several findings using similar paradigms as L&B. Dechovitz (1977) failed to find effects of speaker change for a carrier phrase when two real speakers were used (as opposed to the synthetic manipulation of L&B). Darwin et al. (1989) also failed to find talker-based shifts in several of their manipulations of the L&B paradigm.

Ladefoged and Broadbent later proposed an alternative explanation for their original findings (Broadbent & Ladefoged 1960) that has received less attention in descriptions on extrinsic talker normalization. This explanation was based on adaptation levels (Helson 1948) wherein a participant's judgment of a current stimulus is affected by his/her previous experience with similar stimuli. Broadbent & Ladefoged (1960) suggest that when a listener hears a speaker with high first formants, the adaptation level is raised. This would cause subsequent sounds to be perceived as having a lower first formant value than they actually do. The results of L&B were consistent with this type of adaptation.

An adaptation approach is also consistent with results from Laing et al. (2012). They used the same preceding carrier phrase as L&B: *"Please say what this word is"* but used a /da/ to /ga/ target series, instead of ambiguous /bVt/ targets. They raised or lowered the first or third formant region of their carrier phrase, creating four different carrier phrases. Since the important cue for distinguishing between a /da/ or a /ga/ is the third formant, the authors predicted that the carrier phrases with the raised or lowered third formant would cause a contrastive shift in perception of the /da/-/ga/ targets, but that the carrier phrases with changes in the first formant region would not have any effect on target perception. This is precisely what was found. In a second set of experiments, they preceded the /da/-/ga/ tokens with a series of 17 70-millisecond tones that were matched in average frequency to the higher or lower F3 from the carrier phrases used in the previous speech-only experiments. The same pattern of /da/-/ga/ responses was obtained for the non-speech tone sequences as was obtained for the speech stimuli. All of these shifts could be described as contrastive – higher-frequency stimuli (F3s for speech or average frequencies of tones) resulted in more /ga/ responses, which have a lower F3 onset. Importantly, these shifts can be obtained for speech or non-speech precursors suggesting a general auditory process responsible for the effect as opposed to a speaker-specific or speech-specific process.

The proposal that general representations/processes of the auditory system may be able to accommodate some of the acoustic variability inherent in speech communication is a recurring theme in the work of Harvey Sussman. Sussman has demonstrated how neural processing of acoustic relational properties evident in a number of species may also account for how human listeners can deal with context-dependent variability in phoneme perception (Sussman et al. 1998; Sussman 2013). Similarly, we propose that there are auditory processes present in other species that can accommodate speaker-dependent variability in speech perception (Lotto et al. 1997; Lotto & Sullivan 2007). This LTAS (Long-Term Average Spectrum) model assumes that the listener calculates a running average of the spectral content of acoustic input. This LTAS serves as a baseline referent for the acoustic environment. Sounds whose structure deviates from that referent are enhanced through contrast. This process would provide enhanced perception of novel sounds in an environment but would also lead to the types of effects detailed by L&B when applied to speech. As Laing et al. (2012) demonstrated, the effects are not dependent on the preceding context being speech (see also Holt 2005, 2006). By comparing the LTAS of preceding stimuli (speech or non-speech) with the target speech sound, one is able to make predictions about which phrases will shift the perception of the target sound. If a carrier phrase's LTAS has a peak in frequency that is close to the cue important for the target's identification (such as a formant), then the LTAS could affect the perception of that phoneme – such as the frequency of F1 for the vowels used by L&B. For instance, if the LTAS peak is lower in frequency than a subsequent target vowel's F1, it could effectively raise the perception of that target's F1 and change the listener's perception of it – a spectral contrast effect (Lotto & Holt 2006). This means that LTAS comparisons predict not only when there will be an effect on perception, but also how perception is affected (i.e., in what direction the target's perception will be shifted).

We present here a set of experiments that test the predictions of this general LTAS model of extrinsic talker normalization. The experiments test three main predictions of the model: (1) that the direction of the shift in perception on a target sound can be predicted by comparing the LTAS of the carrier phrase to the target sound; (2) that comparing the LTAS of different talkers can also show which talkers will lead to an effect on perception and which will not; and (3) that non-speech contexts can affect perception, if they have energy in regions that would be predicted to do so. The final experiment is designed to provide more specific information about the characteristics of the signal that are important for the LTAS comparison.

5.2 General Methodology

Participants. All participants were recruited from the University of Arizona and received either course credit or monetary compensation for their time. All reported no history of hearing loss, and English as their native language.

Stimuli. The stimuli in each experiment consisted of a carrier phrase (speech or non-speech) followed by one member of a target series that varied perceptually from "bit" to "bet." The details of each are explained further below with their relevant experiment. The inter-stimulus-interval between the carrier phrase and target was always 50 ms.

Procedure. Participants were run in groups of one to four on separate computers in a large soundproof booth. On each trial, they were presented with a single randomly-selected carrier phrase + target stimulus over circumaural headphones (Sennheiser HD 280) at approximately 75 dB SPL. They were asked to identify the target as either "bit" or "bet" by using a mouse to click one of two labeled boxes on a monitor. The next trial did not begin until the participant responded. The stimuli were split into blocks with a certain number of stimulus repetitions in each block (order counterbalanced). This gave participants the opportunity to take short breaks between blocks, if needed. Each experimental session, including consent and debriefing, took no more than one hour. Stimulus presentation and data collection were controlled by the ALVIN software program (Hillenbrand & Gayvert 2005).

Predictions. Predictions for each experiment were derived from comparisons of the average spectral energy for each carrier phrase with that of the ambiguous member of the target series (the fifth member = bVt5, identified in a small pilot study). The LTAS comparisons show the frequency regions surrounding the first formant (0–1200 Hz). This is because the first formant is the important cue for distinguishing between the vowels in "bit" and "bet." An /ɪ/, like in "bit," has a lower first formant than an /ɛ/, like in "bet."

Generally, if the LTAS of the carrier phrase had a trough (low amplitude) in the region of the ambiguous target's formant and a frequency peak lower or higher than that formant, that carrier phrase was expected to have an effect on target perception. Figure 5.3 shows an example of an LTAS comparison with both of these characteristics. The carriers are the phrase "*He had a rabbit and a*" (explained and used in Experiments 1 and 2) and the ambiguous target, bVt5. Note that the ShortVT phrase has a higher frequency average peak in the F1 region than the target and the LongVT phrase has a peak that largely overlaps with the target. Based on this figure, the LTAS model would predict that the ShortVT phrase would cause an effective lowering of the F1 in the target, making it more "bit" like. Thus, a test of the prediction would be whether there are more "bit" responses for the ShortVT versus the LongVT contexts. It is important to note that while the spectral comparisons are referred to as "LTAS" comparisons, the images actually use a combination of LTAS, linear-predictive coding (LPC) and discrete Fourier transform (dFT) spectral representations. The choices are based on the length and spectral content of the carrier phrase, as well as the quality of the image visually.

Results. Depending on the experiment, separate paired-sample *t*-tests or ANOVAs (Analysis of Variance) were conducted to show whether shifts in target perception were significant. The dependent variable for the perceptual studies was the percentage of "bit" responses collapsed across all series members (for Experiments 1 and 2) and across the five middle targets (for Experiment 3). As the middle of the series contains the more ambiguous targets, it was determined that collapsing across these is more sensitive to shifts in target perception than collapsing across the entire series. The five middle targets for the bit/bet series were bVt4–bVt8. The carrier phrase served as the independent variable.

5.3 Experiment 1

This experiment tested the first two predictions mentioned above: (1) the direction of the shift in perception on a target sound can be predicted by comparing the LTAS of the carrier phrase to the target sound and (2) comparing the LTAS can also show which talkers will lead to an effect on perception and which will not.

Participants. Sixteen listeners participated in this study.

Stimuli. The carrier phrases and targets were synthesized using the TubeTalker model (Story 2013). This is a computational model based on MRI images of sustained phoneme productions from a male vocal tract (Story et al. 1996) and so is constrained by the principles of real vocal tract shapes in its ability to "produce" sound. It can be thought of as a tube or filter that is manipulated in a time-varying fashion to mirror the shape changes that take place during the production of real speech. The source for this filter is based on a kinematic model of the vocal folds that allows manipulations of a number of parameters, including fundamental frequency (Titze 1984, 2006). This model allows for the specification of the shape and length of each vocal tract and control of all other aspects such as the source, the timing and the relative place of all articulations. As a result, we can create different "talkers" with known vocal tract shapes/sizes, even when producing different phrases. We can also match the talkers on speaking rate, source (fundamental frequency and voice quality) and pattern of articulations. Thus, the model allows us to create stimuli with sufficient control while also resulting in an acoustic output more similar to typical speech.

With this model, we created four different "talkers" by imposing changes to the overall, starting shape of the vocal tract or filter of the model (referred to as the "Standard"). The Standard vocal tract (VT) length is 17.5 cm. Two of the new talkers were created by manipulating the length to create the LongVT (20 per cent longer, 21 cm) and the ShortVT (20 per cent shorter, 14 cm). The other pair of vocal tracts was created by keeping the length constant at 17.5 cm but manipulating the cavity size, instead. The ratios of the cross-sectional areas of the oral and pharyngeal cavities were increased or decreased by 20 per cent from the StandardVT. One had an expanded oral cavity but a constricted pharyngeal cavity (O+P–), while the other had the opposite: constricted oral cavity, expanded pharyngeal cavity (O–P+). The phrase synthesized from all four was *"He had a rabbit and a"*[2] (1.4 s), using the exact same source and pattern of constrictions and shape changes (relative to the overall length of each tract) for each of the four "talkers." The voiced source was given an F0 contour based on analysis of a recording of the phrase and varied from 95 Hz to 134 Hz. Figure 5.1 shows the spectrograms of the phrase for each talker appended to one of the members of the target series. The targets consisted of the 12-step "bit" to "bet" series (250 ms each) synthesized from the StandardVT. Instead of changing in equal formant intervals (as is typical in target series creation), the targets changed in equal area or articulation steps from the vocal tract shape considered a good "bit" to the vocal tract shape considered a good "bet." However, the F1 and F2 values for each member of the series are plotted in Figure 5.2. All stimuli were generated with a sampling rate of 44,100 Hz and written to a 16 bit wave format audio file. This created a total of 48 stimuli (4 vocal tracts × 12 series steps).

2 This phrase was chosen from a limited set of options. The creation of intelligible phrases using this complex vocal tract model is a difficult task as each constriction and overall shape change must be specified independently. The chosen phrase is very intelligible for all four vocal tracts. Note that the final vowel in "rabbit" is realized as [ʌ] and not as /ɪ/, as in the target "bit." This phrase was originally developed for a conference presentation (Story 2008).

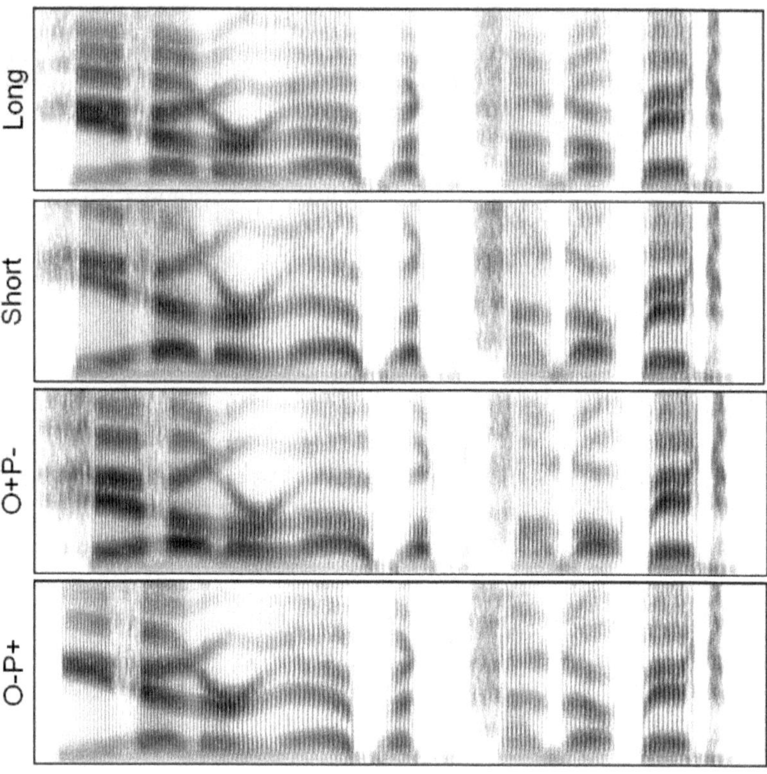

Figure 5.1. Spectrograms of "He had a rabbit and a" appended to the ambiguous target in the "bit" to "bet" series (bVt5). Each version was produced by a different synthetic vocal tract.

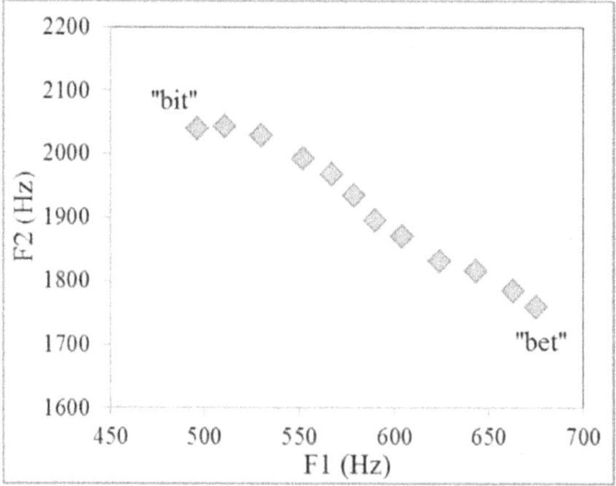

Figure 5.2. F1xF2-vowel space of the vowel portion (at .082 s) of the 12-step "bit" to "bet" target series.

Procedure. The phrases were separated into blocks. The LongVT and ShortVT carrier phrases + target were in Block 1. The O+P– and O–P+ VT carrier phrases + target were in Block 2. Each block contained 5 repetitions of each of the 12 target stimuli preceded by each of the two carrier phrases and participants went through each block twice (480 total trials). Participants had an opportunity to take a break after each block.

Predictions. Based on the LTAS in the region of the first formant, it was predicted that the ShortVT would lead to more "bit" responses than the LongVT (Figure 5.3). The LTAS comparison did not predict any shift between the O+P–VT and the O–P+VT.

The O–P+VT peaks in the same region as the first formant of the ambiguous target and the O+P–VT peaks within the ambiguous target's peak, as well. Although it is slightly higher in frequency than O–P+VT, it does overlap with the ambiguous target more than the ShortVT and so we would predict no difference in perception between these two carrier phrases (Figure 5.4).

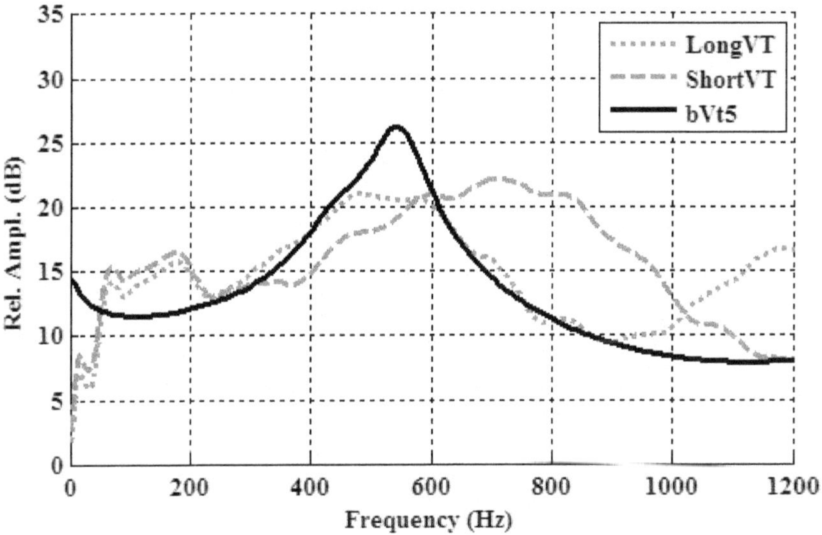

Figure 5.3. LTAS comparison between the carrier phrases "He had a rabbit and a" of the LongVT and ShortVT and the ambiguous target from the "bit" to "bet" series (bVt5) in the region surrounding F1. (LTAS = LongVT, ShortVT; LPC = bVt5).

Results. Separate paired-sample t-tests supported the LTAS predictions. Listeners perceived "bit" significantly more often following the ShortVT's carrier phrase than when the targets followed the LongVT's carrier phrase [$t(15) = -5.42, p < .001$] and there was no significant difference between the O+P– and O–P+ VTs [$t(15) = .69, p > .05$]. Figures 5.5 and 5.6 show these results.

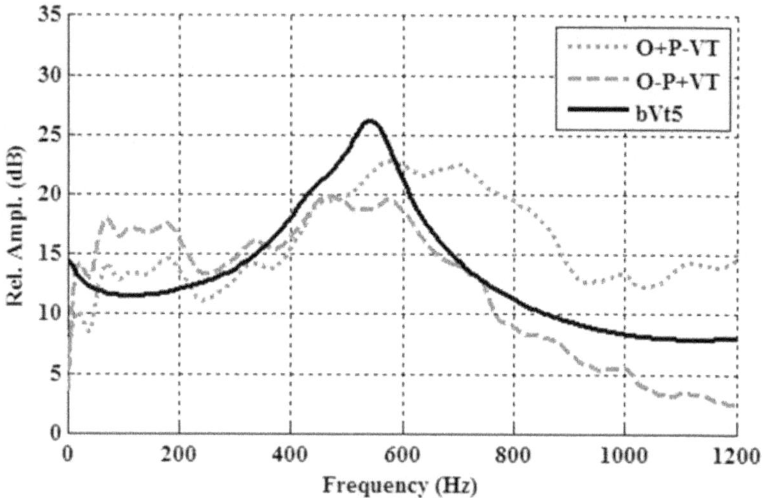

Figure 5.4. LTAS comparison between the carrier phrases "He had a rabbit and a" of the O+P–VT and O–P+VT and the ambiguous target from the "bit" to "bet" series (bVt5) in the region surrounding F1 (LTAS = O+P–, O–P+; LPC = bVt5).

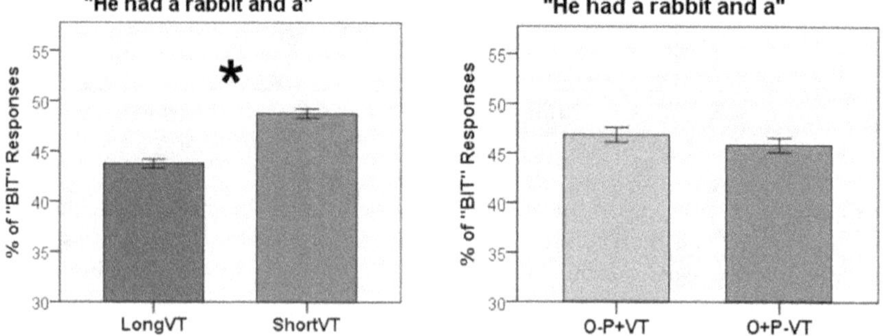

Figures 5.5 and 5.6. Results for Experiment 1: Mean per cent "bit" responses for the LongVT and ShortVT (left) and for O–P+VT and O+P–VT (right) synthesized versions of "He had a rabbit and a." Error bars indicate standard error of the mean.

Discussion. The fact that listeners changed their categorization of target vowels as a function of talker is consistent with proposals that listeners are sensitive to a change in talker. However, the context-dependent changes were not sensitive to all changes of talker (oral-pharyngeal ratio), even though this change in shape does lead to a change in vowel space (increasing the oral/pharyngeal ratio lowers F1 and raises F2, as seen in Figure 5.1). Thus, these results support the LTAS account by demonstrating the power of this model to predict which talker differences will result in shifts in target perception and which talker changes will not, and its ability to predict the direction of the shift. As mentioned previously, this is not the first case of a change in talker not leading to a change in perception of a target sound (Dechovitz 1977; Darwin et al. 1989). If LTAS comparisons were made with these stimuli, it would be expected that the carrier phrases used would not differ substantially in their average energy and no spectral contrast effect would be predicted.

5.4 Experiment 2

According to the LTAS account, a stimulus that differs from the carrier phrase but maintains the same LTAS should result in a similar shift in target responses. Since the forward and backward speech would have equivalent LTAS, they should result in equivalent effects. This prediction was tested using reversed versions of some of the carrier phrases. These phrases would not be intelligible but would have identical LTAS.

Participants. Sixteen listeners participated in this study.

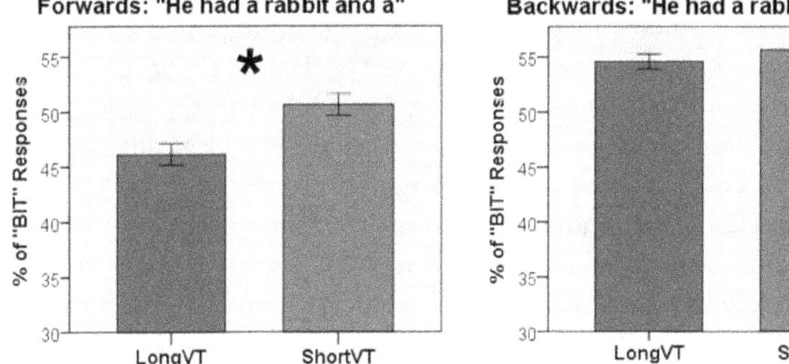

Figures 5.7 and 5.8. Results for Experiment 2: Mean per cent "bit" responses for the LongVT and ShortVT synthesized forward (left) and backward (right) versions of *"He had a rabbit and a."* Error bars indicate standard error of the mean.

Stimuli. The carrier phrases were the same as in Experiment 1 (*"He had a rabbit and a"*) played both forward and backward. Only the LongVT and ShortVT were used, since their LTAS comparison showed an effect in the previous experiment.

Procedure. The stimuli were split into two blocks (Block 1 = forward stimuli; Block 2 = backward stimuli). There were five repetitions of each stimulus per block and participants were run in each block twice for a total of 480 trials.

Predictions. The predictions are the same as for the LongVT and ShortVT of Experiment 1. The ShortVT should result in more "bit" responses whether it is played forward or in reverse.

Results. A 2×2 within-subjects ANOVA was used to analyze the data. The factors were vocal tract (LongVT, ShortVT) and direction (forward, backward). There was not a main effect of vocal tract [$F(1,15) = 3.00$, $p > .05$]. There was a main effect of direction [$F(1,15) = 17.09$, $p < .05$] and a significant interaction [$F(1,15) = 8.73$, $p < .05$]. Planned comparisons showed that listeners heard "bit" significantly more often following the ShortVT than following the LongVT [$F(1,15) = 5.17$, $p < .05$] when the phrases were played forward, but there was no significant difference when the phrases were played backward [$F(1,15) = .58$, $p > .05$]. The results are shown in Figures 5.7 and 5.8.

Discussion. The significant interaction means that the effect size of phrase was not equal for the forward and backward presentations. The forward effect was larger than the backward effect. These results conflict with the LTAS theory, as it predicted that a phrase played backward should have the same effect as when it is played forward. One possible explanation is that there is a temporal window over which the LTAS is computed. That is, only the acoustic information within that window of time is used in the calculation of the LTAS. The information prior to that has no effect on target perception. This window may be shorter than the duration of the carrier phrases used. When the stimuli were played backward, the local spectral information (i.e., the average spectral energy closest to the target) may have been different than when they were played forward, causing different effects in the backward and forward condition. It could also be the case that there is a temporal window but that the window is weighted, meaning the spectral information closer to the target has a greater representation in the LTAS than the spectral information more distant in time. Either one of these would explain this discrepancy in the results without discounting the LTAS theory. A third possibility is that carrier phrases without phonetic content do not elicit talker normalization effects. Sjerps et al. (2011) carried out a number of studies investigating what types of context phrases would and would not elicit effects on a target series. They found that the more dissimilar the context was from speech, the less likely it was to elicit an effect on target perception. This is in contrast to the finding of Holt and colleagues (Holt 2005, 2006; Laing et al. 2012) who found shifts in perception with non-speech contexts. Whereas the first two possibilities suggest a change in how one calculates the LTAS for the current model, the last possibility would require a substantial reformulation, as the model is considered to be a general perceptual process and not specific to speech.

One of the downfalls of the LTAS model is that all of the predictions thus far (in the above two experiments and in other papers) have been rather coarse. In general, they have been made by looking at the relative frequency position of peaks in the LTAS and comparing them to a particular formant peak frequency in the ambiguous vowel. Specifically, if two criteria are met an effect has been predicted. These are: (1) that the spectral energy of the carrier phrase has a trough (low energy) in the region of the formant of interest and (2) that the energy from the trough gradually increases and peaks higher or lower in frequency than the formant of interest. For the most part, these two criteria have been successful in predicting LTAS effects. However, it is necessary to develop a model that can make specific, quantitative predictions that are based on knowledge of the LTAS mechanism, rather than on "eye-balling" the LTAS comparisons. For instance, it is not clear how close in frequency the peak of the carrier phrase and the target's formant need to be for the carrier phrase to have an effect on the target's perception. It could be that outside of a certain frequency range of the target's formant, the carrier no longer has an effect, even if it does have a peak higher or lower in frequency. To examine this possibility, so that the LTAS model is capable of making more specific predictions, this next experiment parametrically explores how previous spectral energy affects target responses.

5.5 Experiment 3

This experiment seeks to determine how close a peak in frequency needs to be to the formant of a target to have an effect on that target's perception. Seven harmonic complexes were created. Each complex had a different peak in frequency that moved in 100 Hz steps from 300 to 900 Hz. The ambiguous target from the "bit" to "bet" series (bVt5) was used. The peak of the complexes was matched in amplitude to the peak of the first formant of the ambiguous target. It was expected that the harmonic complexes with peaks closest to the first formant would cause a shift in target perception, while the ones that were further away would not. Again, these are all very coarse predictions with no true standard for what is considered "further away" or "closer." It was hoped that this experiment would start to refine these into true definable measures.

Participants. Twenty participants ran in this experiment.

Stimuli. The carrier phrases were seven harmonic complexes created in MATLAB. They were 500 ms in length with a 50 ms amplitude ramp at the beginning and end of the stimulus. Each harmonic was a multiple of 100 Hz and the complex was composed of 12 harmonics (100–1200 Hz) that had one peak in frequency. The peak in frequency changed from 300 Hz to 900 Hz. The steepness of the peak was determined by measuring the change in amplitude between the harmonics in the first formant (down-slope) of the ambiguous target of the "bit"-"bet" series (bVt5). The peak harmonic was matched in amplitude to the amplitude of the first formant in the ambiguous target. The harmonics immediately lower and higher in frequency were 10 dB lower and the rest of the harmonics were 15 dB lower than the highest harmonic. Figure 5.9 shows an example – the spectra of the harmonic complex with a peak at 700 Hz and the ambiguous target.

The targets were still the "bit"-"bet" series, except that only the first 11 were used to shorten the experiment length. With the harmonic complexes, there were 77 stimuli in total.

Procedure. The stimuli were not split up into separate blocks, but played in the same block. Each stimulus was repeated 3 times per block and participants ran in this block 4 times for a total of 924 trials (7 harmonic

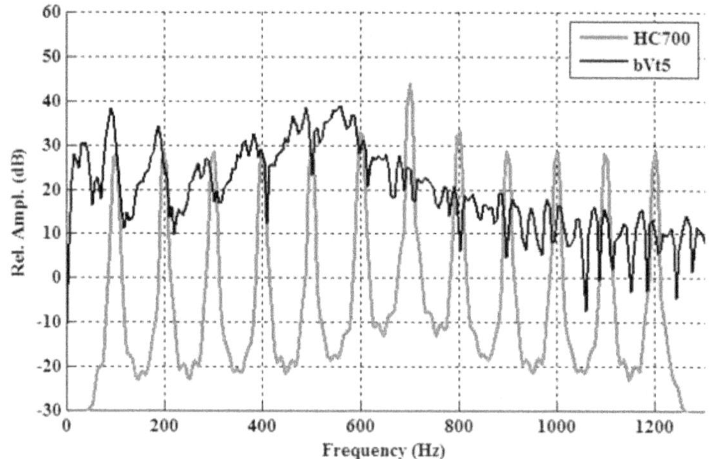

Figure 5.9. The spectra of the harmonic complex with a peak at 700 Hz and the ambiguous target, bVt5.

complexes × 11 targets × 12 repetitions.) All other aspects were the same as Experiment 1 and 2.

Predictions. If the peak in the LTAS needs to be within a certain frequency range of a target's formant to have an effect on perception, then peaks outside that range should not have an effect. The harmonic complexes were created in an attempt to determine what this range is. The harmonic complexes within this range should shift the target's perception. In the case of this particular ambiguous target (bVt5), the region around the first formant is the region of interest, since the first formant is important for the distinction between a "bit" and a "bet." If the harmonic complex peaks higher in frequency, the first formant of the ambiguous target should be perceived as having a lower frequency and, thus, get more "bit" responses. If the harmonic complex peaks lower in frequency, then the opposite should happen and it should get more "bet" responses. The harmonic complexes outside the range should not have an effect on the target.

Results. A one-way ANOVA was used to test for differences in per cent "bit" responses at seven different frequency peaks. The percentage of "bit" responses was determined in the same way as previous experiments (averaged across repetitions of the five middle members of the target series). The results were not significantly different across the seven different frequencies [$F(6,114) = 1.41, p > .05$]. Figure 5.10 shows the results graphically. Figure 5.11 shows the individual data, as well as the average for each condition.

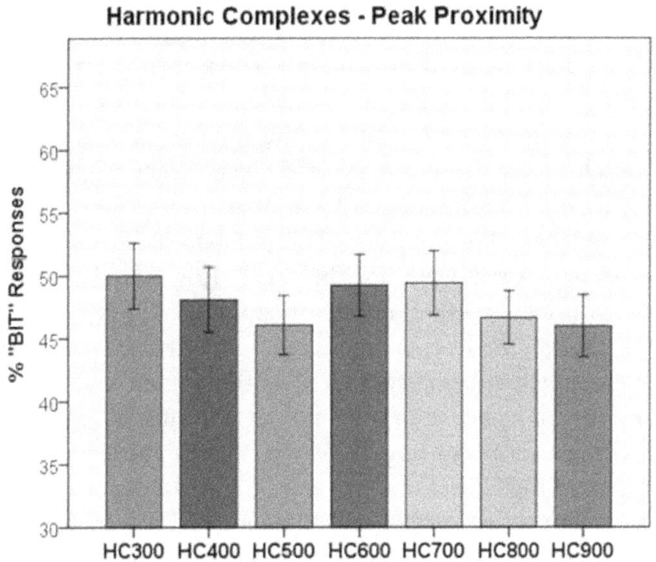

Figure 5.10. Results for Experiment 3: Mean per cent "bit" responses for seven different harmonic complexes. Error bars indicate standard error of the mean.

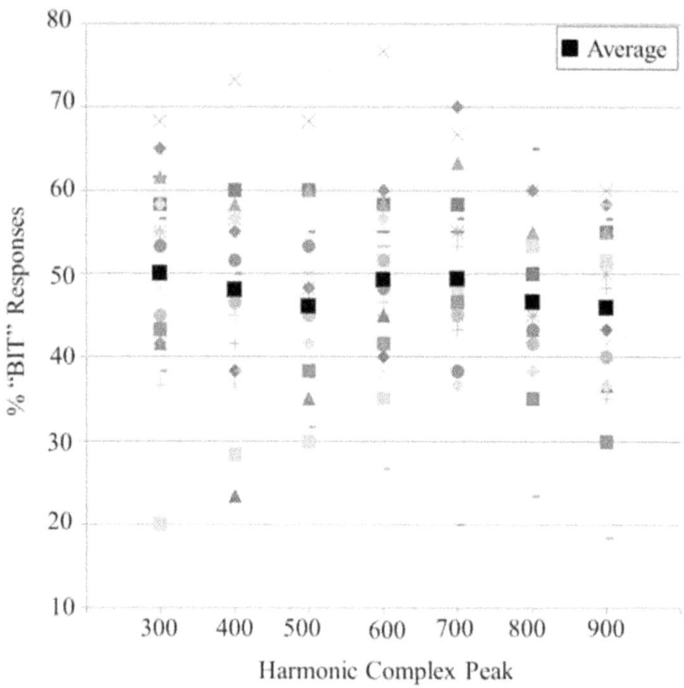

Figure 5.11. Experiment 3: Individual differences for each harmonic complex.

Discussion. Unexpectedly, the ANOVA showed no significant differences between harmonic complexes. Looking at Figure 5.11, it is apparent that there is a huge amount of variation between subjects. One possible reason for this variation could be that listeners differ on their boundary between the vowels /ɪ/ and /ɛ/. That is, the ambiguous target could be different across listeners. For some, it could be an earlier target in the series; for others, it could be one that is later. That means the same harmonic complex could have the opposite effect on two listeners' perception if their ambiguous targets were not the same. This may not have affected the results of previous experiments, since there were typically only two different carrier phrases being compared – so only two frequency peaks were of concern when being compared to the target's first formant. This would have less of a chance of washing out any effects, because only the listeners whose ambiguous target was near one of those peaks may have been affected. In this case, the peaks were every 100 Hz so more discriminable differences between listeners' ambiguous targets could have caused any effects to disappear. For this reason, two more ANOVAs were run. The average of per cent "bit" responses across all conditions was found (grand mean) and the averages for each subject across all conditions were determined. If the subject's average was higher than the grand mean, they were put into one group and if it was lower, they were put into another group. This was thought to separate the participants by whether they had a lower or higher ambiguous target. These separate ANOVAs did not find a significant interaction, either [above grand mean: $F(6,42) = 1.94, p > .05$; below grand mean: $F(6,66) = .49, p > .05$). The individual differences seem like they are quite complex and cannot simply be accounted for by dividing the participants into two groups.

Another possibility is that seven carrier phrases were, in some sense, overwhelming to the participant. Not knowing how the LTAS mechanism works, it could have "tired" the auditory system by stimulating the same frequencies within a certain region continuously for up to an hour. The auditory system could have also segregated the harmonic complexes and identified them as another auditory event than they did the target. If so, then the harmonic complexes may not have been able to affect the target.

5.6 Conclusion

In the spirit of Harvey Sussman's explanation for the perceptual accommodation of context-dependent variability in speech acoustics (Sussman et al. 1998; Sussman 2013), we have proposed a general auditory account of talker normalization. The proposal is based on previous work with human listeners and non-speech sounds (Holt 2005, 2006) and with non-human animals and speech sounds (Lotto et al. 1997). The Long-Term Average Spectrum model proposes that listeners compute a running spectral average of acoustic input and enhance differences from this average through contrast. For the specific case of extrinsic talker normalization such as demonstrated by Ladefoged & Broadbent (1957), this model hypothesizes that listeners calculate the LTAS of carrier phrases and that the shift in target perception is a result of spectral contrast (Lotto & Holt 2006) between this LTAS and the spectral characteristics of the target.

The results of the first experiment demonstrate the predictive power of the LTAS model for speech perception. By comparing the LTAS of the carrier phrases for four simulated talkers with the formant values for the target stimuli, we were able to predict which talker changes would result in a shift in target categorization and which talker changes would lead to no shift. However, the results of Experiment 2 were contradictory to a central prediction of the simplest form of the LTAS model – that only the LTAS of the carrier phrase matters for determining any perceptual shift for the target. The carrier phrases presented forward or backward in time have equivalent LTAS and yet did *not* result in equivalent shifts in target responses. The results of Experiment 3 are also problematic for a simple LTAS model as simple harmonic complexes varying in frequency of the spectral peak were not sufficient to engender context-sensitive shifts in target responses.

The failures of prediction for Experiments 2 and 3 suggest that the LTAS model is wrong in its most simple (and strongest) form. Modifications to this model are necessary to accommodate these findings. Alternatively, it is clearly possible that the model is fundamentally wrong. However, the model *does* correctly predict when and in what directions target shifts will occur for speech contexts. Further, the model is based on findings from non-speech sound perception by humans and auditory perception from non-human animals. The logic of the model flows from an understanding of the neural representation of sound and an analysis of the demands placed on audition by the acoustic environment. This continuity of function from general auditory processing and ecological considerations up through speech communication are strengths of the approach previously developed by Sussman to explain accommodation of variability in speech perception (Sussman 2013). It is hoped that a similar model that does not require a discontinuous theoretical development may be developed, to explain many of the phenomena in speech perception – such as talker normalization (Holt & Lotto 2008).

References

Broadbent, D.E., & P. Ladefoged. (1960). Vowel judgements and adaptation level. *Proceedings of the Royal Society of London. Series B, Biological Sciences*, 151(944), 384–99. http://dx.doi.org/10.1098/rspb.1960.0005

Darwin, C.J., J. Denis McKeown & D. Kirby. (1989). Perceptual compensation for transmission channel and speaker effects on vowel quality. *Speech Communication*, 8(3), 221–34. http://dx.doi.org/10.1016/0167-6393(89)90003-4

Dechovitz, D.R. (1977). Information conveyed by vowels: A negative finding. *Journal of the Acoustical Society of America*, 61(S1), S39. http://dx.doi.org/10.1121/1.2015624

Helson, H. (1948). Adaptation-level as a basis for a quantitative theory of frames of reference. *Psychological Review*, 55(6), 297–313. http://dx.doi.org/10.1037/h0056721

Hillenbrand, J.M., & R.T. Gayvert. (2005). Open source software for experiment design and control. *Journal of Speech, Language, and Hearing Research (JSLHR)*, 48(1), 45–60. http://dx.doi.org/10.1044/1092-4388(2005/005)

Holt, L.L. (2005). Temporally nonadjacent nonlinguistic sounds affect speech categorization. *Psychological Science*, 16(4), 305–12. http://dx.doi.org/10.1111/j.0956-7976.2005.01532.x

Holt, L.L. (2006). The mean matters: Effects of statistically defined nonspeech spectral distributions on speech categorization. *Journal of the Acoustical Society of America*, 120(5), 2801–17. http://dx.doi.org/10.1121/1.2354071

Holt, L.L., & A.J. Lotto. (2008). Speech perception within an auditory cognitive science framework. *Current Directions in Psychological Science*, 17(1), 42–6. http://dx.doi.org/10.1111/j.1467-8721.2008.00545.x

Ladefoged, P., & D.E. Broadbent. (1957). Information conveyed by vowels. *Journal of the Acoustical Society of America*, 29(1), 98–104. http://dx.doi.org/10.1121/1.1908694

Laing, E.J., R. Liu, A.J. Lotto & L.L. Holt. (2012). Tuned with a tune: Talker normalization via general auditory processes. *Frontiers in Psychology*, 3, 203. http://dx.doi.org/10.3389/fpsyg.2012.00203

Lotto, A.J., & L.L. Holt. (2006). Putting phonetic context effects into context: A commentary on Fowler. *Attention, Perception & Psychophysics*, 68(2), 178–83. http://dx.doi.org/10.3758/BF03193667

Lotto, A.J., K.R. Kluender & L.L. Holt. (1997). Perceptual compensation for coarticulation by Japanese quail (*Coturnixcoturnix japonica*). *The Journal of the Acoustical Society of America*, 102(2), 1134–40.

Lotto, A.J., & S.C. Sullivan. (2007). Speech as a sound source. In W.A. Yost, R.R. Fay & A.N. Popper (eds.), *Auditory Perception of Sound Sources* (pp. 281–305). New York: Springer Science and Business Media, LLC. http://dx.doi.org/10.1007/978-0-387-71305-2_10

Sjerps, M.J., H. Mitterer & J.M. McQueen. (2011). Constraints on the processes responsible for the extrinsic normalization of vowels. *Attention, Perception & Psychophysics*, 73(4), 1195–215. http://dx.doi.org/10.3758/s13414-011-0096-8

Story, B.H. (2008). Simulation of speech production with kinematic models of the vocal tract and vocal folds. Paper presented at the International Conference on Vocal Fold Physiology and Biomechanics, Tampere, Finland.

Story, B.H. (2013). Phrase-level speech simulation with an airway modulation model of speech production. *Computer Speech & Language*, 27(4), 989–1010. http://dx.doi.org/10.1016/j.csl.2012.10.005

Story, B.H., I.R. Titze & E.A. Hoffman. (1996). Vocal tract area functions from magnetic resonance imaging. *Journal of the Acoustical Society of America*, 100(1), 537–54. http://dx.doi.org/10.1121/1.415960

Sussman, H.M. (2013). Neuroethology in the service of neurophonetics. *Journal of Neurolinguistics*, 26(5), 511–25. http://dx.doi.org/10.1016/j.jneuroling.2013.02.004

Sussman, H.M., D. Fruchter, J. Hilbert & J. Sirosh. (1998). Linear correlates in the speech signal: The orderly output constraint. *Behavioral and Brain Sciences*, 21(02), 241–59. http://dx.doi.org/10.1017/S0140525X98001174

Titze, I.R. (1984). Parameterization of the glottal area, glottal flow, and vocal fold contact area. *Journal of the Acoustical Society of America*, 75(2), 570–80. http://dx.doi.org/10.1121/1.390530

Titze, I.R. (2006). *The Myoelastic Aerodynamic Theory of Phonation*. Salt Lake City, UT: National Center for Voice and Speech.

6
Music Training and the Neural Processing of Speech: A Critical Review of the Literature

Bharath Chandrasekaran, Zilong Xie and Rachel Reetzke[1]

6.1 Introduction

In recent years there has been a proliferation in studies examining the effects of music training on brain plasticity and cognitive function. There are clear practical implications of this line of work, as music therapy has been used as an effective intervention tool for diverse clinical populations with physical, psychological, behavioral, cognitive and/or social disorders (AMTA 2014). The myriad of available music therapy methods often fall into one of two broad categories: (1) *passive*, which requires little to no action from the participant, or (2) *active*, which requires physical action from the participant (Montello & Coons 1998; Treurnicht Naylor et al. 2010; Pacchetti et al. 2000). Passive music therapy (e.g. listening to pre-recorded music) has been implemented to reduce anxiety and promote relaxation in both pediatric and adult hospital patients (for reviews, see Evans 2002; Klassen et al. 2008). Active music therapy (e.g. instrument improvisation and melodic intonation therapy) has been found to promote functional behavior, communication and socialization in children with neurodevelopment disorders such as autism spectrum disorder (for a review, see Accordino et

1 Bharath Chandrasekaran is an associate professor in the Department of Communication Sciences and Disorders, Psychology, and Linguistics, Institute for Neuroscience, at the University of Texas at Austin.
Zilong Xie is a doctoral student in the Department of Communication Sciences and Disorders, Moody College of Communication, at the University of Texas at Austin.
Rachel Reetzke is a doctoral student in the Department of Communication Sciences and Disorders, Moody College of Communication, at the University of Texas at Austin.

al. 2007; Wan et al. 2010) as well as elderly populations with neurodegenerative disorders, such as dementia (for a review, see Koger et al. 1999).

The goal of this review article is to critically examine the literature investigating the effects of music training on the domain of speech processing. Speech processing requires a finely tuned peripheral auditory system to process the complex spectrotemporal properties of speech signals as well as a robust central nervous system capable of extracting discrete, higher-level information from a highly variable acoustic signal. Deficits in speech processing have been evidenced in several clinical populations, including individuals with dyslexia (for a review, see Farmer & Klein 1995; Schulte-Körne et al. 1998). Understanding the mechanisms by which music training influences speech processing may have critical implications for the use of active music training to enhance disordered speech perception.

Here we examine several research works wherein musicians have been studied as models of experience-dependent neuroplasticity, as "auditory experts." The primary aim of this line of inquiry is to examine the extent to which long-term music training elicits cross-domain effects. To date, clear neuroanatomical and neurophysiological differences between musicians and non-musicians have been established through studies implementing a descriptive-comparative approach, whereby groups with enriched relative to impoverished music experiences are compared (e.g. musicians vs non-musicians). Several studies using this design have examined the extent to which music training impacts the neural processing of speech signals. The general conclusion is that lifelong music training positively impacts the encoding of speech signals, even at relatively early neural stages of processing. However, whether an early encoding advantage translates to a real-world advantage in speech perception remains an open question. We critically evaluate the burgeoning literature on music training and brain plasticity, with a specific focus on the cortical and subcortical mechanisms underlying the musician advantage in speech perception. The extent to which neural encoding enhancement in musicians transfers to a functional benefit in speech perception is examined. We also evaluate a recent proposal (i.e., the *OPERA hypothesis*) that suggests a theoretical scaffolding to better clarify the musician advantage in speech processing. Our goal is to construct an improved understanding of the mechanisms underlying experience-dependent brain plasticity to speech signals. A fundamental identification of mechanisms is critical before music training can be truly prescribed as a remedial solution for a variety of speech and auditory processing deficits (Chandrasekaran & Kraus 2010; Kraus &Chandrasekaran 2010; Overy 2000). We begin by evaluating the literature on music training and brain plasticity.

6.2 Neuroplasticity Associated with Music Training: Changes in Structure and Function

Testing the general claim that musicians are "auditory experts," several studies examine the effects of musical expertise on brain plasticity. We have summarized several of these studies in the Appendix. These investigations have revealed structural differences between musicians and age-matched non-musicians in key auditory cortical regions such as the planum temporale (PT) (Bermudez & Zatorre 2005; Keenan et al. 2001; Schlaug et al. 1995; Zatorre et al. 1998) and Heschl's gyrus (Bermudez et al. 2009; Gaser & Schlaug 2003; Hyde et al. 2009; Schneider et al. 2002). For example, Schneider et al. (2002) found that the gray matter volume of the antero-medial portion of Heschl's gyrus in both hemispheres is larger in professional musicians than in non-musicians, with amateur musicians showing intermediate gray matter volume. Importantly, gray matter volume positively correlated strongly with musical aptitude. Later studies revealed similar results, but only differed in the exact part of Heschl's gyrus that showed morphological changes: the right superior temporal area, centered on the postero-lateral aspect of Heschl's gyrus (Bermudez et al. 2009), or the medial portion of left Heschl's gyrus (Gaser & Schlaug 2003).

With regard to functionality, the effect of musical expertise and musical training on cognitive processing in the auditory cortex has been convincingly demonstrated by numerous studies using electroencephalography (EEG) and magnetoencephalography (MEG) methods (see Pantev and Herholz 2011, for review). The cortical evoked responses were shown to be larger for musicians than for non-musicians toward musically relevant sounds such as instrumental tones (Baumann et al. 2008; Meyer et al. 2011; Pantev et al. 1998, 2001; Shahin et al. 2003, 2007), major chords (Koelsch et al. 1999), melodic patterns (Fujioka et al. 2004, 2005; Magne et al. 2006; Moreno et al. 2009), harmonically rich tones (Seppänen 2012a, b) as well as abstract tonal patterns (Herholz et al. 2009; van Zuijen et al. 2004, 2005). Impressively, short-term musical training results in a significant enlargement of cortical responses to musical relevant sounds relative to a control group (Fujioka et al. 2006; Lappe et al. 2008, 2011). In addition, cortical representations for tones of different timbre are enhanced preferentially for timbres of the instrument on which the musician was trained (Pantev et al. 2001; Shahin et al. 2008). Consistent with a domain-general benefit, the cortical plastic changes are not confined to music related sounds, but also extend to speech processing (Chobert et al. 2011; Kühnis et al. 2013;

Magne et al. 2006; Marie et al. 2011; Marques et al. 2007; Moreno et al. 2009; Schön et al. 2004). For example, musical experience enhanced cortical pitch processing for speech signals (Magne et al. 2006; Marie et al. 2011; Marques et al. 2007; Moreno et al. 2009; Schön et al. 2004), and enhanced cortical processing of critical acoustic features in speech (Chobert et al. 2011; Kühnis et al. 2013).

The aforementioned studies demonstrate that music training modulates auditory cortical circuitry. A related question of whether music training enhanced subcortical auditory processing of speech sounds was posed by Wong et al. (2007). This study used the frequency following response (FFR) as an index of experience-dependent plasticity. The FFR reflects sustained, phase-locked activity from neural ensembles within the auditory brainstem (Chandrasekaran & Kraus, 2010; Smith et al. 1975; Sohmer et al. 1977). Relative to the more abstract auditory cortical responses, the FFR reflects the stimulus with high fidelity. For example, when scalp-recorded FFRs to words are collected and played back as wave files, listeners can often recognize the words with a high degree of precision. The FFRs encode stimulus related information with high temporal and spectral precision, and provide a valuable aperture into how musical training can transform the representation of auditory signals.

Using FFR as an index to quantify effects of musical expertise on musical information, previous studies have shown that musicians had a more accurate encoding of musical pitch patterns such as chordal arpeggios (Bidelman et al. 2011c) and musical pitch interval (Bidelman et al. 2011b; Lee et al. 2009) than non-musicians. Musicians also revealed superior encoding of lexical pitch patterns in Mandarin relative to non-musicians (Bidelman et al. 2011b; Wong et al. 2007). Further, as reflected by the FFR, musicians show less sluggish encoding of critical speech events relative to non-musicians, especially when speech is presented in background noise (Parbery-Clark et al. 2012b). A body of work using the FFR demonstrates that musicians have faster neural response timing to auditory events (Parbery-Clark et al. 2012a and b), higher neural response consistency (Parbery-Clark et al. 2012b), more robust encoding of the fundamental frequency (*F0*) of a speech syllable (Bidelman & Krishnan 2010) and harmonics in the vowel in both quiet and noise conditions (Bidelman & Krishnan 2010; Parbery-Clark et al. 2012b), and better neural representation of the stimulus envelope and the vowel (Parbery-Clark et al. 2012b). Musicians additionally show enhanced neural distinction of contrastive speech syllables such as /ba/ and /ga/ (Parbery-Clark et al. 2012c; Strait et al. 2013). Finally, musicians show enhanced context-dependent modulation of speech signals at the level of the auditory brainstem (Parbery-Clark et al. 2011b).

6.3 Neuroplasticity Associated with Music Training: Behavior

The literature reviewed in section 6.2 clearly demonstrates structural and functional brain differences between musicians and non-musicians. These brain changes reflect enhanced neural encoding of speech signals at multiple levels of auditory processing. In this section we address studies that have demonstrated *behavioral* differences as a function of music training. Typically, neuroimaging studies have used correlational analyses to link music training indices (e.g., years of music training, age of onset) to functional benefits in speech processing. For example, FFR indices have been linked to higher speech intelligibility in challenging listening conditions across the lifespan in typical hearing individuals (Parbery-Clark et al. 2009b, 2011b), middle-aged musicians with normal hearing (Parbery-Clark et al. 2011a, 2012b), as well as those with hearing loss (Parbery-Clark et al. 2013). However, a speech perception benefit in challenging listening conditions for musicians is not a consistent finding. A recent behavioral study (Ruggles et al. 2014) directly compared a group of normal hearing young adult musicians and non-musicians in various speech-in-noise tests, including those reported in Parbery-Clark et al. (2009b), and showed that, at least in normal hearing young adults, musical training does not produce benefits in understanding speech in noise. Future studies would need to address these divergent findings.

Music training has also been linked to enhanced learning of non-native speech sounds. For example, Cooper & Wang (2012) found that non-tonal language listeners (English) with musical experience had higher Cantonese tone word learning proficiency than those English listeners without musical experience, and the musical aptitude scores were significantly correlated with their word learning success. Similarly, Wong & Perrachione (2007) showed that musicians required fewer sessions to learn non-native speech patterns, a finding they linked to enhanced brain encoding of speech signals. Also, two years of music training resulted in enhanced speech segmentation, which is an important skill linked to language learning (François et al. 2012).

Playing a musical instrument requires the integration of information from visual, auditory and motor systems, and therefore is a prime example of multisensory processing. The extent to which multisensory training experiences transfer across domains has been examined by several studies. Musicians showed more robust FFRs to speech and music stimuli under audiovisual conditions (Musacchia et al. 2007). Further, Lee

& Noppeney (2011) showed that behaviorally musicians demonstrated a narrower temporal integration window, enhanced neural responses to audiovisual asynchrony and increased effective connectivity within the auditory-motor circuitry in the brain. And for audiovisual integration of abstract congruency rules in musical stimuli, musicians exhibit higher performance for incongruency judgment, and increased activity mainly in frontal regions in response to multisensory incongruencies (Paraskevopoulos et al. 2012).

Behavioral studies also lend support to an association between musical training and enhanced working memory. For example, relative to non-musicians, musicians demonstrated better performance in measures of auditory and visual short-term memory (Fujioka et al. 2006; Lee et al. 2007; Parbery-Clark et al. 2009b), non-word span (Lee et al. 2007), operation span (ibid.), spatial span (ibid.), and verbal WM span (Chan et al. 1998; Parbery-Clark et al. 2009b). By combining behavioral and neurophysiological methods, George and Coch (2011) showed that musicians outperformed non-musicians in various measures of WM, and these behavioral benefits for musical training were reflected by differences in a neural index of WM, the P300 component (a positive event-related component that peaks ~300 ms post event onset). Musicians exhibited shorter P300 latency and larger amplitude relative to non-musicians. In the auditory domain, the brain networks for verbal WM and tonal WM differed between non-musicians and musicians: in non-musicians, there are considerable overlaps with the brain regions between tonal and verbal WM, with verbal WM involved additional structures; in contrast, musicians showed a larger overlap of structures for the two subsystems of auditory working memory, and a recruitment of diverse structures exclusively for either verbal or tonal WM (Schulze & Koelsch 2012; Schulze et al. 2011).

6.4 Neuroplasticity Associated with Music Training: A Predisposition or Experience-Dependent?

As discussed in section 6.3, a number of studies confirm a difference in brain structure and function as well as behavioral performance between musicians and non-musicians. An important question is the extent to which music training is causally linked to these changes. For example, are those with a more effective auditory cortex predisposed to be musicians, or are the changes a result of the music training? This question cannot be addressed by descriptive-comparative designs and requires a randomized-control study (RCT) design. A recent RCT study randomly grouped children with no prior formal musical training into a 15-month musical training group or a matched control group (Hyde et al. 2009), and found structural changes in the right primary auditory region that positively correlated with improvements in auditory-musical skills. Another line of evidence that supports the view of experience-dependent changes are studies that have demonstrated timbre-specificity enhancement of brain activity for instruments that the musician was trained with (e.g., Gebel et al. 2013; Pantev et al. 2001; Shahin et al. 2008; Strait et al. 2012). In these studies the experimental and control groups are formed by musicians with matched training profiles.

Assuming that neuroplasticity seen in musicians is indeed experience-dependent, an interesting, practically-relevant question is how long such plastic changes persist after musical training stops. A recent study from Skoe & Kraus (2012) addressed this question using a retrospective design. In their study, young adult participants were assigned into three groups based on self-report of years of formal instrumental music instruction: 0, 1–5, and 6–11 years. The individuals in both the musically trained groups started training at around 9 years of age, and had stopped training for an average of about 7 years and 3 years respectively. The two trained groups showed more robust FFRs to complex sounds relative to the untrained group. Moreover, the signal-to-noise ratio of the FFR negatively correlated with the number of years individuals had stopped instrumental training. These results suggest that a relatively short period of music training (3 years) during childhood alters brain networks, and such neural plastic changes persist in adulthood after auditory training has ceased (7 years later), but may fade over time to some extent.

Evidence reviewed thus far indicates a cross-domain benefit for musicians. With respect to speech processing, musicians have been shown to encode speech signals with higher fidelity, and also show behavioral advantages in speech processing under challenging listening environments as well as in learning new speech patterns. In the next section we critically discuss a recent proposal (the OPERA hypothesis) that discusses the mechanisms underlying the impact of music training on speech processing.

6.5 Neuroplasticity Associated with Music Training: A Theoretical Framework

Various frameworks have been proposed to delineate the mechanisms underlying the neuroplasticity associated with music training. For example, Kraus & Chandrasekaran (2010) hypothesized that the musician's brain is better able to track regularities in the incoming stimulus stream (e.g., speech sounds), and this is likely due to enhanced corticofugal function. Besson et al. (2011) suggest that music training enhances executive function (e.g., attention and working memory), which contributes to the transfer of training effects to the speech domain. While these hypotheses have provided important insights into understanding the transfer of training from music to speech, the recent OPERA (overlap, precision, emotion, repetition and attention) hypothesis presents itself as a broader theoretical approach that addresses the conditions that lead to music-related plasticity to speech signals. The OPERA hypothesis argues that music training enhances speech processing because (a) there is a significant overlap in the auditory and cognitive circuitry between the two domains (music and speech), (b) music training requires greater precision relative to speech, (c) music is inherently rewarding, (d) music training involves repetition and focused attention that is previously shown to be associated with neural plasticity (Patel 2011, 2012, 2014). Expanding on the OPERA hypothesis, a recent proposal suggests that an important determiner of cross-domain transfer is that music training places a greater demand on the common neural circuitry between music and speech (Patel 2014). The OPERA hypothesis is a more general theoretical framework relative to models developed by Besson and colleagues as well as Kraus and colleagues. The latter models have largely established reasons for specific empirical results. Therefore, the OPERA hypothesis provides a useful scaffolding to begin a more systematic study of the mechanisms underlying music training-related neuroplasticity (Kraus & Chandrasekaran 2010). In this section we critically evaluate the individual components of the OPERA hypothesis.

6.5.1 Overlap in Neural Circuitry vs Modular Processing

As per the OPERA hypothesis, a key reason for the domain-general transfer is the degree of neural overlap between music and speech during sensory and cognitive processing (Patel 2011). Here we critically examine this claim. In examining the extent of overlap between these two domains, we discuss the acoustic similarities between the two domains as well as the overlap in neural real-estate. Acoustically, both music and speech use pitch, timing and timbre cues to convey behavioral information (Barrett et al. 2013; Kraus 2012; Kraus & Chandrasekaran 2010). For example, in English, pitch is extensively used to convey intonational and emotional information. In tonal languages, apart from intonation, pitch movement within a syllable is also used to modify meaning. In tonal languages, pitch contours play a role similar to segmental (vowels and consonants) information. Critical timing information within the sound can also convey important cues for speech perception. The classic example is voice-onset-time, a feature that is important in distinguishing stop sounds such as /b/ and /p/. This is a timing-based feature that requires high temporal resolution – differences in the order of a few milliseconds can change the percept of a stop consonant. Timbre in speech is critical to differentiating talkers. Music also uses these three basic sound attributes to convey information (Patel 2011). However, note that a recent modification to the OPERA hypothesis argues that despite these essential commonalities between speech and music in terms of the use of pitch, timing and timbre cues, the relative use of these cues likely differs between the two domains (Patel 2012, 2014).

The alternative view, that music and speech are processed autonomously, has a rich and controversial history. Literatures in both music and speech have addressed issues related to modularity, that is, the extent to which autonomous perceptual-cognitive modules operate to process music/speech information (Liberman & Mattingly 1989; Peretz & Coltheart 2003). In the speech sciences, previous studies have argued that a "closed loop" phonetic module of sound localization is independent from "open loop" processing of pitch, timbre, and timing (Liberman & Mattingly 1989). Similarly, in the music domain Peretz & Coltheart (2003) argue for a partially dissociable modular network for processing music. They base their predictions on lesion studies that show spared musical abilities in individuals with brain lesions that affect speech and language. The findings that musicians have superior neural encoding of speech signals are not easily resolved by models that advocate significant modularity in brain processing. Similarly, speakers of a tone language show enhanced neural encoding of musical information, suggesting that the cross-domain transfer is not unidirectional (Bidelman et al. 2011a). These studies suggest neural circuitry that is not organized in as strictly hierarchical processing modules for music and speech, and that at least early in the neural processing of speech and music, there is overlap between domains. Figure 6.1, which is constructed from meta-analyses of neuroimaging studies on speech and

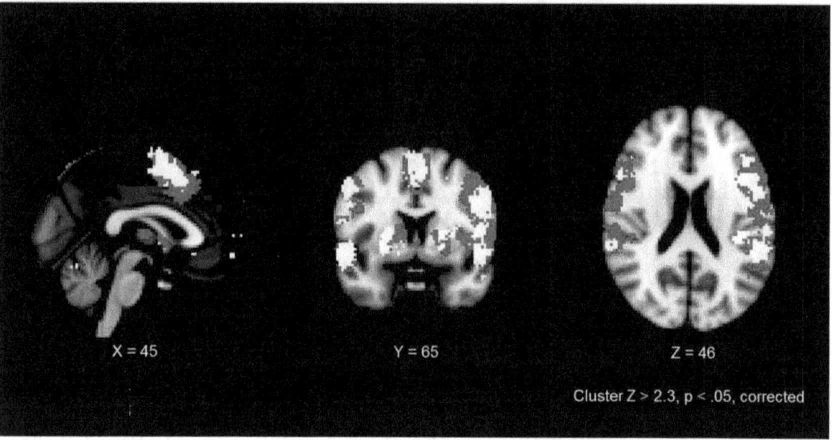

Figure 6.1. The database Neurosynth (http://neurosynth.org/) was used to conduct a meta-analysis of neuroimaging studies containing keywords music (white pixilated area, constructed from 59 studies) and speech (grey pixilated area, constructed from 133 studies). As seen from the figure, there is considerable overlap in the networks for music and speech. These overlaps can be seen in sensory (bilateral auditory cortex and thalamus) regions as well as regions associated with higher-level cognitive function (e.g. bilateral prefrontal cortex, medial frontal gyrus).

music, clearly shows an overlapping sensory-cognitive network underlying speech and music.

Does this mean there is no modularity during early auditory processing of speech or music signals? Examining the complexity of the auditory system may help us better inform this discussion. Sounds reach the external ear as longitudinal pressure waves and set the tympanic membrane into mechanical vibration. A transduction to a neural code occurs at the cochlea, which breaks down the complex signals by frequency. This neural code is processed at multiple auditory stages including the cochlear nucleus, lateral lemniscus, inferior colliculus, auditory thalamus and the auditory cortex. At the auditory cortex and beyond, the auditory object is reconstructed and processed by a complex cortical network that extracts meaning from the acoustic content (Pickles 1988). Given that music and speech are primarily auditory events that convey behaviorally-relevant information, the claim that there is substantial overlap in sensory circuitry is definitely true if the auditory system is strictly viewed as a hierarchical processor. However, a key feature of the auditory system that sets it apart from other sensory systems is the extent of top-down (corticofugal) connectivity (Suga 2008; Suga et al. 1997, 2000; Winer 2005; Winer et al. 1998). Through this extensive back-projection, the cortex has the capability of fine-grain control of the so-called "lower-level" auditory structures (Suga 2008). Animal models demonstrate that auditory signals deemed to be behaviorally-relevant are processed more efficiently by lower-level structures, a process that is actively driven by the cortex ("egocentric selection") (Suga 2008; Suga et al. 1997). When the cortex identifies the signal as music or speech, it is possible that the circuits are controlled in a manner that is domain-specific. The large overlap between the two domains (e.g., see Figure 6.1) seen in neuroimaging studies could simply be a resolution issue. The neuroimaging methodology, which relies on blood flow/oxygenation changes, may not have the resolution to capture the fine-grained dynamics of the neural code for speech or music. One possibility, not currently addressed by the OPERA hypothesis, is that the influence of music training may not be a result of shared sensory/cognitive substrates (Chandrasekaran et al. 2013). Rather, years of music training could hone in the efficiency of the top-down corticofugal circuitry that aids in the "clean-up" of the incoming sounds as a form of egocentric selection (ibid.). Consistent with this view, neural encoding of speech signals in musicians and non-musicians are similar in quiet conditions (Parbery-Clark et al. 2009a). It is possible therefore that the neural representation of speech is similar in musicians and non-musicians, but the ability to "clean up" the signal in adverse listening conditions differ between the two groups. This proposal invokes both overlap as well as a certain degree of modularity. The initial sensory circuitry activated may be related to the acoustics (domain-general). Once the domain is established (i.e., music vs speech) at the cortex (i.e., after the auditory object is constructed), the top-down circuitry may activate more domain-specific modules. The functioning of the top-down corticofugal circuitry may be superior in musicians, as a consequence of years of focused attention to sound.

6.5.2 Precision

The original OPERA hypothesis posited that music demanded greater auditory precision within the shared neural circuitry. Therefore, the greater rigor required translates to enhanced encoding of speech signals in musicians. Relative to most musical instruments, the range and variability in human speech acoustics is staggering. The human vocal tract, for example, can be likened to a highly irregular shaped, dynamically changing resonator. Given the complexity and variability in vocal fold/tract size and shape in humans, speech acoustics are inherently variable across talkers and contexts. Thus, computationally the brain is required to tolerate a large amount of variability and compromise on precision during speech perception. In fact, as classic "categorical perception" experiments demonstrate, expert listeners lose sensitivity to fine-grained acoustics (e.g., MacKain et al. 1981). Instead, speech categories dominate perception even if the acoustic cues are only in the ball-park. Contrast this to music – in tuning a violin, the musician needs to be acoustically precise. So the tenet that precision is of greater need in music is indeed possible. As discussed before, several studies have demonstrated minute differences in sensory encoding between musicians and non-musicians (e.g., neural encoding advantages in the order of few milliseconds). Whether such a small enhancement in precision is epiphenomenal and at all useful to speech perception is still unresolved. One possibility is that this improved precision in early sensory coding may simply be an incidental consequence of enhanced corticofugal tuning in musicians and may not have a functional role in speech perception.

6.5.3 Emotion, Repetition and Attention

These components within the OPERA hypothesis are not specific to music training, but are argued to be important conditions under which music results in neuroplasticity. The OPERA hypothesis argues that music is inherently rewarding and engages the reward learning circuitry, resulting in dopamine release. However, the studies that demonstrate the activation of the reward circuitry in music were conducted in non-musicians (Salimpoor et al. 2009, 2011, 2013). Therefore, it is unclear whether musicians, who process music more analytically, derive the same benefits as non-musicians. The argument here is not that music is rewarding – indeed, the socio-cultural appeal and universality of music argues that it is. But whether the reward circuitry is more engaged (or more consistently engaged as a function of training) in musicians is still an unanswered empirical question. One possibility is that learning to play a musical instrument and the instant feedback from playing an instrument engages the reward circuitry more consistently. Further studies will be needed to validate this prediction.

The extent to which focused attention is important for speech is also an unresolved question. Speech in infancy as well as adulthood is optimally learned through implicit learning mechanisms (Chandrasekaran et al. 2014). Focused attention may negatively impact speech learning by not allowing the implicit learning system to operate effectively (Maddox et al. 2013). In contrast to learning speech, extracting speech under challenging listening environments is an effortful task, and may indeed require selective attention, but whether music "trains up" the specific cognitive circuitry involved in parsing out speech under challenging listening conditions is unclear. One of the main functions of the corticofugal system may be to enhance the signal-to-noise of the incoming sensory stimuli (Luo et al. 2008). The superior performance in speech-in-noise tasks may therefore reflect a higher-functioning corticofugal circuitry, rather than general attentional processes.

6.6 Neuroplasticity Associated with Music Training: Specificity

We began this chapter with the practical implications of music therapy. In reviewing the vast literature on the topic, there is converging evidence from a variety of neuroimaging methods that intense music training results in changes in neural structure and function. However, a marginal number of these studies implemented longitudinal, randomized control experimental designs. To confirm that music training, and not a general predisposition, drives brain plasticity, it is imperative for future investigations to implement more stringent experimental methodology. Moreover, in order to better prescribe music training as a rehabilitation measure or a means of enhancing speech processing, an important confirmation to make is that music training is *better* or at least comparable to available evidence-based training procedures. The current control guidelines applied to test music training benefit consist of a rudimentary criterion: no-training or experience with a non-auditory training task (e.g. drama lessons). Therefore, the control group that music training needs to be tested against should not broadly be non-musicians, but rather non-musicians who have spent an equivalent amount of focused time on another challenging auditory task. Both music training and linguistic training studies have demonstrated gains in functional speech and language. Therefore, having a clearer definition of a non-musician control group has practical implications. For example, to improve speech perception, should a therapist simply focus on speech perception, or will music training be more effective? Or perhaps a "cocktail" of training methods that include music training?

What is then an appropriate "control" group that musicianship can be contrasted with? We propose linguistic training as a viable alternative treatment for music training to be tested against. Similar to studies investigating the effects of intensive music training, significant evidence reveals that highly proficient bilingual speakers experience enhanced structural and functional changes in the brain. This has been revealed through studies that indicate enhanced neural encoding of fundamental frequency in highly proficient bilinguals at the level of the brainstem (Krizman et al. 2012); cognitive reserve from neurodegenerative disorders, as shown in the delayed onset of symptoms related to dementia in elderly lifelong bilingual speaking populations (Bialystok et al. 2007; Schweizer et al. 2012); as well as higher-level cognitive gains in executive function, as demonstrated through enhanced selective attention task performance in highly proficient bilinguals relative to monolingual counterparts (Krizman et al. 2012).

Within the theoretical framework of OPERA, the overlap between two languages is greater than the overlap between music and speech; spoken language is emotive and is strongly associated with the striatal reward circuitry. Learning a second language is an effortful process and requires sustained attention and repetition. However, music may require a greater degree of focused auditory attention and repetition. It is important to note here another profound similarity between bilingualism and musicianship, and that is that both categories cannot be considered as binary measures. Many factors contribute to the level of attention and focus that are exerted by a member of either group. For example, the context in which the musician plays, just as the context in which the bilingual speaks, has a role in attention and greater executive function ability.

Based upon the current similarities in cognitive benefit evidence found across both populations, future investigations should examine the short-term benefit of music training, relative to the short-term benefit of linguistic training. These studies should additionally take significant consideration in clearly defining targeted populations of musicians and bilinguals in order to control for: age of onset, level of proficiency, daily use etc. This experimental design has the potential to further facilitate understanding of the specific mechanisms underlying training-related neuroplasticity and cognitive function gains.

6.7 Neuroplasticity Associated with Music Training: Conclusion and Future Directions

Music training has significant promise as a neuroprotective and a rehabilitative tool for a wide range of populations. However, on a cautionary note, it is critical that we first have a better understanding of the mechanisms underlying the specific effects of music training. To do this, it is imperative that an operational definition of "musician" is further refined (Levitin 2012), along with the definition of "non-musician." By comparing groups of participants with enriched relative to impoverished music training, we are likely *exaggerating* the effects of musicianship. Current neuroscience research has primarily focused on individuals who have undertaken private music lessons outside of the school curriculum. Therefore, a gap in knowledge remains regarding the effects of school music training on neuroplasticity and cognitive control. Private music instruction is expensive and this criterion for musicianship may result in discrepancies in socioeconomic status, a factor that is known to modulate brain plasticity on its own, and is rarely controlled in studies comparing musicians and non-musicians.

In conclusion, the last 10 years have seen stimulated interest in the topic of the impact of music on brain plasticity and cognitive function, both among scientists and the general public. These brain changes likely lead to enhanced music processing, but also to advantages outside the domain of music (e.g., speech processing). However, currently there is a dearth of evidence demonstrating *non-laboratory* transfer of short-term music training benefits to long-term gains in other domains, such as those responsible for speech and cognitive control. Future work will need to address the neural mechanisms underlying brain plasticity related to music training as well as develop more refined operational definitions of musicianship.

Acknowledgments

Research reported in this publication was supported by the National Institute on Deafness and Other Communication Disorders of the National Institutes of Health under Award Number R01DC013315 (awarded to BC). The content is solely the responsibility of the authors and does not necessarily represent the official views of the National Institutes of Health.

Appendix. Summary of studies examining the effects of musical expertise on brain plasticity.

Focused topics	Study	Definition of musicians						Definition of non-musicians		Main findings related to the focused topic
		Age (mean ± SD, range etc.)	Onset of training (mean ± SD, range etc.)	Daily or weekly training time (mean ± SD, range etc.)	Total years of training (mean ± SD, range etc.)	Music types	Instrument types (if instrumentalists)	Age (mean ± SD, range etc.)	Definition	
Cortical structural plasticity	Bermudez & Zatorre (2005)	N/A	N/A	N/A	> = 10 years	N/A	N/A	NA	No specific definition	Greater gray matter concentration in planum temporale in AP and non-AP musicians than non-musicians
	Keenan et al. (2001)	AP Musicians: 26.74 ± 6.73 years	5.06 ± 1.14 years	N/A	21.68 ± 6.55 years	Instrumentalist	Mainly keyboard, some also string instruments	24.89 ± 5.75 years	No formal musical training or never having played a musical instrument	Stronger leftward planum temporale asymmetry and smaller right planum temporale size for AP musicians than non-musicians or non-AP musicians
		Non-AP Musicians: 26.32 ± 9.94 years	5.09 ± 0.97 years	N/A	21.23 ± 9.92 years	N/A	N/A			
	Schlaug et al. (1995)	AP Musicians: 27 ± 5 years	N/A	N/A	N/A	N/A	N/A	26 ± 3 years	NA	Stronger leftward planum temporale asymmetry for AP musicians than non-musicians or non-AP musicians; larger left planum temporal size for musicians than non-musicians
		Non-AP Musicians: 26 ± 4 years	N/A	N/A	N/A	N/A	N/A			
	Zatorre et al. (1998)	AP Musicians: 24.5 ± 4.1 years	N/A	N/A	18.2 ± 6.3 years	N/A	N/A	N/A	N/A	A larger left planum temporale in AP musicians than non-AP musicians
		Non-AP Musicians: 24.8 ± 6.6 years	N/A	N/A	13.1 ± 6.9 years	N/A	N/A			

Focused topics	Study	Definition of musicians						Definition of non-musicians		Main findings related to the focused topic
		Age (mean ± SD, range etc.)	Onset of training (mean ± SD, range etc.)	Daily or weekly training time (mean ± SD, range etc.)	Total years of training (mean ± SD, range etc.)	Music types	Instrument types (if instrumentalists)	Age (mean ± SD, range etc.)	Definition	
	Bermudez et al. (2009)	AP Musicians: 23.2 ± 3.5 years	5.4 ± 1.7 years	15.4 ± 10.5 hours/week	17.0 ± 3.9 years	Instrumentalist	N/A	24.4 ± 4.9 years	< = 3 years of musical training	Greater right-lateralized gray matter concentration in postero-lateral Heschl's gyrus in musicians than non-musicians
		Non-AP Musicians: 23.2 ± 3.9 years	7.6 ± 3.2 years	13.9 ± 9.7 hours/week	15.0 ± 4.3 years	Instrumentalist	N/A			
	Gaser & Schlaug (2003)	Professional Musicians: 23.5 ± 3.83 years	6.0 ± 1.81 years	2.23 ± 0.91 hours/day	average 17.5 years	Instrumentalist	Keyboard	26.92 ± 4.90 years	Never having played a musical instrument	Increased gray matter volume in motor, auditory (including left Heschl's gyrus) and visual–spatial brain regions for professional musicians than for amateur musicians and non-musicians
		Amateur Musicians: 25.95 ± 5.61 years	7.65 ± 4.17 years	1.15 ± 1.0 hours/day	average 15.5 years					
	Hyde et al. (2009)	6.32 ± 0.82 years at the start of study	6.32 ± 0.82 years	0.5 hour/week	15 months	Private instrumental training	Keyboard	5.9 ± 0.54 years at the start of study	Never having received any instrumental musical training during the 15 months period, but participated in a weekly 40 min group music class in school consisting of singing and playing with drums and bells	After training, greater relative voxel size in motors areas, such as the right precentral gyrus, and corpus callosum, as well as in the right lateral aspect of Heschl's gyrus were found for musical trained group than the control group. These changes correlated with behavioral improvements on motor and auditory-musical tests

Focused topics	Study	Definition of musicians						Definition of non-musicians		Main findings related to the focused topic
		Age (mean ± SD, range etc.)	Onset of training (mean ± SD, range etc.)	Daily or weekly training time (mean ± SD, range etc.)	Total years of training (mean ± SD, range etc.)	Music types	Instrument types (if instrumentalists)	Age (mean ± SD, range etc.)	Definition	
	Schneider et al. (2002)	Professional Musicians: 29–55 years	N/A	N/A	N/A	With a diploma in music education and actively performing when tested	N/A	26–43 years	Never having played a musical instrument other than school musical education	Greater gray matter volume in the antero-medial portion of Heschl's gyrus for musicians than non-musicians
		Amateur Musicians: 24–62 years	N/A	N/A	N/A	Received special instruction in one or more musical instruments.	N/A			
Cortical functional plasticity	Baumann et al. (2008)	25.6 ± 3.4 years	7.7 ± 2.7 years	1–5 hours/day	N/A	Most of the musicians played multiple instruments	Piano, violin, trumpetand saxophone	26.2 ± 1.5 years	No formal musical training and no history of musical instrument performance	Enhanced cortical N1 responses to instrumental sounds and sinusoidal sounds in musicians than non-musicians
	Meyer et al. (2011)	10 ± 1.61 years	4.80 ± 1.46 years	217.22 ± 116.26 mins/week	5.19 ± 1.46 years	Instrumentalist	Violin	9.78 ± 1.62	Most had not received formal instrumental education; none played violin	Enhanced MMN responses to violin tones for musicians than non-musicians, and diminished MMN responses to sinusoidal tones for musicians than non-musicians
	Pantev et al. (1998)	AP Musicians: 29 ± 6 years	N/A	27 ± 14 hours/week in the 5 years preceding the study	21 ± 6 years	Instrumentalist	Piano, woodwind and strings	26 ± 4 years	Never having played a musical instrument	Larger cortical representations for piano tones, but not for pure tones was found in musicians than non-musicians; this increment was associated with onset of musical training; no differences between AP and non-AP musicians
		Non-AP Musicians: 26 ± 5 years	N/A	23 ± 12 hours/week in the 5 years preceding the study	15 ± 3 years					

Focused topics	Study	Definition of musicians						Definition of non-musicians		Main findings related to the focused topic
		Age (mean ± SD, range etc.)	Onset of training (mean ± SD, range etc.)	Daily or weekly training time (mean ± SD, range etc.)	Total years of training (mean ± SD, range etc.)	Music types	Instrument types (if instrumentalists)	Age (mean ± SD, range etc.)	Definition	
	Pantev et al., (2001)	Violinists: 23.8 ± 2.8 years	N/A	24.9 ± 13.1 hours/ week in the 5 years preceding the study	15.1 ± 3.3 years	Instrumentalist	Violin and piano	N/A	N/A	For each group, N1m responses were larger for timbres of the trained instrument; N1m responses to instrumental tones were larger than that of pure sine tones in both groups
		Trumpeters: 26.8 ± 3.0 years	N/A	18.4 ± 8.0 hours/ week in the 5 years preceding the study	15.3 ± 3.2 years		Trumpet and piano			
	Shahin et al. (2003)	Violinists: 24.3 ± 2.2 years	N/A	34.7 ± 20.8 hours/ week	17 ± 3.7 years	Instrumentalist	Violin	22.2 ± 3.4 years	No formal musical training and no history of musical instrument performance	Larger N1c and P2 responses to three types of tonal stimuli (violin tones, piano tones, and pure tones) for both musician groups relative to non-musicians
		Pianists: 23 ± 2.5 years	N/A	17.9 ± 11.1 hours/ week	16.6 ± 4.0 years		Piano			
	Shahin et al. (2007)	28 ± 8 years	7 ± 3 years	9 ± 5 hours/week for principle instrument	15 ± 7 years	Instrumentalist	Piano, flute and percussion	29 ± 4 years	No formal musical training and no history of musical instrument performance	Auditory evoked responses in the anterior temporal cortex to instrumental tones are larger in musicians than non-musicians
	Koelsch et al. (1999)	23–27 years	N/A	N/A	> = 12 years	Instrumentalist	Violin	19–26 years	No musical expertise	Occurrence of MMN responses to deviant major chords in musicians but not in non-musicians
	Fujioka et al. (2004)	19–33 years	N/A	N/A	10–23 years	Instrumentalist	N/A	19–40 years	Almost no musical training other than school musical lessons	Larger MMNm responses to deviant melodic contour and interval structure in musicians than non-musicians

Focused topics	Study	Definition of musicians						Definition of non-musicians		Main findings related to the focused topic
		Age (mean ± SD, range etc.)	Onset of training (mean ± SD, range etc.)	Daily or weekly training time (mean ± SD, range etc.)	Total years of training (mean ± SD, range etc.)	Music types	Instrument types (if instrumentalists)	Age (mean ± SD, range etc.)	Definition	
	Fujioka et al. (2005)	20–35 years	N/A	N/A	> = 10 years	Instrumentalist	N/A	23–34 years	Almost no musical training other than school musical lessons	Larger MMNm responses to deviant polyphonic melodies in musicians than non-musicians
	Magne et al. (2006)	8 ± 1 years	N/A	3–4 hours/week	4 ± 1 years	Instrumentalist	Violin, guitar, flute, clarinet, harp and piano	8 ± 1 years	No musical training but having had other regular extracurricular activities	The occurrence of early negative ERP responses to weakly incongruent melodies and late positive ERP responses to weakly incongruent pitch in sentences was only found in musicians
	Moreno et al. (2009)	101.1 ± 4.3 months at the start of study	101.1 ± 4.3 months	75 mins/week	24 weeks	Musical training based on a combination of Kodaly, Orff and Wuytack methodologies and included training on rhythm, melody, harmony and timbre	N/A	98.8 ± 4.7 months at the start of study	Painting training	Improved the amplitude of the N300 responses to weakly incongruent melodies and sentences was found in the musical training group, but not in the painting training group
	Seppänen et al. (2012a)	25 ± 5 years	8 ± 3 years	N/A	Average 17 years	Instrumentalist	N/A	24 ± 3 years	None having had professional music training; Most had played a instrument over a year during school; Some currently playing 0.5–1 hour/week	Enhanced rapid plasticity of N1 and P2 response to harmonically rich tones in musicians than non-musicians

Focused topics	Study	Definition of musicians						Definition of non-musicians		Main findings related to the focused topic
		Age (mean ± SD, range etc.)	Onset of training (mean ± SD, range etc.)	Daily or weekly training time (mean ± SD, range etc.)	Total years of training (mean ± SD, range etc.)	Music types	Instrument types (if instrumentalists)	Age (mean ± SD, range etc.)	Definition	
	Seppänen et al. (2012b)	21–39 years	8 ± 3 years	4–28 hours/week	Average 17 years	Instrumentalist	N/A	19–31 years	None having had professional music training; most had played a instrument over a year during school; some currently playing 0.5–1 hour/week	Enhanced short-term plasticity of P3a/P3b to harmonically rich sounds in musicians than non-musicians
	Herholz et al. (2009)	25.6 ± 3.4 years	N/A	N/A	> = 10 years	Instrumentalist	N/A	27 ± 2.4 years	< = 2 years of musical training other than school music education	More leftward-lateralized MMN responses to deviant tone sequence patterns in musicians than non-musicians
	van Zuijen et al. (2004)	22–28 years	4–3 years	Average 4.2 hours/day	Average 4 years	Instrumentalist; having reached at least the level of acceptance into a music academy	N/A	19–26 years	Never received formal musical training; None played an instrument on a daily basis at the time of study; Some played an instrument as an amateur	The occurrence of MMN responses to tone sequences that can be grouped based on pitch continuation was found in musicians, but not in non-musicians
	van Zuijen et al. (2005)	Average 24.7 years	Average 6 years	4 hours/day	Average 7 years	Instrumentalist; having reached at least the level of acceptance into a music academy	Piano, flute, organ, bassoon and guitar	Average 21.8 years	Never received formal musical training; never played an instrument at a professional level; most had received school music lessons	The occurrence of MMN responses to violations of the numerical regularity in tone sequences was found in musicians, but not in non-musicians

Focused topics	Study	Definition of musicians						Definition of non-musicians		Main findings related to the focused topic
		Age (mean ± SD, range etc.)	Onset of training (mean ± SD, range etc.)	Daily or weekly training time (mean ± SD, range etc.)	Total years of training (mean ± SD, range etc.)	Music types	Instrument types (if instrumentalists)	Age (mean ± SD, range etc.)	Definition	
	Fujioka et al. (2006)	Average 65.7 month at the start of study	Average 65.7 month at the start of study	N/A	0.75–2.5 months	Attended Suzuki music schools	Violin and piano	Average 66.7 month at the start of study	No music lessons outside of school	Larger and earlier N250m peak in the left hemisphere in response to the violin sounds in musically trained group than untrained children; pronounced morphological change in musically trained children but only with violin stimuli; comparable changes were present in the untrained group regardless of stimulus type
	Lappe et al. (2008)	24–38 years	N/A	25 mins/day	8 days within two weeks	No formal musical training before study other than compulsory school lessons; trained to play a musical sequence on the piano	Piano	24–38 years	No formal musical training before study other than compulsory school lessons; trained to listen to and judge the sequence played by the participants from the musician group	Enhanced MMNm responses to piano sequences in the musically trained group than the untrained group

Focused topics	Study	Definition of musicians						Definition of non-musicians		Main findings related to the focused topic
		Age (mean ± SD, range etc.)	Onset of training (mean ± SD, range etc.)	Daily or weekly training time (mean ± SD, range etc.)	Total years of training (mean ± SD, range etc.)	Music types	Instrument types (if instrumentalists)	Age (mean ± SD, range etc.)	Definition	
	Lappe et al. (2011)	24–38 years	N/A	30 mins/day	8 days within two weeks	No formal musical training before study other than compulsory school lessons; trained to play a musical sequence on the piano	Piano	24–38 years	No formal musical training before study other than compulsory school lessons; trained to listen to and judge the sequence played by the partici-pants from the musician group	Enhanced MMN and P2 responses to piano sequences in the musi-cally trained group than the untrained group
	Shahin et al. (2008)	Violinists: 24.3 ± 2.2 years	N/A	34.6 ± 20.8 hours/week	17 ± 3.7 years	Instrumentalist	Violin	22.2 ± 3.4 years	No formal musi-cal training	Enlargement of induced gamma band activity specifically to their instrument of practice in adult and child musicians; more pronounced evoked gamma band activity in adult musicians than adult non-musicians
		Pianists: 23 ± 2.5 years	N/A	17.9 ± 11.1 hours/week	16.6 ± 4.0 years		Piano			
		Suzuki children: 4.6 ± 0.4 years at the start of study	N/A	N/A	N/A	N/A	N/A	4.8 ± 0.4 years		
	Chobert et al. (2011)	9.4 ± 1.4 years	N/A	N/A	4 ± 1 years	Instrumentalist	Violin, piano, string-bass, oboe, flute, cello and horn	9.0 ± 1.6 years	No formal musical training other than school music classes	Larger MMN responses to duration and VOT deviants in CV syllables in musicians than non-musicians
	Kühnis et al. (2013)	24.7 ± 6.8 years	5.56 ± 1.44 years	2.79 hours/day	N/A	Instrumentalist	Violin, viola and cello	27.0 ± 8.2 years	No formal musi-cal education	Increased MMN responses to spectral and temporal variations (VOT and duration) in CV syllables in musicians

Focused topics	Study	Definition of musicians						Definition of non-musicians		Main findings related to the focused topic
		Age (mean ± SD, range etc.)	Onset of training (mean ± SD, range etc.)	Daily or weekly training time (mean ± SD, range etc.)	Total years of training (mean ± SD, range etc.)	Music types	Instrument types (if instrumentalists)	Age (mean ± SD, range etc.)	Definition	
	Marie et al. (2011)	24 ± 2.6 years	7 ± 1.6 years	N/A	16 ± 3.8 years	Instrumentalist	Saxophone, guitar bass, accordion, double bass, violin, piano, flute, bassoon, clarinet, organ and harp	23 ± 1.9 years	No formal musical training other than school music classes; none played an instrument	Larger and earlier N2/N3 responses to tonal variations in Mandarin Chinese were found in musicians than non-musicians; enhanced P3b responses to both tonal and segmental variations in musicians than in non-musicians
	Marques et al. (2007)	38.33 ± 14 years	N/A	N/A	> = 14 years	Instrumentalist	N/A	26.61 ± 2.08 years	No formal musical training; not music-lovers	Enhanced and earlier responses to weakly pitch violations in Portuguese sentences were found in musicians than non-musicians
	Schön et al.(2004)	Average 31 years	N/A	N/A	Average 15 years	N/A	N/A	Average 31 years	N/A	Larger and earlier responses to music and language pitch deviants in musicians than non-musicians; distinct scalp distribution of an early negativity in the linguistic tasks for both groups: largest over temporal sites bilaterally for musicians, and largest centrally and over left temporal sites for non-musicians

Focused topics	Study	Definition of musicians						Definition of non-musicians		Main findings related to the focused topic
		Age (mean ± SD, range etc.)	Onset of training (mean ± SD, range etc.)	Daily or weekly training time (mean ± SD, range etc.)	Total years of training (mean ± SD, range etc.)	Music types	Instrument types (if instrumentalists)	Age (mean ± SD, range etc.)	Definition	
Sub-Cortical Functional Plasticity	Bidelman et al. (2011c)	22.63 ± 2.15 years	8.7 ± 1.4 years	N/A	12.4 ± 1.8 years	Instrumentalist; with formal private or group lessons for the past 5 years before the study; current playing	Trumpet, piano, saxophone, guitar, clarinet, violin, string bass, trombone, tuba and bassoon	22.82 ± 3.40 years	< = 1 year of formal music training on any combination of instruments; not having received any music instruction within the past 5 years before the study	Faster and stronger brainstem responses to the third of the triadic arpeggios regardless whether the sequence was in or out of tune were found in musicians than non-musicians; stronger brainstem encoding for the tuned than the detuned chords in musicians than non-musicians
	Bidelman et al. (2011a)	23.2 ± 2.3 years	7.8 ± 2.3 years	N/A	12.2 ± 2.4 years	Instrumentalist; with formal private or group lessons for the past 5 years before the study; current playing	Trumpet, piano, saxophone, guitar, violin, string bass and trombone	24.7 ± 2.9 years	< = 3 years of formal music training on any combination of instruments; not having received any music instruction within the past 5 years before the study	Higher pitch-tracking accuracy to in musicians than non-musicians to iterated rippled noise homologues of a musical pitch interval and a lexical tone; more robust pitch strength in musicians than non-musicians
	Lee et al. (2009)	Average 25.8 years	< = 7 years	N/A	> = 10 years	Instrumentalists and vocalists	Piano and violin	Average 23.5 years	< 3 years of musical training	Enhanced responses to the harmonics of the upper tone in a musical interval in musicians than non-musicians; more precise encoding of temporal envelop in musicians than non-musicians

Focused topics	Study	Definition of musicians						Definition of non-musicians		Main findings related to the focused topic
		Age (mean ± SD, range etc.)	Onset of training (mean ± SD, range etc.)	Daily or weekly training time (mean ± SD, range etc.)	Total years of training (mean ± SD, range etc.)	Music types	Instrument types (if instrumentalists)	Age (mean ± SD, range etc.)	Definition	
	Wong et al. (2007)	N/A	< = 12 years	N/A	> = 6 years	Instrumentalists and vocalists	Clarinet, piano and trumpet	N/A	< = 3 years of musical training	More robust and faithful encoding of lexical tones in musicians than non-musicians
	Parbery-Clark et al. (2012a)	55.2 ± 4.97 years	< 9 years	A minimum of 3 times a week engaged in musical activities (practice, performance, or teaching	Average 49 years	Instrumentalists	Violin, piano, French horn, cello, viola, saxophone, clarinet and trombone	57.3 ± 5.39 years	< 4 years of musical training	Higher brainstem encoding of speech in quiet and noise conditions in musicians than non-musicians, which included faster neural response timing, higher neural response consistency, more robust encoding of speech harmonics, and greater neural precision
	Parbery-Clark et al. (2012b)	Young musicians: 18–32 years Older musicians: 45–65 years	< 9 years	A minimum of 3 times a week engaged in musical activities (practice, performance or teaching	N/A	N/A	N/A	18–32 years 45–65 years	< 3 years of musical training	Age-related delay in brainstem response timing to the formant transition in CV syllables was reduced in musicians
	Bidelman & Krishnan (2010)	22.4 ± 2.0 years	7.8 ± 1.6 years	N/A	12.0 ± 1.8 years	Instrumentalist; with formal private or group lessons for the past 5 years before the study; current playing	Piano, saxophone, viola, trumpet, clarinet, guitar and flute	22.0 ± 2.7 years	< = 3 years of formal music training on any combination of instruments; not having received any music instruction within the past 5 years before the study	More robust brainstem encoding of F1 harmonics and F0 in musicians in all quiet and all reverberation settings in musicians than non-musicians; this neural enhancement related to behavioral performances about discrimination of vowel pitch and first formant

Focused topics	Study	Definition of musicians						Definition of non-musicians		Main findings related to the focused topic
		Age (mean ± SD, range etc.)	Onset of training (mean ± SD, range etc.)	Daily or weekly training time (mean ± SD, range etc.)	Total years of training (mean ± SD, range etc.)	Music types	Instrument types (if instrumentalists)	Age (mean ± SD, range etc.)	Definition	
	Parbery-Clark et al. (2012c)	18–32 years	5.14 ± 1.03 years	A minimum of three times a week engaged in musical activities	15.9 ± 4.0 years	Instrumentalists	Bassoon, piano, cello, flute, horn, percussion and violin	18–32 years	< 3 years of musical training	Improved subcortical discrimination of closely related speech sounds in terms of response timing was found in musicians relative to non-musicians; this neural distinction linked with the ability to perceive speech in noise
	Strait et al. (2013)	Adult musicians: 18–30 years	5.4 ± 0.75 years	Weekly instruction average 1.12 hours/week; > = 3 days/week for > = 1 hour/session	16.7 ± 3.5 years	Instrumentalists	N/A	18–30 years	< 3 years of musical training	Musicians demonstrated improved neural differentiation of stop consonants early in life even with as little as a few years of training; this distinction associated with auditory working memory and attention
		School-aged musicians: 7–13 years	4.9 ± 0.81 years	Weekly instruction average 1.12 hours/week; > = 20 mins/day for 5 days/week	7.2 ± 2.43 years			7–13 years		
		Pre-school musicians: 3–5 years	N/A	Weekly instruction average 1.12 hours/week; home practice > = 4 days/week	3.3 ± 1.6 years			3–5 years	No musical training during the year of study; < 6 months of musical training in their lives	
	Parbery-Clark et al. (2011b)	18–30 years	5 1 ± 1.2years	N/A	16.4 ± 3.4 years	Instrumentalists	N/A	18–30 years	< 3 years of musical training	Musicians demonstrated enhanced neural responses to fundamental frequency in a predictable compared to a variable context; this enhancement in neural sensitivity relates to the ability to perceive speech in noise

Abbreviations: AP = absolute pitch; MMN = mismatch negativity; MMNm = magnetic mismatch negativity; N/A = no available information.

References

Accordino, R., R. Comer & W.B. Heller. (2007). Searching for music's potential: A critical examination of research on music therapy with individuals with autism. *Research in Autism Spectrum Disorders*, 1(1), 101–15. http://dx.doi.org/10.1016/j.rasd.2006.08.002

American Music Therapy Association (AMTA) (2014). Definition and Quotes about Music Therapy. From http://www.musictherapy.org/about/quotes/

Barrett, K.C., R. Ashley, D.L. Strait & N. Kraus. (2013). Art and science: How musical training shapes the brain. *Frontiers in Psychology*, 4, 713. http://dx.doi.org/10.3389/fpsyg.2013.00713

Baumann, S., M. Meyer & L. Jäncke. (2008). Enhancement of auditory-evoked potentials in musicians reflects an influence of expertise but not selective attention. *Journal of Cognitive Neuroscience*, 20(12), 2238–49. http://dx.doi.org/10.1162/jocn.2008.20157

Bermudez, P., J.P. Lerch, A.C. Evans & R.J. Zatorre. (2009). Neuroanatomical correlates of musicianship as revealed by cortical thickness and voxel-based morphometry. [Research Support, Non-U.S. Govt]. *Cerebral Cortex*, 19(7), 1583–96. http://dx.doi.org/10.1093/cercor/bhn196

Bermudez, P., & R.J. Zatorre. (2005). Differences in gray matter between musicians and nonmusicians. [Research Support, Non-U.S. Govt]. *Annals of the New York Academy of Sciences*, 1060(1), 395–99. http://dx.doi.org/10.1196/annals.1360.057

Besson, M., J. Chobert & C. Marie. (2011). Transfer of training between music and speech: Common processing, attention, and memory. *Frontiers in Psychology*, 2. doi: Artn 94. Doi 10.3389/Fpsyg.2011.00094

Bialystok, E., F.I. Craik & M. Freedman. (2007). Bilingualism as a protection against the onset of symptoms of dementia. *Neuropsychologia*, 45(2), 459–64.

Bidelman, G.M., J.T. Gandour & A. Krishnan. (2011a). Cross-domain effects of music and language experience on the representation of pitch in the human auditory brainstem. *Journal of Cognitive Neuroscience*, 23(2), 425–34. http://dx.doi.org/10.1162/jocn.2009.21362

Bidelman, G.M., J.T. Gandour & A. Krishnan. (2011b). Musicians demonstrate experience-dependent brainstem enhancement of musical scale features within continuously gliding pitch. [Research Support, N.I.H., Extramural]. *Neuroscience Letters*, 503(3), 203–7. http://dx.doi.org/10.1016/j.neulet.2011.08.036

Bidelman, G.M., & A. Krishnan. (2010). Effects of reverberation on brainstem representation of speech in musicians and non-musicians. [Comparative Study Research Support, N.I.H., Extramural]. *Brain Research*, 1355, 112–25. http://dx.doi.org/10.1016/j.brainres.2010.07.100

Bidelman, G.M., A. Krishnan & J.T. Gandour. (2011c). Enhanced brainstem encoding predicts musicians' perceptual advantages with pitch. [Research Support, N.I.H., Extramural]. *European Journal of Neuroscience*, 33(3), 530–8. http://dx.doi.org/10.1111/j.1460-9568.2010.07527.x

Chan, A.S., Y.C. Ho & M.C. Cheung. (1998). Music training improves verbal memory. *Nature*, 396(6707), 128. http://dx.doi.org/10.1038/24075

Chandrasekaran, B., & N. Kraus. (2010). Music, noise-exclusion, and learning. *Music Perception*, 27(4), 297–306. http://dx.doi.org/10.1525/mp.2010.27.4.297

Chandrasekaran, B., E. Skoe & N. Kraus, N. (2013). An integrative model of subcortical auditory plasticity. *Brain Topography*, 27(4), 539–52. http://dx.doi.org/10.1007/s10548-013-0323-9

Chandrasekaran, B., H.G. Yi & W.T. Maddox. (2014). Dual-learning systems during speech category learning. *Psychonomic Bulletin & Review*, 21(2), 488–95. http://dx.doi.org/10.3758/s13423-013-0501-5

Chobert, J., C. Marie, C. François, D. Schön & M. Besson. (2011). Enhanced passive and active processing of syllables in musician children. *Journal of Cognitive Neuroscience*, 23(12), 3874–87. http://dx.doi.org/10.1162/jocn_a_00088

Cooper, A., & Y. Wang. (2012). The influence of linguistic and musical experience on Cantonese word learning. [Research Support, Non-U.S. Govt]. *Journal of the Acoustical Society of America*, 131(6), 4756–69. http://dx.doi.org/10.1121/1.4714355

Evans, D. (2002). The effectiveness of music as an intervention for hospital patients: A systematic review. *Journal of Advanced Nursing*, 37(1), 8–18. http://dx.doi.org/10.1046/j.1365-2648.2002.02052.x

Farmer, M.E., & R.M. Klein. (1995). The evidence for a temporal processing deficit linked to dyslexia: A review. *Psychonomic Bulletin & Review*, 2(4), 460–93. http://dx.doi.org/10.3758/BF03210983

François, C., B. Tillmann & D. Schön. (2012). Cognitive and methodological considerations on the effects of musical expertise on speech segmentation. [Research Support, Non-U.S. Gov't Review]. *Annals of the New York Academy of Sciences*, 1252(1), 108–15. http://dx.doi.org/10.1111/j.1749-6632.2011.06395.x

Fujioka, T., B. Ross, R. Kakigi, C. Pantev & L.J. Trainor. (2006). One year of musical training affects development of auditory cortical-evoked fields in young children. [Research Support, Non-U.S. Govt]. *Brain: A Journal of Neurology*, 129(10), 2593–608. doi: 10.1093/brain/awl247

Fujioka, T., L.J. Trainor, B. Ross, R. Kakigi & C. Pantev. (2004). Musical training enhances automatic encoding of melodic contour and interval structure. *Journal of Cognitive Neuroscience*, 16(6), 1010–21. http://dx.doi.org/10.1162/0898929041502706

Fujioka, T., L.J. Trainor, B. Ross, R. Kakigi & C. Pantev. (2005). Automatic encoding of polyphonic melodies in musicians and nonmusicians. *Journal of Cognitive Neuroscience*, 17(10), 1578–92. http://dx.doi.org/10.1162/089892905774597263

Gaser, C., & G. Schlaug. (2003). Brain structures differ between musicians and non-musicians. *Journal of Neuroscience*, 23(27), 9240–5.

Gebel, B., C. Braun, E. Kaza, E. Altenmuller & M. Lotze. (2013). Instrument specific brain activation in sensorimotor and auditory representation in musicians. [Research Support, Non-U.S. Govt]. *NeuroImage*, 74, 37–44. http://dx.doi.org/10.1016/j.neuroimage.2013.02.021

George, E.M., & D. Coch. (2011). Music training and working memory: An ERP study. [Research Support, Non-U.S. Govt]. *Neuropsychologia*, 49(5), 1083–94. http://dx.doi.org/10.1016/j.neuropsychologia.2011.02.001

Herholz, S.C., C. Lappe & C. Pantev. (2009). Looking for a pattern: An MEG study on the abstract mismatch negativity in musicians and nonmusicians. [Comparative Study Research Support, Non-U.S. Govt]. *BMC Neuroscience*, 10(1), 42. http://dx.doi.org/10.1186/1471-2202-10-42

Hyde, K.L., J. Lerch, A. Norton, M. Forgeard, E. Winner, A.C. Evans & G. Schlaug. (2009). Musical training shapes structural brain development. [Comparative Study Research Support, Non-U.S. Govt Research Support, U.S. Govt, Non-P.H.S.]. *Journal of Neuroscience*, 29(10), 3019–25. http://dx.doi.org/10.1523/JNEUROSCI.5118-08.2009

Keenan, J.P., V. Thangaraj, A.R. Halpern & G. Schlaug. (2001). Absolute pitch and planumtemporale. *NeuroImage*, 14(6), 1402–8. http://dx.doi.org/10.1006/nimg.2001.0925

Klassen, J.A., Y. Liang, L. Tjosvold, T.P. Klassen & L. Hartling. (2008). Music for pain and anxiety in children undergoing medical procedures: A systematic review of randomized controlled trials. *Ambulatory Pediatrics*, 8(2), 117–28. http://dx.doi.org/10.1016/j.ambp.2007.12.005

Koelsch, S., E. Schröger & M. Tervaniemi. (1999). Superior pre-attentive auditory processing in musicians. *Neuroreport*, 10(6), 1309–3. http://dx.doi.org/10.1097/00001756-199904260-00029

Koger, S.M., K. Chapin & M. Brotons. (1999). Is music therapy an effective intervention for dementia? A meta-analytic review of literature. *Journal of Music Therapy*, 36(1), 2–15. http://dx.doi.org/10.1093/jmt/36.1.2

Kraus, N. (2012). Biological impact of music and software-based auditory training. *Journal of Communication Disorders*, 45(6), 403–10. http://dx.doi.org/10.1016/j.jcomdis.2012.06.005

Kraus, N., & B. Chandrasekaran. (2010). Music training for the development of auditory skills. *Nature Reviews: Neuroscience*, 11(8), 599–605. http://dx.doi.org/10.1038/nrn2882

Krizman, J., V. Marian, A. Shook, E. Skoe & N. Kraus. (2012). Subcortical encoding of sound is enhanced in bilinguals and relates to executive function advantages. *Proceedings of the National Academy of Sciences*, 109(20), 7877–81.

Kühnis, J., S. Elmer, M. Meyer & L. Jancke. (2013). The encoding of vowels and temporal speech cues in the auditory cortex of professional musicians: An EEG study. [Research Support, Non-U.S. Govt]. *Neuropsychologia*, 51(8), 1608–18. http://dx.doi.org/10.1016/j.neuropsychologia.2013.04.007

Lappe, C., S.C. Herholz, L.J. Trainor & C. Pantev. (2008). Cortical plasticity induced by short-term unimodal and multimodal musical training. [Research Support, Non-U.S. Govt]. *Journal of Neuroscience*, 28(39), 9632–9. http://dx.doi.org/10.1523/JNEUROSCI.2254-08.2008

Lappe, C., L.J. Trainor, S.C. Herholz & C. Pantev. (2011). Cortical plasticity induced by short-term multimodal musical rhythm training. *PloSOne*, 6(6). doi: ARTN e21493DOI 10.1371/journal.pone.0021493

Lee, H., & U. Noppeney. (2011). Long-term music training tunes how the brain temporally binds signals from multiple senses. [Research Support, Non-U.S. Govt]. *Proceedings of the National Academy of Sciences of the United States of America*, 108(51), E1441–50. http://dx.doi.org/10.1073/pnas.1115267108

Lee, K.M., E. Skoe, N. Kraus & R. Ashley. (2009). Selective subcortical enhancement of musical intervals in musicians. [Research Support, Non-U.S. Gov't Research Support, U.S. Govt, Non-P.H.S.]. *Journal of Neuroscience*, 29(18), 5832–40. http://dx.doi.org/10.1523/JNEUROSCI.6133-08.2009

Lee, Y., M. Lu & H. Ko. (2007). Effects of skill training on working memory capacity. *Learning and Instruction*, 17(3), 336–44. http://dx.doi.org/10.1016/j.learninstruc.2007.02.010

Levitin, D.J. (2012). What does it mean to be musical? *Neuron*, 73(4), 633–7. http://dx.doi.org/10.1016/j.neuron.2012.01.017

Liberman, A.M., & I.G. Mattingly. (1989). A specialization for speech perception. *Science*, 243(4890), 489–94. http://dx.doi.org/10.1126/science.2643163

Luo, F., Q. Wang, Q., A. Kashani & J. Yan. (2008). Corticofugal modulation of initial sound processing in the brain. *Journal of Neuroscience*, 28(45), 11615–21. http://dx.doi.org/10.1523/JNEUROSCI.3972-08.2008

MacKain, K.S., C.T. Best &W. Strange. (1981). Categorical perception of English /r/ and /l/ by Japanese bilinguals. *Applied Psycholinguistics*, 2(4), 369–90. http://dx.doi.org/10.1017/S0142716400009796

Maddox, W.T., B. Chandrasekaran, K. Smayda & H.G. Yi. (2013). Dual systems of speech category learning across the lifespan. *Psychology and Aging*, 28(4), 1042–56. http://dx.doi.org/10.1037/a0034969

Magne, C., D. Schön & M. Besson. (2006). Musician children detect pitch violations in both music and language better than nonmusician children: Behavioral and electrophysiological approaches. *Journal of Cognitive Neuroscience*, 18(2), 199–211. http://dx.doi.org/10.1162/jocn.2006.18.2.199

Marie, C., F. Delogu, G. Lampis, M.O. Belardinelli & M. Besson. (2011). Influence of musical expertise on segmental and tonal processing in Mandarin Chinese. *Journal of Cognitive Neuroscience*, 23(10), 2701–15. http://dx.doi.org/10.1162/jocn.2010.21585

Marques, C., S. Moreno, S.L.Castro & M. Besson. (2007). Musicians detect pitch violation in a foreign language better than nonmusicians: Behavioral and electrophysiological evidence. *Journal of Cognitive Neuroscience*, 19(9), 1453–63. http://dx.doi.org/10.1162/jocn.2007.19.9.1453

Meyer, M., S. Elmer, M. Ringli, M.S. Oechslin, S. Baumann & L. Jancke. (2011). Long-term exposure to music enhances the sensitivity of the auditory system in children. [Research Support, Non-U.S. Govt]. *European Journal of Neuroscience*, 34(5), 755–65. http://dx.doi.org/10.1111/j.1460-9568.2011.07795.x

Montello, L., & E.E. Coons. (1998). Effects of active versus passive group music therapy on preadolescents with emotional, learning, and behavioral disorders. *Journal of Music Therapy*, 35(1), 49–67. http://dx.doi.org/10.1093/jmt/35.1.49

Moreno, S., C. Marques, A. Santos, M. Santos, S.L. Castro & M. Besson. (2009). Musical training influences linguistic abilities in 8-year-old children: More evidence for brain plasticity. [Comparative Study Research Support, Non-U.S. Govt]. *Cerebral Cortex*, 19(3), 712–23. http://dx.doi.org/10.1093/cercor/bhn120

Musacchia, G., M. Sams, E. Skoe & N. Kraus. (2007). Musicians have enhanced subcortical auditory and audiovisual processing of speech and music. [Research Support, N.I.H., Extramural Research Support, U.S. Got, Non-P.H.S.]. *Proceedings of the National Academy of Sciences of the United States of America*, 104(40), 15894–8. http://dx.doi.org/10.1073/pnas.0701498104

Overy, K. (2000). Dyslexia, temporal processing and music: The potential of music as an early learning aid for dyslexic children. *Psychology of Music*, 28(2), 218–29. http://dx.doi.org/10.1177/0305735600282010

Pacchetti, C., F. Mancini, R. Aglieri, C. Fundarò, E. Martignoni & G. Nappi. (2000). Active music therapy in Parkinson's disease: An integrative method for motor and emotional rehabilitation. *Psychosomatic Medicine*, 62(3), 386–93. http://dx.doi.org/10.1097/00006842-200005000-00012

Pantev, C., & S.C. Herholz. (2011). Plasticity of the human auditory cortex related to musical training. *Neuroscience & Biobehavioral Reviews*, 35(10), 2140–54.

Pantev, C., R. Oostenveld, A. Engelien, B. Ross, L.E. Roberts & M. Hoke. (1998). Increased auditory cortical representation in musicians. *Nature*, 392(6678), 811–14. http://dx.doi.org/10.1038/33918

Pantev, C., L.E. Roberts, M. Schulz, A. Engelien & B. Ross. (2001). Timbre-specific enhancement of auditory cortical representations in musicians. *Neuroreport*, 12(1), 169–74. http://dx.doi.org/10.1097/00001756-200101220-00041

Paraskevopoulos, E., A. Kuchenbuch, S.C. Herholz & C. Pantev. (2012). Musical expertise induces audiovisual integration of abstract congruency rules. [Research Support, Non-U.S. Govt]. *Journal of Neuroscience*, 32(50), 18196–203. http://dx.doi.org/10.1523/JNEUROSCI.1947-12.2012

Parbery-Clark, A., S. Anderson, E. Hittner & N. Kraus. (2012a). Musical experience offsets age-related delays in neural timing. *Neurobiology of Aging*, 33(7). doi. *ARTN, 1483*, e1.http://dx.doi.org/10.1016/j.neurobiolaging.2011.12.015

Parbery-Clark, A., S. Anderson, E. Hittner & N. Kraus. (2012b). Musical experience strengthens the neural representation of sounds important for communication in middle-aged adults. *Frontiers in Aging Neuroscience*, 4, 30.http://dx.doi.org/10.3389/fnagi.2012.00030

Parbery-Clark, A., S. Anderson & N. Kraus. (2013). Musicians change their tune: How hearing loss alters the neural code. [Research Support, U.S. Govt, Non-P.H.S.]. *Hearing Research*, 302, 121–31. http://dx.doi.org/10.1016/j.heares.2013.03.009

Parbery-Clark, A., E. Skoe & N. Kraus. (2009a). Musical experience limits the degradative effects of background noise on the neural processing of sound. [Research Support, U.S. Govt, Non-P.H.S.]. *Journal of Neuroscience*, 29(45), 14100–7. http://dx.doi.org/10.1523/JNEUROSCI.3256-09.2009

Parbery-Clark, A., E. Skoe, C. Lam & N. Kraus. (2009b). Musician enhancement for speech-in-noise. *Ear and Hearing*, 30(6), 653–61. http://dx.doi.org/10.1097/AUD.0b013e3181b412e9

Parbery-Clark, A., D.L. Strait, S. Anderson, E. Hittner & N. Kraus. (2011a). Musical experience and the aging auditory system: Implications for cognitive abilities and hearing speech in noise. *PloSOne*, 6(5).doi: ARTN e18082 DOI 10.1371/journal.pone.0018082

Parbery-Clark, A., D.L. Strait & N. Kraus. (2011b).Context-dependent encoding in the auditory brainstem subserves enhanced speech-in-noise perception in musicians. [Research Support, U.S. Govt, Non-P.H.S.]. *Neuropsychologia*, 49(12), 3338–45. http://dx.doi.org/10.1016/j.neuropsychologia.2011.08.007

Parbery-Clark, A., A. Tierney, D.L. Strait & N. Kraus. (2012c). Musicians have fine-tuned neural distinction of speech syllables. [Research Support, N.I.H., Extramural Research Support, U.S. Govt, Non-P.H.S.]. *Neuroscience*, 219, 111–19. http://dx.doi.org/10.1016/j.neuroscience.2012.05.042

Patel, A.D. (2011). Why would musical training benefit the neural encoding of speech? The OPERA hypothesis. *Frontiers in Psychology*, 2, 142. http://dx.doi.org/10.3389/fpsyg.2011.00142

Patel, A.D. (2012). The OPERA hypothesis: Assumptions and clarifications. [Research Support, Non-U.S. Govt Review]. *Annals of the New York Academy of Sciences*, 1252(1), 124–8. http://dx.doi.org/10.1111/j.1749-6632.2011.06426.x

Patel, A.D. (2014). Can nonlinguistic musical training change the way the brain processes speech? The expanded OPERA hypothesis. *Hearing Research*, 308, 98–108.http://dx.doi.org/10.1016/j.heares.2013.08.011

Peretz, I., & M. Coltheart. (2003). Modularity of music processing. *Nature Neuroscience*, 6(7), 688–91. http://dx.doi.org/10.1038/nn1083

Pickles, J.O. (1988). *An Introduction to the Physiology of Hearing* (Vol. 2). London: Academic Press.

Ruggles, D.R., R.L. Freyman & A.J. Oxenham. (2014). Influence of musical training on understanding voiced and whispered speech in noise. *PLoS One*, 9(1), e86980. http://dx.doi.org/10.1371/journal.pone.0086980

Salimpoor, V.N., M. Benovoy, K. Larcher, A. Dagher & R.J. Zatorre. (2011). Anatomically distinct dopamine release during anticipation and experience of peak emotion to music. *Nature Neuroscience*, 14(2), 257–62. http://dx.doi.org/10.1038/nn.2726

Salimpoor, V.N., M. Benovoy, G. Longo, J.R. Cooperstock & R.J. Zatorre. (2009). The rewarding aspects of music listening are related to degree of emotional arousal. *PLoS One*, 4(10), e7487. http://dx.doi.org/10.1371/journal.pone.0007487

Salimpoor, V.N., I. van den Bosch, N. Kovacevic, A.R. McIntosh, A. Dagher & R.J. Zatorre. (2013). Interactions between the nucleus accumbens and auditory cortices predict music reward value. *Science*, 340(6129), 216–19. http://dx.doi.org/10.1126/science.1231059

Schlaug, G., L. Jancke, Y. Huang & H. Steinmetz. (1995). In vivo evidence of structural brain asymmetry in musicians. *Science*, 267(5198), 699–701. http://dx.doi.org/10.1126/science.7839149

Schneider, P., M. Scherg, H.G. Dosch, H.J. Specht, A. Gutschalk & A. Rupp. (2002). Morphology of Heschl's gyrus reflects enhanced activation in the auditory cortex of musicians. *Nature Neuroscience*, 5(7), 688–94. http://dx.doi.org/10.1038/nn871

Schön, D., C. Magne & M. Besson. (2004). The music of speech: Music training facilitates pitch processing in both music and language. [Clinical Trial Research Support, Non-U.S. Govt]. *Psychophysiology*, 41(3), 341–9. http://dx.doi.org/10.1111/1469-8986.00172.x

Schulte-Körne, G., W. Deimel, J. Bartling & H. Remschmidt. (1998). Auditory processing and dyslexia: Evidence for a specific speech processing deficit. *Neuroreport*, 9(2), 337–40. http://dx.doi.org/10.1097/00001756-199801260-00029

Schulze, K., & S. Koelsch. (2012). Working memory for speech and music. [Review]. *Annals of the New York Academy of Sciences*, 1252(1), 229–36. http://dx.doi.org/10.1111/j.1749-6632.2012.06447.x

Schulze, K., S. Zysset, K. Mueller, A.D. Friederici & S. Koelsch. (2011). Neuroarchitecture of verbal and tonal working memory in nonmusicians and musicians. [Research Support, Non-U.S. Govt]. *Human Brain Mapping*, 32(5), 771–83. http://dx.doi.org/10.1002/hbm.21060

Schweizer, T.A., J. Ware, C.E. Fischer, F.I. Craik & E. Bialystok. (2012). Bilingualism as a contributor to cognitive reserve: Evidence from brain atrophy in Alzheimer's disease. *Cortex*, 48(8), 991–6.

Seppänen, M., J. Hamalainen, A.K. Pesonen & M. Tervaniemi. (2012a). Music training enhances rapid neural plasticity of n1 and p2 source activation for unattended sounds. *Frontiers in Human Neuroscience*, 6, 43. http://dx.doi.org/10.3389/fnhum.2012.00043

Seppänen, M., A.K. Pesonen & M. Tervaniemi. (2012b). Music training enhances the rapid plasticity of P3a/P3b event-related brain potentials for unattended and attended target sounds. [Research Support, Non-U.S. Govt]. *Attention, Perception & Psychophysics*, 74(3), 600–12. http://dx.doi.org/10.3758/s13414-011-0257-9

Shahin, A., D.J. Bosnyak, L.J. Trainor & L.E. Roberts. (2003). Enhancement of neuroplastic P2 and N1c auditory evoked potentials in musicians. *Journal of Neuroscience*, 23(13), 5545–52.

Shahin, A.J., L.E. Roberts, W. Chau, L.J. Trainor & L.M. Miller. (2008). Music training leads to the development of timbre-specific gamma band activity. [Research Support, Non-U.S. Govt]. *NeuroImage*, 41(1), 113–22. http://dx.doi.org/10.1016/j.neuroimage.2008.01.067

Shahin, A.J., L.E. Roberts, C. Pantev, M. Aziz & T.W. Picton. (2007). Enhanced anterior-temporal processing for complex tones in musicians. *Clinical Neurophysiology*, 118(1), 209–20. http://dx.doi.org/10.1016/j.clinph.2006.09.019

Skoe, E., & N. Kraus. (2012). A little goes a long way: How the adult brain is shaped by musical training in childhood. *The Journal of Neuroscience*, 32(34), 11507–10.

Smith, J.C., J.T. Marsh & W.S. Brown. (1975). Far-field recorded frequency-following responses: Evidence for the locus of brainstem sources. *Electroencephalography and Clinical Neurophysiology*, 39(5), 465–72. http://dx.doi.org/10.1016/0013-4694(75)90047-4

Sohmer, H., H. Pratt & R. Kinarti. (1977). Sources of frequency following responses (FFR) in man. *Electroencephalography and Clinical Neurophysiology*, 42(5), 656–64. http://dx.doi.org/10.1016/0013-4694(77)90282-6

Strait, D. L., K. Chan, R. Ashley & N. Kraus. (2012). Specialization among the specialized: Auditory brainstem function is tuned in to timbre. [Letter Research Support, N.I.H., Extramural Research Support, U.S. Govt, Non-P.H.S.]. *Cortex; A Journal Devoted to the Study of the Nervous System and Behavior*, 48(3), 360–2. doi: 10.1016/j.cortex.2011.03.015

Strait, D.L., S. O'Connell, A. Parbery-Clark & N. Kraus. (2013). Musicians' enhanced neural differentiation of speech sounds arises early in life: Developmental evidence from ages 3 to 30. *Cerebral Cortex*. http://dx.doi.org/10.1093/cercor/bht103

Suga, N. (2008). Role of corticofugal feedback in hearing. *Journal of Comparative Physiology A: Neuroethology, Sensory, Neural, and Behavioral Physiology*, 194(2), 169–83. http://dx.doi.org/10.1007/s00359-007-0274-2

Suga, N., E. Gao, Y. Zhang, X. Ma & J.F. Olsen. (2000). The corticofugal system for hearing: Recent progress. *Proceedings of the National Academy of Sciences of the United States of America*, 97(22), 11807–14. http://dx.doi.org/10.1073/pnas.97.22.11807

Suga, N., J. Yan & Y. Zhang. (1997). Cortical maps for hearing and egocentric selection for self-organization. *Trends in Cognitive Sciences*, 1(1), 13–20. http://dx.doi.org/10.1016/S1364-6613(97)01002-4

Treurnicht Naylor, K., S. Kingsnorth, A. Lamont, P. McKeever & C. Macarthur. (2010). The effectiveness of music in pediatric healthcare: A systematic review of randomized controlled trials. *Evidence-Based Complementary and Alternative Medicine*, 2011, Article ID 464759, 18 pages. doi:10.1155/2011/464759.

van Zuijen, T.L., E. Sussman, I. Winkler, R. Naatanen & M. Tervaniemi. (2004). Grouping of sequential sounds: An event-related potential study comparing musicians and nonmusicians. *Journal of Cognitive Neuroscience*, 16(2), 331–8. http://dx.doi.org/10.1162/089892904322984607

van Zuijen, T.L., E. Sussman, I. Winkler, R. Naatanen & M. Tervaniemi. (2005). Auditory organization of sound sequences by a temporal or numerical regularity: A mismatch negativity study comparing musicians and non-musicians. [Comparative Study Research Support, N.I.H., Extramural Research Support, Non-U.S. Gov't Research Support, U.S. Gov't, P.H.S.]. *Brain Research: Cognitive Brain Research*, 23(2–3), 270–6. http://dx.doi.org/10.1016/j.cogbrainres.2004.10.007

Wan, C.Y., K. Demaine, L. Zipse, A. Norton & G. Schlaug. (2010). From music making to speaking: Engaging the mirror neuron system in autism. *Brain Research Bulletin*, 82(3–4), 161–8. http://dx.doi.org/10.1016/j.brainresbull.2010.04.010

Winer, J.A. (2005). Decoding the auditory corticofugal systems. *Hearing Research*, 207(1–2), 1–9. http://dx.doi.org/10.1016/j.heares.2005.06.007

Winer, J.A., D.T. Larue, J.J. Diehl & B.J. Hefti. (1998). Auditory cortical projections to the cat inferior colliculus. *Journal of Comparative Neurology*, 400(2), 147–74. http://dx.doi.org/10.1002/(SICI)1096-9861(19981019)400:2<147::AID-CNE1>3.0.CO;2-9

Wong, P., & T.K. Perrachione. (2007). Learning pitch patterns in lexical identification by native English-speaking adults. *Applied Psycholinguistics*, 28(4), 565–85. http://dx.doi.org/10.1017/S0142716407070312

Wong, P.C., E. Skoe, N.M. Russo, T. Dees & N. Kraus. (2007). Musical experience shapes human brainstem encoding of linguistic pitch patterns. [Research Support, N.I.H., Extramural Research Support, Non-U.S. Govt Research Support, U.S. Govt, Non-P.H.S.]. *Nature Neuroscience*, 10(4), 420–2. http://dx.doi.org/10.1038/nn1872

Zatorre, R.J., D.W. Perry, C.A. Beckett, C.F. Westbury & A.C. Evans. (1998). Functional anatomy of musical processing in listeners with absolute pitch and relative pitch. *Proceedings of the National Academy of Sciences of the United States of America*, 95(6), 3172–7.http://dx.doi.org/10.1073/pnas.95.6.3172

7 Effects of Syllable Complexity on Vowel Formant Variability in Acquired Apraxia of Speech

Sarah Key-DeLyria, Adam Jacks and Thomas P. Marquardt[1]

7.1 Introduction

Apraxia of speech (AOS) is a disorder of speech production characterized by reduced ability to program speech movements in the absence of significant muscular weakness or paralysis.[2] AOS most often occurs as a result of left anterior brain damage involving the inferior frontal cortex (Duffy 2012; Hillis et al. 2004; McNeil et al. 1997; Richardson et al. 2012). Speakers with apraxia demonstrate phonetic distortions (Duffy 2012), reduced speech rate (Deger & Ziegler, 2002; Haley & Overton 2001), groping for articulatory targets (Darley et al. 1975; Deger& Ziegler 2002; Duffy 2012), prosodic errors (Kent & Rosenbek 1982) and increasing speech errors with increasing word and phrase length. Errors may differ from production to production during voluntary speech (Deger & Ziegler 2002; Dogil & Mayer

1 Sarah Key-DeLyria is an assistant professor in the Department of Speech and Hearing Sciences at Portland State University, Oregon.
Adam Jacks is an associate professor in the Division of Speech and Hearing Sciences, Department of Allied Health Sciences, at the University of North Carolina at Chapel Hill.
Thomas P. Marquardt is a professor in the Department of Communication Sciences and Disorders at Moody College of Communication, the University of Texas at Austin.

2 Apraxia of speech (AOS) is primarily used to refer to apraxia acquired in adulthood, while childhood apraxia of speech (CAS) is the preferred term for apraxia of speech in childhood (see American Speech-Language-Hearing Association 2007). CAS and AOS share an underlying impairment of motor programming that is not explained by muscular weakness or paralysis, but CAS is congenital and has different diagnostic features in comparison to AOS.

1998; Freed 2000; Haley et al. 2013, but see McNeil et al. 1995). Automatic speech, such as counting to 20 or saying "hello", is generally unimpaired.

Lesions causing AOS have been reported in a wide range of brain areas (Collins 1989; Dronkers 1996; Duffy 2012), though the strongest evidence links AOS to damage to the left inferior frontal gyrus. The importance of this region was noted by Broca in his reports of patients with impaired speech production (Dronkers et al. 2007), and has received more recent support through advanced structural brain analysis methods. In particular, Richardson et al. (2012) found that presence and severity of AOS was best predicted by damage and reduced blood flow to the pars opercularis of the left inferior prefrontal cortex, the posterior portion of Broca's area. Although various other regions may be involved in speech programming (see Tourville & Guenther 2011), lesions affecting the left inferior frontal cortex most frequently cause AOS.

7.2 Characteristics of Apraxia of Speech

Prosodic abnormalities help to distinguish AOS from other speech production disorders (Duffy 2012). The prosodic impairment in AOS is characterized by slow rate, prolonged consonant and vowel segments, extended pauses between words and reduced stress patterns (Kent & Rosenbek 1982; Wambaugh et al. 2006). In some speakers, syllables are produced in a scanning, one-at-a-time fashion. Speech fluency also may be impaired, with a halting rhythm, frequent revisions or self-corrections, and groping or searching for articulatory placement.

Segmental speech errors are a consistently identified feature of AOS (Duffy 2012; Haley & Overton 2001; Odell et al. 1990). These errors have been observed in both consonant and vowel articulation and are based on temporal or spatial distortions and imprecisions in producing target segments (Kent & Rosenbek 1983; McNeil et al. 1989; Odell et al. 1990; Ziegler & von Cramon 1985).

Several studies have shown that error frequency increases as motor complexity increases (Dunlop & Marquardt 1977; Kent & Rosenbek 1982; McNeil et al. 1997; but see Dogil & Mayer 1998). If patients with AOS encode sounds into movements online, as suggested by Whiteside & Varley (1998), more complex segments would be expected to have more errors. A study comparing 7 speakers with AOS with 7 neurotypical speakers found that as the distance between points of articulation increased, errors in place of articulation increased for speakers with apraxia (Kent & Rosenbek 1983).

Speakers with AOS tend to substitute less complex consonants for more complex consonants (Marquardt et al. 1979; Wolk 1986). Consonant complexity can be estimated from markedness, developmental ordering, distance metrics and the direction of complexity change. The complexity of consonants based on markedness analysis predicts overall accuracy of production and substitution patterns in apraxic speech (Marquardt et al. 1979; Wolk 1986). Error patterns in AOS also reflect developmental complexity (Ireland et al. 1977), with greater consonant errors for speech sounds that children acquire later. Significant correlations between per cent correct production of consonants by 3-year-old children and error frequency were found for speakers with apraxia (Marquardt et al. 1979).

Vowels are perceived less categorically than consonants, and listeners are less readily affected by variability in vowel production (Pisoni 1975). Perhaps partially for this reason, many early studies of vowel production in AOS found fewer vowel errors than consonant errors (La Pointe & Johns 1975; Monoi et al. 1983). These findings, however, may reflect difficulty in vowel perception. Studies using narrow transcription (Haley et al. 2001a; Odell et al. 1991) or acoustic analysis (Kent & Rosenbek 1983) have found some abnormal production characteristics. Several acoustic studies have found longer vowel durations, but only in multisyllabic words (Haley & Overton 2001; Kent & Rosenbek 1983; Ryalls 1981).

Considerable debate exists on the importance of speech variability for a diagnosis of AOS, based on transcription of repeated speech productions. While early researchers observed that repeated productions of a word might result in both correct and incorrect productions (Johns & Darley 1970), an influential report by McNeil and colleagues found that speech errors were consistent in place and location in four speakers with AOS (McNeil et al. 1995). Recent work has shown that the degree of speech variability observed in a speaker depends on the overall severity of speech impairment (Haley et al. 2013) and how variability is defined, with some individuals showing high levels of word level variability but consistency in the location and types of errors produced (Haley et al. submitted).

The varied results from transcription-based variability studies suggest that these measures are not likely useful for diagnosis of AOS (e.g. Haley et al. 2013; Staiger et al. 2012). However, a number of studies have observed that speakers with AOS are indeed variable when acoustic and kinematic measures of multiple productions are compared. For example, kinematic studies have found varied movement patterns on multiple productions of a phrase (e.g. Itoh & Sasanuma 1984; McNeil et al. 1989). Acoustic analysis of voiced and voiceless stops has also shown variability in voice onset time of speakers with AOS (Blumstein et al. 1977; Hoit-Dalgaard et al. 1983). These studies, examining instrumental variability of consonants or articulatory gestures at the phrase level, suggest that speech patterns are notably variable in adults with AOS.

Studies of vowel formant variability, reflecting trial-to-trial differences in articulatory positioning, have yielded conflicting results. For example, some studies have reported greater formant variability in speakers with AOS or Broca's aphasia (Jacks 2008; Ryalls 1986), while others have found no difference in comparison to neurologically healthy speakers (Haley et al. 2001a; Jacks et al. 2010). Notably, these findings were based on single syllable words in a simple context (hVd), which may result in lower variability due to relatively low motor complexity. In contrast, a case study investigating vowel production in both single syllables and in sentence and question frames (Whiteside et al. 2010) found that vowel space was nearly collapsed in the sentence and question contexts for the speaker with AOS. It is therefore possible that greater variability of vowel production might be observed in more complex phonetic contexts.

Phonetic distance metrics are used to define the difference between consonants based on phonetic features (Juola & Zimmermann 1996; Kondrak 2003; Somers 1998). In the context of single-syllable words with CVC structure, the distance between the initial and final consonant in terms of phonetic features or place of articulation may affect vowel production. The distance between places of articulation also could affect production. For example, while the distance between the place of articulation for /s/ and /ʃ/ may be small, the distance between /t/ and /k/ would be expected to have more of an effect. The difference in distance may affect vowel production in one direction more than the other. For example, articulatory movement from front to back (e.g., /t/ to /k/) may be easier and have less of an effect on production than back to front (e.g., /k/ to /t/).

Purpose. The goal of this study was to determine the effect of consonant context complexity on vowel formant variability in CVC syllables. Specifically, we piloted stimuli that were designed to systematically explore distance in terms of number of distinctive phonetic features between initial and final consonants in CVC syllables. Based on the frequent reports of reduced consistency of speech production in AOS, we predicted greater variability for vowels in complex consonantal environments for speakers with AOS compared to neurotypical speakers.

7.3 Method

Participants. Four adults participated in the study, including two with AOS and two with no history of neurological deficits (i.e., neurotypical). See

Table 7.1 for participant information. Participants were native speakers of American English; three with Northern Cities and one with Southern American dialect (Labov et al. 2005). Audiometric screening confirmed consistent responses to frequencies at 500, 1000, and 2000 Hz at 30 dB or lower in at least one ear.

Table 7.1. Participant demographic and test information.

		Participant (AOS)	
		A1	**A2**
Gender		F	M
Regional dialect		Northern	Southern
Age		76	58
Years;months post-onset		10;8	1;8
Site of lesion		Left basal ganglia and internal capsule	Left basal ganglia, insula, frontal operculum and superior temporal gyrus
Apraxia battery for adults	Overall severity	Moderate	Mild
Diadochokinesis		Mild	None
Increasing word length (1–3 syllables)		Moderate	Mild
Increasing word length (2–5 syllables)		‡	Moderate
Limb apraxia		None	None
Oral apraxia		None	None
Repeated trials		Moderate	None
Western aphasia battery	Aphasia quotient	93	96
Comprehension		100	100
Naming		87	91
Hearing screening	Right/Left screening threshold (dB)	45/30	20/25
		Participant (Neurotypical)	
		N1	N2
Gender		F	M
Regional dialect		Northern	Northern
Age		53	60
Hearing screening	Right/Left threshold (dB)	20/20	35/20

The participants with AOS had a history of left-hemisphere damage due to cerebrovascular accident at least 6 months prior to the study. AOS was diagnosed based on criteria reported by Kent and Rosenbek (1983), including effortful articulatory groping and difficulty initiating speech with attempts at self-correction, inconsistent errors on repeated trials, slow rate and dysprosody. The participants with AOS were administered the *Apraxia Battery for Adults* (ABA-II, Dabul 2000) and the *Western Aphasia Battery* (Kertesz 1982). Results showed mild to moderate apraxia of speech and mild aphasia with agrammatism and anomia.

Two neurotypical participants with no history of speech disorders or neurological disease were matched to the AOS participants on the basis of age and sex. They were recruited from volunteers expressing interest in participation in research studies. The participants were screened for speech and language impairment on the basis of interview and conversational speech observations (Questionnaire for Verifying Stroke-Free Status, Jones et al. 2001).

Stimuli. Stimuli were 13 single-syllable real words and 23 single-syllable nonsense words, including 12 words for each of three vowels, /i/, /a/ and /u/ (See Table 7.2). In each group of 12, four CVC words had consonants that reflected a place change (e.g., "cot"), four items where consonants differed in place and manner of articulation (e.g., "sock"), and four words with consonants that differed in place, manner and voicing (e.g., "keys"). The constraints of developing CVC syllables with the desired phonetic changes

Table 7.2. Word and nonword stimuli.

Vowels	**Place change**	**Place + Manner change**	**Place + Manner + Voice change**
"ee" /i/	*Nonwords*: deeg, keet, geed *Words*: teak	*Nonwords*: zeeg, geez *Words*: seek, quiche	*Nonwords*: seeg, zeek *Words*: geese, keys
"ah" /a/	*Nonwords*: dahg *Words*: tock, god, cot	*Nonwords*: goz, koss, zog *Words*: sock	*Nonwords*: zock, kahz *Words*: gosh, shod
"oo" /u/	*Nonwords*: doog, tuke, gude *Words*: coot	*Nonwords*: suke, gooz, zoog, koos	*Nonwords*: zuke, soog, kooz *Words*: goose

Note: CVC stimuli were constructed to reflect increases in syllable complexity for each of the vowels based on place, manner and voicing changes. Front to back and back to front place changes (i.e., "geese" keys) were included for each of the stimulus conditions.

required the use of both nonsense words and real words. Stimulus complexity was based on feature changes in consonants of the syllables for each vowel. For example, "cot" with only a place change between the consonants produced was considered less complex than "shod" that included place, manner, and voicing changes. Digital recordings of the words were made by a 60-year-old male speaker of American English (Northern dialect).

Procedure. Each participant repeated the 36 stimuli to ensure correct articulation and understanding of the task. One nonsense item, "dahg," was problematic because of its similarity to the real word "dog." Participants were required to produce "dahg" with the same vowel as in the word, "cot" to continue with testing. No participant had difficulty producing this word or any of the stimuli.

Participants were seated in front of a computer monitor in a quiet room. Stimuli were presented randomly through the open-source presentation software, *Alvin* (Hillenbrand & Gayvert 2005). The 36 CVCs were repeated 7 times for a total of 252 productions. Productions were recorded directly to a computer using a one-point, directional stereo microphone (Sony Model # ECM-MS57) and a high-quality PC sound card. Recordings were digitized as .wav files at a sampling rate of 16 KHz with 16-bit quantization.

Analysis. Quantitative and qualitative data analysis procedures were employed to investigate the effect of articulatory complexity on vowel formant variability in AOS. Vowel and consonant productions were analyzed for accuracy. Only correct vowels were acoustically analyzed for formant frequencies. Vowels were deemed correct if they matched the target vowel perceptually, if they did not match a different vowel and if the individual vowels matched the perceptual quality of other vowels of the intended target. The first and second formants were measured at the vowel nucleus. The vowel nucleus was chosen as a combination of three features: maximum intensity, maximum first formant and the middle of the vowel duration. If there was a clear off-glide (i.e., diphthong), the nucleus was selected from the first portion of the duration only. Jacks (2006) found measures of the first and second formants at the vowel nucleus to be highly reliable between two investigators with Pearson's correlations of $r^2 = .97$ for F1 and $r^2 = .93$ for F2.

The first five correct productions of the stimuli by each participant were selected for analysis. Analysis was completed using *Praat* (Boersma & Weenink 2005), using a script to partially automate the management of sound files, the display of analysis windows, the selection of vowel formants and the recording of numeric data to text files. Fast Fourier transform (FFT) spectra and linear prediction coding (LPC) spectral envelopes were generated for each of the measurement points, using a Gaussian-like analysis window with a 50 ms analysis window, time steps of 5 ms, and a pre-emphasis frequency of 50 Hz. Formant measurements were obtained both from manual selection based on FFT spectra and LPC envelopes and from values derived automatically based on default formant tracking settings. Manually selected formants were used to verify results where available. However, manually selected formants for N1 were not saved in the original data file, so for this participant, the reported values represent the automatically selected formants. Comparison of manually and automatically selected formants in the other 3 participants did not reveal large differences.

Measurement procedures yielded mean and standard deviations for formant frequencies across the repeated trials of each stimulus. Coefficients of variation were calculated (standard deviation/mean) to examine the effects of participants (AOS vs neurotypical), vowel type and complexity on formant variability.

7.4 Results

First and second formants for each production of the vowels by AOS and neurotypical participants are shown in Figure 7.1. There was no vowel

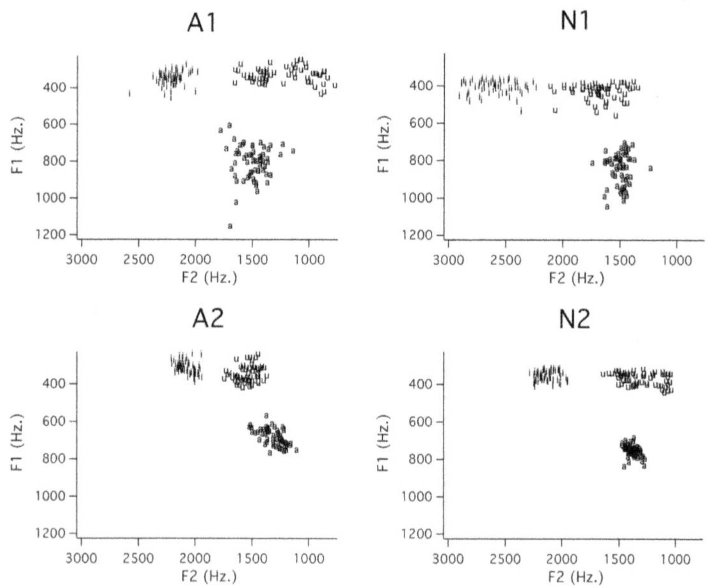

Figure 7.1. Vowel formant frequency (F1, F2) scatterplots for apraxia of speech (A1, A2) and neurotypical (N1, N2) speakers.

overlap for either the AOS or the neurotypical participants; AOS productions were within ranges comparable to the neurotypical participants.

Coefficients of variation (COVs) for F1 and F2, averaged across consonant change within the syllable, are shown in Figure 7.2 for the AOS and neurotypical participants. Increased COVs did not correspond predictably with increases in feature complexity. Each participant varied in terms of which complexity change demonstrated the largest and smallest COVs. For example, participant A1 had the largest COV for the place change of velar to alveolar (F1 COV = 0.21) and the smallest COV for the place and manner change of fricative to stop (F1 COV = 0.08). In contrast, participant A2 had the largest COV for the place, manner and voice change of stop to fricative (F1 COV = 0.10) and the smallest COV for the place change of alveolar to velar (F1 COV = 0.07). Consonant complexity did not result in greater vowel formant variability in CVC syllables for either the AOS or neurotypical participants.

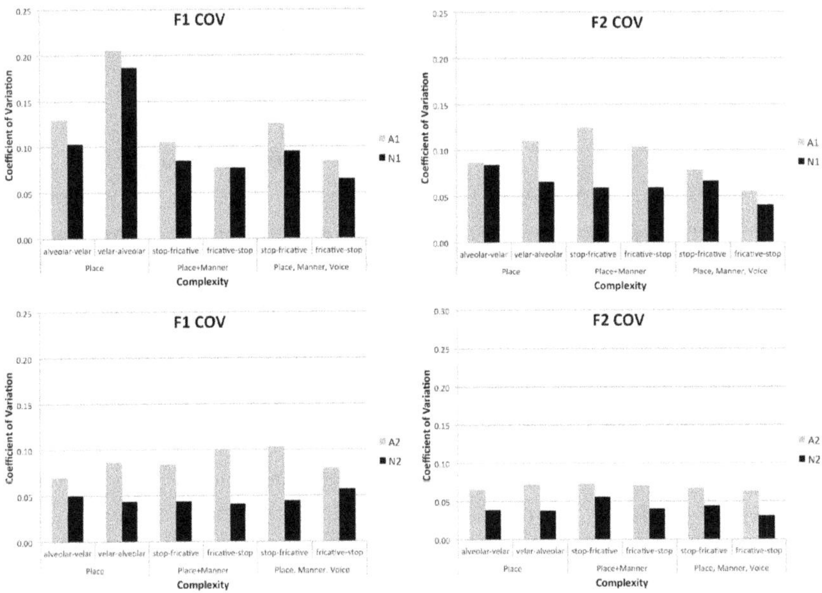

Figure 7.2. Vowel formant coefficients of variation for stimuli with increasing motor complexity for apraxia of speech (A1, A2) and neurotypical (N1, N2) speakers.

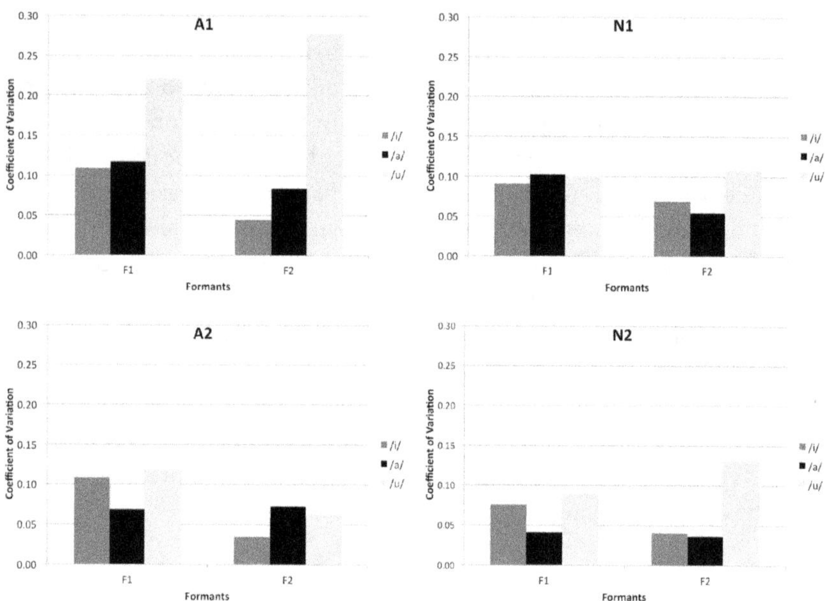

Figure 7.3. Vowel formant (F1, F2) coefficients of variation for three vowels produced by apraxia of speech (A1, A2) and neurotypical (N1, N2) speakers.

Mean COVs for F1 and F2 are shown in Figure 7.3 for each of the three vowels produced by A1 and N1 and by A2 and N2, respectively. The participants with AOS generally had greater variability for each vowel than neurotypical participants. Average COVs were larger for participants A1 and A2 than N1 and N2 overall, with the greatest variability demonstrated for the vowel /u/ (F2 COV A1: /u/ = 0.28; N1: /u/ = 0.11). There was one exception to the overall trend for participants with AOS and neurotypical participants. Participant A1 had a lower COV than participant N1 for F2 in the /i/ vowel (F2 COV A1: /i/ = 0.04; N1: /i/ = 0.07). In summary, syllable complexity did not predict vowel variability, but participants with AOS demonstrated greater formant frequency variability than the neurotypical participants.

The COVs for F1 and F2 averaged across vowels for each participant with AOS and each neurotypical participant are shown in Figure 7.4. Variation was higher for F1 than for F2 for participants A1 (F1 = 0.15, F2 = 0.14), A2 (F1 = 0.10, F2 = 0.06) and N1 (F1 = 0.10, F2 = 0.08). Participant N2 had equivalent COVs for F2 and F1 (0.07). Overall, the average COVs were greater for the participants with AOS.

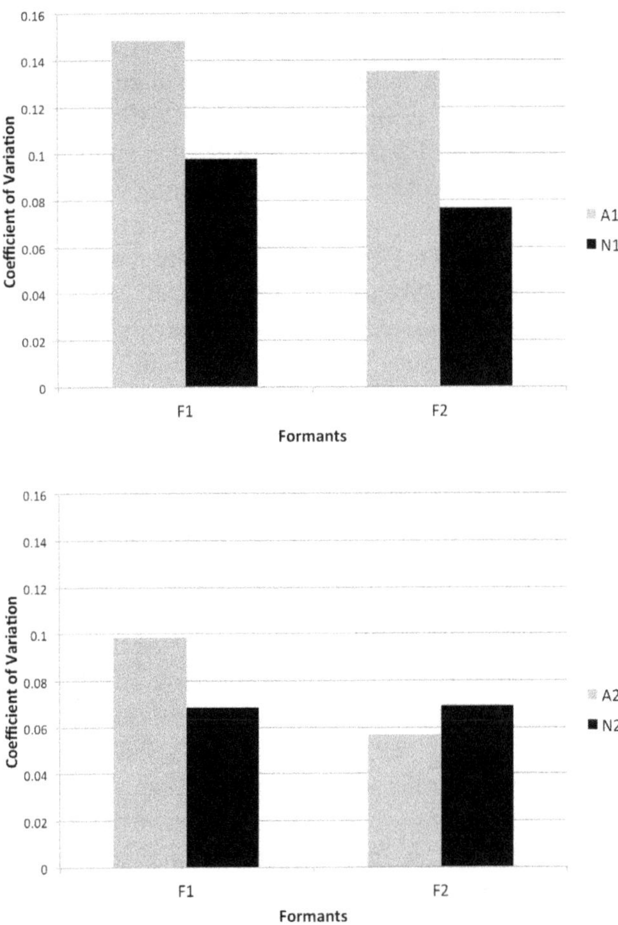

Figure 7.4. Mean vowel formant (F1, F2) coefficients of variation for apraxia of speech (A1, A2) and neurotypical (N1, N2) speakers.

7.5 Discussion

The study found that vowels produced by participants with AOS were more variable than those produced by unimpaired speakers. The vowel /u/ was the most unstable across speakers; however, participants demonstrated differing patterns of production variability for the vowels /i/ and /a/. Finally, variability in vowel production was not consistently predicted by CVC contextual complexity. The discussion will focus on these three main findings of the study.

Speaker variability was determined for vowel formants from a series of CVC productions varying in complexity. Greater variability was expected for the speakers with AOS because the disorder often is characterized by inconsistent speech sound errors on repeated trials (Deger & Ziegler 2002; Dogil & Mayer 1998; Freed 2000; but see McNeil et al. 1995). The participants with AOS were generally more variable than neurologically normal speakers.

Point vowels were used to develop stimuli without differences expected in production consistency. Skenes & Trullinger (1988) did not find a significant difference in the production of consonant errors between the vowels /i/, /a/ and /u/. Other studies have noted individual variability in vowel production without noting an effect of target vowel (Haley et al. 2000, 2001b; Haley & Overton 2001). Results from these studies indicated common errors in vowel height and duration with significant variation between speakers in the production of vowel errors.

The vowel /u/ tended to be the least consistent across speakers, and both participants with AOS had the highest variability for F2 of the vowel /u/. Participants demonstrated different patterns of variability in production of vowels. For example, participant A1 demonstrated the lowest variability for the vowel /i/, while participant A2 demonstrated the lowest variability for the vowel /a/. Patterns of individual variability extended to an exception to the overall higher variability observed in speakers with AOS, with participant A1 demonstrating lower variability than the matched neurotypical participant N1 for the vowel /i/. Nevertheless, the general results as a function of vowel target are in agreement with previous studies of vowel production in AOS speakers (e.g. Jacks et al. 2010; Kent & Rosenbek 1983; Ryalls 1986).

Formant variability was analyzed in terms of the feature complexity of surrounding consonants. Increased coefficients of variation were expected with increases in the complexity of the consonant context. There were differences in variability between contexts but they were not consistent. Notably, participant A1 demonstrated greatest variability in less complex contexts, and participant A2 demonstrated greatest variability in more complex contexts. In both cases, there was not an increase in vowel formant inconsistency with increases in predicted stimulus complexity. Feature complexity was not a predictor of vowel production consistency based on formant frequency coefficients of variability.

7.5.1 Implications

AOS is a disorder of motor programming (Duffy 2012; Edmonds & Marquardt 2004; Freed 2000; McNeil et al. 1997). Varley & Whiteside (2001) hypothesized that speakers with AOS have lost access to the syllabary in motor programming and must use a subsyllabic route for speech production. However, Aichert & Ziegler (2004) found syllable effects on production errors by speakers with AOS suggesting at least partially maintained access to the syllabary. An effect of consonant complexity on vowel stability would have supported the notion of a subsyllabic route to production in apraxic speech. The consonantal complexity effect might also have implied that the complexity of a consonant increases the overall load on motor programming and disrupts production of following phonemes.

Two previous research findings supplied the rationale for exploring whether complexity also affected surrounding phonemes. First, vowel production is more disrupted in sentence and question contexts than in single syllables (Whiteside et al. 2010). Second, previous research found a positive relationship between complexity and isolated consonant errors (Marquardt et al. 1979; Wolk 1986). Thus, consonant complexity was a potential contextual factor that could affect vowel production.

Vowels may be less variable than consonants, despite impaired motor programming. However, it is also possible that vowels are variable both in neurologically healthy and impaired speakers, and that this variance is tolerated due to widely ranging differences in speaker dialect, age and sex. While consonant errors are more frequently observed clinically, this may be due to greater perceptual sensitivity to the acoustic cues for consonants than for vowels. Since some studies have shown similar vowel variability in neurologically healthy and AOS speakers, this may indicate that vowel production is somewhat robust to motor programming disruption. In this case, when a speaker *does* exhibit high levels of vowel variability in comparison to neurotypical speakers (as observed in this study), this may reflect more significant motor programming involvement.

7.5.2 Limitations

The current study focused on whether vowel formant frequencies in correctly repeated CVC syllables were affected by the complexity of the surrounding consonants in two participants with AOS. The most obvious limitation of this study was the small number of participants. Further collection of productions of the CVC stimuli should be completed with additional participants with AOS and neurotypical controls.

The participants in this study with AOS both had mild to moderate apraxia severity with mild concomitant aphasia. Participant A1 had higher severity on subtests of the ABA than participant A2. Participant A1 also demonstrated greater variability in vowel production. Analyzing vowel formants in the CVC stimuli produced by speakers with more systematically variable levels of severity would also benefit the interpretation of findings. The difficulty in including participants with more severe AOS is that participants must be able to produce the stimuli without extensive training. However, the inclusion of a larger number of participants with either carefully described mild or moderate AOS would be beneficial.

Participants should be better matched for dialect and age. The participants were more than 50 years old; however, participant A1 was 18 years older than participant A2 and A1 was 23 years older than N1. Participants A1 and N1 also differed in dialect. Both age and dialect affect measures of vowel production (Hillenbrand et al. 1995).

The effects of complexity on vowel durations warrant further study due to temporal variability in apraxic speech (Kent & Rosenbek 1983). Speech in AOS is characteristically slow and halting, and vowel duration could be affected by consonantal complexity. But, repetition of unfamiliar and decontextualized stimuli may slow speech rate. The slow rate may create artifacts in formant as well as durational data. The CVC stimuli restricted the possible complexity effects to the phonemic level in order to control for the extra effect of the syllable boundary. Given that complexity effects were not found for the vowels, the production of consonant-vowel-consonant vowel (CVCV) disyllable stimuli would allow for the study of complexity effects across syllable boundaries. Manipulation of the consonants and vowels in CVCV stimuli would provide information about the effects of complexity on the stability of vowels within and across syllable boundaries.

This study did not examine vowel variability in relation to individual consonant complexity, instead focusing on complexity change from initial to final consonant. Previous findings that different measures of complexity predict variability in consonant production (Marquardt et al. 1979; Wolk 1986) suggest that the effect of individual consonant complexity on vowel production warrants further study. Further, due to constraints in developing stimuli with specific changes in phonetic complexity, order of acquisition (Ireland et al. 1977) for the consonants used was variable and did not change systematically across each group of stimuli.

Complexity was defined in this study as the number of distinctive features that changed between initial and final consonants (Juola &

Zimmermann 1996; Kondrak 2003; Somers 1998) and does not necessarily reflect true articulatory complexity. In particular, producing stops in both the initial and final positions of a CVC, which requires the involvement of multiple articulatory systems, may be more difficult or complex than transitioning from a stop in the initial position to a fricative in the final position. In future studies, consideration of different complexity metrics, including those based on articulatory kinematics of speech, may be useful in determining the relative difficulty of speech production stimuli.

Lexicality effects were not examined in the study. Real words and nonsense words were used in order to create a list of stimuli, which reflected a range of complexity changes from initial to final consonant. The real word syllables and not the nonsense syllables could theoretically be stored in a syllabary of commonly used syllables (Levelt et al. 1999). The decreased cognitive load on speech production in producing stored syllables may affect vowel formant and duration variability. Lexicality effects should be examined in future analyses.

Finally, the specific phonemes used in the study may have been resistant to effects of variability. According to Stevens (1989), the two point vowels used, /i/ and /a/, may resist variability in speech production. Naturally increased stability of the jaw during the production of the vowels /i/ and /a/ may also result in reduced variability. The greater variability of the vowel /u/ observed in all speakers supports the notion of the relative stability of /i/ and /a/. The vowels chosen, /i/, /a/ and /u/, had been used in previous studies of vowel production in AOS (e.g., Skenes & Trullinger 1988); however, other vowels were excluded due to higher known variability in production. For example, the vowel /o/ is usually a diphthong in American English and, therefore, was excluded from the study. The schwa, /ə/, was excluded because speakers with AOS demonstrate fewer speech errors in the unstressed syllables in which the vowel /ə/ is produced (Hillenbrand et al. 1995). Schwa is likely highly variable based on its defining feature of taking on the features of surrounding phonemes (Ziegler & von Cramon 1985, 1986). The reasons for the exclusion of schwa could also justify inclusion. Schwa is rarely produced in error, as desired for variability measures.

7.6 Conclusion

Vowels were more variable in the two participants with AOS than in the two neurotypical participants. However, there were no consistent effects of complexity observed for vowel production variability. These findings are not consistent with the hypothesized effect of consonant complexity on vowel production. Lack of complexity effects could mean that errors are not dependent on the complexity or variability measures used in the study. Interpretation of the findings should be tempered by a number of limitations of the study design, including the small number of participants and the specific stimuli used. The vowels used in this study or vowels in general may be resistant to effects of complexity. Further study of the effect of complexity on vowel durations and vowel formants in multisyllabic stimuli is warranted due to the current absence of a significant effect of complexity on vowel formants in CVC stimuli.

References

Aichert, I., & W. Ziegler. (2004). Syllable frequency and syllable structure in apraxia of speech. *Brain and Language,* 88(1), 148–59. http://dx.doi.org/10.1016/S0093-934X(03)00296-7

American Speech-Language-Hearing Association. (2007). *Childhood apraxia of speech* [Position Statement]. Available from www.asha.org/policy

Blumstein, S.E., W.E. Cooper, E.B. Zurif & A. Caramazza. (1977). The perception and production of voice-onset time in aphasia. *Neuropsychologia,* 15(3), 371–83. http://dx.doi.org/10.1016/0028-3932(77)90089-6

Boersma, P., & D. Weenink. (2005). *Praat: Doing phonetics by computer (Version 4.3.14)* [Computer software and manual]. Retrieved July 1, 2006, from http://www.praat.org

Collins, M.J. (1989). Differential diagnosis of aphasic syndromes and apraxia of speech. In P. Square-Storer (ed.), *Acquired Apraxia of Speech in Aphasic Adults: Theoretical and Clinical Issues* (vol. xvii, pp. 87–114). Hillsdale, NJ: Lawrence Erlbaum Associates.

Dabul, B. (2000). *Apraxia Battery for Adults* (2nd ed.). Austin, TX: Pro-Ed.

Darley, F.L., A.E. Aronson & J.R. Brown. (1975). *Motor Speech Disorders.* Philadelphia, PA: W.B. Saunders Company.

Deger, K., & W. Ziegler. (2002). Speech motor programming in apraxia of speech. *Journal of Phonetics,* 30(3), 321–35. http://dx.doi.org/10.1006/jpho.2001.0163

Dogil, G., & J. Mayer. (1998). Selective phonological impairment: A case of apraxia of speech. *Phonology,* 15(2), 143–88. http://dx.doi.org/10.1017/S095267579800356X

Dronkers, N.F. (1996). A new brain region for coordinating speech articulation. *Nature,* 384(6605), 159–61. http://dx.doi.org/10.1038/384159a0

Dronkers, N.F., O. Plaisant, M.T. Iba-Zizen, & E.A. Cabanis. (2007). Paul Broca's historic cases: High resolution MR imaging of the brains of Leborgne and Lelong. *Brain,* 130(5), 1432–41. http://dx.doi.org/10.1093/brain/awm042

Duffy, J. (2012). *Motor Speech Disorders: Substrates, Differential Diagnosis, and Management*. St. Louis, MI: Mosby.

Dunlop, J.M., & T.P. Marquardt. (1977). Linguistic and articulatory aspects of single word production in apraxia of speech. *Cortex*, 13(1), 17–29. http://dx.doi.org/10.1016/S0010-9452(77)80050-6

Edmonds, L.A., & T.P. Marquardt. (2004). Syllable use in apraxia of speech: Preliminary findings. *Aphasiology*, 18(12), 1121–34. http://dx.doi.org/10.1080/02687030444000561

Freed, D. (2000). *Motor Speech Disorders: Diagnosis and Treatment*. San Diego, CA: Thomson Learning-Singular Publishing Group.

Haley, K.L., G.L. Bays & R.N. Ohde. (2001a). Phonetic properties of aphasic–apraxic speech: A modified narrow transcription analysis. *Aphasiology*, 15(12), 1125–42. http://dx.doi.org/10.1080/02687040143000537

Haley, K. L., K.T. Cunningham, C.T. Eaton & A. Jacks. (submitted). Sound error variability in acquired apraxia of speech is multidimensional.

Haley, K.L., A. Jacks & K.T. Cunningham. (2013). Error variability and the differentiation between apraxia of speech and aphasia with phonemic paraphasia. *Journal of Speech, Language, and Hearing Research (JSLHR)*, 56(3), 891–905. http://dx.doi.org/10.1044/1092-4388(2012/12-0161)

Haley, K.L., R.N. Ohde & R.T. Wertz. (2000). Single word intelligibility in aphasia and apraxia of speech: A phonetic error analysis. *Aphasiology*, 14(2), 179–201. http://dx.doi.org/10.1080/026870300401540

Haley, K.L., R.N. Ohde & R.T. Wertz. (2001b). Vowel quality in aphasia and apraxia speech: Phonetic transcription and formant analyses. *Aphasiology*, 15(12), 1107–23. http://dx.doi.org/10.1080/02687040143000519

Haley, K.L., & H.B. Overton. (2001). Word length and vowel duration in apraxia of speech: The use of relative measures. *Brain and Language*, 79(3), 397–406. http://dx.doi.org/10.1006/brln.2001.2494

Hillenbrand, J., & R. Gayvert. (2005). Open source software for experiment design and control. *Journal of Speech, Language, and Hearing Research (JSLHR)*, 48(1), 45–60. http://dx.doi.org/10.1044/1092-4388(2005/005)

Hillenbrand, J., L.A. Getty, M.J. Clark & K. Wheeler. (1995). Acoustic characteristics of American English vowels. *Journal of the Acoustical Society of America*, 97(5), 3099–111. http://dx.doi.org/10.1121/1.411872

Hillis, A.E., M. Work, P.B. Barker, M.A. Jacobs, E.L. Breese & K. Maurer. (2004). Re-examining the brain regions crucial for orchestrating speech articulation. *Brain*, 127(7), 1479–87. http://dx.doi.org/10.1093/brain/awh172

Hoit-Dalgaard, J., T. Murray & H.G. Kopp. (1983). Voice onset time production and perception in apraxic subjects. *Brain and Language*, 20(2), 329–39. http://dx.doi.org/10.1016/0093-934X(83)90048-2

Ireland, J.V., R.J. Klich & J.M. Panagos. (1977). Is there phonemic regression in aphasic speech? *Perceptual and Motor Skills*, 44(3c), 1042. http://dx.doi.org/10.2466/pms.1977.44.3c.1042

Itoh, M., & S. Sasanuma. (1984). Articulatory movements in apraxia of speech. In J.C. Rosenbek, M.R. McNeil &A.E. Aronson (eds.), *Apraxia of Speech:*

Physiology, Acoustics, Linguistics, Management (pp. 135–65). San Diego, CA: College-Hill Press.

Jacks, A. (2006). Vowel targeting and perception in apraxia of speech. Unpublished doctoral dissertation, The University of Texas at Austin.

Jacks, A. (2008). Bite block vowel production in apraxia of speech. *Journal of Speech, Language, and Hearing Research (JSLHR)*, 51(4), 898–913. http://dx.doi.org/10.1044/1092-4388(2008/066)

Jacks, A., K.A. Mathes & T.P. Marquardt. (2010). Vowel acoustics in adults with apraxia of speech. *Journal of Speech, Language, and Hearing Research (JSLHR)*, 53(1), 61–74. http://dx.doi.org/10.1044/1092-4388(2009/08-0017)

Johns, D. F., & F.L. Darley. (1970). Phonemic variability in apraxia of speech. *Journal of Speech, Language, and Hearing Research (JSLHR)*, 13(3), 556–83.

Jones, W.J., L.S. Williams & J.F. Meschia. (2001). Validating the questionnaire for Verifying Stroke-Free Status (QVSFS) by neurological history and examination. *Stroke*, 32(10), 2232–36. http://dx.doi.org/10.1161/hs1001.096191

Juola, P., & P. Zimmermann. (1996). Whole-word phonetic distances and the PGPfone alphabet. *Proceedings of the International Conference on Spoken Language Processing*, 96. http://dx.doi.org/10.1109/ICSLP.1996.607046

Kent, R.D., & J.C. Rosenbek. (1982). Prosodic disturbance and neurologic lesion. *Brain and Language*, 15(2), 259–21. http://dx.doi.org/10.1016/0093-934X(82)90060-8

Kent, R.D., & J.C. Rosenbek. (1983). Acoustic patterns of apraxia of speech. *Journal of Speech and Hearing Research*, 26(2), 231–49. http://dx.doi.org/10.1044/jshr.2602.231

Kertesz, A. (1982). *Western Aphasia Battery*. New York: Grune & Stratton.

Kondrak, G. (2003). Phonetic alignment and similarity. *Computers and the Humanities*, 37(3), 273–91. http://dx.doi.org/10.1023/A:1025071200644

La Pointe, L.L., & D.F. Johns. (1975). Some phonemic characteristics in apraxia of speech. *Journal of Communication Disorders*, 8(3), 259–69. http://dx.doi.org/10.1016/0021-9924(75)90018-0

Labov, W., S. Ash & C. Boberg. (2005). *Atlas of North American English: Phonetics, Phonology, and Sound Change*. New York: Mouton de Gruyer. http://dx.doi.org/10.1515/9783110206838

Levelt, W.J., A. Roelofs & A.S. Meyer. (1999). A theory of lexical access in speech production. *Behavioral and Brain Sciences*, 22(1), 1–38. http://dx.doi.org/10.1017/S0140525X99001776

Marquardt, T.P., J.B. Reinhart & H.A. Peterson. (1979). Markedness analysis of phonemic substitution errors in apraxia of speech. *Journal of Communication Disorders*, 12(6), 481–94. http://dx.doi.org/10.1016/0021-9924(79)90011-X

McNeil, M.R., M. Caligiuri & J.C. Rosenbek. (1989). A comparison of labiomandibular kinematic durations, displacements, velocities, and dysmetrias in apraxic and normal adults. In *Clinical Aphasiology: Proceedings of the Conference* (pp. 173–93). San Diego: College-Hill Press.

McNeil, M.R., K.H. Odell, S.B. Miller & L. Hunter. (1995). Consistency, variability, and target approximation for successive speech repetitions among apraxic, conduction aphasic, and ataxic dysarthric speakers. *Clinical Aphasiology*, 23, 39–55.

McNeil, M.R., D.A. Robin & R.A. Schmidt. (1997). Apraxia of speech: Definition, differentiation, and treatment. In M.R. McNeil (ed.), *Clinical Management of Sensorimotor Speech Disorders* (pp. 311–44). New York: Thieme Medical Publishers.

Monoi, H., Y. Fukusako, M. Itoh & S. Sasanuma. (1983). Speech sound errors in patients with conduction and Broca's aphasia. *Brain and Language*, 20(2), 175–94. http://dx.doi.org/10.1016/0093-934X(83)90041-X

Odell, K., M. McNeil, J.C. Rosenbek & L. Hunter. (1990). Perceptual characteristics of consonant production by apraxic speakers. *Journal of Speech and Hearing Disorders*, 55(2), 345–59. http://dx.doi.org/10.1044/jshd.5502.345

Odell, K., M. McNeil, J.C. Rosenbek & L. Hunter. (1991). Perceptual characteristics of vowel and prosody production in apraxic, aphasic, and dysarthric speakers. *Journal of Speech and Hearing Research*, 34(1), 67–80. http://dx.doi.org/10.1044/jshr.3401.67

Pisoni, D.B. (1975). Auditory short-term memory and vowel perception. *Memory & Cognition*, 3(1), 7–18. http://dx.doi.org/10.3758/BF03198202

Richardson, J.D., P. Fillmore, C. Rorden, L.L. LaPointe & J. Fridriksson. (2012). Re-establishing Broca's initial findings. *Brain and Language*, 123(2), 125–30. http://dx.doi.org/10.1016/j.bandl.2012.08.007

Ryalls, J.H. (1981). Motor aphasia: Acoustic correlates of phonetic disintegration in vowels. *Neuropsychologia*, 19(3), 365–74. http://dx.doi.org/10.1016/0028-3932(81)90066-X

Ryalls, J.H. (1986). An acoustic study of vowel production in aphasia. *Brain and Language*, 29(1), 48–67. http://dx.doi.org/10.1016/0093-934X(86)90033-7

Skenes, L.L., & R.W. Trullinger. (1988). Error patterns during repetition of consonant-vowel-consonant syllables by apraxic speakers. *Journal of Communication Disorders*, 21(3), 263–9. http://dx.doi.org/10.1016/0021-9924(88)90034-2

Somers, H.L. (1998). Similarity metrics for aligning children's articulation data. *Proceedings of COLING-ACL '98: 36th Annual Meeting of the Association for Computational Linguistics and 17th International Conference on Computational Linguistics* (pp. 1227–32).

Sony (n.d.). One-point stereo microphone Model #ECM-MS57 [Hardware]. New York: Sony Corporation of America.

Staiger, A., W. Finger-Berg, I. Aichert & W. Ziegler. (2012). Error variability in apraxia of speech: A matter of controversy. *Journal of Speech, Language, and Hearing Research (JSLHR)*, 55(5), S1544–61. http://dx.doi.org/10.1044/1092-4388(2012/11-0319)

Stevens, K.N. (1989). On the quantal nature of speech. *Journal of Phonetics*, 17(1–2), 3–45.

Tourville, J.A., & F.H. Guenther. (2011).The DIVA model: A neural theory of speech acquisition and production. *Language and Cognitive Processes*, 26(7), 952–81. http://dx.doi.org/10.1080/01690960903498424

Varley, R., & S.P. Whiteside. (2001). What is the underlying impairment in acquired apraxia of speech? *Aphasiology*, 15(1), 39–84.

Wambaugh, J.L., J.R. Duffy, M.R. McNeil, D.A. Robin & M.A. Rogers. (2006). Treatment guidelines for acquired apraxia of speech: A synthesis and evaluation of the evidence. *Journal of Medical Speech-Language Pathology*, 14(2), xv–xxxiii.

Whiteside, S.P., S. Grobler, F. Windsor & R. Varley. (2010). An acoustic study of vowels and coarticulation as a function of utterance type: A case of acquired apraxia of speech. *Journal of Neurolinguistics*, 23(2), 145–61. http://dx.doi.org/10.1016/j.jneuroling.2009.12.002

Whiteside, S.P., & R.A. Varley. (1998). A reconceptualisation of apraxia of speech: A synthesis of evidence. *Cortex*, 34(2), 221–31. http://dx.doi.org/10.1016/S0010-9452(08)70749-4

Wolk, L. (1986). Markedness analysis of consonant error productions in apraxia of speech. *Journal of Communication Disorders*, 19(2), 133–60. http://dx.doi.org/10.1016/0021-9924(86)90016-X

Ziegler, W., & D. von Cramon. (1985). Anticipatory coarticulation in a patient with apraxia of speech. *Brain and Language*, 26(1), 117–30.

Ziegler, W., & D. von Cramon. (1986). Disturbed coarticulation in apraxia of speech: Acoustic evidence. *Brain and Language*, 29(1), 34–47.

8
Speed and Accuracy of Picture Naming in Adults Who Stutter: The Influence of Phonetic Complexity

Courtney T. Byrd, Geoffrey A. Coalson, Jie Yang and Kirsten Moriarty[1]

8.1 Introduction

Stuttering is a disorder that affects approximately 1 per cent of the adult population (almost 3 million people) and can impose potentially negative academic, vocational and societal consequences (for WHO-ICF description, see Yaruss & Quesal 2004). The observable properties of stuttering include atypical disruptions in the forward momentum of speech, characterized by sound repetitions (e.g., "b-b-b-backpack"), syllable repetitions (e.g., "back...back...backpack"), monosyllabic word repetitions (e.g., "my... my...my... my backpack), audible sound prolongations (e.g., "mmmmmmy backpack) and/or inaudible blocks (e.g., "[b] – – backpack"; Yairi & Ambrose 2005). The EXPLAN model of stuttering (EX: execution, PLAN: planning; Howell 2011: 2267–73) argues that these disfluencies characteristic of

1 Courtney T. Byrd is an associate professor in the Department of Communication Sciences and Disorders at Moody College of Communication, the University of Texas at Austin.
Geoffrey A. Coalson is an assistant professor in the Department of Communication Sciences and Disorders at Louisiana State University.
Jie Yang is an assistant professor in the Department of Communication Sciences and Disorders at Moody College of Communication, the University of Texas at Austin.
Kirsten Moriarty is a recent graduate in speech-language pathology from the Department of Communication Sciences and Disorders at Moody College of Communication, the University of Texas at Austin.

stuttering occur because individuals who stutter have insufficient time to plan for speech. As a result, motor execution is initiated prior to the completion of the speech plan. Howell and colleagues (Dworzynski & Howell 2004; Howell & Dworzynski 2005) suggest that stuttering is more likely to occur with increased phonetic complexity because more complex articulatory movements require additional time to formulate the speech plan.

Until recently, the Index of Phonetic Complexity (IPC; Jakielski 1998) was the primary measurement tool used (and available) to investigate the influence of phonetic complexity on stuttered speech (Dworzynski & Howell 2004; Howell & Au-Yeung 2007; Howell et al. 2006; LaSalle & Wolk 2011). The IPC is an unpublished eight-factor index of phonetic complexity based on the speech output of infants ($N = 5$; 7 to 36 months of age) which assigns numerical value to words based on select phonetic properties [i.e., (1) consonant place, (2) consonant manner, (3) vowel types, (4) word shapes, (5) word length, (6) consonant reduplication versus variegation, (7) singletons versus clusters and (8) cluster types; see Table 8.1 for an IPC

Table 8.1. Categories of phonological complexity and scoring criteria for the Index of Phonetic Complexity and Word Complexity Measure.

IPC points	IPC	WCM points	WCM
1	Dorsals	1	Velars/dorsals
1	Fricatives	1	Fricatives
	X	1	Voiced fricatives
1	Affricates	1	Affricates
	X	1	Voiced affricates
1	Liquids	1	Liquids/syllabic liquids
1	Place variegations of consonants within word		X
1	Rhotics	1	Rhotics
1	Word-final consonant	1	Word-final consonant
1	> 2 syllables	1	> 2 syllables
1	Consonant clusters (intra-syllabic)	1	Consonant clusters (intra-syllabic)
1	Consonant clusters (inter-syllabic)		X
1	Place variegations within clusters		X
	X	1	Non-initial stress

Note. IPC = Index of Phonetic Complexity (Jakielski 1998); WCM = Word Complexity Measure (Stoel-Gammon 2010).

scoring rubric]. Unpublished data report that IPC scores of verbal output increase in children 1 to 3 years of age (Jakielski 2002; Jakielski et al. 2006) and serve as a metric of developmental advancements in the articulatory system during this time.

The relationship between phonetic complexity, as measured by the IPC, and stuttered speech has been demonstrated in older children and adults, but not in younger children (Dworzynski & Howell 2004: 6 years and older; Howell & Au-Yeung 2007: 6 years of age or older; Howell et al. 2006: 11 to 18 years of age; LaSalle & Wolk 2011: 14 years of age). These findings are unexpected as one would presume that younger children would be more vulnerable to the phonetic complexity of their spoken output while their articulatory systems are still in the early developmental stage. These findings also appear to contradict research that suggests that the phonetic plan does not appear to differ in stuttered speech. Sussman et al. (2011) examined the acoustic properties of fluent and stuttered tokens that included initial consonant-vowel (CV) onsets. Results indicated that the phonetic properties between initial consonant and vowels of stuttered tokens remained relatively intact and similar to non-stuttered CV tokens. Authors interpreted findings to suggest that phonetic properties are preserved once phonological plans become available to the articulatory system. Perhaps, as suggested by Bernstein Ratner (2005), past findings that suggested phonetic complexity as a significant contributor to stuttered speech were compromised by one or more confounding factors.

To begin with, the application of the IPC at any age beyond babbling is questionable given that the basic constructs were developed on prelinguistic speech. In addition, lexical factors such as word frequency and phonological neighborhood properties were not accounted for in past studies that examined the role of phonetic complexity as measured by the IPC. There also has been no consideration of the length and complexity of the utterances from which the words were extracted for analysis. Bernstein Ratner (2005) suggested that an experimental paradigm might be the preferred method for exploring the potential for a link between stuttering and phonetic complexity as, at present, there are limited data in the broad literature to suggest that phonetic complexity delays speech planning or production in individuals who do or do not stutter.

Coalson et al. (2012) recently addressed three of the four concerns outlined by Bernstein Ratner (2005) in their analysis of phonetic complexity in stuttered versus fluent words produced by children during parent-child interactions (age range: 2 years 7 months to 5 years 9 months). First, instead of using the IPC, Coalson and colleagues used the Word Complexity Measure (WCM: Stoel-Gammon 2010), a measure that is comparable to the IPC but is more appropriate for use as this tool is based on speech properties of children beyond the stage of babbling and closer to the age at which stuttering is often reported to begin. For example, in contrast to the IPC, the WCM does *not* award points for certain phonetic constructs that are typically mastered by preschool-aged children (e.g., inter-syllabic clusters and place variegation of consonants or consonant clusters) but *does* award points for later developing constructs (e.g., voiced fricatives and affricates; see Table 8.1 for IPC vs WCM scoring rubrics). Also unlike the IPC, the clinical utility of the WCM is supported in published studies of typically developing children (Macrae 2013) and children with phonological disorders (Anderson & Cohen 2012). Second, using logistic regression analysis, Coalson et al. accounted for multiple lexical properties in addition to phonetic complexity, including word frequency, segmental and biphone phonotactic probability, neighborhood density, neighborhood frequency and grammatical classification. Third, utterance length, syntactic complexity and utterance-position were included as additional predictor variables. Of the variables considered in their regression analysis, Coalson and colleagues reported that only utterance-level variables (i.e., length, syntactic complexity and utterance-initial position) significantly influenced the likelihood of stuttered speech.

Data from Coalson et al. (2012) provide a reasonable account for the observed influence of phonetic complexity on the stuttered speech of older children and adults and the lack thereof in young children. Compared to younger children, older children and adults are more likely to speak in longer and more complex utterances, two factors known to exacerbate stuttered speech (Logan & Conture 1997; Tsiamtsiouris & Cairns 2013; Yaruss 1999; Zackheim & Conture 2003). However, as acknowledged by Coalson and colleagues, their findings do not entirely negate the potential influence of phonetic complexity on stuttered speech, but rather highlight relevant factors to consider during future interpretation of conversational data. Coalson et al. further suggested, in agreement with the fourth concern raised by Bernstein Ratner (2005), that the subtle influence of phonetic complexity may be more evident during controlled experimental tasks that allow syntactic as well as lexical variables to be controlled.

Lexical variables such as word frequency (i.e., how frequently an individual word occurs in a native language: Dell 1990; Jescheniak & Levelt 1994), neighborhood density (i.e., the number of words that differ from the target word by the addition, substitution or deletion of one phoneme: Luce & Pisoni 1998) and neighborhood frequency (i.e., the average word frequency of neighboring words: ibid.), are known contributors to the *accuracy* and *speed* of responses for AWNS (e.g., Newman & German 2005; Vitevitch 2002; Vitevitch & Sommers 2003). Specific to adults who stutter (AWS), Newman & Bernstein Ratner (2007: 206–7) found an overall greater number of naming errors compared to AWNS for real word stimuli that varied by word frequency, neighborhood density and neighborhood frequency, although error patterns mirrored those of adults who do not stutter (AWNS) and no significant interactions were observed. They also reported that although increase in errors produced by both talker groups for words of low versus high neighborhood density (and balanced for word and neighborhood frequency) were observed, differences diminished for both groups upon removal of stimuli with consonant clusters. As discussed by Newman & Bernstein Ratner, the effects of certain lexical properties may be confounded to a degree by phonetic properties, and vice versa, during real word production.

In terms of speed of production, Huinck et al. (2004) found AWS were slower to initiate bisyllabic nonwords with homorganic clusters relative to AWNS when these clusters flanked the syllable boundary. Upon subsequent analysis, results were not affected by removal of stimuli with high-frequency clusters (ibid.: 18). These findings suggest that, when controlling for specific phonological properties (i.e., cluster frequency), certain phonetic properties may serve as an independent factor to speed of response in AWS. However, the contribution of additional lexical factors, such as word frequency, could not be measured with a nonword paradigm, and as noted by Vitevitch & Luce (2005), reaction time latencies during repetition of nonwords are not immune to its overall phonological properties (e.g., mean-weighted neighborhood density). Thus, further isolation of phonetic from lexical properties may inform data that suggest speech *fluency* of real word production in AWS may be mitigated by lexical factors (word frequency: Anderson 2007; Dayalu et al. 2002; Newman & Bernstein Ratner 2007; neighborhood density: LaSalle & Wolk 2011; cf. Arnold et al. 2005; neighborhood frequency: Anderson 2007; cf. Newman & Bernstein Ratner 2007) as well as phonetic factors (Dworzynski & Howell 2004; Howell & Au-Yeung 2007; Howell et al. 2006; LaSalle & Wolk 2011; cf. Coalson et al. 2012).

In sum, the purpose of the present study is to investigate the effects of phonetic complexity, if any, on the speed and accuracy of picture naming in AWS and AWNS. Specifically, we employed the most valid tool currently available in the literature to measure phonetic complexity: the WCM. To control for utterance-based factors, we employed a single-word picture naming paradigm. In addition, to account for lexical factors, we constructed word lists of high and low phonetic complexity that were balanced relative to word frequency, neighborhood density and neighborhood frequency properties. Based on the limitations of past research, we predict that present findings will lend further support to our position that the speech fluency of persons who stutter is uniquely compromised by phonetic complexity.

8.2 Method

8.2.1 Participants

Participants included 14 AWS and 14 AWNS who were matched for age (+/– 3 years) and gender. Participants included 3 females and 11 males in each group, with ages ranging from 18 years 1 month to 46 years 11 months (AWS: Mean age = 28;8; AWNS: Mean age = 28;6). Participants were paid volunteers who were unfamiliar with the purpose and protocol of the study. Approval for the study was attained by the first author through the Institutional Review Board of the University of Texas at Austin, and informed consent was obtained for each participant.

Prior to experimental testing, a battery of standardized tests was administered to all participants. The *Peabody Picture Vocabulary Test: Third Edition* or *Fourth Edition* (PPVT-III: Dunn & Dunn 1997; PPVT-IV: Dunn & Dunn 2007) and the *Expressive Vocabulary Test* and *Expressive Vocabulary Test-Revised* (EVT: Williams 1997; EVT-2: Williams 2007) were used to assess receptive and expressive vocabulary. Both editions were used as when the study began authors did not have access to the most recent edition of each test (i.e., PPVT-IV and EVT-2). In addition, the Nonword Repetition and Rapid Digit Naming subtests of the *Comprehensive Test of Phonological Processing* (CTOPP: Wagner et al. 1999) were administered to assess working memory capacity and phonological information retrieval. Each participant and age/gender matched counterpart scored within 10 mean standard score points on the PPVT, 11 on the EVT, 3 on Rapid Digit Naming, and 2 on Nonword Repetition subtests. A summary of participants' characteristics and performance on standardized measures is found in Tables 8.2 and 8.3.

Table 8.2. Participant characteristics for adults who stutter.

PN	CA	Stg %	Stg scale	SSI-3	PPVT	EVT	CTOPP (RD)	CTOPP (NR)	Tx
1	20;5	0	2	Very Mild	114	120	11	8	Y
2	38;1	0	3	Mild	101	100	7	8	N
3	21;2	1.25	3	Mild	130	118	7	5	Y
4	44;6	0	2	Very Mild	106	116	*	*	Y
5	23;7	17.5	7	Sev	140	129	6	9	Y
6	40;4	5	4	Mild/Mod	107	106	*	*	Y
7	23;11	16.3	7	Sev	106	97	9	5	Y
8	28;7	11.3	6	Mod/Sev	115	97	10	6	Y
9	24;1	2.5	3	Mild	122	116	16	7	N
10	18;1	10	6	Mod/Sev	120	134	9	10	Y
11	27;1	6.3	4	Mild/Mod	124	125	9	7	Y
12	21;3	8.8	5	Mod	107	111	12	9	N
13	33;3	5	4	Mild/Mod	108	105	13	10	N
14	39;0	0	2	Very Mild	112	118	14	10	Y
M	28;8	6.0	4		115	114	10	8	Y = 10
SD	8;4	5.8	2		11	11	3	2	N = 4

Table 8.3. Participant characteristics for adults who do not stutter.

PN	CA	PPVT	EVT	CTOPP (RD)	CTOPP (NR)
1	27;6	106	97	13	10
2	20;8	117	114	17	8
3	21;9	104	105	9	6
4	22;9	124	114	13	9
5	38;8	107	101	12	7
6	37;5	105	115	7	8
7	20;5	117	118	9	8
8	46;11	110	120	12	6
9	27;9	101	116	10	10
10	26;7	106	114	11	8
11	21;1	117	114	12	15
12	30;1	112	122	10	11
13	19;8	97	96	8	6
14	39;11	99	91	10	8
M	28;6	109	109	11	9
SD	8;2	8	10	2	2

Note: * = scores unavailable; PN = participant number; CA = chronological age; Stg = stuttering; Mod = moderate; Sev = severe; PPVT = Peabody Picture Vocabulary Test; EVT = Expressive Vocabulary Test; CTOPP = Comprehensive Test of Phonological Processing; RD = Rapid Digit Naming; NW = Nonword Repetition; Tx = treatment; M = mean; SD = standard deviation; Y = yes; N = no.

In addition to performing within normal limits on these standardized tests, participants were required to meet the following criteria: (a) native monolingual English speaker (*n* = 12 for AWS group, *n* = 13 for AWNS group) or speak English as their primary language and with native competency (*n* = 2 for AWS group, *n* = 1 for AWNS group); (b) between the ages of 17 and 50 years; (c) no speech or language disorders (apart from stuttering in AWS group); and (d) no present or past history of psychiatric, social or emotional disturbances.

Three participants (i.e., 2 AWS and 1 AWNS) initially recruited failed to meet one or more of the inclusion criteria. One AWS participant did not speak English with native competency, and two participants, one AWS and one AWNS, did not meet the standardized testing score criteria.

The *AWS participants* had to meet the following additional criteria to be included in the present study: (1) confirmed diagnosis of stuttering from a certified speech-language pathologist specializing in stuttering (through evaluation of conversational and narrative discourse type yielding behaviors indicative of stuttering including audible as well as inaudible sound prolongations and repetitions of monosyllabic words, sounds and syllables wherein the iterations varied in timing and tension: Yairi & Ambrose 2005); (2) self-identification as an AWS with reported onset prior to age 7; (3) no history of traumatic brain injury and/or any form of cerebral insult that could potentially impact speech production or reaction time; and (4) no report of current medication use that could impact speech production or reaction time. Further confirmation of the identified stuttering behavior was established by the fourth author during severity analysis.

Stuttering severity. Analysis of stuttering severity was completed using a modified version of a rating scale originally developed by O'Brian et al. (2004). Stuttering severity was measured using a 9-point scale (i.e., 1 = no stuttering, 5 = moderate stuttering, 9 = extremely severe stuttering). The mean rating for the total 14 participants was 4 (SD = 2, range 2 to 7), with six participants receiving a rating of 2 to 3, four participants receiving a rating of 4 to 5, and four participants receiving a rating of 6 to 7 (see Table 8.2). The fourth author and a graduate student trained in disfluency count analysis independently rated the unstructured conversational samples for 36 per cent of the total AWS participants (*n* = 5 of 14). Inter-judge ratings were exact for 80 per cent (*n* = 4) of the participants, and within one scale point for the remaining 20 per cent (*n* = 1). Intra-rater ratings were completed by the fourth author with the same scale point assigned for her first and second rating across 5 participants (100 per cent agreement).

In addition to this rating scale the fourth author also completed the Stuttering-Severity Instrument-3 on each participant (SSI-3: Riley 1994). The severity rating results using this tool yielded the exact same findings as reported with the 9-point scale above, with the exception of three participants who were rated as "mild" receiving a score of "very mild" on the SSI-3.

Treatment history. Of the AWS participants, 71 per cent (n = 10) were currently receiving speech therapy, and/or had received speech therapy in the past. The remaining AWS participants (29 per cent, n = 4) were not enrolled in therapy at the time of the experiment and reportedly had not received speech therapy in the past. The authors chose not to exclude adults on the basis of treatment history for two key reasons. First, there was no reason to suspect that exposure to fluency therapy would differentially affect an individual adult's performance on the tasks employed in the study. Second, it is not uncommon for AWS to report participation in fluency therapy, particularly during school years. Thus, inclusion of adults who had participated in therapy adds to the ecological validity of this study (see Byrd et al. 2012, for a similar argument regarding inclusion of participants who stutter who had history of treatment).

8.2.2 Stimuli Selection

Two lists of 14 content words were selected based on phonetic and lexical properties. One list comprised words with high phonetic complexity (HPC) and the other list with low phonetic complexity (LPC), both as measured by the WCM. Of the 14 words within each list, 7 were high in word frequency, neighborhood density and neighborhood frequency, while the remaining 7 were considered to have low word frequency, neighborhood density and neighborhood frequency. Word frequency, neighborhood density and neighborhood frequency values were obtained from the Hoosier Mental Lexicon (HML) adult database (see Luce et al. 1990; Luce & Pisoni 1998; available at http://128.252.27.56/neighborhood/Home.asp). Per the HML, word frequency values were defined as the log frequency of the word in the database corpus. Neighborhood density values were defined as the raw number of words that differed by one phoneme from the target word. Neighborhood frequency was defined as the mean word frequency of the neighboring words. See Tables 8.4 and 8.5 for the phonetic and lexical values related to each target word.

Table 8.4. High phonetic complexity (HPC) stimuli with word frequency, neighborhood density, neighborhood frequency and phonetic complexity values.

Target Word	Word frequency	Neighborhood density	Neighborhood frequency	WCM
	High			
Corn	2.53	14.00	2.05	4.00
Hat	2.75	31.00	2.44	2.00
Leg*	2.76	14.00	2.00	3.00
Ring	2.69	21.00	2.02	3.00
Shirt	2.43	14.00	1.91	4.00
Sink	2.36	12.00	1.96	5.00
Swing	2.38	10.00	1.76	4.00
	Low			
Desk	2.81	2.00	2.22	4.00
Dinosaur	1.00	1.00	1.00	4.00
Dresser*	1.00	0.00	0.00	4.00
Giraffe	1.00	1.00	1.00	6.00
Guitar	2.28	1.00	1.00	4.00
Umbrella	1.90	0.00	0.00	5.00
Zebra	1.00	1.00	1.00	4.00
M	2.06	8.64	1.38	4.07
Maximum	2.81	31.00	2.44	6.00
Minimum	1.00	0.00	0.00	2.00
SD	0.74	9.59	0.88	1.00

Note: * = removed from final analysis; WCM = Word Complexity Measure (Stoel-Gammon 2010).

Table 8.5. Low phonetic complexity (LPC) stimuli with word frequency, neighborhood density, neighborhood frequency and phonetic complexity values.

Target Word	Word frequency	Neighborhood density	Neighborhood frequency	WCM score
	High			
Goat*	1.78	20.00	1.99	2.00
Moon	2.78	19.00	2.23	1.00
Pen	2.26	25.00	1.96	1.00
Rain	2.90	28.00	2.02	2.00
Shoe	2.15	21.00	2.60	1.00
Sun	3.44	24.00	2.50	2.00
Tree	2.77	11.00	2.11	2.00
	Low			
Banana	1.60	0.00	0.00	2.00
Camel	1.00	7.00	1.72	3.00
Helmet	1.00	0.00	0.00	3.00
Onion	2.18	0.00	0.00	1.00
Panda	1.00	1.00	1.00	0.00
Penguin	1.00	0.00	0.00	2.00
Waffle*	1.00	6.00	1.08	3.00
M	1.92	11.57	1.38	1.79
Maximum	3.44	28.00	2.60	3.00
Minimum	1.00	0.00	0.00	0.00
SD	0.85	10.81	1.00	0.89

Note: * = removed from final analysis; WCM = Word Complexity Measure (Stoel-Gammon 2010).

Black-on-white pictures that represented target words were selected from a list of picture stimuli compiled by the International Picture Naming Project (Szekely et al. 2004). Picture stimuli were presented to participants on a computer screen via the assessment program E-Prime®, created by Psychology Software Tools, Inc.

8.3 Procedure

Training and experimental tasks. Participants were asked to sit in front of a Dell Intel Pentium Processor with a Dell 12-inch Flat Panel Monitor located in a sound treated room. A microphone was placed approximately two to five inches from the participant's face. A scripted protocol was read to each participant, stating that one by one, pictures would appear on the screen and the participant was to say the word that corresponded to the picture as quickly as possible. The participants were instructed to press a designated key on the keyboard after producing the target word to advance the program to the next picture. The third and fourth authors were both present in the room to transcribe each response. A portable Olympus digital recording device was also used to record each participant during the task for later analysis and confirmation of the online recordings.

Prior to experimental testing, participants were shown four practice pictures (i.e., two HPC and two LPC) during two rounds to familiarize them with the structure of the experiment. Each of the four pictures was balanced relative to the properties of the experimental stimuli (i.e., word frequency, neighborhood density and neighborhood frequency). After training was completed, participants were presented with 56 black-on-white line drawings (i.e., two rounds of 28 target words). This provided participants with two opportunities to produce the correct word and increased the likelihood for usable target productions. Picture order was randomized by the E-Prime® program for both the first and second round for each participant. Speech reaction times (SRTs) were recorded by E-Prime® software for each word produced by each participant. The experimental task took approximately 10 to 15 minutes.

8.3.1 Coding, Reliability and Outliers

Response coding. For the purposes of analysis, responses were coded similar to other studies (e.g., Anderson 2008; Byrd et al. 2007; Newman & Bernstein Ratner 2007) and included the following error types:

(a) Naming Error: participant responded with a word that was not the desired target word (e.g., produced "dog" for the target word "goat").
(b) Intelligibility Error: either participant's response was unintelligible to researchers, or participant did not arrive at any response corresponding to the picture presented (e.g. "I don't know").

(c) Program Error: the recorded SRT of a production was not a reliable time (e.g. recorded as 0 or –5) with no previous error coding for response, or participant's response was not detected by the program and participant had to repeat target.

Coding reliability. The third author confirmed correct coding for all of participants' responses by listening to the audio digital recording against the coded spreadsheet. Any discrepancy in the coding that occurred during testing that was noted during review was corrected to ensure accurate coding of disfluent versus fluent productions as well as error type.

Participant outliers. Given the nature of this study we pre-determined that any participant whose mean reaction time and/or mean error production exceeded 2 SDs from the mean of the condition (i.e., HPC or LPC) within their talker group (i.e., AWS or AWNS) would be excluded from the final data corpus. Only one participant initially recruited for participation, an AWS, met this outlier criterion. This participant and his AWNS age match were removed prior to final analysis, resulting in our final reported number of 14 participants per talker group.

Stimuli outliers. Word stimuli were excluded if mean errors or reaction times exceeded 2 SDs from the mean of the condition (i.e., HPC or LPC) for both talker groups (i.e., AWS and AWNS). No tokens had to be removed for this purpose. Two tokens were excluded based on excessive naming errors in both talker groups and were removed from final analysis (i.e., high lexical properties: *leg*, low lexical properties: *dresser*). To maintain balance between word lists, two tokens of low phonetic complexity were removed with the highest error rate from each lexical group (i.e., high lexical properties: *goat*, low lexical properties: *waffle*). Upon removal of these four tokens, the stimuli set contained 24 words (HPC: n = 12; LPC: n = 12; 6 words with high and low lexical properties included in each list). Stimuli lists are provided in Tables 8.4 and 8.5.

Stimuli properties. Upon removal of outliers, words within each list were analyzed to ensure desired phonetic and lexical properties were maintained. A significant difference was observed between lists for phonetic complexity (HPC: M = 4.08, SD = 1.00; LPC: M = 1.67, SD = .89; $t = 6.27$, $p < .001$) but no significant differences between lists were observed for word frequency (HPC: M = 2.09, SD = .70; LPC: M = 2.01, SD = .87; $t = .27$, $p = .787$), neighborhood density (HPC: M = 8.92, SD = 9.96; LPC: M = 11.33, SD = 11.35; $t = -.55$, $p = .585$) or neighborhood frequency (HPC: M = 1.45, SD = .83; LPC: M = 1.35, SD = 1.07; $t = .26$, $p = .800$). See Tables 8.4 and 8.5 for the phonetic and lexical values related to each target word.

8.3.2 Analysis

The initial data corpus included 1,344 unique responses (i.e., 24 words × 2 trials × 28 participants; HPC: $n = 672$; LPC: $n = 672$). Program errors (HPC: $n = 38$; LPC: $n = 45$) or intelligibility errors (HPC: $n = 0$; LPC: $n = 2$) were considered unusable and excluded from the initial data corpus, resulting in a total of 1,259 total usable tokens in the final data corpus (HPC: $n = 634$; LPC: $n = 625$).

8.4 Results

To recap, the purpose of the present study was to explore the influence of phonetic complexity as measured by the WCM on the speed and accuracy of naming pictures from two lists of target words. The two lists differed in that one set included only words with high WCM scores and the other set included words with low WCM scores. Each set contained equal numbers of words with high and low word frequency, neighborhood density and neighborhood frequency.

8.4.1 Speed of Production

A mixed-model repeated-measures analysis of variance (ANOVA) was conducted to assess the impact of high and low phonetic complexity on SRTs, with talker group (i.e., AWS and AWNS) as the between-subjects factor and phonetic complexity (i.e., LPC and HPC) as the within-subjects factor. As illustrated in Figure 8.1, the main effect of talker group was significant, $F(1, 26) = 7.28$, $p = .012$, $\eta\rho^2 = .22$, with AWS exhibiting overall slower response times. However, no significant interaction between talker group and phonetic complexity was found, Wilks' Lambda = .96, $F(1, 26) = 1.04$, $p = .318$, $\eta\rho^2 = .04$. There was also no significant main effect of phonetic complexity ($F < 1$), with both groups responding with comparable speed to words with low and high phonetic complexity.

To explore possible interactions between phonetic and lexical factors, a mixed-model repeated-measures ANOVA was conducted, with talker group (i.e., AWS and AWNS) as between-group factors, and word subgroups (i.e., LPC and HPC with high lexical values, LPC and HPC with low lexical values) as within-group factors. In addition to the significant main effect for talker group, $F(1, 26) = 7.29$, $p = .012$, $\eta\rho^2 = .22$, a significant effect for word subtype was observed, $F(3, 24) = 4.68$, $p = .010$, $\eta\rho^2 = .37$. Planned

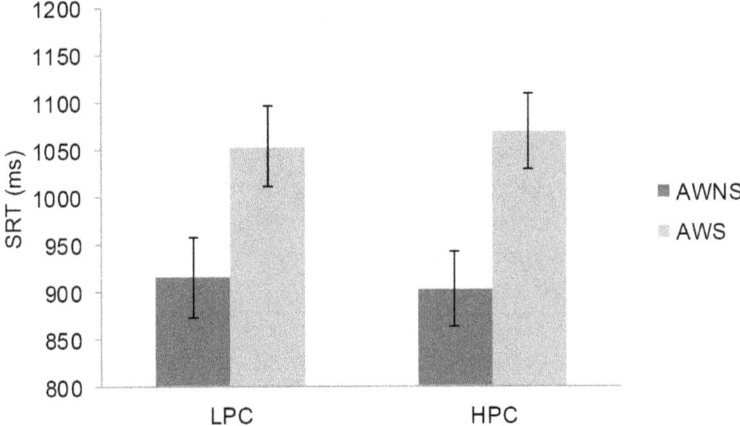

Figure 8.1. Mean speech reaction time (SRT) for adults who stutter (AWS) and adults who do not stutter (AWNS) when naming pictures with low phonetic complexity (LPC) and high phonetic complexity (HPC). Error bars represent the standard error of the mean.

comparisons found AWS produced low complexity words with high lexical values significantly faster (M = 996.04, SE = 46.32) than high complexity words with similar lexical values (M = 1070.01, SE = 42.95) or words with lows lexical values, regardless of complexity (LPC: M = 1111.40, SE = 45.98; HPC: M = 1070.47, SE = 41.18). No significant differences in SRT were found for AWNS across word subtype (see Figure 8.2).

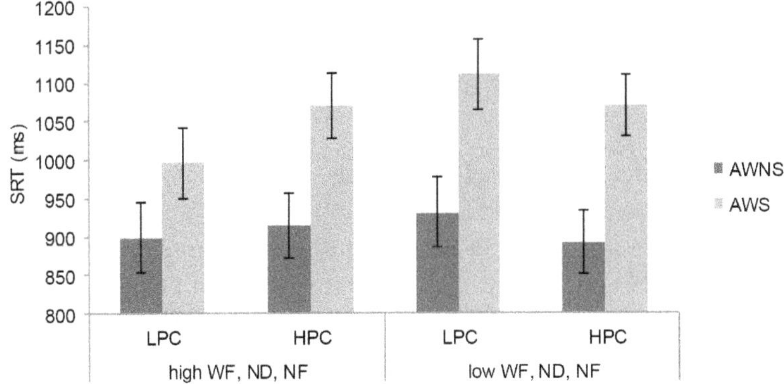

Figure 8.2. Mean speech reaction time (SRT) for adults who stutter (AWS) and adults who do not stutter (AWNS) when naming pictures of low phonetic complexity (LPC) and high phonetic complexity (HPC) with low or high word frequency (WF), neighborhood density (ND) and neighborhood frequency (NF). Error bars represent the standard error of the mean.

8.4.2 Accuracy of Production

A mixed-model repeated-measures ANOVA was conducted to assess the impact of high and low phonetic complexity on error production, with talker group (i.e., AWS and AWNS) as the between-subjects factor and phonetic complexity (i.e., LPC and HPC) as the within-subjects factor. As illustrated in Figure 8.3, significant interaction between talker group and phonetic complexity approached, but did not reach significance, Wilks' Lambda = .88, $F(1, 26) = 3.58$, $p = .070$, $\eta\rho^2 = .12$. The main effect of talker group was also not significant, $F(1, 26) = 1.09$, $p = .306$, $\eta^2 = .04$, with adults who stutter exhibiting overall errors comparable to AWNS. There was no significant main effect of word type ($F < 1$), with both groups responding with comparable accuracy to words with low and high phonetic complexity in both conditions.

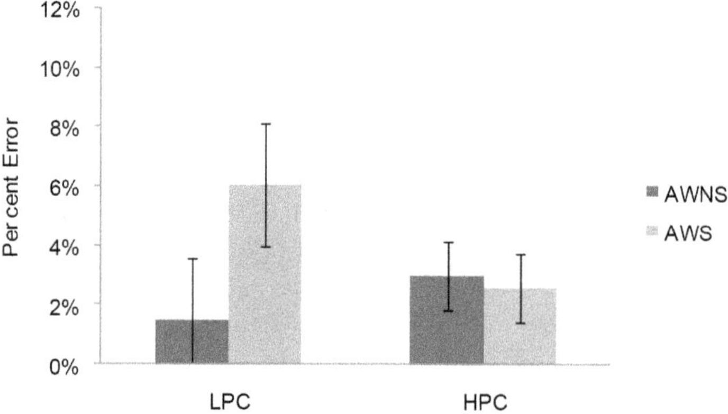

Figure 8.3. Mean number of naming errors for adults who stutter (AWS) and adults who do not stutter (AWNS) when naming pictures with low phonetic complexity (LPC) and high phonetic complexity (HPC). Error bars represent the standard error of the mean.

To explore possible interaction between phonetic and lexical factors, a mixed-model repeated-measures ANOVA was conducted, with talker group (i.e., AWS and AWNS) as between-group factors, and word sub-groups (i.e., LPC and HPC with high lexical values, LPC and HPC with low lexical values) as within-group factors. No main effect was found for word subtype, ($F < 1$), or talker group, $F(1, 26) = 1.09$, $p = .306$, $\eta\rho^2 = .04$. Planned comparisons found no significant differences, although differences between words of high and low phonetic complexity with low lexical values approached significance in AWS ($p = .081$). Again, no significant differences in accuracy were found for AWNS across word subtype (see Figure 8.4).

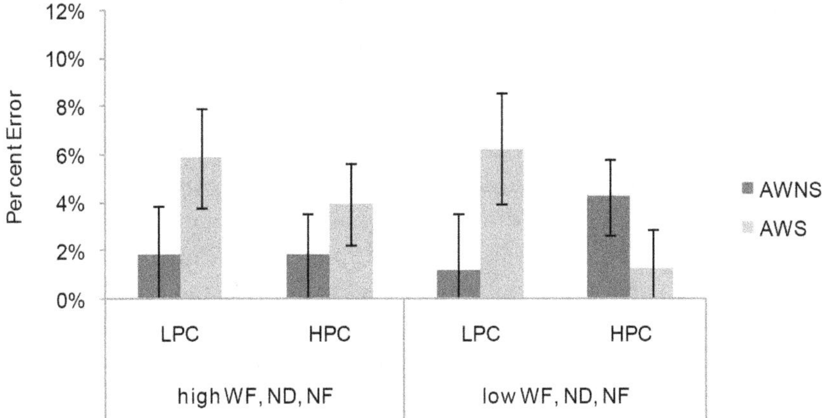

Figure 8.4. Mean number of naming errors for adults who stutter (AWS) and adults who do not stutter (AWNS) when naming pictures of low phonetic complexity (LPC) and high phonetic complexity (HPC) with low or high word frequency (WF), neighborhood density (ND) and neighborhood frequency (NF). Error bars represent the standard error of the mean.

8.5 Discussion

The present study was designed to evaluate whether the phonetic complexity of a word differentially influences the speed and accuracy of speech production in AWS relative to AWNS. There was no significant difference in SRT when naming words of high versus low phonetic complexity between or within talker groups, but the SRT of AWS was significantly slower than AWNS when naming all pictures. In addition, no significant differences were found in the number of naming errors between AWS and AWNS.

8.5.1 Speed of Production

Phonetic complexity did not significantly influence the speed of production for either talker group. Comparisons with previous studies must be made with caution due to inconsistent criteria used to measure phonetic complexity. For example, Huinck et al. (2004) found significantly longer SRTs for nonwords with homorganic medial clusters, but not intra-syllabic or heterorganic medial clusters. Given that consonant clusters in the current study, when they occurred, were comprised almost entirely of intra-syllabic or heterorganic, inter-syllabic clusters (i.e., 10/12 clusters across conditions), non-significant differences in SRTs between groups are similar to those found by Huinck and colleagues.

Another possible contributor to the non-significant differences could be the number of factors included in the measurement tool. Although the WCM is the most valid measure of phonetic complexity currently available to researchers, the breadth of factors included may potentially obscure key phonetic factors in the adult stuttering population. Howell et al. (2006: 714) made a similar argument with respect to the IPC and noted that certain aspects of the previously used IPC may be more relevant to AWS than others (i.e., consonant place, manner, word length and clusters). They further suggested modifications may be necessary, such as adjusting a factor to capture the effects of contiguous consonant strings at the syllabic boundary with divergent gestural patterns. In light of Huinck et al.'s (2004) results, similar modifications may apply for the WCM. In the WCM, consonant clusters serve as one of eight indexed factors in the WCM and value is assigned only to intra-syllabic clusters with no distinction of gestural configuration. Thus, the unique influence of an inter-syllabic cluster would not be scored, while a factor with less empirical support (e.g., liquids, rhotics) would be credited a point. Perhaps only certain aspects of phonetic complexity, at certain syllabic positions, hold greater potential to disrupt speech in AWS relative to AWNS.

Mediation, as defined by Baron & Kenny (1986), suggests that observed relationship between predictor and criterion occurs *only if* additional factors are present. When mediated by high word frequency, neighborhood density and neighborhood frequency, our preliminary data indicate significantly faster SRTs emerged between phonetically simple words, but not complex words (see Figure 8.4). Complexity-based differences were not observed for words with low lexical properties, nor when lexical factors were balanced across sets (see Figure 8.1). The observed influences of reduced phonetic complexity on the speed of production in AWS may become evident only in the presence of a third mediating variable, such as high lexical values. Further investigation and replication of this relationship between lexical and phonetic factors on the speed of speech production is warranted in future studies and may provide greater specificity to the unexpected findings of previous studies which proposed complexity-based accounts of stuttering without considering the potential influence of lexical properties.

8.5.2 Accuracy of Production

There were no significant differences between groups relative to naming accuracy in either the low or the high phonetic complexity condition. These findings are congruent with previous findings by Huinck et al. (2004) in that accuracy remained intact relative with fluctuations in phonetic complexity Thus, the results of this study may simply serve as additional support for the limited impact of phonetic complexity (as measured by the WCM) on speech production accuracy between talker groups. Results do not negate Newman & Bernstein Ratner's (2007) suggestion that increased naming errors emerge specific to complexity when the person is engaged in circumlocution; rather they suggest that our participants were not actively engaging in avoidance behaviors when completing our picture naming task.

If increased phonetic complexity does indeed require additional processing, as suggested by Howell (2011), the attentional resources necessary to efficiently operate other levels of processing, such as lexical-semantic selection and/or inhibition (e.g. Maxfield et al. 2010, 2012), may be re-allocated to phonological-phonetic systems and result in either (a) a delayed cascade of activation prior to speech, or (b) a notable increase in naming errors. Non-significant differences in naming accuracy in the current study provide additional support for the assumption that non-significant observed naming latencies are not a product of atypical semantic processing in AWS, and together, lend further support to position that the unique influence of phonetic properties, if any, may manifest at a level more peripheral and independent from the lexical processing system.

Finally, unlike SRT data that supported the possible relevance of phonetic complexity in the presence of a third variable, this was not the case for AWS for accuracy of responses. That is, phonetic complexity did not contribute to production accuracy when balanced for lexical factors, or when grouped by both phonetic and lexical factors. These findings are consistent, in part, with error data reported by Newman & Bernstein Ratner (2007), who observed no significant interactions between talker group and word frequency or neighborhood frequency data, both of which did not differ in WCM values. That is, similar to the current study, words with similar phonetic complexity and dissimilar lexical properties did not increase or decrease error production for either group.

In contrast to the current exploratory data, Newman & Bernstein Ratner (2007) observed greater error production for AWS than AWNS across word-types, and all participants produced significantly greater errors for words with low lexical properties. One possible explanation for inconsistent results may be larger sample size ($N = 25$ AWS, 25 AWNS) and number of tokens ($N = 22$ to 24 per analysis). A more likely explanation for this discrepancy is discordant error criteria used between studies. Unlike the current study, Newman & Bernstein Ratner included alternative word choices (e.g., *puppy* for *dog*) and elaborations (e.g., *birthday cake* for *cake*) as accurate responses during error analysis. Given these methodological differences, caution should be applied when comparing error data between studies.

8.5.3 Implications for EXPLAN Model

To review, according to the EXPLAN model, stuttering occurs due to incomplete or delayed completion of the speech plan prior to motoric execution, and considers planning and execution stages to be relatively independent from each other (Howell 2011). It is difficult to apply findings at the single-word level directly to the EXPLAN model, as stuttered speech within this model is thought to rely largely on the properties of the upcoming word during connected speech. However, single words still require planning prior to execution, and stuttered speech does occasionally occur on single-word productions. Thus, findings can be applied to single-word productions in a modified fashion.

If, as Howell suggested (2011), increased phonetic complexity of words is considered a sufficient indicator of planning speed and stuttered speech, the present findings do not support the EXPLAN theory as described; instead, they validate the concerns raised by Bernstein Ratner (2005) that the data which suggest phonetic complexity as a critical contributor are compromised. In the present study, increased phonetic complexity did not appear to affect the speed of production when lexical variables were controlled within complex and simple words. On the other hand, if as reported by Smith et al. (2010) phonetic complexity is considered a factor more relevant to motoric execution abilities, rather than speech planning abilities as suggested by Howell, then the preliminary findings in the current study make the EXPLAN model more tenable.

Smith et al. (2010) found stimuli of increased phonetic complexity (e.g., WCM scores of 4, similar to the high complexity words in this study) resulted in decreased motoric stability during execution in AWS, while words with minimal phonetic complexity (WCM score ≤ 2, similar to the low complexity words in this study) were produced with stability comparable to AWNS. If it takes AWS longer to retrieve lexical information or access the phonological spell-out, and the speaker is particularly vulnerable to speech breakdown when producing motor movements that are more complex and unstable, this combined instability of processing and production would seemingly present the ideal environment for stuttered speech (Sussman et al. 2011).

Perhaps the most striking pattern supporting atypical processing in AWS in the current study is that any observed differences were unique to AWS participants; AWNS did not exhibit any discernible statistical or qualitative patterns of mediation or moderation. Nonetheless, caution should be taken when interpreting this data, as the precise nature of these interactions needs to be explored more explicitly in future studies. For example, the influence of lexical factors as they were grouped in the current study is consistent in speech production patterns in AWNS. In AWNS, SRTs are faster for words of high lexical properties (word frequency: Jescheniak & Levelt 1994; neighborhood density: Luce & Pisoni 1998; neighborhood frequency: Vitevitch & Sommers 2003), while accuracy of production is decreased by low lexical properties (word frequency: Newman & German 2005; neighborhood density: Vitevitch 2002; neighborhood frequency: Newman & Bernstein Ratner 2007). However, due to the potential differences in lexical and phonological processing in AWS, the individual lexical properties may exert differential impact (e.g., Anderson 2007) or minimal impact (e.g., Arnold et al. 2005; Coalson et al. 2012) on speech production. Thus, grouped lexical properties of similar values may mask the full effect of individual lexical properties in AWS, relative to phonetic properties. Future studies targeting these and other relevant factors (e.g., word familiarity: Hubbard & Prins 1994, Newman & German 2005; phonotactic probability: Anderson & Byrd 2008) in isolation and at the single-word level, relative to phonetic complexity, would provide greater specificity to the planning factors that may or may not result in disfluencies within the EXPLAN model.

8.6 Conclusion

Present results do not support phonetic complexity as an independent predictor of speech production in AWS or AWNS, at least not when measured by the WCM. Instead, present findings indicate that phonetic complexity, by itself, does not affect reaction time or accuracy. Preliminary data suggest consideration of lexical and phonetic variables is necessary to discern the impact of either in AWS. Together, these findings support the possibility that, when lexical values are not accounted for during analysis as in previous studies examining conversational data, observed differences in phonetic complexity in AWS may be an epiphenomenon of an interaction between lexical and phonetic factors, in addition to utterance-based factors. Future studies should further investigate the influence with regard to the speed, accuracy, *and* fluency of single word production and validate if, and to what degree, the combined contribution of lexical and phonetic factors contribute to speech production at the word level in AWS.

Acknowledgments

This research was funded in part by the grant F32 DC006755–01 (Phonological Encoding of Children who Stutter) from the National Institutes of Health (NIH). We would like to thank Elizabeth Hampton, MS, CCC-SLP, who assisted us with the recruitment and testing of participants as well as the graduate students who assisted with the testing, transcription and data coding process. We would also like to thank Dr Michael Mahometa for his assistance with the statistical analyses. Most of all, we are grateful to the adults who do and do not stutter who were willing to give their time to participate in this study and help us to further our knowledge of the underlying nature of stuttering.

References

Anderson, J.D. (2007). Phonological neighborhood and word frequency effects in the stuttered disfluencies of children who stutter. *Journal of Speech, Language, and Hearing Research (JSLHR)*, 50(1), 229–47. http://dx.doi.org/10.1044/1092-4388(2007/018)

Anderson, J.D. (2008). Age of acquisition and repetition priming effects on picture naming of children who do and do not stutter. *Journal of Fluency Disorders*, 33(2), 135–55. http://dx.doi.org/10.1016/j.jfludis.2008.04.001

Anderson, J.D., & C.T. Byrd. (2008). Phonotactic probability effects in children who stutter. *Journal of Speech, Language, and Hearing Research (JSLHR)*, 51(4), 851–66. http://dx.doi.org/10.1044/1092-4388(2008/062)

Anderson, C., & W. Cohen. (2012). Measuring word complexity in speech screening: Single-word sampling to identify phonological delay/disorder in preschool children. *International Journal of Language & Communication Disorders*, 47(5), 534–41. http://dx.doi.org/10.1111/j.1460-6984.2012.00163.x

Arnold, H.S., E.G. Conture & R.N. Ohde. (2005). Phonological neighborhood density in the picture naming of young children who stutter: Preliminary study. *Journal of Fluency Disorders*, 30(2), 125–48. http://dx.doi.org/10.1016/j.jfludis.2005.01.001

Baron, R.M., & D.A. Kenny. (1986). The moderator-mediator variable distinction in social psychological research: Conceptual, strategic, and statistical considerations. *Journal of Personality and Social Psychology*, 51(6), 1173–82. http://dx.doi.org/10.1037/0022-3514.51.6.1173

Bernstein Ratner, N. (2005). Is phonetic complexity a useful construct in understanding stuttering? *Journal of Fluency Disorders*, 30(4), 337–41. http://dx.doi.org/10.1016/j.jfludis.2005.09.002

Byrd, C.T., E.G. Conture & R.N. Ohde. (2007). Phonological priming in young children who stutter: Holistic versus incremental processing. *American Journal of Speech-Language Pathology*, 16(1), 43–53. http://dx.doi.org/10.1044/1058-0360(2007/006)

Byrd, C.T., M. Vallely, J.D. Anderson & H. Sussman. (2012). Nonword repetition and phoneme elision in adults who do and do not stutter. *Journal of Fluency Disorders*, 37(3), 188–201. http://dx.doi.org/10.1016/j.jfludis.2012.03.003

Coalson, G.A., C.T. Byrd & B.L. Davis. (2012). The influence of phonetic complexity on stuttered speech. *Clinical Linguistics & Phonetics*, 26(7), 646–59. http://dx.doi.org/10.3109/02699206.2012.682696

Dayalu, V.N., J. Kalinowski, A. Stuart, D. Holbert & M.P. Rastatter. (2002). Stuttering frequency on content and function words in adults who stutter: A concept revisited. *Journal of Speech, Language, and Hearing Research (JSLHR)*, 45(5), 871–8. http://dx.doi.org/10.1044/1092-4388(2002/070)

Dell, G.S. (1990). Effects of frequency and vocabulary type on phonological speech errors. *Language and Cognitive Processes*, 5(4), 313–49. http://dx.doi.org/10.1080/01690969008407066

Dunn, L.M., & D.M. Dunn. (1997). *Peabody Picture Vocabulary Test – III (PPVT-III)* (3rd ed.). San Antonio, TX: Pearson Education, Inc.

Dunn, L.M., & D.M. Dunn. (2007). *Peabody Picture Vocabulary Test – IV (PPVT-IV)* (4th ed.). San Antonio, TX: Pearson Education, Inc.

Dworzynski, K., & P. Howell. (2004). Predicting stuttering from phonetic complexity in German. *Journal of Fluency Disorders*, 29(2), 149–73. http://dx.doi.org/10.1016/j.jfludis.2004.03.001

Howell, P. (2011). *Recovery from Stuttering*. New York: Taylor and Francis Group.

Howell, P., J. Au-Yeung, S.J. Yaruss & K. Eldridge. (2006). Phonetic difficulty and stuttering in English. *Clinical Linguistics & Phonetics*, 20(9), 703–16. http://dx.doi.org/10.1080/02699200500390990

Howell, P., & J. Au-Yeung. (2007). Phonetic complexity and stuttering in Spanish. *Clinical Linguistics & Phonetics*, 21(2), 111–27. http://dx.doi.org/10.1080/02699200600709511

Howell, P., & Dworzynski, K. (2005). Planning and execution processes in speech control by fluent speakers and speakers who stutter. *Journal of Fluency Disorders*, 30(4), 343–54. http://dx.doi.org/10.1016/j.jfludis.2005.09.005

Hubbard, C.P., & D. Prins. (1994). Word familiarity, syllabic stress, and stuttering. *Journal of Speech and Hearing Research*, 37(3), 564–71. http://dx.doi.org/10.1044/jshr.3703.564

Huinck, W.J., P.H.H.M. Van Lieshout, H.F.M. Peters &W. Hulstijn. (2004). Gestural overlap in consonant clusters: Effects on the fluent speech of stuttering and non-stuttering subjects. *Journal of Fluency Disorders*, 29(1), 3–25. http://dx.doi.org/10.1016/j.jfludis.2003.09.001

Jakielski, K.J. (1998). Motor organization in the acquisition of consonant clusters. PhD dissertation, The University of Texas at Austin.

Jakielski, K.J. (2002, November). A new method for measuring articulatory complexity. Paper presented at the annual convention of the American Speech-Language-Hearing Association, Atlanta, GA.

Jakielski, K.J., R. Maytasse & E. Doyle. (2006, November). Acquisition of phonetic complexity in children 12–36 months of age. Poster session presented at the annual convention of the American Speech-Language-Hearing Association, Miami, FL.

Jescheniak, J.D., & W.J. Levelt. (1994). Word frequency effects in speech production: Retrieval of syntactic information and phonological form. *Journal of Experimental Psychology. Learning, Memory, and Cognition*, 20(4), 824–43. http://dx.doi.org/10.1037/0278-7393.20.4.824

LaSalle, L.R., & L. Wolk. (2011). Stuttering, cluttering, and phonological complexity: Case studies. *Journal of Fluency Disorders*, 36(4), 285–9. http://dx.doi.org/10.1016/j.jfludis.2011.04.003

Logan, K.J., & E.G. Conture. (1997). Selected temporal, grammatical, and phonological characteristics of conversational utterances produced by children who stutter. *Journal of Speech, Language, and Hearing Research (JSLHR)*, 40(1), 107–20. http://dx.doi.org/10.1044/jslhr.4001.107

Luce, P.A., D.B. Pisoni & S.D. Goldfinger. (1990). Similarity neighborhoods of spoken words. In G.T.M. Altmann (ed.), *Cognitive Models of Speech Processing: Psycholinguistic and Computational Perspective* (pp. 122–47). Cambridge, MA: The MIT Press.

Luce, P.A., & D.B. Pisoni. (1998). Recognizing spoken words: The Neighborhood Activation Model. *Ear and Hearing*, 19(1), 1–36. http://dx.doi.org/10.1097/00003446-199802000-00001

Macrae, T. (2013). Lexical and child-related factors in word variability and accuracy in infants. *Clinical Linguistics & Phonetics*, 27(6–7), 497–507. http://dx.doi.org/10.3109/02699206.2012.752867

Maxfield, N.D., J.L. Huffman, S.A. Frisch & J.J. Hinckley. (2010). Neural correlates of semantic activation spreading on the path to picture naming in adults who stutter. *Clinical Neurophysiology*, 121(9), 1447–63. http://dx.doi.org/10.1016/j.clinph.2010.03.026

Maxfield, N.D., A.A. Pizon-Moore, S.A. Frisch & J.L. Constantine. (2012). Exploring semantic and phonological picture-word priming in adults who stutter using event-related potentials. *Clinical Neurophysiology*, 123(6), 1131–46. http://dx.doi.org/10.1016/j.clinph.2011.10.003

Newman, R.S., & N. Bernstein Ratner. (2007). The role of selected lexical factors on confrontation naming accuracy, speed, and fluency in adults who do and do not stutter. *Journal of Speech, Language, and Hearing Research (JSLHR)*, 50(1), 196–213. http://dx.doi.org/10.1044/1092-4388(2007/016)

Newman, R.S., & D.J. German. (2005). Life span effects of lexical factors on oral naming. *Language and Speech*, 48(2), 123–56. http://dx.doi.org/10.1177/00238309050480020101

O'Brian, S., A. Packman, M. Onslow & N. O'Brian. (2004). Measurement of stuttering in adults: Comparison of stuttering-rate and severity-scaling methods. *Journal of Speech, Language, and Hearing Research (JSLHR)*, 47(5), 1081–7. http://dx.doi.org/10.1044/1092-4388(2004/080)

Riley, G. (1994). *Stuttering Severity Instrument for Children and Adults – 3 (SSI-3)* (3rd ed.). Austin, TX: Pro-Ed.

Smith, A., N. Sadagopan, B. Walsh & C. Weber-Fox. (2010). Increasing phonological complexity reveals heightened instability in inter-articulatory coordination in adults who stutter. *Journal of Fluency Disorders*, 35(1), 1–18. http://dx.doi.org/10.1016/j.jfludis.2009.12.001

Stoel-Gammon, C. (2010). The Word Complexity Measure: Description and application to developmental phonologic and disorders. *Clinical Linguistics & Phonetics*, 24(4–5), 271–82. http://dx.doi.org/10.3109/02699200903581059

Sussman, H., C. Byrd & B. Guitar. (2011). The integrity of anticipatory coarticulation in fluent and non-fluent utterances of adults who stutter. *Clinical Linguistics & Phonetics*, 25(3), 169–86. http://dx.doi.org/10.3109/02699206.2010.517896

Szekely, A., T. Jacobsen, S. D'Amico, A. Devescovi, E. Andonova, D. Herron, ... & E. Bates. (2004). A new on-line resource for psycholinguistic studies. *Journal of Memory and Language*, 51(2), 247–50. http://dx.doi.org/10.1016/j.jml.2004.03.002

Tsiamtsiouris, J., & H.S. Cairns. (2013). Effects of sentence-structure complexity on speech initiation time and disfluency. *Journal of Fluency Disorders*, 38(1), 30–44. http://dx.doi.org/10.1016/j.jfludis.2012.12.002

Vitevitch, M.S. (2002). The influence of phonological similarity neighborhoods on speech production. *Journal of Experimental Psychology: Learning, Memory, and Cognition*, 28(4), 735–47. http://dx.doi.org/10.1037/0278-7393.28.4.735

Vitevitch, M.S., & P.A. Luce. (2005). Increases in phonotactic probability facilitate spoken nonword repetition. *Journal of Memory and Language*, 52(2), 193–204. http://dx.doi.org/10.1016/j.jml.2004.10.003

Vitevitch, M.S., & M.S. Sommers. (2003). The facilitative influence of phonological similarity and neighborhood frequency in speech production in younger and older adults. *Memory & Cognition*, 31(4), 491–504. http://dx.doi.org/10.3758/BF03196091

Wagner, R.K., J.K. Torgesen & C.A. Rashotte. (1999). *Comprehensive Test of Phonological Processing (CTOPP)*. Austin, TX: Pro-Ed.

Williams, K.T. (1997). *Expressive Vocabulary Test (EVT)*. Circle Pines, MN: American Guidance Services.

Williams, K.T. (2007). *Expressive Vocabulary Test-2 (EVT-2)* (2nd ed.). Minneapolis, MN: Pearson Assessments.

Yaruss, J.S. (1999). Utterance length, syntactic complexity, and childhood stuttering. *Journal of Speech, Language, and Hearing Research (JSLHR)*, 42(2), 329–44. http://dx.doi.org/10.1044/jslhr.4202.329

Yaruss, J.S., & R.W. Quesal. (2004). Stuttering and the international classification of functioning, disability, and health (ICF): An update. *Journal of Communication Disorders*, 37(1), 35–52. http://dx.doi.org/10.1016/S0021-9924(03)00052-2

Yairi, E., & N.G. Ambrose. (2005). *Early Childhood Stuttering: For Clinicians, By Clinicians*. Austin, TX: Pro-Ed.

Zackheim, C.T., & E.G. Conture. (2003). Childhood stuttering and speech disfluencies in relation to children's mean length of utterance: A preliminary study. *Journal of Fluency Disorders*, 28(2), 115–42. http://dx.doi.org/10.1016/S0094-730X(03)00007-X

9
Linguistic Considerations for Rehabilitation of Persons with Hearing Loss

Linda Thibodeau[1]

9.1 Introduction

The field of linguistics has relevance to many professions, but perhaps one often overlooked is audiology. Given that linguistics involves an interaction between sound and meaning through systems of phonetics, grammar, semantics and pragmatics, it is logical that research in these areas provides a framework for determining the rehabilitative needs of persons with impaired hearing. There are two main effects of hearing loss: (1) loss of absolute sensitivity, one's ability to detect sound, and (2) loss of differential sensitivity, one's ability to detect changes in sound. For mild-to-moderate hearing loss, the main effect is primarily the loss of audibility which can be restored fairly successfully with amplification devices. For more severe hearing loss, there may be reductions in both absolute and differential sensitivity. Most manufacturers of amplification devices have focused on restoring audibility with few efforts to develop technology to address the loss of differential sensitivity. Sussman and colleagues (Burlingame et al. 2005; Marion et al.1993; Thibodeau & Sussman 1979) have emphasized the relationship between perception and production particularly in the developmental years. Observations from these studies suggest that the acoustic features of speech must be a primary focus in the attempt to restore perception in persons with hearing loss. However, to focus on restoring just audibility of acoustic features as a means to improve communication is aiming for success for only those persons with mild-to-moderate hearing

1 Linda Thibodeau is professor at the Advanced Hearing Research Center, Callier Center for Communication Disorders, School of Behavioral and Brain Sciences, at the University of Texas at Dallas.

loss. Those individuals often delay seeking amplification because they are able combine auditory cues with visual cues on the speaker's face and manage to function similar to a person with normal hearing.

However, from a linguistic perspective, one must be concerned with the second main effect of hearing loss, the deficits in differential sensitivity that may impact the perception of certain features of sounds. For example, poor temporal resolution of speech may result in the inability to distinguish voicing cues. Also, poor frequency resolution may impact the ability to distinguish second formant transitions that cue place of articulation. The focus of this chapter is on research that relates linguistic processes to the advances in fitting assistive technology and rehabilitative techniques for persons with hearing loss. This linguistic impact can be illustrated by research in two areas: short-term speech characteristics and auditory training techniques.

9.2 Implications of Short-Term Speech Characteristics in Hearing Aid Design

When a hearing loss is suspected, generally the first action involves seeking a standard audiometric evaluation that focuses on assessment of absolute sensitivity. Based on these pure-tone thresholds along with the patient's subjective reports regarding communication challenges, the need for amplification is determined. When audibility of the signal is reduced, the effects on recognition of specific speech features can be well predicted by the absolute thresholds for pure tones (Dubno & Levitt 1981). Current fitting algorithms for the available advanced hearing aid circuitry also focus on restoring the listener's audibility for speech (Bagatto et al. 2005). Often the effects of the hearing loss are explained by plotting the hearing threshold levels on a graph with representations of speech sounds, commonly referred to as the speech banana because the intensity of specific sounds varies across frequencies. The individual can then see the sounds that are more difficult or even impossible to hear without amplification. When counseling adults with hearing loss, the effect of hearing loss on hearing specific sounds is often simplified into two frequency regions. The reduction in audibility of low-frequency information interferes with perception of cues for nasality, while a reduction in audibility of high-frequency information interferes with perception of cues for sibilants and fricatives.

There are, however, two main flaws with this approach that linguistically-trained audiologists would note immediately. The sounds on the speech banana are represented as if they are produced in isolation. The effects of coarticulation (Agwuele et al. 2008; Lindblom & Sussman 2012) and masking effects by neighboring sounds are not accounted for in this two-dimensional representation. Furthermore, if the degree of hearing loss exceeds a moderate level, individuals often demonstrate reductions in differential sensitivity, adding more challenges to speech recognition (Hall & Grose 1989; Thibodeau 1991a, b; Thibodeau & Van Tasell 1987; Van Tasell et al. 1987). Therefore, even when amplification is provided that restores audibility of these speech features, one may still experience poor speech recognition because of these factors beyond audibility that affect one's ability to distinguish speech sounds. This was clearly illustrated in two case studies presented by Skinner et al. (1982) where the thresholds were nearly the same, yet the speech recognition scores differed significantly as bandwidth of the amplification was increased. When a noisy environment is added to the communication challenge, the problems are even further compounded beyond that predicted solely by audibility.

The perception of fine acoustic distinctions in speech is also affected by the often long-standing nature of hearing loss in adults. Because hearing loss is typically gradual as one ages, awareness of the loss may be minimal. However, as there is a gradual increase over time in auditory deprivation in regions of hearing loss, there can be reorganization of the cortical responses to sound. As a consequence, there are difficulties associated with cortical reorganization of frequency representation occurring in conjunction with auditory deprivation (Dietrich et al. 2001). The tonotopic organization of the auditory cortex may become altered so that greater cortical areas respond to frequencies in the regions of normal hearing adjacent to the hearing loss and smaller cortical areas respond to frequencies in the hearing loss region (Irvine 2000; Irvine & Rajan 1997). Introduction of amplification leads to further reorganization of the auditory system and possibly a remediation of deprivation effects (Willott 1996).

Therefore, it is important in the hearing instrument fitting process that evaluations are performed not only of absolute sensitivity but also of differential sensitivity, in particular frequency and temporal resolution (Reed et al. 2008). Psychoacoustic studies have shown moderate to strong correlations between speech recognition and frequency resolution (Thibodeau & Van Tasell 1987; Tyler et al. 1982b) and temporal resolution (Festen & Plomp 1983; Tyler et al. 1982a). When speech recognition is lower than expected based on threshold information, the reduced performance might be related to a reduction in differential sensitivity.

9.3 Considerations for Assessment of Speech Processing

In the typical clinical assessment of speech processing, the effects of reduced absolute and differential sensitivity cannot be separated. Unless the signal is spectrally shaped to ensure complete audibility, the combined effects of these deficits will be represented in a single score. One way to quantify the deficits that might result from changes in absolute sensitivity is through a procedure known as the Articulation Index (AI) (French & Steinberg 1947). The AI is calculated based on an individual's hearing sensitivity relative to the long-term average speech spectrum. High frequencies receive more credit because of their significant contribution to speech intelligibility. An AI of .90 would mean that someone would have access to 90 per cent of the speech information and excellent speech recognition, whereas an AI of .50 would suggest considerably more difficulty. By comparing actual speech recognition performance to that predicted by the AI, one can gain an estimate of the speech processing problems that may remain even after accounting for reduced audibility. Knowing this information may lead to more appropriate counseling regarding the benefits an individual might receive from amplification.

As hearing aid technology has moved beyond the basic premise of restoring audibility, the demand for more sensitive speech assessment procedures has increased. For example, the benefits of circuits designed to address poor frequency resolution may not be evident by measuring per cent correct recognition of word lists but require a more sensitive measure, such as discrimination of high-frequency second-formant transitions. Thibodeau & Van Tasell (1987) studied adults with hearing loss and found that measures of frequency resolution at 2000 Hz were not correlated with per cent correct scores for consonant-vowel-consonant identification, but were correlated with one's ability to discriminate second-formant transitions in the same 2000-Hz region.

Without the consideration for the short-term speech characteristics, erroneous conclusions regarding performance may be made. Use of only phonetically-balanced word lists to quantify speech recognition difficulties limits the opportunity to determine the possible cause of speech recognition difficulties. When research employs additional tools such as confusion matrices and feature analysis (Dubno & Levitt 1981), particular speech recognition difficulties may be identified as more spectral or temporal in nature. This information could lead to more appropriate hearing aid design and fitting.

Analyses of consonant confusion matrices obtained from normal-hearing persons who listened to speech through a variety of filtering conditions has determined that voicing and manner cues are carried across the frequency spectrum, but place of articulation is cued primarily in high-frequency information (Dubno & Levitt 1981). Therefore, one would expect a patient with a high-frequency hearing loss to have the most difficulty with place information. These predicted error patterns were confirmed by Olsen & Matkin (1979), who also reported that consonant errors were likely to be substitutions rather than omissions. When omissions did occur they were most likely for final consonant sounds.

9.4 Considerations of Temporal Aspects of Speech

One type of hearing aid technology that may have an effect on the temporal characteristics of the speech signal is known as adaptive compression. For this technology, it is important to consider the temporal characteristics of sounds, syllables and pauses between words in sentences. To evaluate the potential benefits of adaptive compression circuits that alter the signal in the temporal domain, the duration of the speech stimuli must be considered in relationship to temporal processing. For example, an adaptive compression system in a hearing instrument that is designed to vary the release time relative to the duration of the signal that caused it to go into compression must be evaluated with speech stimuli that would allow observation of this effect. Presenting lists of monosyllabic words of relatively equal duration to a person with hearing loss would probably not be sensitive to the effects of such a circuit. On the other hand, presenting connected speech in the presence of background noise with an average duration between words of 200 ms might reveal differences in speech recognition between an adaptive compression circuit and one with a fixed release time less than 150 ms.

To illustrate the effects of compression in the hearing aid on these short-term temporal characteristics, consider a typical speaking situation. If the speaking rate were 200 words per minute with a pause rate of 50 per cent, the average word and pause duration would be about 150 ms each. It is possible that hearing aids with fast-acting compression circuits, i.e., release times of 40–50 ms, would potentially allow background noise to be amplified during pauses (Teder 1993). Therefore, when determining the benefit of circuits such as adaptive release time, one must include speech stimuli of appropriate durations for the electroacoustic effect, or lack thereof, to be experienced. An evaluation of this type would require connected speech test materials and ideally include some type of background noise.

When designing hearing aid circuitry for persons with hearing loss, the important temporal characteristics to consider include not only the duration of pauses between words and syllables but also the duration of specific speech sounds. Pickett (1999) provided an overview of how the duration of individual sounds depended on their position relative to pauses, syllables, stress, linguistic content and acoustic features. Vowels can range from 52 to 212 ms but average 70 to 130 ms when in unstressed or stressed syllables, respectively (Klatt 1976). Vowels are about 20 ms shorter when followed by a voiceless-stop consonant (Umeda 1975). Consonants are generally shorter and vary from 25 ms for a stop consonant that precedes a stressed vowel, to 86 ms for a nasal consonant in the initial stressed syllable of a word. As with vowels, consonant duration can be about 20 to 40 ms longer in words having higher content meaning (Umeda 1977). Consonants such as /s/ can range from a duration greater than 200 ms at the end of a phrase to 50 ms in a consonant cluster. These values are important considerations relative to the compression features of the hearing aid. For some individuals, if the gain of the hearing aid is reduced for intense vowel sounds, the weaker intensity consonants that followed may still be affected by the gain reduction and consequently not be audible. Therefore, some hearing aid designs employ circuits with fast release times (< 50 ms), a feature known as syllabic compressions.

Syllable duration is also important with respect to compression characteristics of hearing aids. It can be influenced by stress and proximity to pauses. Initial syllables typically range from 130 to 483 ms compared to final syllables preceding a pause that may range from 243 to 516 ms (Crystal & House 1990). The rate of conversational speech is typically 200 words per minute which may cause great difficulty for persons with hearing loss. However, if speakers are instructed to speak "clearly," the rate is typically 100 words per minute which can be extremely beneficial (Picheny et al. 1989). Pauses that occur among syllables, words, and sentences are naturally related to speaking rate. Because pauses allow time for processing speech information and full activation of compression release times, they are extremely valuable to those with impaired hearing.

9.5 Consideration of the Role of Visual Cues in Speech Processing

The inability to resolve fine acoustic distinctions is particularly challenging when visual cues regarding the speech sounds are also indistinct. For example, there is little differentiation in the visual cues for the speech sounds /p/, /b/ and /m/ and one must rely more on the acoustic signal for differentiation. One phenomenon that has been instrumental in helping to illustrate the relative effects of auditory and visual speech cues with respect to short-term speech characteristics is the McGurk Effect (McGurk & MacDonald, 1976). An auditory illusion occurs when the visual representation of one sound is paired with the auditory representation of a second sound to create the perception of a third sound. For example "ba" is presented auditorially at the same time that the visual presentation is a speaker producing "ga." Viewers typically perceive "da." If viewers report perceiving "ga" in this condition, the interpretation is is that they rely more on visual than on auditory cues. Rouger et al. (2008) studied the McGurk Effect in adults with hearing loss and determined that they relied more on visual information than on auditory information as one might expect. In other words, they were not as affected by the conflicting auditory and visual information. The outcomes of these experiments with short-term auditory and visual representations are a reminder that persons with hearing loss do not rely solely on their hearing aids for perception. They use a multitude of cues, both visual and auditory and on occasion olfactory and tactile, to draw conclusions about what was presented by a speaker. Therefore, even when the reduction in audibility can be completely addressed through amplification, it is still possible that conflicting visual information may impair perception. In particular, for those with impairments in differential sensitivity that cannot be restored with current hearing aid technology, relying on visual information may be a primary source of information to achieve accurate perception.

In summary, the short-term characteristics of the speech signal must be considered when evaluating the effects of hearing loss or determining the benefits of new hearing assistive technology. Use of inappropriate speech stimuli may lead to inaccurate conclusions regarding benefit. When assisting persons with hearing loss, it must be remembered that much of the auditory communication occurs with accompanying visual information from the speaker's face. The person with hearing loss may attribute different values to the auditory and visual information received compared to persons with normal hearing. Persons with hearing loss often find it impossible, given the typical rate of speech, to focus on resolving individual sounds and must concentrate on following the main topic of the conversation.

9.6 Linguistic Implications for Auditory Training for Those with Impaired Hearing

In addition to restoring audibility with hearing instruments, individuals with hearing loss may benefit from auditory training programs. The potential benefit of auditory training is supported by the findings that new hearing aid users experience a gradual improvement in speech recognition over time with performance typically peaking between 6 and 12 weeks following hearing aid fitting (Gatehouse 1992). The continual improvement appears related to neural reorganization of the auditory system following the reintroduction of auditory input through amplification. Research with cats has shown that auditory training results in the expansion of cortical representations of the trained frequencies, and results in perceptual and neurophysiological changes in less than 10 days (Irvine 2000).

One way to facilitate this process of neural reorganization is to engage in some auditory training that will stimulate the frequency area of reorganization in a repetitive manner such that the cortical representations for the restored auditory information can be strengthened. There are several types of auditory training programs for persons with hearing loss. Many involve sentence repetition in quiet and in progressive levels of background noise. Some have been developed for use with a computer so that persons might be encouraged to do the training more frequently (Sweetow & Sabes 2006). These programs typically involve sentences or phrases in varying degrees of noise and are not focused on any particular acoustic cue.

Based on the premise that following amplification, auditory training with signals in the previously deprived frequency regions facilitates improvements in speech recognition, Scott & Thibodeau (2006) designed a study to explore the benefits of auditory training in a specific frequency region. Given that cortical expansion is occurring in the previously deprived frequency region, they concluded that it would be most productive to determine the acoustic features of speech related to that frequency region. Rather than training on complete sentences as done in most of the existing programs, they reasoned that specific training on the acoustic features might be more productive.

Ten adults with hearing loss who had not experienced amplification before were fitted with hearing aids and enrolled in a program of seven hours of auditory training that focused on the frequency region in which audibility had been restored, i.e., primarily high frequencies. The acoustic cue most relevant to training in that region is the second formant transition that cues place of articulation. After fitting adults with high-frequency hearing loss with hearing aids that restored high-frequency audibility, frequency discrimination at 2000 Hz was assessed. Thereafter each participant was enrolled in an auditory training program for frequency-sweep discrimination at 2000 Hz for half an hour per day for 10 days. Scott & Thibodeau (2006) found that these newly-amplified listeners made significant improvements in frequency discrimination as well as speech recognition in noise. These improvements were greater than those made by young adults with normal hearing who completed the same amount of training. Perception of consonant-vowel-consonant syllables was related to the training in the 2000-Hz region with greater effects shown for perception of place cues than for nasality cues. Perceived hearing aid benefit also significantly improved following training.

In early 2000, there was a shift from restoring audibility by simply increasing gain in proportion to the hearing loss, to ensuring that a critical region of the spectrum was coded in a way that could be audible despite severe-to-profound hearing loss in that region. This special hearing aid feature was developed with a regard for the importance of linguistic features of speech and is known as frequency transposition. Researchers noted the importance of high-frequency information in the development of speech and language (Stelmachowicz et al. 2001). Because the most common configuration of hearing loss involves a loss in the high frequencies, hearing aid manufacturers developed several techniques to make the acoustic information in this region audible. By using frequency transposition, the speech information in the high-frequency region is moved to a lower-frequency region where there is less hearing loss. More recently, hearing aid designs have included frequency compression where those frequencies above a specified cutoff frequency are compressed within a lower frequency region so that they can be perceived in one's region of residual hearing.

Research has shown that this hearing aid feature has made a significant impact on the production of high-frequency sibilants (Glista et al. 2009). These improvements appear, however, after a period of therapeutic intervention in which auditory training activities are conducted to help the listener learn to interpret the new acoustic information and then relate it to motor commands to accurately produce high-frequency sounds. Had there not been attention given to this linguistic feature in hearing aid design accompanied by specific intervention, many children with hearing loss would not have mastered production of these high-frequency sounds which are critical to language development.

In the past 10 years, there has been a shift in auditory training from an emphasis on identifying specific linguistic features in quiet to listening to all speech features in noise. It was determined that when there are pauses in the noise as might occur in the real world, the listener could get a "glimpse" of the message. Rhebergen et al. (2008) found that adults with normal hearing could make significant gains when auditory training was conducted in the presence of interrupted versus continuous background noise. Because this training effect was significant in adults, Sullivan et al. (2012, 2013) speculated that it might be a key component in auditory training for children. They compared the benefits of seven hours of auditory training in continuous versus interrupted noise in children with bilateral hearing loss. They determined that auditory training in interrupted noise yielded greater benefits in speech recognition in noise than training in continuous noise. Furthermore, these benefits significantly exceeded the slight gains in speech recognition in noise made by the control group who completed the same amount of training on a visual perception task.

These studies, taken together, suggest that a linguistic approach focused on absolute and differential sensitivity for specific speech features can result in significant gains in speech recognition in noise and speech production by persons with hearing loss. In fact, recent research suggests that new hearing aid designs should include access to auditory training within the circuitry worn at the ear level. These hearing instruments could be designed to not only receive sound and provide amplification, but also to serve as an auditory training platform. The hearing instrument might be programmed to present phonetic contrasts in a training paradigm to facilitate the acclimatization process. In addition, convenient access to auditory training in an ear-level device could aid neuronal organization that occurs for adults who are adjusting to amplification and for children who are developing speech and language. The success of the "training hearing aid" will be achieved by the collaboration of acoustic engineers, audiologists and linguists.

9.7 Summary

In summary, the speech recognition challenges one faces with hearing loss may be reduced through amplification circuits that are designed to restore audibility in the frequency regions corresponding to the hearing loss. However, if one takes a linguistic perspective to account for the specific speech features that are affected by the hearing loss, either by reduced audibility or reduced differential sensitivity, the rehabilitative benefits will be far greater. This linguistic approach to rehabilitation begins with the assessment of the effects of hearing loss on the psychoacoustic processing of the temporal and spectral features of speech. With this information, specific features of the hearing aid design may be selected such as adaptive compression or frequency compression based on the individual's needs. Furthermore, these results may guide the rehabilitative efforts to be focused on restoring audibility of the features as well as training one's ability to distinguish the features first in quiet and then in noise.

Just as many athletes have excelled after significant injury by following the suggestions of a collaborative team of specialists looking at the micro-mechanics of the injury and designing specific rehabilitative techniques, so must persons with hearing loss excel by experiencing the advances in technology and training that will undoubtedly prevail when the collaborative team of experts includes a linguistic focus. Harvey Sussman has set the stage for generations of scientists to explore the relationships across disciplines to advance understanding of normal and disordered systems. Without his collaborative work across the fields of linguistics and communicative disorders, the students he mentored would not have discovered new applications of linguistic research to their own scientific pursuits.

References

Agwuele, A., H.M. Sussman & B. Lindblom. (2008). The effect of speaking rate on consonant vowel coarticulation. *Phonetica*, 65(4), 194–209. http://dx.doi.org/10.1159/000192792

Bagatto, M.P., S. Moodie, S.D. Scollie, R.C. Seewald, K. Moodie, J. Pumford & K.P.R. Liu. (2005). Clinical protocols for hearing instrument fitting in the Desired Sensation Level method. *Trends in Amplification*, 9(4), 199–226. http://dx.doi.org/10.1177/108471380500900404

Burlingame, E., H.M. Sussman, R.B. Gillam & J.F. Hay. (2005). An investigation of speech perception in children with SLI on a continuum of formant transition duration. *Journal of Speech, Hearing, and Language Research*, 48, 805–16.

Crystal, T.H., & A.S. House. (1990). Articulation rate and the duration of syllables and stress groups in connected speech. *Journal of the Acoustical Society of America*, 88(1), 101–12. http://dx.doi.org/10.1121/1.399955

Dietrich, V., M. Nieschalk, W. Stoll, P. Rajan, & C. Pantev. (2001). Cortical reorganization in patients with high frequency cochlear hearing loss. *Hearing Research*, 158(1–2), 95–101. http://dx.doi.org/10.1016/S0378-5955(01)00282-9

Dubno, J., & H. Levitt. (1981). Predicting consonant confusions from acoustic analysis. *Journal of the Acoustical Society of America*, 69(1), 249–61. http://dx.doi.org/10.1121/1.385345

Festen, J., & R. Plomp. (1983). Relations between the auditory functions in impaired hearing. *Journal of the Acoustical Society of America*, 73(2), 652–62. http://dx.doi.org/10.1121/1.388957

French, N.R., & J.C. Steinberg. (1947). Factors governing the intelligibility of speech sounds. *Journal of the Acoustical Society of America*, 19(1), 90–119. http://dx.doi.org/10.1121/1.1916407

Gatehouse, S. (1992). The time course and magnitude of perceptual acclimatization to frequency responses: Evidence from monaural fitting of hearing aids. *Journal of the Acoustical Society of America*, 92(3), 1258–68. http://dx.doi.org/10.1121/1.403921

Glista, D., S. Scollie, M. Bagatto, R. Seewald, V. Parsa & A. Johnson. (2009). Evaluation of nonlinear frequency compression: Clinical outcomes. *International Journal of Audiology*, 48(9), 632–44. http://dx.doi.org/10.1080/14992020902971349

Hall, J.W., & J.H. Grose. (1989). Spectrotemporal analysis and cochlear hearing impairment: Effects of frequency selectivity, temporal resolution, signal frequency, and rate of modulation. *Journal of the Acoustical Society of America*, 85(6), 2550–62.http://dx.doi.org/10.1121/1.397749

Irvine, D.R. (2000). Injury- and use-related plasticity in the adult auditory system. *Journal of Communication Disorders*, 33(4), 293–312. http://dx.doi.org/10.1016/S0021-9924(00)00026-5

Irvine, D.R., & R. Rajan. (1997). Injury-induced reorganization of frequency maps in adult auditory cortex: The role of unmasking of normally-inhibited inputs. *Acta Otolaryngolica Supplement*, 532, 39–45.

Klatt, D. (1976). Linguistic uses of segmental duration in English: Acoustic and perceptual evidence. *Journal of the Acoustical Society of America*, 59(5), 1208–21. http://dx.doi.org/10.1121/1.380986

Lindblom, B., & H.M. Sussman. (2012). Dissecting coarticulation: How locus equations happen. *Journal of Phonetics*, 40(1), 1–19.

Marion, M.J., H.M. Sussman & T.P. Marquardt. (1993). The perception and production of rhyme in normal and developmentally apraxic children. *Journal of Communication Disorders*, 26(3), 129–60. http://dx.doi.org/10.1016/0021-9924(93)90005-U

McGurk, H., & J. MacDonald. (1976). Hearing lips and seeing voices. *Nature*, 264(5588), 746–8. http://dx.doi.org/10.1038/264746a0

Olsen, W.O., & N. Matkin. (1979). Speech Audiometry. In W. Rintelmann (ed.), *Hearing Assessment*. Baltimore, MD: University Park Press.

Picheny, M., N. Durlach & L. Braida. (1989). Speaking clearly for the hard of hearing III: An attempt to determine the contribution of speaking rate to differences in intelligibility between clear and conversational speech. *Journal of Speech and Hearing Research*, 32(3), 600–3. http://dx.doi.org/10.1044/jshr.3203.600

Pickett, J.M. (1999). *The Acoustics of Speech Communication: Fundamentals, Speech Perception Theory, and Technology*. Boston: Allyn and Bacon.

Reed, C.M., L.D. Braida & P.M. Zurek. (2008). Review article: Review of the literature on temporal resolution in listeners with cochlear hearing impairment: A critical assessment of the role of suprathreshold deficits. *Trends in Amplification*, 13(1), 4–43. http://dx.doi.org/10.1177/1084713808325412

Rhebergen, K.S., N.J. Versfeld & W.A. Dreschler. (2008). Learning effect observed for the speech reception threshold in interrupted noise with normal hearing listeners. *International Journal of Audiology*, 47(4), 185–8. http://dx.doi.org/10.1080/14992020701883224

Rouger, J., B. Fraysse, O. Deguine & P. Barone. (2008). McGurk effects in cochlear- implanted deaf subjects. *Brain Research*, 1188, 87–99. http://dx.doi.org/10.1016/j.brainres.2007.10.049

Scott, J., & L. Thibodeau. (2006).The effects of auditory training on hearing aid acclimatization. Paper presented at the American Acoustic Society, Phoenix, AZ. http://dx.doi.org/10.1121/1.4781399

Skinner, M., M. Karstaedt & J. Miller. (1982). Amplification bandwidth and speech intelligibility for two listeners with sensorineural hearing loss. *Audiology*, 21(3), 251–68. http://dx.doi.org/10.3109/00206098209072743

Stelmachowicz, P.G., A.L. Pittman, B.M. Hoover & D.L. Lewis. (2001). The effect of stimulus bandwidth on the perception of /s/ in normal- and hearing-impaired children and adults. *Journal of the Acoustical Society of America*, 110(4), 2183–90. http://dx.doi.org/10.1121/1.1400757

Sullivan, J.R., L.M. Thibodeau & P.F. Assmann. (2012). Performance intensity function in interrupted and continuous noise for children with hearing impairment. *Journal of Educational Audiology*,18, 6–12.

Sullivan, J.R., L.M. Thibodeau & P.F. Assmann. (2013). Auditory training of speech recognition with interrupted and continuous noise maskers by children with hearing impairment. *Journal of the Acoustical Society of America*, 133(1), 495–501. http://dx.doi.org/10.1121/1.4770247

Sweetow, R.W., & J.H. Sabes. (2006). The need for and development of an adaptive listening and communication enhancement (LACE) program. *Journal of the American Academy of Audiology*, 17(8), 538–58. http://dx.doi.org/10.3766/jaaa.17.8.2

Teder, H. (1993). Compression in the time domain. *American Journal of Audiology*, 2(2), 41–6. http://dx.doi.org/10.1044/1059-0889.0202.41

Thibodeau, L. (1991a). Performance of hearing-impaired persons on auditory enhancement tasks. *Journal of the Acoustical Society of America*, 89(6), 2843–50. http://dx.doi.org/10.1121/1.400722

Thibodeau, L. (1991b). Exploration of factors beyond audibility that may influence speech recognition. *Ear and Hearing*, 12(Suppl.), 109S–15S. http://dx.doi.org/10.1097/00003446-199112001-00004

Thibodeau, L., & H. Sussman. (1979). Performance on a test of categorical perception of speech in normal and communication disordered children. *Journal of Phonetics*, 7, 375–91.

Thibodeau, L., & D. Van Tasell. (1987). Frequency resolution and speech reception in persons with sensori-neural hearing loss. *Journal of the Acoustical Society of America*, 82(3), 864–73. http://dx.doi.org/10.1121/1.395285

Tyler, R., A. Summerfield, E. Wood & M. Fernandes. (1982a). Psychoacoustic and phonetic temporal processing in normal and hearing impaired listeners. In G. van den Brink & F. Bilsen (eds.), *Psychophysical, Physiological, and Behavioural Studies in Hearing* (pp. 458–65). Holland: Delft University Press. http://dx.doi.org/10.1121/1.388254

Tyler, R., E. Wood & M. Fernandes. (1982b). Frequency resolution and hearing loss. *British Journal of Audiology*, 16(1), 45–63. http://dx.doi.org/10.3109/03005368209081507

Umeda, N. (1975). Vowel duration in American English. *Journal of the Acoustical Society of America*, 58(2), 434–445. http://dx.doi.org/10.1121/1.380688

Umeda, N. (1977). Consonant duration in American English. *Journal of the Acoustical Society of America*, 61(3), 846–58. http://dx.doi.org/10.1121/1.381374

Van Tasell, D., D. Fabry & L. Thibodeau. (1987). Vowel identification and vowel masking patterns in normal and hearing impaired listeners. *Journal of the Acoustical Society of America*, 81, 1586–97. http://dx.doi.org/10.1121/1.394511

Willott, J.F. (1996). Physiological plasticity in the auditory system and its possible relevance to hearing aid use, deprivation effects, and acclimatization. *Ear and Hearing*, 17(Suppl. 1), 66S–77S.http://dx.doi.org/10.1097/00003446-199617031-00007

10
The Locus Equation as an Index of Auditory Access for Children with Hearing Loss

Helen Morrison[1]

10.1 Introduction

The development of spoken language production proceeds along three dimensions: physical-motor, perceptual-cognitive and social-communicative. Infants and young children acquire motor speech skill and control through general processes of maturation and specific practice creating vocal sounds (Green et al. 2002). Infants form phonological categories from perceptual input delivered by the ambient language (Kuhl 2004). Perceptual and motor domains develop synergistically as the infant matches productive output to caregiver models (Callan et al. 2000). As infants and young children bond and interact with caregivers, they learn to communicate and construct a lexicon that shapes the productive phonemic inventory along with syllabic shape and content (see Stoel-Gammon 2011 for a review).

The role that auditory perception plays in the development of speech production is not easily investigated in the laboratory setting. Hearing loss, on the other hand, provides a means for investigating the relationship between auditory perception and speech production. The locus equation derived from the second formant (F2) transition onset and mid-vowel in consonant-vowel (CV) syllables is well suited to serve as a measure for observing the role of audition in speech production because F2 is particularly vulnerable to hearing loss. Sensorineural hearing loss tends to be greatest in the frequency range encompassed by F2, reducing acoustic

1 Helen Morrison is a retired Associate Professor in the Department of Communication Sciences and Disorders at Texas Christian University, and the owner of Listening and Spoken Language Coaching and Professional Development.

access. In cases of severe and profound hearing loss, F2 may be completely inaudible even with the use of hearing aids. Finally, F2 varies with tongue movement, an aspect of production that is far more difficult to speech-read than lip or jaw movement, necessitating acoustic access to F2 for unambiguous perception.

10.2 Childhood Hearing Loss in the 21st Century

The first publication of Sussman's locus findings in 1991 (Sussman et al. 1991) and investigations that followed over the next two decades took place during a transformative period in the lives of children with hearing loss. Technological advances leading to the development of portable auditory brainstem test equipment and instrumentation for the assessment of otoacoustic emissions made possible accurate and cost-effective universal newborn hearing screening (UNHS). In 1990 Hawaii passed the first state legislation mandating UNHS. Today all 50 states and the United States territories mandate infant hearing screening (National Center for Hearing Assessment and Management 2013). Digital hearing aids that process sound with greater versatility than analog instruments were introduced in the 1990s. In 1990 the Food and Drug Administration (FDA) approved cochlear implantation in children as young as 2 years. Since 1990, the FDA has lowered the minimum age for cochlear implantation to 12 months, and today 38,000 children in the United States wear cochlear implants (National Institutes of Health 2013).

As a consequence, children with hearing loss in the 21st century are fit with hearing technology that provides essential auditory access to the speech spectrum at sufficiently young ages to enable listening and spoken language acquisition to proceed in synchrony with other developmental domains (Yoshinaga-Itano et al. 1998; Yoshinaga-Itano 2003). Today's children with hearing loss can potentially follow the same developmental trajectory, and reach listening and spoken language benchmarks at ages equivalent to typically developing peers (Davis et al. 2005; Morrison & Russell 2012; Eriks-Brophy et al. 2013).

Intervention strategies that in the past employed alternative sensory inputs (e.g., vision or touch) and focused on the remediation of abnormal patterns lose relevance for today's population of children with hearing loss. Intervention has shifted toward approaches that follow a typical developmental trajectory, target the establishment of an auditory-based phonological system acquired by listening to ambient language input, and monitor for the emergence of atypical patterns that may require remediation (Morrison 2012a; Morrison & Russell 2012).

This shift adds another dimension to the usefulness of investigating locus functions in the speech produced by persons with hearing loss. Due to the vulnerability of F2 to the impact of hearing loss, locus functions can potentially serve as a "canary in the coal mine" for intervention. Atypical locus measures can indicate inadequacy in hearing technology, insufficient spoken language models from the adults in the child's daily life, or an over-emphasis on visual aspects of production in intervention to the detriment of auditory learning.

The following describes the outcomes and clinical implications of two locus investigations of speech produced by individuals with hearing loss. The first, involving 4 young adult speakers with profound hearing loss, explores how the lack of auditory access to F2 manifests in speech production (Morrison 2008). The second examines the interaction between auditory and motor development in speech acquisition by 3 young children who wore hearing technology that enabled auditory access to F2, but were fitted with their technology at different ages and stages of motor experience (Morrison 2012b).

10.3 When Spoken Language Is Auditorially Inaccessible

Slopes and *y*-intercepts in locus functions derived from CVs produced by speakers with normal hearing vary with consonant place of production, and are contrastive in the acoustic plane described by the relationship between F2-onset and F2-midvowel (Sussman et al. 1998). This was not the case for locus functions derived from the productions of 4 young adults with profound hearing loss and little to no auditory access to speech with hearing aids (Morrison 2008). Euclidean distances calculated from plots of locus slopes along normalized *y*-intercepts derived from syllables initiated by [b], [d] and [g] were 4 times greater in productions from normally hearing speakers compared to speakers with profound deafness. The vowels produced by this group were marked by limited F2 range and attendant vowel neutralization, a common productive pattern in speakers with profound hearing loss (Angelocci et al. 1964; Monsen 1976; McCaffrey &

Sussman 1994). The limited vowel F2 range in turn constrained the extent to which locus functions were differentially represented across consonant place. One speaker in the Morrison (2008) study further reduced contrastiveness of locus functions across consonant place by producing high levels of anticipatory coarticulation in contexts where coarticulation is typically low. Speech intelligibility decreased with decreased differentiation of locus slopes across speakers.

Data from locus investigations of speech produced by adults with profound loss highlight the importance of establishing a full range of vowels in order to build a foundation for intelligible speech by facilitating the development of contrastive coarticulatory patterns that contribute to intelligibility. The failure to acquire a full range of vowels may indicate problems of acoustic access with hearing technology, or other causes for reliance on visual cues to the diminution of auditory development, such as an intervention approach that fails to support listening as a goal.

10.4 Auditory Access, Motor Experience and Hearing Age

Lindblom (1983) predicted that anticipatory coarticulation is a product of maturing motor control of the syllable. Locus functions derived from CVs produced by typically developing infants and children in 4 longitudinal and cross-sectional investigations explored the developmental trajectory of coarticulation from the onset of canonical babble to attainment of adult levels (Gibson & Ohde 2007; Sussman et al. 1992, 1996, 1999). Morrison (2012b) plotted the locus slopes obtained in these 4 investigations across chronological age (7 months to 5 years), constructing separate plots for slopes obtained from CVs initiated by [b], [d] and [g]. Locus function slopes reached adult values at around 48 months.

The developmental trajectory, however, varied with consonant place. The extent of anticipatory coarticulation increased over time in syllables initiated by [b], promoted by increased vowel types in the phonetic inventory. Coarticulation decreased over time in syllables initiated by [d] and [g] as Frame Content (Davis & MacNeilage 1995) constraints released tendencies toward coupling of the jaw and tongue to enable a variety of vowels along the front/back dimension to be produced at these places of occlusion, with the tongue placement for the consonant remaining stable.

In order to examine the role of auditory perception on the development of coarticulation, Morrison (2012b) derived locus functions from acoustic analysis of CV syllables in babble and early words produced by 3 children with hearing loss. Each child was fitted with hearing aids within the first 5 months of life, but only one child (S1) obtained auditory access to the speech spectrum with his hearing aids. The two others, children with profound hearing loss, did not obtain functional auditory access to speech with their hearing aids. Rather, they received auditory access with cochlear implants that were activated at 19 months (S2) and 39 months (S3) of age.

The children were recorded at intervals, at approximately 6 months and 1 year after fitting with hearing aids (S1) or cochlear implants (S2 and S3). Children S2 and S3 were also recorded one month prior to cochlear implant activation. Locus functions were compared to measures obtained from productions by typically developing children (Gibson & Ohde 2007; Sussman et al. 1992, 1996, 1999) that were matched according to two different "ages": (1) chronological age and (2) hearing age, or the duration of time that a child has worn hearing technology that provides auditory access to the speech spectrum.

The child with auditory access to the speech spectrum from early infancy produced [d]+vowel syllables almost exclusively across recording sessions. The slope of locus functions derived from this syllable type matched values from productions by typically developing peers with the same chronological age. This is a finding that was rarely obtained prior to the 1990s. In the past, children with hearing loss who reached "normal" levels of production ordinarily did so by progressing more slowly than typically developing children and experiencing a delay in attaining benchmarks. In the case of S1, audition developed in synchrony with other developmental domains and speech production (in this case anticipatory coarticulation) was comparable to same-age typically developing peers.

More complex results were obtained from the two children who received later auditory access via cochlear implants. Locus slopes derived from syllables that were present pre-implantation were more similar to slopes from syllables produced by children with the same chronological age. These included CVs initiated by [b] produced by both S2 and S3, and CVs initiated by [g] produced by S3. With limited auditory access prior to implantation, alternative sensory inputs may have taken precedence to trigger the emergence of these syllable types, enabling motor practice and the development of coarticulation similar to children of equivalent chronological age. The visible labial consonants have been reported to dominate consonant inventories in the productive output of other young children with profound hearing loss prior to or in the earliest months of cochlear implant use (McCaffrey et al. 1999; Davis et al. 2005; Schramm et al. 2009). The high proportion of [g] + vowel syllables produced by S3 may have been a consequence of tactile feedback available for production of this consonant.

Conversely, locus slopes from syllable types that were triggered by auditory experience following cochlear implant activation were closer to values from children matched by hearing age than chronological age. These included CVs initiated by [d] in productions by both S2 and S3, and CVs initiated by [g] produced by S2. The emergence of CVs initiated by [d] or [g] has been reported in accounts of changes in phonetic inventories post-implantation (McCaffrey et al. 1999; Davis et al. 2005; Schramm et al. 2009).

The contrastiveness of locus functions across place of production of the initiating consonant was assessed in the data obtained from speakers S2 and S3 at 1 year post-implantation. Locus slopes were plotted against normalized *y*-intercepts derived from syllables initiated by [b], [d] and [g], and compared to plots of slopes and *y*-intercepts derived from productions of children of the same chronological age and the same hearing age. At 1 year post-implantation, the separation of place categories more closely resembled chronological age peers than hearing age peers. Furthermore, these graphs illustrated greater separation of place categories than that produced by young adults with profound hearing loss and minimal auditory access to speech in Morrison's 2008 investigation.

Several clinical implications can be drawn from locus findings with children who received auditory access via cochlear implants. Despite newborn identification of hearing loss and hearing aid fitting within the first weeks of life, infants with profound hearing loss typically wait until age 12 months for cochlear implant surgery in accord with FDA guidelines. As a consequence, parents and interventionists may consider the period prior to implantation to be a time when little can be accomplished. The findings from Morrison's (2012b) study that revealed coarticulatory patterns were established prior to implantation indicate that there is value to continuing to direct spoken language input to the infant in ordinary caregiver-child contexts and to encourage and reinforce vocal behavior. Productive patterns that have been established prior to cochlear implant activation should be assessed for atypical characteristics that may have resulted from formation via non-auditory models and feedback. Once cochlear implants are activated it may be necessary to re-establish production using auditory stimulation and auditory models with words and phrases that include speech targets that developed prior to auditory access.

After cochlear implant activation young children have the potential to establish auditory-based production in essentially the same manner as typically developing children. The expected time course for achievement of benchmarks will be guided by the child's hearing age, or reference to the time course followed by typically developing children whose chronological age is equivalent to the duration that the child has been listening with the cochlear implants.

10.5 Summary

Locus functions derived from the relationship between F2 at the onset of the CV transition and F2 at midvowel serve as an index of the degree of anticipatory coarticulation in CV production. The F2 frequency range is vulnerable to the impact of sensorineural hearing loss and locus functions derived by productions by speakers with hearing loss may serve as an index of the auditory accessibility of F2 for these speakers.

References

Angelocci, A.A., G.A. Kopp & A. Holbrook. (1964). The vowel formants of deaf and normal-hearing eleven- to fourteen-year-old boys. *Journal of Speech and Hearing Disorders*, 29(2), 156–70. http://dx.doi.org/10.1044/jshd.2902.156

Callan, D.E., R.D. Kent, F.H. Guenther & H.K. Vorperian. (2000). An auditory-feedback- based neural network model of speech production that is robust to developmental changes in size and shape of the articulatory system. *Journal of Speech, Language, and Hearing Research (JSLHR)*, 43(3), 721–36. http://dx.doi.org/10.1044/jslhr.4303.721

Davis, B.L., & MacNeilage, P.F. (1995). The articulatory basis of babbling. *Journal of Speech, Language, and Hearing Research (JSLHR)*, 38(6), 1199–1211. http://dx.doi.org/10.1044/jshr.3806.1199

Davis, B.L., H.M. Morrison, D. von Hapsburg & A. Warner-Czyz. (2005). Early vocal patterns in infants with varied hearing levels. *Volta Review*, 105, 151–73.

Eriks-Brophy, A., S. Gibson & S. Tucker. (2013). Articulatory error: Patterns and phonological process use of preschool children with and without hearing loss. *Volta Review*, 113, 87–125.

Gibson, T., & R. Ohde. (2007). F2 locus equations: Phonetic descriptors of coarticulation in 17- to 22-month-old children. *Journal of Speech, Language, and Hearing Research (JSLHR)*, 50(1), 97–108. http://dx.doi.org/10.1044/1092-4388(2007/008)

Green, J.R., C.A. Moore & K.J. Reilly. (2002). The sequential development of jaw and lip control for speech. *Journal of Speech, Language, and Hearing Research (JSLHR)*, 45(1), 66–79. http://dx.doi.org/10.1044/1092-4388(2002/005)

Kuhl, P. (2004). Early language acquisition: Cracking the speech code. *Nature Reviews: Neuroscience*, 5(11), 831–43. http://dx.doi.org/10.1038/nrn1533

Lindblom, B. (1983). Economy of speech gestures. In P.F. MacNeilage (ed.), *The Production of Speech* (pp. 217–45). New York: Springer-Verlag. http://dx.doi.org/10.1007/978-1-4613-8202-7_10

McCaffrey, H.A., B.L. Davis, P.F. MacNeilage & D. von Hapsburg. (1999). Multichannel cochlear implantation and the organization of early speech. *Volta Review*, 101, 5–29.

McCaffrey, H.A., & H.M. Sussman. (1994). An investigation of vowel organization in speakers with severe and profound hearing impairment. *Journal of Speech and Hearing Research*, 17(4), 938–51. http://dx.doi.org/10.1044/jshr.3704.938

Monsen, R.B. (1976). Second formant transitions of selected consonant-vowel combinations in the speech of deaf and normal-hearing children. *Journal of Speech and Hearing Research*, 19, 279–89.

Morrison, H.M. (2008). The locus equation as an index of coarticulation in syllables produced by speakers with profound hearing loss. *Clinical Linguistics & Phonetics*, 22, 726–40.

Morrison, H.M. (2012a). How do children acquire speech without studying mouth and/or face movements in auditory-verbal therapy and education? In Warren Estabrooks (ed.), *101 Frequently Asked Questions about Auditory-Verbal Practice* (pp. 184–7). Washington, DC: A.G. Bell.

Morrison, H.M. (2012b). Coarticulation in early vocalizations by children with hearing loss: A locus perspective. *Clinical Linguistics & Phonetics*, 26(3), 288–309. http://dx.doi.org/10.3109/02699206.2011.614718

Morrison, H.M., & A. Russell. (2012). What is meant by a "developmental approach" to speech production in auditory-verbal therapy and education? In Warren Estabrooks (ed.), *101 Frequently Asked Questions about Auditory-Verbal Practice* (pp. 437–41). Washington, DC: A.G. Bell.

National Center for Hearing Assessment and Management (2013). EHDI legislation: Overview. Retrieved from http://www.infanthearing.org/legislation

National Institutes of Health (2013). Cochlear implants. Retrieved from http://www.nidcd.nih.gov/health/hearing/pages/coch.aspx

Schramm, B., A. Bohnert & A. Keilmann. (2009). The prelexical development in children implanted by 16 months compared with normal hearing children. *International Journal of Pediatric Otorhinolaryngology*, 73(12), 1673–81. http://dx.doi.org/10.1016/j.ijporl.2009.08.023

Stoel-Gammon, C. (2011). Relationships between lexical and phonological development in young children. *Journal of Child Language*, 38(1), 1–34. http://dx.doi.org/10.1017/S0305000910000425

Sussman, H.M., C. Duder, E. Dalston & A. Cacciatore. (1999). An acoustic analysis of the development of CV coarticulation: A case study. *Journal of Speech,*

Language, and Hearing Research (JSLHR), 42(5), 1080–96. http://dx.doi.org/10.1044/jslhr.4205.1080

Sussman, H.M., D. Fruchter, J. Hilbert & J. Sirosh. (1998). Linear correlates in the speech signal: The Orderly Output Constraint. *Behavioral and Brain Sciences*, 21(2), 241–99. http://dx.doi.org/10.1017/S0140525X98001174

Sussman, H.M., K. Hoemeke & H.A. McCaffrey. (1992). Locus equations as an index of coarticulation for place of articulation distinctions in children. *Journal of Speech, Language, and Hearing Research (JSLHR)*, 35(4), 769–81. http://dx.doi.org/10.1044/jshr.3504.769

Sussman, H.M., H.A. McCaffrey & S.A. Matthews. (1991). An investigation of locus equations as a source of relational invariance for stop place categorization. *Journal of the Acoustical Society of America*, 90(3), 1309–25. http://dx.doi.org/10.1121/1.401923

Sussman, H.M., F. Minifie, E. Buder, C. Stoel-Gammon & J. Smith. (1996). Consonant–vowel interdependencies in babbling and early words: Preliminary examination of a locus equation approach. *Journal of Speech, Language, and Hearing Research (JSLHR)*, 39(2), 424–33. http://dx.doi.org/10.1044/jshr.3902.424

Yoshinaga-Itano, C. (2003). From screening to early identification and intervention: Discovering predictors to successful outcomes for children with significant hearing loss. *Journal of Deaf Studies and Deaf Education*, 8(1), 11–30. http://dx.doi.org/10.1093/deafed/8.1.11

Yoshinaga-Itano, C., A.L. Sedey, D. Coulter & A. Mehl. (1998). The language of early- and later-identified children with hearing loss. *Pediatrics*, 102(5), 1161–71. http://dx.doi.org/10.1542/peds.102.5.1161

11
Person-Centeredness, Culture and Communication in Dementia Care: Attitudes among Medical Students

Tony Johnstone Young, Ellen St. Clair Tullo, and Richard Philip Lee[1]

11.1 Introduction: The Challenge of Dementia Care

Providing effective care for a person/people living with dementia[2] (PLWD) is one of the greatest social, economic and health challenges currently facing societies. There are now about 40 million PLWD worldwide: best current estimates indicate a doubling of numbers every 20 years, with a rise to around 115 million by 2050 (Alzheimer's Disease International 2011). Recent research and policy responses have been largely confined to "the west" – North America, Western Europe and Australasia (NIHCE-SCIE 2007; Beer et al. 2009; Alzheimer's Disease International 2012; Alzheimer's Society 2012), although similar initiatives are beginning to emerge more widely as numbers of older people in populations increase and the global scale of the challenge becomes apparent (Alfonso et al. 2010; Alzheimer's Disease International 2012). Research has identified

1 Tony Johnstone Young is Senior Lecturer in Language and Communication in the School of Education, Communication and Language Sciences at Newcastle University.
Ellen St. Clair Tullo is a teaching and research fellow at the Newcastle NIHR Biomedical Research Centre in Ageing and Chronic Disease, Institute for Ageing and Health, Newcastle University.
Richard Philip Lee is senior research associate at the Institute of Health & Society, Newcastle University.

2 This is the first of two reports of the study on medical students' views. Here we lay emphasis on cross-cultural analysis.

communicative practices by professionals involved in dementia care as a key, cost-effective area for improvement, and evidence, discussed below, indicates that improvements in communication between PLWD and those involved in their care can promote positive changes in practice; and that this has a direct impact on the ability of people to live well, or otherwise, with dementia.

One of the more research-active environments with regard to dementia care has been the United Kingdom (UK). Here, the majority of healthcare professionals working in both hospitals and in the community have frequent contact with PLWD, but the care they provide has come under increasing scrutiny and criticism (National Audit Office 2007; Royal College of Psychiatrists 2011). About 25 per cent of all National Health Service (NHS) beds are currently occupied by PLWD, although the majority of PLWD live in the community under the care of General Practitioners (GPs) and Primary Care teams (Alzheimer's Society 2012). In terms of community care, a recent survey of GPs found that only 31 per cent felt that they had sufficient dementia training (National Audit Office 2007).

With regard to hospital care, recent reports have uncovered a number of inequities faced by PLWD (Alzheimer's Society 2009; The Patients Association 2011; Care Quality Commission 2012). Areas of dissatisfaction for PLWD and family members relate to a lack of person-centeredness and poor communication practices by staff. These included general neglect of PLWD on wards; a lack of opportunity for social interaction by PLWD; not as much involvement in decision-making as wished for (for both the PLWD and family); and PLWD being treated by staff with a lack of dignity and respect. Once admitted, PLWD tend to spend considerably more time as inpatients than do patients without dementia receiving treatment for similar medical conditions. There are considerable cost implications for this, and lengthy inpatient stays are also associated with a negative impact on PLWD's dementia symptoms, physical health and wellbeing. Areas of concern identified by staff themselves include difficulties communicating with PLWD, and dealing with problematic behaviors such as wandering.

There is evidence to indicate that poor communication by care staff with PLWD may cause them significant harm. The over-use of antipsychotic medication for PLWD has been highlighted by a number of authorities, with suggestions that more effective communication practices might lessen the perceived need for such medication (Department of Health 2009). "Talking down" to PLWD, or not attempting to engage them in meaningful interaction, can have the effect of reinforcing perceived deficits at the expense of retained abilities, producing a downward communication spiral and a self-fulfilling perception that PLWD are, at best, to be engaged with like young children, at worst not engaged with meaningfully at all (Young and Manthorp 2009). This is despite the fact that a small but growing body of research suggests that optimizing carers' communicative practices can positively influence the quality of life of PLWD (Peterson et al. 2002; Worral & Hickson 2003; Savundranayagam et al.. 2007; Young et al. 2011a).

11.2 Person-Centered Care (PCC)

As a means of optimizing care practices, the notion of person-centeredness has become highly influential in recent years, particularly in the care of older people (Edvardsson and Innes 2010). PCC has at its core attempts to reconfigure care practices away from the strictly biomedical and more toward the individual patient – essentially, away from the condition and onto the person (Kitwood 1993, 1997). A person-centered approach is realized through appropriate communicative practices by those caring for PLWD. It attempts to incorporate recognition and acknowledgment of a person's life history, beliefs, values and individual wants, needs and preferences into interaction. To be successfully applied, a person-centered approach depends on a positive and affirming attitude on the part of carers, and an aspiration by them to recognize and support a PLWD's individuality, agency and sense of self. Efficacious communication practices by carers are key to this recognition and support, and to supporting and promoting wellbeing (Department of Health 2009).

PCC is, however, vaguely conceptualized, and has been variously realized in care models (Brooker 2007). In addition, very little investigation of the outcomes of the application of person-centered approaches to care has been conducted (Gibson 1999; Davis 2004). PCC has also been criticized for a possibly overly individualistic, "Western" orientation, which might make its applicability problematic outside this context. Possible cultural inappropriateness and ethnocentricity may be revealed by PCC's emphasis on support for the agency of the individual, essentialized, self (Young and Manthorp 2009). It may also be difficult for the very large numbers of people influenced by a more collectivistic, non-Western cultural background who work in Western care contexts to operationalize (Young et al. 2011b).

11.3 Medical Education about Dementia

In terms of improving healthcare for PLWD, there is a strong current of opinion among a range of stakeholders internationally that medical education about dementia needs to be improved for both undergraduate and postgraduate medical students. Concern has been expressed at policy level that negative attitudes, along with gaps in knowledge and skills among healthcare professionals may contribute to the generally prevalent less than optimal care of PLWD, with communicative practices being a particular focus for recommended improvement. (Department of Health 2009, 2011; Alzheimer's Disease International 2011; Alzheimer's Society 2012; Care Quality Commission 2012).

Improving education about dementia worldwide will require multiple approaches. Central among these will be becoming better informed about healthcare professionals' approaches to dementia care in general, and more specifically to communication and person-centered care for PLWD. To our knowledge, no previous research has specifically addressed issues relating to undergraduate medical students' attitudes toward communicating with PLWD. A better understanding of how medical students internationally approach communication with PLWD will enable us to see how this key group of professionals-to-be are orientated regarding PCC, facilitating the design and delivery of appropriate teaching and learning about PCC. It will also allow insight into the nature of the challenges that are likely to occur in implementing person-centeredness for PLWD in different countries.

11.3.1 The Study

The aim of this study was to provide internationally and transculturally relevant information comparing attitudes and approaches to communicating with PLWD between medical students in different year groups, and in different national locations, who were following the same core curriculum. The two locations of the study were the UK and Malaysia: the former is a relatively prosperous, Western, country with an older, and aging, population; the latter a middle-income, developing country with a younger but rapidly aging population. The need for strategies to provide efficacious cost-effective dementia care is being felt internationally, but is likely to be particularly acute in low- and middle-income countries like Malaysia. Around 58 per cent of PLWD now live in such countries, with an anticipated rise to 71 per cent by 2050, with those in Asia likely to show the highest increase (Alzheimer's Disease International 2010). Since the vast majority of research about dementia care has been conducted in "the West" (Prince 2010), we aim to make a contribution to redressing this balance by locating our study in these two, contrasting, countries.

11.4 Methods

The study had a mixed methods design. Quantitative data was gathered using the Dementia Communication Questionnaire (DCQ). This was supplemented by qualitative data collected from focus groups of questionnaire participants.

11.4.1 Participants

The study involved students in years one and three at a medical school with UK and Malaysian sites. The school's largest facility is based in the UK, but a smaller facility recently opened in Malaysia. Year-one students in Malaysia were the first entry-level group at the new site. Year-three students in Malaysia had spent the first two years of their program of study in the UK, and had moved back to the Malaysian site in 2011 to continue and complete their studies. UK-based students were either entry-level-year ones, or year-threes who had completed the first two years of their program in the UK.

11.4.2 Questionnaire

As no instrument specifically addressing attitudes toward communication with PLWD existed, the authors produced a "Dementia Communication Questionnaire" (DCQ). This consisted of 12 questions, each related to one of 12 aspects of effective communicative behavior identified in the "Dementia Toolkit for Effective Communication" (DEMTEC), itself the basis for a "Dementia Model for Effective Communication" (DeMEC, Table 11.1). This model was developed in the UK between 2009 and 2011 after a series of iterative investigations, and is an attempt to encapsulate best current communicative practice with PLWD in social-care and healthcare contexts (Young et al. 2011a, b; Young et al. 2013). Unlike most dementia communications advice (Levy-Storms 2008), it is conceptually grounded, specifically, on theory related to Communication Accommodation Theory (Giles & Ogay 2007) and gerontological derivatives such as the Communicative Predicament of Aging Model (Hummert et al. 1998). DeMEC is also empirically derived, as it draws on the views and preferences of PLWD and a spectrum of other experienced stakeholders, including family members, social carers, social-care professionals, speech and language therapists, dementia specialist nursing staff and old-age psychiatrists. Although a product of UK-based research projects, DeMEC was explicitly designed to be translatable and transculturally applicable, and has been so far been translated for Spanish- and Catalan-speaking audiences (Young et al. 2010). Its pre-suppositions are based primarily on "Western" perspectives, but are explicitly stated, and are intended to be adaptable by people in other socio-cultural and care contexts to their own needs and circumstances. The centrality of the views of PLWD are also highlighted in DeMEC. As these views have, historically, been under-represented, we felt that this gave DeMEC additional validity as a conceptual framework.

Table 11.1. Overview of Dementia Model for Effective Communication (DeMEC, adapted from Young et al. 2013).

Level Three	Actual communication involving people living with dementia, their care plans, guidance for informal careers and guidance and training for health- and social-care providers.							
↑ ↑ ↑ ↑ *which guide and inform* ↑ ↑ ↑ ↑								
↑ Level Two	1 Conver-sation	2 Non-verbal commu-nication/ body language	3 Environ-mental consider-ations	4 Anxiety reduc-tion	5 Mindful-ness and empathy	6 Under-standing beha-viors	7 Retain-ing a sense of self	8 Check-ing under-standing
Eight components of good communicative practice, each consisting of a "What" (definition), a "Why" (rationale for inclusion) and a "How" (specific considerations and behaviors).								
↑ ↑ ↑ ↑ *which guide and inform* ↑ ↑ ↑ ↑								
↑ Level One	Beliefs and principles about the importance of communication to quality of life. Approaches to communication which acknowledge personhood and aim to promote agency and empowerment.							

The DCQ items surveyed related to orientations and communicative behaviors identified as efficacious in Levels One and Two of DeMEC (Table 11.1). The first item related to preferred terminology and gave participants a range of options. These included possibilities that prior research (Young et al. 2011a) had indicated that PLWD was felt to be person-centered and non-stigmatizing ("person living with dementia", and, to a lesser extent, "person with dementia"), and that other options were more biomedically-focused ("person living with a dementing illness" and "a dementia sufferer"), or that were possibly stigmatizing ("a demented person"). The other 11 items consisted of statements to which participants were asked to indicate their level of agreement. The first of these asked whether older people deserved great respect, to glean information about the orientation of participants toward older people in general, and to DeMEC Level One, which emphasizes the importance of a positive and affirmative attitude in carers. The other items explored views on specific aspects of person-centered communication identified as key in Level Two of DeMEC, which details specific components of communicative practice. These included views on the degree to which conversation is an important part of treatment and whether it can reduce anxiety; the extent to which very confused speech might hold meaning; the appropriateness of the use of prompts and clues as reminders of who and where people are; whether lying was acceptable if the truth might be upsetting for people to hear; the importance of checking understanding; the perceived importance of nonverbal communication, including the appropriate use of touch, gestures and posture; the efficacy or otherwise of staff wearing uniforms; and whether it was better to speak to a family member first. Items are scored using a five-point Likert scale ranging from "strongly agree" to "strongly disagree." Higher scores reflect a greater level of agreement with the person-centered communicative approaches advocated in DeMEC, although some items are reverse coded to minimize the risk of acquiescence bias (Oppenheim 2000).

As students were located across institutional sites in the UK and Malaysia, for practical, access-related reasons some variation in questionnaire administration was necessary. UK-based year-one students were approached at the end of a lecture for the whole year group and invited to complete a paper-based questionnaire. UK-based year-three students were widely dispersed at hospitals across the region, so three cohorts of students undertaking a psychiatry rotation were approached during seminars and similarly invited to complete the same paper-based questionnaire. All year-three medical students at this institution completed the same psychiatry rotation, and the profile of the participant group in terms of age and gender balance was similar to that of the wider cohort, so participant groups were not atypical. The same questionnaire was converted to an electronically administered instrument and all year-one and -three students based in Malaysia were contacted by email and invited to complete the questionnaire online. Medical students at both the UK-based and Malaysian sites speak English, the language of instruction, to a high minimum standard, either as their first language, or to at least band seven in the International English Language Testing System (IELTS 2012) or an equivalent, indicating "fully operational command of the language." The content and phrasing of the DCQ statements were reviewed with Malaysian staff during piloting and no problems were reported with comprehension for any items in the questionnaire.

11.4.3 Focus Groups

Students who completed the DCQ were invited to attend a focus group to discuss issues arising from the questionnaire. Focus groups are a complementary method to questionnaire administration since they allow participants the opportunity to expand and reflect on the more immediate responses inherent to brief questionnaires (Barbour 2005; Green & Thorogood 2009). Moreover, this method was felt to be suitable for this study in order to promote an interactive exchange between students during which they could consider both group norms and divergent opinions (Lingard & Kennedy 2010). The focus groups were semi-structured; students had access to a copy of the DCQ statements and the focus group moderator used the statements as prompts for discussion. Students were encouraged to discuss in more detail the statements that they found the most interesting or challenging.

Focus groups held in the UK and Malaysia were audio-recorded, transcribed and anonymized. A thematic content analysis was then conducted (Braun & Clarke 2006). Content was initially categorized and divided using the DCQ statements as major theme headings, with related subthemes emerging. For each DCQ statement, text was then independently coded. Thematic analysis of communication issues was undertaken by two of the authors (ET and TY), while the third author (RL) interrogated the thematic analysis and considered narrative and interactional aspects of these findings. Coded data was organized using N-Vivo 9™ and the authors compared their codings. Where there was disagreement over an appropriate code for each section of text, these examples were further discussed until consensus was reached.

11.4.4 Ethics

Students at both sites were advised that completion of the questionnaires was voluntary and anonymous. Students who expressed an interest in taking part in a focus group were provided with further information about the format and topic of discussion before confirming whether or not they would like to attend. Written consent was then obtained. Recordings were kept in a secure location. The project met the ethical assessment guidelines for the relevant University's School of Education, and approval was confirmed by its Medical Board of Studies.

11.5 Findings

11.5.1 Demographics of Respondents

A total of 326 questionnaires were collected from the UK and Malaysian sites; 283 were completed by year-one students, representing roughly 87 per cent of the year group at the two sites, and 43 were completed by year-three students, representing approximately 13 per cent of the year group at the two sites (see Table 11.2). For the practical reasons discussed above, samples sizes of year-three students were smaller, but the response rate of year-three students approached was 81 per cent. Fifty-five per cent of the respondents were female. 270 of the respondents were based in the UK, 56 in Malaysia.

Table 11.2. DCQ responses by location and year group.

Group		UK	Malaysia	Total
Year 1	(responses/group size)	238/245	45/57	283/302
	% group	97%	79%	94%
Year 3	(responses/group size)	32/300	11/20	43/320
	% group	11%	55%	13%
Total		270	56	326

Table 11.3. Responses to DCQ 8 (*It is acceptable to lie to them if you think the truth might be upsetting to hear*) by year and location.

	UK	**Malaysia**	**Significance**
Year 1 (n) (mean rank)	237148.62	45103.99	0.000
Year 3 (n) (mean rank)	3220.38	1126.73	0.154
Overall (n) (mean rank)	269169.03	56134.03	0.007

11.5.2 Statistical Analysis

A Kolmogorov-Smirnov test of normality confirmed that our data was non-normal, so group comparisons were made using appropriate non-parametric tests including Chi-square and Mann-Whitney U. If a questionnaire had missing data for a category required in a particular analysis it was not used. To avoid type I error, a Bonferroni correction was applied to the Mann-Whitney U tests – results are only therefore presented as significant if the p value is less than 0.00076.

11.5.3 Terminology Question

The preferred term shared across all groups was "person with dementia" (54 per cent). Comparison of terminology choice between students based in the UK and in Malaysia was significantly different, at year one ($X^2 = 33.6$, $p < 0.001$). Year-one students based in Malaysia were more likely to select "other" as preferred terminology than year-one students based in the UK, and less likely to select "person living with dementia" than students based in the UK.

11.5.4 Responses to Other DCQ Items

Overall, the majority of students in all year groups and locations agreed or strongly agreed with the majority of the DCQ statements – median responses in most cases scored 4 out of 5, and there were no significant differences between the responses from different year groups and locations. The only exceptions to this overall confirmatory pattern were DCQ 8 and 11. Student response to DCQ 8 and 11 was most often scored 3 – "neither agree nor disagree," although the range of responses in both cases included all of the Likert categories (see Figures 11.1 and 11.2).

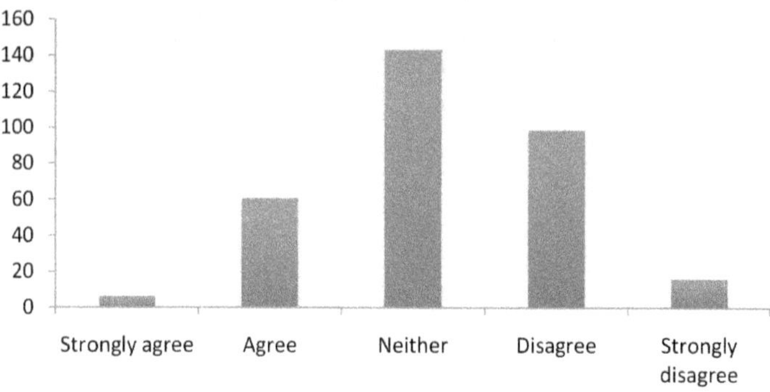

Figure 11.1. Responses to DCQ 8.

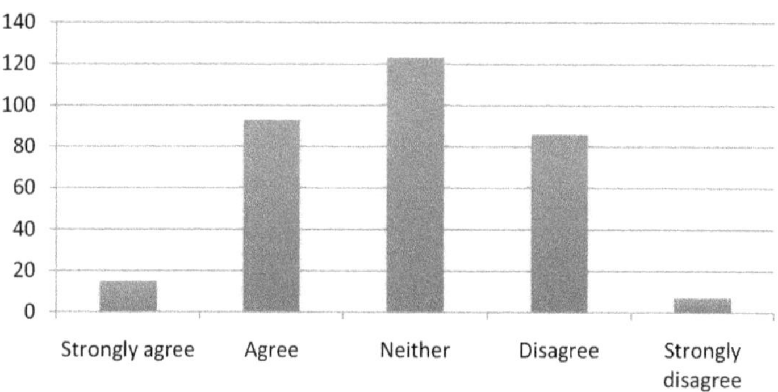

Figure 11.2. Responses to DCQ 11.

There were no significant differences in responses to any of the DCQ items between students in years one and three. However, responses to DCQ 8 ("It is acceptable to lie to them if you think the truth might be upsetting to hear") and DCQ 11 ("It is preferable to try to talk to a member of their family first, before speaking to them") were significantly different between students based in the UK and in Malaysia (see Tables 11.3 and 11.4). Students based in Malaysia were more likely to agree with DCQ 8 than students in the UK. However, after Bonferroni correction, this was only significant for year-one students; i.e., for. year-three students, the difference in response to DCQ 8 was no longer significant (Table 11.3).

Table 11.4. Responses to DCQ 11 (*It is preferable to try to talk to a member of their family first, before speaking to them*) by year and location.

	UK	Malaysia	Significance
Year 1 (n) (mean rank)	237149.74	4598.08	0.000
Year 3 (n) (mean rank)	3122.69	1118.14	0.295
Overall (n) (mean rank)	268171.77	56118.12	0.000

Similarly, students based in Malaysia were more likely to agree with DCQ 11, about speaking to a member of the family first, than students in the UK. Once again, after Bonferroni correction, this was only significant for year-one students. By year three, the difference in response to DCQ 11 was no longer significant (Table 11.4).

11.5.5 Focus Groups

A total of 21 students contributed to one of six focus groups held in the UK and Malaysia (Table 11.5). Group size ranged from 2 to 5 students. For reasons of participant availability two separate year-one focus groups were held in the UK and in Malaysia. Focus group identifiers relate to location and stage of study (e.g. FGUK1a being UK-based year-one students, FGM3 Malaysia-based year three students).

The focus groups enabled further exploration of the issues featured in the DCQ concerning communication and person-centered care, and the topic guide for the focus groups invited the students to elaborate upon their questionnaire responses in a group dynamic. Communication issues discussed across the focus groups included: appropriate terms for PLWD; the role of conversation (in checking understanding, expression of feelings, providing reminders/clues, determining meaning); the role of nonverbal communication (NVC) or "body language"; the role of touching; and the impact of uniforms. Space does not permit detailed discussion of all of

Table 11.5. Student participation in focus groups.

	UK	Malaysia	Total
Year 1	3 (FGUK1a) + 4 (FGUK1b)	2 (FGM1a) + 4 (FGUK1b)	13
Year 3	4 (FGUK3)	4 (FGM3)	8
Total	11	10	21

these findings. Instead, this section provides some concise summaries of the focus group data. An emergent theme, "challenges of communicative engagement," is also developed.

11.5.6 Appropriate Terms for PLWD

Discussion of the appropriate terms for describing PLWD turned on issues related to "connotations of madness" [FGUK1a], being "derogatory" [FGUK1a & FGUK3] and "PC" (political correctness) [FGUK1a]. Two UK-based year-one students discussed these latter possibilities with the focus group moderator:

> 17. I put the, erm, the person living with dementia, just because, I think the others, some of them are a bit kind of derogatory [I: okay] and it's like part of their life, so they are living with it. And it just seems less, like kind of neutral, like it isn't derogatory. It isn't making them seem like patients as such.
>
> I: Yeah. Okay, so it's less, it's less like a patient [FR: yeah] with a, an illness.
>
> 14: I'd probably tend towards a person with dementia, erm, just for the first, the living bit, maybe seems a little bit, erm, going in a way too PC.
>
> I: Okay.
>
> [FGUK1a]

Student 17 recognized PLWD as being the description furthest away from more "derogatory" terms (which strongly classify people in terms of their condition) and "neutral" on assigning a sick role to people. However, for student 14 the "living" aspect of the term was a step too far, and another participant subsequently supported this position, suggesting that denying the illness is to deliberately mis-specify a person's situation.

11.5.7 The Role of Conversation

Conversation was discussed by students in a number of ways. An exchange between year-one Malaysia-based students centered upon how conversation can be used by health professionals to check understanding and provide reminders or clues for PLWD [FGM1a]. However, in a different focus group, one student expressed unease over clue-giving as coercion [FGM1b]. Conversation was also considered to be important in allowing PWLD to express (and for health professionals to understand) how they feel and why they do so [FGM1b], and to address feelings of isolation [FGUK1b]. There was general consensus that even confused speech could hold meaning, that it was the healthcare professional's job to "find" meaning in confused speech [FGM1a], and that active listening could help in this situation [FGM1a; FGUK1b]. The challenges of communicative engagement are further explored in a later section.

11.5.8 Non-Vocal Communication and Touching

The duty to find meaning was also discussed in relation to maintaining positive NVC by UK-based year-one students. Showing interest and providing "another sort of stimulus" through NVC were considered to be important parts of overall communication [FGUK1b]. For one Malaysia-based year-one student, NVC was seen as a means of comforting the PWLD while having doubts about the "true meaning" of the dialogue [FGM1b]. The same student also felt that touching denoted close feeling, a notion supported by another participant who likened it to "really car[ing]." The quality of touching was also discussed, with some suggesting a "gentle" touch being preferable [FGUK1b] or "touch a little bit" [FGUK1a], while for others a touch could give rise to anxiety [FGUK1a].

11.5.9 Uniforms

Discussion of the role uniforms play in communicating with PWLD focused upon the need to "differentiate" [FGUK1b] and "identify" [FGM3], and, more negatively, on the creation of barriers [FGM1b; FGUK1a], the masking of "personality" [FGM1b] and an overly "clinical" environment [FGUK1b]. For one UK-based year-three student, identification through a white coat was recognized as the embodiment of expertise and reassurance:

FI: Is that, is that true of, more do you think of people with dementia, or relevant to?

21: I don't know really, I think, people with dementia, I suppose generally are older, [MI: mm] and so they generally, sort of, have this sort of, perhaps more of a respect towards doctors than people who are younger. So then, it might be more intimidating, but at the same time, it might be more comforting to know that there are doctors there looking after them, so that's why they're in this, this building.

[FGUK3]

Here a perception that PLWD will have particular (generational) expectations fitted with this student's concerns (raised earlier in the discussion) over the lack of an identifiable doctor's uniform.

11.5.10 Communicating with Family Members and Truth-Telling

In correspondence with the findings from the questionnaire data, discussions over lying/truth-telling and interaction with family members generated considerable debate. Year-one students based in UK and Malaysia considered the role family members play in providing initial information about the PLWD. For students in FGUK1b, extended discussion took place over the importance of getting insights from family members being balanced with getting "first-hand" [FGUK1b] and "blank slate" [FGUK1b] impressions directly from the PLWD. A Malaysia-based year-one student referred to family members as "shap[ing] our mind" [FGM1a] in advance of interaction with the PLWD. In the following extract from a lengthy discussion, two UK students consider the implications of talking to a family member first and (for 12) the uncertainty involved in initiating a conversation with a PWLD:

11: ...I think it is important not to judge someone before you meet them. I think it's, I think, yeah, talking to someone and having your own opinion is extremely important.

12: The family might give you a, if it's a family who are caring for someone, so they might have quite a different view if they're living with them, like, all the time. Obviously, then, that also has a place because if you see a snapshot of a patient with dementia you might see them on their best five minutes of that week...yeah, I agree with what was said about, if you can get the information from them first, but then clarification and sort of extra information from family might be very, very helpful.

[FGUK1b]

For some, relationships between family members and the PWLD raise difficult questions over truth-telling. In one UK-based year-one focus group, a long discussion took place over the dilemmas of truth-telling as a health professional – both in terms of communicating with a PWLD and their family – and an appreciation of the nuances of truth-telling in a medical context. In this extract two students consider such a dilemma:

17: Yeah. I mean, what if, like, the medical profession lie to them and then a family member told them the truth, [I: okay] then that's just, yeah.

I: Okay.

16: Trust is, like, important. I think it's diff-, like, as a doctor you, you can't really lie. I mean as a health professional, you've got to tell the truth, but I'd say it's probably a bit different with, like, family and things.

[FGUK1a]

Student 16 went on to describe personal circumstances which had given them some insight into these trade-offs. Following this, another student raised the issue of "little white lies" which they suggested nursing staff sometimes use:

> 14: ... which I think, a lot of the time, you can just, it can help, erm, at the moment, but sometimes they can, I think, do more harm in the long run, in a couple of, in some cases, but...

A fourth student in the focus group developed this notion of "little white lies" in terms of how the benefit for the lie is distributed; whether it simply makes work easier for health professionals, is focused on the care of the PLWD, or is mutually beneficial. Data from focus groups in both locations and across year groups showed students wrestling with the ethics of lying, or avoiding truths which might negatively received, and with the problems of balancing the need for therapeutically-directed interactions with the need for absolute integrity as a professional.

11.5.11 The Challenges of Communicative Engagement

Across the focus group data it was evident that students recognized that delivering appropriate and effective dementia care was likely to be among the greatest professional challenges they would face. When asked about communicating with PWLD relative to other communication situations, UK-based year-three students agreed it was very challenging, with student 20 stating: "It's up there with the most difficult things you have to deal with" (FGUK3).

The analysis revealed that communicative engagement with PLWD was fraught with practical, professional and ethical challenges for students. Although they expressed positive attitudes toward communicating with PWLD, these challenges – both perceived and experienced – highlighted the importance of students experiencing and reflecting on dementia care in practice during their training trajectory.

11.6 Discussion

Our main research focus was on the hitherto unexplored question of whether the views of medical students regarding communication with

PLWD conformed to a PCC approach. We found that, in the two locations we investigated, medical students' views did conform, on the whole, to those informing the communicative approaches in a person-centered care communication model (Young et al. 2011a, b, 2013). Appropriate attitudes and intentions toward communication are important if person-centeredness is to be realized, and so we regard these as positive findings (cf. Kitwood 1993, 1997; Woods 2001).

DCQ findings generally showed a strong preference for positions which adhered closely to a PCC approach: for example, a large majority of students expressed views that indicated respect for older people; recognized the importance of real engagement with PLWD through conversation and appropriate nonverbal communication; and recognized the importance of identity-reinforcement through the use of cues and reminders. Focus group findings gave us a complementary, detailed and fine-grained picture which tended to confirm the prevalence of these positive views, but which also gave access to a nuanced perspective. Students demonstrated awareness of the scale of the challenge in their future professional careers in caring effectively for PLWD, and of the desirability of real communicative engagement, while also having an awareness of the complexities, and sometimes the perplexities, of achieving this engagement, for example balancing an awareness of the therapeutic value of touch with an awareness of the need for appropriateness, and of the potential benefits of uniforms as a cue to PLWD, balanced with an awareness that they might also serve as a barrier between PLWD and doctor.

Findings relating to the three most controversial items in the DCQ items further highlighted the complexities of perspectives toward communication and PCC. These three debated items are: preferred terminology to be used to categorize PLWD; attitudes toward truth-telling; and attitudes toward speaking to a family member first, before speaking to a PLWD. Concurrently, in line with our secondary interest, these three items highlighted differences between students based in Malaysia and the UK. We argue that these findings are essentially supportive of the principle of person-centeredness in care, while also providing important confirmatory evidence that the notion still needs further development conceptually, in terms of defining its possible limitations and paradoxes, and in terms of making it applicable in different locations by hard-pressed practitioners in real-life, real-time care practice.

We first discuss the choice of appropriate terminology. Although this has not, as far as we can discern, been the subject of any prior investigation, anecdotal evidence suggests that a group self-designation conforming to a structure "person living with" + acute, chronic and serious condition, is a growing phenomenon, particularly in North America and Western Europe. Examples in English include "person/people living with HIV" (e.g. Coates et al. 2008) and "person/people living with cancer" (e.g. Macmillan 2012). This phenomenon seems related to the notion arising from Self Categorization Theory in social psychology (Turner et al. 1987) that people will self-organize and act cooperatively around perceived similarity, especially where a group is the subject of stereotyping and/or social stigma. An important part of this self-organizing is self-designation which resists stigma and which attempts to frame a group identity in an assertive and affirming way.

PLWD and family carers belonging to mutual support groups who participated in the research that developed DeMEC (Young et al. 2011a) strongly preferred "person living with dementia" while health- and social-care professional participants tended to prefer "person with dementia" – in line with most policy and psycho-social research documents (e.g., Brodaty et al. 2003; Department of Health 2009). Our finding that 86 per cent of questionnaire participants preferred one of these two designations, also reflected in focus group discussion around this topic, indicates that one of these two non-stigmatizing designations are strongly preferred by medical students across the two national locations we investigated. This seems supportive of the idea that possible stigmatization of dementia, a growing issue in some parts of the world (e.g. Kontos 2004, Alzheimer's Disease International, 2012), is recognized but is likely to be resisted by a majority of medical students, certainly by those who have been exposed to medical education up to year three. The fact that year-one students based in Malaysia were more likely to select another preferred terminology compared to year-one students based in the UK may indicate that sensitivity in Malaysia to the issue among entry-point medical students – and by implication among young people in the wider society – is less developed than in the UK. This may reflect societal changes occurring in Malaysia, which are common to many other developing East and Southeast Asian countries (Alfonso et al. 2010; Chiu et al. 2010).

The population in Malaysia is young compared to countries in "the West," but is aging rapidly – the population is currently around 29 million, with only around 5 per cent of the population aged 65 or over. Malaysia is fourth in the world in terms of the projected percentage growth of people aged 65 by 2040, with an expected rapid expansion of PLWD from the current estimate of around 50,000 (Alzheimer's Disease Foundation Malaysia 2010). In common with other developing countries, research into dementia care in Malaysia has been less common than in the West, with no work prior to this study focusing specifically on communication. There is, however, agreement that care patterns are changing here as the proportion of older people increases, young women – traditionally, the main caregivers – go out to work in greater numbers, and increasing urbanization means less space for older dependents (Nikmat et al. 2011). The social-care system in Malaysia is relatively under-developed, and there is a growing concern that, as with the UK, PLWD will spend unnecessarily extended periods in acute care settings as families and the social-care system struggle to cope (Kua 2010). There is also concern that social stigmatization and attitudinal negativity toward dementia is prevalent and increasing (Nikmat et al. 2011).

An encouraging sign from our findings is that, while preference for non-stigmatizing terminology is lower among entry-level students in Malaysia than in the UK, preferences change by year three to a more person-centered position. There may be a need to address issues of general public knowledge of and attitudes toward dementia if care is to be optimized in Malaysia. It should be noted that all year-three Malaysia-based participants had been exposed to a UK medical school curriculum. A UK medical education curriculum may positively influence attitudes and inform more positive approaches: future study could usefully examine the comparative effects of medical education where a curriculum not based on this model is followed.

Related to the second point of contention emerging from our analysis, there is a considerable literature on the efficacy or otherwise of truth-telling in dementia care. There is some suggestion that patients potentially benefit from lying or deception in certain circumstances – for example, about spousal death or concern about impact of a diagnosis (Elvish et al. 2010; Marzanski 2000). The bulk of opinion seems to correspond to a view that lying has to be a last resort, and that a validation of feelings, and redirection, are a way through the thicket of problems and possible paradoxes identified by our participants (Tuckett 2012). The fact that none of our participants had knowledge of a clear schema or protocol guiding the application of reality orientation indicates a pressing need for issues around "white lying" and deception to be explored and addressed in medical training.

Our participants also showed a significant degree of uncertainty and a broad range of opinion relating to whether they should speak to a member of the family first. This issue also points to some of the potential problems in defining and realizing person-centeredness, and the need for situation-specific guidance and training. The fact that Malaysia year-one students were more likely to accept lying, and speaking to family members first, than any other group might indicate a slight societal bias away from an individualized idea of person-centeredness, and toward the idea of the central importance of family in that national context. These findings are indications that further research is needed to determine any predispositions toward the level of individualization in person-centeredness, and any alternative models of care used internationally and interculturally. Further analysis is currently being undertaken to explore the issues of truth-telling and the efficacy or otherwise of speaking to family members first.

The changes in opinion demonstrated between years one and three may indicate a direct influence of medical education on perceptions of person-centered care and approaches to communication with PLWD. It is known that communication skills training for medical students in general, can result in a positive change in knowledge, attitudes and skills (Aspegren 1999), however, it remains unclear to what extent undergraduate students' attitudes relating to person-centered communication in care for PLWD are translated into professional behavior in the clinical context. In the post-graduate environment, communication skills training for old-age psychiatrists caring for people with dementia has been shown to have an impact on subjective, self-reported clinical practice (Robinson et al. 2010). Further research could usefully compare the expressed attitudes and intentions of healthcare professionals interacting with PLWD with directly observed practice in clinical contexts or with patient satisfaction. While policy documents cited above have suggested that healthcare staff hold negative attitudes toward PLWD, an alternative hypothesis arising from our findings is that there are difficulties in translating positive attitudes and intentions into good care in the clinical environment. It is also possible that attitudes erode in the later years of medical school or when staff have completed undergraduate training. This again warrants further investigation.

11.6.1 Limitations

The practical difficulties of administering a survey across international sites led to differences in sample sizes between year-one and -three students, with fewer responses from year-three students. However we believe the sample of year-three students to be representative of their year group in both UK and Malaysian sites. Focus group participants were self-selected and were likely to have direct interest in dementia care. This may have introduced bias toward expression of more positive comments and consensus, but the breadth of responses among participants highlighted both positive and negative attitudes.

Statement of Ethical Approval

The project met the relevant University's Preliminary ethical assessment guidelines for the School of Education, Communication and Language Sciences and approval was confirmed by its Medical Board of Studies.

Declaration of Contribution of Authors

Authors 1 and 2 designed the study, carried out data collection, and contributed to analysis and to the drafting of the article. Author 3 contributed to analysis and to drafting the article.

Statement of Conflict of Interest

Author 2 is funded by the National Institute for Health Research (NIHR) Newcastle Biomedical Research Centre based at Newcastle upon Tyne Hospitals NHS Foundation Trust and Newcastle University. The views expressed are those of the authors and not necessarily those of the UK National Health Service, the NIHR or the Department of Health.

References

Alfonso, T., E.S. Krishnamoorthy & K. Gomez. (2010). Caregiving for dementia: Global perspectives and transcultural issues. In E.S. Krishnamoorthy, M.J. Prince & J.L. Cummings (eds.), *Dementia: A Global Approach* (pp. 99–106). Cambridge: Cambridge University Press. http://dx.doi.org/10.1017/CBO9780511780615.011

Alzheimer's Disease Foundation Malaysia. (2010). *About Alzheimer's*. Available online at: http://www.adfm.org.my/Home/about-alzheimer-s. Accessed April 2014.

Alzheimer's Disease International. (2010). *World Alzheimer Report: The Global Economic Impact of Dementia*. Available online at http://www.alz.co.uk/research/world-report. Accessed April 2014.

Alzheimer's Disease International. (2011). *World Alzheimer Report: The Benefits of Early Diagnosis and Intervention.* Available online at http://www.alz.co.uk/research/world-report. Accessed April 2014.

Alzheimer's Disease International. (2012). *World Alzheimer Report: Overcoming the Stigma of Dementia.* Available online at http://www.alz.co.uk/research/world-report. Accessed April 2014.

Alzheimer's Society. (2009). *Counting the Cost: Caring for People with Dementia on Hospital Wards.* Available online at http://www.alzheimers.org.uk/countingthecost. Accessed April 2014.

Alzheimer's Society. (2012). *Dementia 2012: A National Challenge.* Available online at http://www.alzheimers.org.uk/dementia2012. Accessed April 2014.

Aspegren, K. (1999). Best Evidence Medical Education Guide No. 2: Teaching and learning communication skills in medicine – A review with quality grading of articles. *Medical Teacher,* 21(6), 563–70. http://dx.doi.org/10.1080/01421599978979

Barbour, R. (2005). Making sense of focus groups. *Medical Education,* 39(7), 742–50. http://dx.doi.org/10.1111/j.1365-2929.2005.02200.x

Beer, C., B. Horner, O.P. Almeida, S. Scherer, N.T. Lautenschlager, N. Bretland, P. Flett, F. Schaper & L. Flicker. (2009). Current experiences and educational preferences of general practitioners and staff caring for people with dementia in residential facilities. *BMC Geriatrics,* 9(36), 1–10. http://dx.doi.org/10.1186/1471-2318-9-36

Braun, V., & V. Clarke. (2006). Using thematic analysis in psychology. *Qualitative Research in Psychology,* 3(2), 77–101. http://dx.doi.org/10.1191/1478088706qp063oa

Brodaty, H., A. Green & A. Koschera. (2003). Meta-analysis of psychosocial interventions for caregivers of people with dementia. *Journal of the American Geriatrics Society,* 51(5), 657–64. http://dx.doi.org/10.1034/j.1600-0579.2003.00210.x

Brooker, D. (2007). *Person-Centred Dementia Care: Making Services Better.* London: Jessica Kingsley.

Care Quality Commission. (2012). *The State of Health Care and Adult Social Care in England.* London: CQC.

Chiu, H., J. Tsoh & X. Yu. (2010). Care arrangements for people with dementia: China. In E.S. Krishnamoorthy, M.J. Prince & J.L. Cummings (eds.), *Dementia: A Global Approach* (pp. 107–12). Cambridge: Cambridge University Press. http://dx.doi.org/10.1017/CBO9780511780615.012

Coates, T., M. Weston, B. Hanson, V. Patel, G. Szekeres & R. Remien. 2008. *Living with HIV in the 21st Century.* New York: Ford Foundation.

Davis, D. (2004). Dementia: Sociological and philosophical constructions. *Social Science & Medicine,* 58(2), 369–78. http://dx.doi.org/10.1016/S0277-9536(03)00202-8

Department of Health. (2009). *Living Well with Dementia: A National Dementia Strategy.* London: Department of Health.

Department of Health. (2011). *Core Principles for Supporting People with Dementia.* London: Department of Health.

Edvardsson, D., & A. Innes. (2010). Measuring person-centred care: A critical comparative review of published tools. *Gerontologist,* 50(6), 834–46. http://dx.doi.org/10.1093/geront/gnq047

Elvish, R., I. James & D. Milne. (2010). Lying in dementia care: An example of a culture that decieves in people's best interests. *Aging & Mental Health,* 14(3), 255–62. http://dx.doi.org/10.1080/13607861003587610

Gibson, F. (1999). Can we risk person-centred communication? *Journal of Dementia Care,* 7(5), 20–4.

Giles, H., & T. Ogay. (2007). Communication accomodation theory. In B. Whaley & W. Samter (eds.), *Explaining Communication: Contemporary Theories and Exemplars* (pp. 293–310). Mahwah, NJ: Lawrence Erlbaum.

Green, J., & Thorogood, N. (2009). *Qualitative Methods for Health Research.* London: Sage.

Hummert, M., J. Shaner, T. Garstka & C. Henry. (1998). Communication with older adults: The influence of age stereotypes, context and communicator age. *Human Communication Research,* 25(1), 124–51. http://dx.doi.org/10.1111/j.1468-2958.1998.tb00439.x

IELTS (2012). International English Language Testing System. Available at: http://www.ielts.org/about_us.aspx. Accessed April 2014.

Kitwood, T. (1993). Discover the person, not the disease. *Journal of Dementia Care,* 1(1), 16–17.

Kitwood, T. (1997). *Dementia Reconsidered.* Buckingham: Open University Press.

Kontos, P.C. (2004). Ethnographic reflections on selfhood, embodiment and Alzheimer's Disease. *Ageing and Society,* 24(6), 829–49. http://dx.doi.org/10.1017/S0144686X04002375

Kua, E.H. (2010). The aging brain and mind: Cultural and anthropological perspectives. In E.S. Krishnamoorthy, M.J. Prince & J.L. Cummings (eds.), *Dementia: A Global Approach* (pp. 1–6). Cambridge: Cambridge University Press.

Levy-Storms, L. (2008). Therapeutic communication training in long-term care institutions: Recommendations for further research. *Patient Education and Counseling,* 73(1), 8–21. http://dx.doi.org/10.1016/j.pec.2008.05.026

Lingard, L., & T. Kennedy. (2010). Qualitative research methods in medical education. In T. Swanwick (ed.), *Understanding Medical Education. Evidence, Theory and Practice* (pp. 323–35). Sussex: Wiley-Blackwell. http://dx.doi.org/10.1002/9781444320282.ch22

Macmillan. (2012). Living with cancer: We're here to help. Available at: http://www.macmillan.org.uk/. Accessed April 2014.

Marzanski, M. (2000). Would you like to know what is wrong with you? On telling the truth to patients with dementia. *Journal of Medical Ethics,* 26(2), 108–13. http://dx.doi.org/10.1136/jme.26.2.108

National Audit Office. (2007). *Improving Services and Support for People with Dementia.* London: National Audit Office.

NIHCE-SCIE (National Institute for Health and Clinical Excellence and Social Care Institute for Excellence). (2007). *A NICE-SCIE Guideline on Supporting People with Dementia and Their Carers in Health and Social Care*. London: British Psychological Society.

Nikmat, A.W., G. Hawthorne & S.H. Al-Mashoor. (2011). Dementia in Malaysia: Issues and challenges. *ASEAN Journal of Psychiatry*, 12(1), 1–7.

Oppenheim, A.N. (2000). *Questionnaire Design, Interviewing and Attitude Measurement*. London: Continuum International Publishing.

Peterson, D., M. Berg-Weger, J. McGillick & J. Schwartz. (2002). Basic care 1: The effect of dementia-specific training on certified nursing assistants and other staff. *American Journal of Alzheimer's Disease and Other Dementias*, 17(3), 154–64. http://dx.doi.org/10.1177/153331750201700309

Prince, M.J. (2010). The contribution of cross-cultural research to dementia care and policy. In E.S. Krishnamoorthy, M.J. Prince & J.L. Cummings (eds.), *Dementia: A Global Approach* (pp. 163–82). Cambridge: Cambridge University Press. http://dx.doi.org/10.1017/CBO9780511780615.023

Robinson, L., C. Bamford, R. Briel, J. Spencer & P. Whitty. (2010). Improving patient centred care for people with dementia in medical encounters: An educational intervention for old age psychiatrists. *International Psychogeriatrics*, 22(1), 129–38. http://dx.doi.org/10.1017/S1041610209990482

Royal College of Psychiatrists. (2011). *Report of the National Audit of Dementia Care in General Hospitals*. London: Royal College of Psychiatrists.

Savundranayagam, M., E. Ryan, A. Anas & J. Orange. (2007). Communication and dementia: Staff perceptions of conversational strategies. *Clinical Gerontologist*, 31(2), 47–63. http://dx.doi.org/10.1300/J018v31n02_04

The Patients Association. (2011). *We've Been Listening, Have You Been Learning.* Available at http://www.edva.org/content/patients-association-weve-been-listening-have-you-been-learning. Accessed September 2015..

Tuckett, A. (2012). The experience of lying in dementia care: A qualitative study. *Nursing Ethics*, 19(1), 7–20. http://dx.doi.org/10.1177/0969733011412104

Turner, J., M. Hogg, P. Oakes, S. Reicher & M. Weatherell. (1987). *Rediscovering the Social Group*. Oxford: Basil Blackwell.

Woods, R. (2001). Discovering the person with Alzheimer's disease: Cognitive, emotional and behavioural aspects. *Aging & Mental Health*, 5 (Suppl. 1), 7–16. http://dx.doi.org/10.1080/713650008

Worral, L., & L. Hickson. (2003). *Communication Disability in Ageing: Prevention and Intervention*. San Diego, CA: Singular.

Young, T.J., & C. Manthorp. (2009). Towards a code of practice for effective communication with people with dementing illnesses. *Journal of Language and Social Psychology*, 28(2), 174–89. http://dx.doi.org/10.1177/0261927X08330611

Young, T.J., C. Manthorp & D. Howells (2010). *Communication and Dementia: New Perspectives, New Approaches.* Barcelona: Editorial Aresta

Young, T.J., C. Manthorp, D. Howells & E. Tullo. (2011a). Developing a carer communication intervention to support personhood and quality of life in dementia. *Ageing and Society,* 31(6), 1003–25. http://dx.doi.org/10.1017/S0144686X10001182

Young, T.J., C. Manthorp, D. Howells & E. Tullo. (2011b). Optimizing communication between medical professionals and people living with dementia. *International Psychogeriatrics,* 23(7), 1078–85. http://dx.doi.org/10.1017/S1041610211000652

Young, T.J., C. Manthorp, D. Howells & J. Vines. (2013). *Dementia Talk: Dementia Toolkit for Effective Communication.* Available online at http://www.demtalk.org.uk/. Accessed April 2014.

12
Profiling Individual Differences in Speech Production

Sandra P. Whiteside[1]

12.1 Introduction: F2 Locus Equations

F2 locus equations (F2 LEs) have attracted much debate in the field of speech perception and production (e.g. Fowler 1994; Sussman & Shore 1996; Sussman et al. 1998b). The debate on the role of F2 LEs as invariant cues for place of articulation has led to many studies which have sought to establish whether this is indeed the case (e.g. Sussman et al. 1991; Fowler 1994; Sussman & Shore 1996; Brancazio & Fowler 1998; Tabain 2000, 2002). The evidence presented across a wide range of studies on F2 LEs suggests that they are not a direct measure of place of articulation (Fowler 1994; Brancazio & Fowler 1998), nor are they invariant cues for place of articulation (Fowler 1994; Tabain 2000, 2002). However, they have more recently been advocated as useful phonetic expressions which measure "tongue body synergy," and which can be used in cross-linguistic comparisons, and in the study of typical and atypical speakers (Iskarous et al. 2010: 2031). In addition, despite some evidence to the contrary (Löfqvist 1999; Tabain 2000, 2002), there is support for the use of F2 LEs as effective measures for determining coarticulation resistance and the degree of coarticulation in speech production (Iskarous ct al. 2010).

F2 LEs as phonetic descriptors (Lindblom 1963; Nearey & Shammass 1987; Krull 1989; Duez 1992; Sussman 1994; Sussman et al. 1991, 1992, 1998a, b), depict the linear relationship between the F2-midvowel (or target) frequencies (plotted along the *x*-axis) and F2-(vowel)-onset frequencies (plotted along the *y*-axis) of consonant-vowel (CV) sequences in CVC syllables, for example. Locus equations are expressed by a simple

1 Sandra P. Whiteside is a Reader in the Department of Human Communication Sciences at the University of Sheffield.

regression function as F2-onset = $k \times$ F2-midvowel + c, where k represents the slope of the function and c, the y-intercept. The simple regression functions expressed by F2-onset = $k \times$ F2-midvowel + c, also yield R^2 values and standard errors of estimate (SE). The R^2 values index the level of variance in F2-onset values as a function of F2-midvowel (or target) frequencies; larger R^2 values indicate higher degrees of linearity between these two variables. The SE values provide a metric for the degree of dispersion of the F2-onset and target data points along the regression function; smaller SE values are indicative of lower levels of dispersion along the regression line.

The slopes of these regression lines vary with the place of articulation (Sussman et al. 1991, 1992, 1998a, b), and the steepness of these slopes can be used as a measure of the extent to which consonants and vowels coarticulate (e.g. Krull 1989; Sussman et al. 1991; Duez 1992; Whiteside et al. 2010; Lindblom & Sussman 2012). For example, steeper slopes where there are high levels of covariation between the onset and target values of a vowel in a CV syllable, provide an index of higher degrees of coarticulation (Sussman et al. 1991, 1992, 1998a, b), and also are indicative of lower levels of articulatory resistance (e.g. Whiteside & Rixon 2003; Whiteside et al. 2010). Fast speech has a tendency to be hypoarticulated (e.g. Bakran & Mildner 1995; Agwuele et al. 2008) and is characterized by steeper F2 LE slopes. In contrast, shallower slopes are indicative of low levels of covariation, and therefore, less coarticulation between the onset and target values of a vowel in a CV sequence of a CVC syllable. Higher levels of articulatory resistance are also associated with shallower slopes (e.g. Embarki et al. 2007; Whiteside et al. 2010; Yeou 1997). Further, hyperarticulated speech is characterized by shallower F2 LE slopes (e.g. Bakran & Mildner 1995). Extensive published data show that there is an inverse relationship between slope and y-intercept values (Sussman et al. 1991, 1992, 1998a, b).

Plotting the slope values on the x-axis against normalized y-intercept values of F2 LEs (y-intercept values divided by 2000) on the y-axis has been described as providing "a highly simplified graphic representation of the relative separation of place categories in a higher-order and derived acoustic space" (Sussman et al. 1998a: 219). Calculating Euclidean distances within the higher-order acoustic space also serves, for example, to highlight the contrasts between different stop consonant categories as a function of speaking style (Sussman et al. 1998a). If we accept the views of Iskarous et al. (2010), second-order acoustic expressions also provide information on the synergy between articulators in different phonetic contexts (see also Chennoukh et al. 1997). F2 LE functions and associated higher-order acoustic spaces can therefore be used to profile individual speaker differences across a range of speech tasks. Examples of these are presented and discussed throughout this review.

Despite their importance in speech and phonetics research, studies on F2 LEs have not been specifically focused on assessing and profiling individual speaker differences. The aim of this paper is to re-examine the F2 LE data reported in a range of non-clinical and clinical studies, and to present an overview and assessment of individual speaker differences across the human lifespan from a range of different perspectives. The studies reviewed are not an exhaustive set of accounts which have reported on F2 LEs, but are exemplars which are representative of the metric and associated measures, and their relevance to understanding speech production and speaker-determined variation. The key themes explored in this review of F2 LE data will include: speech development; cross-linguistic comparisons and regional dialect comparisons in Arabic; speech style, rate and speaker adaptation; and speech and language pathology.

12.2 The Development of Speech Gestures in Infants and Young Children

Sussman et al. (1999) investigated F2 LEs in a longitudinal study of a single female infant from age 7 to 40 months. CV sequences with labial ([b]), alveolar ([d]) and velar plosives ([g]) and vocalic/vowel-like sounds were sampled and analyzed, and formed the basis of the study. Data were collected on a longitudinal and regular basis; weekly until age 16 months and monthly thereafter. Given the age of the participant and the time span, the samples consisted of babbling, early words and connected speech. In addition, the babbling phase overlapped with the early words phase until 16 ([b], [g]) and 18 months ([d]). The F2 LE results showed an increase in slope values for the labial plosives from 10 months (.34 – babbling), to 17 months (.675 – words) to 37 months (.753 – speech). In contrast, the alveolar plosives showed decreases in the slope from 10 months (.622 – babbling), to 17 months (.502 – words), to 37 months (.49 – speech). The velar plosives showed an increase from 10 months (.356 – babbling) to 17/18 months (1.003 – words), with a small decrease at 37 months (.958 – speech).

The longitudinal patterns across these three developmental phases indicated that by 37 months, the slope values were approaching those of adults. However, it is evident from the slope values given above that the developmental trajectories varied as a function of the plosive-vowel sequences.

The labial-vowel sequences displayed shallow slopes in the babbling phase compared to the steeper slopes in the speech phase. In contrast, the slopes for the alveolar-vowel sequences started off fairly steep for the babbling phase and then become shallower. The velar plosives were very shallow in the babbling samples, and showed marked increases in the later developmental phases. Sussman et al. (1999) acknowledge that it is difficult to make definite links between F2 LE data and underlying articulatory gestures. However, it is possible to offer some suggestions for the acoustic phonetic observations, and the different developmental patterns are explained by them in terms of the articulatory dynamics required for each CV sequence. During the babbling phase for the labial-vowel sequences, there was evidence of a limited and neutral vowel repertoire. This, coupled with opening and closing jaw movements while maintaining a neutral lingual posture, suggests that during the babbling phase, the young infant had not yet mastered the independent control of the labial and lingual systems that are required for the articulation of the labial-vowel sequences. This therefore gives rise to the flat slope observed for the phonetic context for this developmental phase. However, the increases in the slopes for the words and speech suggest that the child is beginning to achieve independent control of the labial and lingual articulators during the articulation of labial-vowel sequences in a variety of vowel contexts.

Different parts of the lingual system are required for alveolar-vowel sequences. The child must therefore learn to master these different parts of the lingual system separately during the articulation of the alveolar-vowel sequences. This fine motor control is more challenging for alveolar-front-vowel sequences given the linked systems of the tongue tip/blade required for the closure of the plosive, and the body of the tongue body required for the articulation of the vowel. In the alveolar-vowel sequences there was evidence of predominantly front vowels in the babbling phase. This and the higher slopes in the babbling phase are indicative of higher levels of coarticulation and overlap between the alveolar plosive and front vowels and, therefore, poorly differentiated articulatory gestures. The data for the word and speech phases suggest that the vowel repertoire increases with each developmental phase to yield a richer set of alveolar-vowel sequences. In addition, the shallower slopes and therefore lower levels of coarticulation suggest a clearer differentiation between the alveolar plosive and ensuing vowel. This may therefore be indicative of the child achieving increased levels of motor control over the lingual system required for the production of the alveolar-vowel sequences across a wider range of vowels.

The lingual system is also required for the production of velar-vowel sequences; the tongue body is involved in the articulation of both the consonant and vowel. In the babbling phase, more fronted vowels were observed in addition to shallower slopes, indicating less overlap between the consonant and vowel. The slope value for this phase (.356) approximates the adult values for front vowels and the [g]-palatal context (.34) reported by Sussman et al. (1991: 1317, table 2). In contrast, the word and speech phases display a larger repertoire of back vowels and steeper slopes (1.003 and .958), which are indicative of higher levels of coarticulation between the consonant and vowel, and are more reflective of the higher slopes observed for back vowels and the [g] velar context in adult speech (e.g. Sussman et al. 1991, 1998a). The results for the velar data suggest that the control of the tongue body is easier to master in the articulation of velar-vowel sequences compared to the tongue tip/blade and tongue body involved in the articulation of the alveolar-vowel sequences.

In an earlier case study Sussman et al. (1996) investigated F2 LE data in a longitudinal study of another female infant at 12 months and 21 months. The results for the babbling tokens at 12 months revealed slope and *y*-intercept values of .482/659.597, .385/2007.199, and .816/486.326 for /b/, /d/ and /g/, respectively. At 21 months, the slope and *y*-intercept values were .536/576.865, .267/2240.028, and .757/976.53 for /b/, /d/ and /g/, respectively. These data are depicted in Figure 12.1 by place of articulation in the higher-order acoustic space together with the data reported by Sussman et al. (1999), which were discussed above. The data are presented in chronological order for developmental comparisons. What is clear from the acoustic space represented by the slope and normalized *y*-intercept data in Figure 12.1 are the individual differences in the developmental patterns of the two children. The child reported in Sussman et al. (1999), who was discussed in detail above, displays a clear developmental shift in the acoustic space from the babbling phase at 10 months to the word and speech phases at 17 and 37 months, respectively. In contrast, the child reported in Sussman et al. (1996) shows a different pattern of development; the changes are less marked, for example. In addition, although the slopes and *y*-intercept values for the labial and velar plosives displayed a shift toward those which have been observed for adults, this was not the case for the alveolar plosive, which displayed a shift away from the adult target. Furthermore, if we examine the data in Figure 12.1 for the labials in the context of the vowel repertoires expressed in the F2 LEs reported for each of the studies, it is evident that both children display differences in this dimension of their speech production in the babbling phase. While the child in Sussman et al. (1999: 1088, fig. 5) uses a neutral and limited vowel repertoire at 10 months for /b/, the child at 12 months displays a much richer vowel repertoire for this phonetic context (see Sussman et al. 1996:

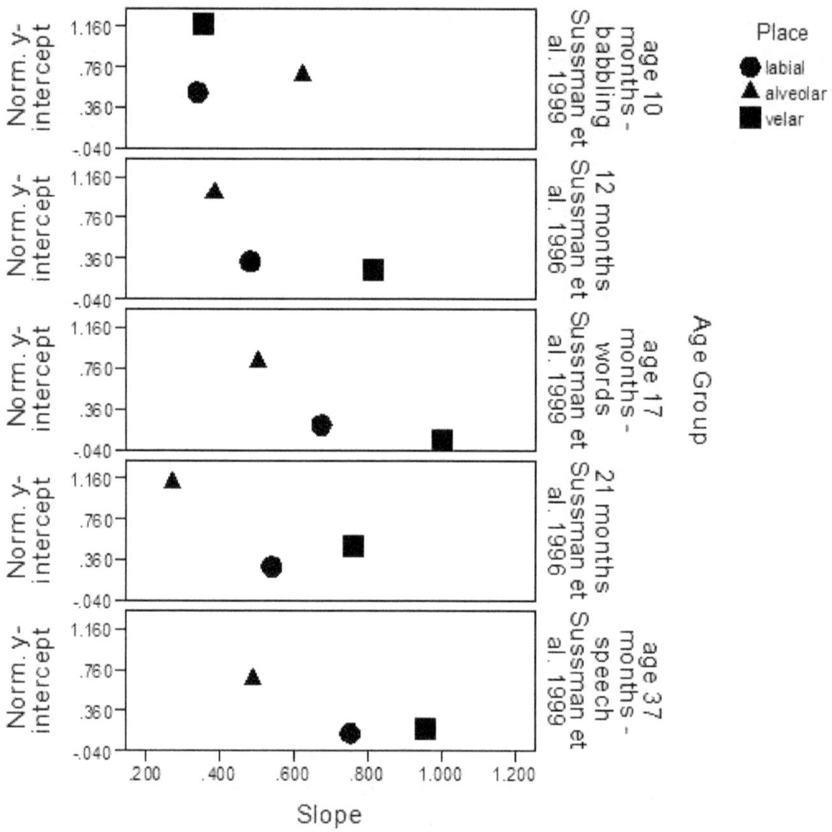

Figure 12.1. Higher-order acoustic space for labial, alveolar and velar plosives as a function of age.

Note: Derived from the data reported in the two longitudinal case studies by Sussman et al. (1996): data at 12 months (babbling) are based on fig. 2, p. 429 – panel 2; data at 21 months are based on fig. 4, p. 431 – panel 4; and Sussman et al. (1999): data at 10 months (babbling – panel 1), 17 months (words – panel 3) and 37 months (speech – panel 5) are based on fig. 5, p.1088, fig. 6, p.1089 and fig. 7, p. 1091.

429, fig. 2). This taken together with the slope values for each child (.34 – Sussman et al. 1999; .482 – Sussman et al. 1996: see fig. 1), suggests that the child in Sussman et al. (1996) is already displaying evidence of articulatory control over the independent gestures required for /bV/ syllables during this phase of speech development, and highlights individual differences in developmental patterns of speech production.

Sussman et al. (1992) investigated F2 LEs in 16 older healthy children aged 3 to 5 years (3-year-olds, n = 2, both F; 4-year-olds, n = 7, 3 M, 4 F; 5-year-olds, n = 7, 6 M, 1 F). The children produced multiple repetitions of /CVt/ syllables using an imitation task. The initial consonants included /b, d, g/ and the medial vowels included 6 vowels representing a range of different vowel qualities. The results across all age groups revealed mean slopes of .84, .46 and .78 for the bilabial, alveolar and velar plosives, respectively. These values indicated the contrasts between both the labial and alveolar places of articulation, and the velar and alveolar places of articulation. However, the slope values for the labial and velar plosives were found to be less contrastive. These patterns are discussed by Sussman et al. (1992) as evidence for the maturation of articulatory gestures; the patterns of maximal coarticulation for the bilabial plosives which were the most similar to those reported for adults, suggest that the independent bilabial gestures coupled with vowel gestures at this stage had been mastered earlier in comparison to alveolar and velar gestures in the /CVt/ syllables. This pattern of speech development can be explained by the fact that the labial articulators required for the plosive are delinked from the lingual system required for the following vowel; the bilabial plosive has lower levels of coarticulation resistance and is therefore free to coarticulate with the ensuing vowel which is controlled independently by the lingual system. These delinked gestures therefore appear to be acquired with relative ease by this stage of development. Alveolar gestures in /CVt/ syllables, however, appear to take longer to master due to the more complex articulatory dynamics underpinning these syllables. The tip/blade and body of the lingual system are involved in the entire syllable; the motor skills required for the production of the syllable's different phases therefore require coordinated, smooth and finely differentiated articulatory gestures between the alveolar plosive, the medial vowel and final alveolar plosive. Differentiating articulatory gestures which share the same articulator (e.g. /di/) is particularly challenging during speech acquisition. This is partly borne out by the results in Sussman et al. (1992). For example, the alveolar plosives displayed the most variable slope and *y*-intercept values across all 16 children (SD = .155, 423 Hz) compared to the labial (SD = .112, 226 Hz) and velar (SD = .123, 294 Hz) places of articulation (Sussman et al. 1992: 776, table 2). Sussman et al. (1992) also examined the allophones of /g/ and found the [g] palatal and [g] velar split in the F2 LE function representing front and back vowels, respectively for all three age groups. This confirms that the control of the tongue body in the articulation of velar-vowel sequences has already been mastered by the 3-year-olds and corroborates the findings of Sussman et al. (1999) which were presented and discussed above.

If we examine the higher-order acoustic space for the 3-, 4- and 5-year-olds alongside adult data (Sussman et al. 1991) as a function of consonant place (see Figure 12.2), it is evident that the developmental changes which occur are neither linear nor uniform across all three places of articulation:

the slope values for the labials decrease from age 3 to 4 years, but are fairly stable thereafter; the alveolars display fluctuating increases and decreases across the age groups; and the velars display an increase from age 3 to 4 years followed by a decrease at age 5 years which is similar to that for the adults. What is also evident from Figure 12.2 is that although there is less separation in the slope values for the labial and velar consonants for the 4-year-olds, there is some separation as a function of the normalized *y*-intercept. In addition, the data indicated that the 5-year-olds displayed values which were closest to those observed for adults (see Figure 12.2).

In summary, the data reviewed here suggest that in addition to providing a useful metric for gauging speech development, F2 LEs and associated higher-order functions highlight the individual differences in the developmental trajectories of infants and young children in CV articulation.

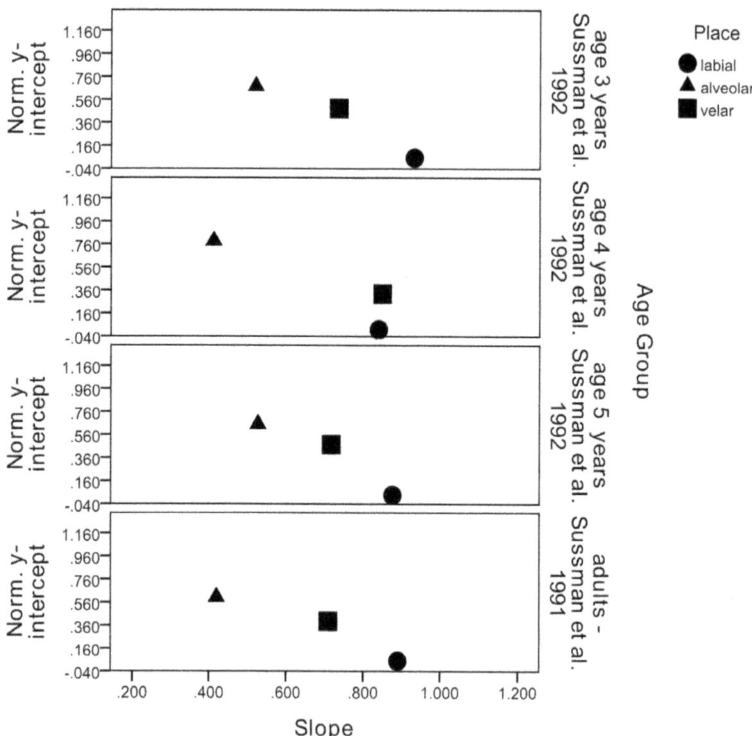

Figure 12.2. Higher-order acoustic space for labial, alveolar and velar plosives as a function of age.

Note: Derived from the data for 3-, 4- and 5-year-olds reported in the study by Sussman et al. (1992): based on values in figs. 1a, 1b and 1c, pp. 774–5; and adult data in Sussman et al. (1991: 1315).

12.3 Cross-Linguistic and Dialect Comparisons in F2 LEs

F2 LEs have been investigated across different languages (e.g. Sussman et al. 1993), and as a function of dialect (Embarki et al. 2007). Here we explore a sample of studies, and examine the extent of the differences and similarities across languages. We also assess the role of F2 LEs in determining regional dialect differences in Arabic (e.g. Embarki et al. 2007), and how these compare with data published on Arabic in an earlier study (Yeou 1997).

12.3.1 Coarticulation Patterns in F2 LEs: A Cross-Linguistic Perspective

Differences in slope and *y*-intercept values in first-order F2 LEs reflect the variation in consonant-vowel articulation across languages. For example, Sussman et al. (1993) examined F2 LEs in Thai, Cairene Arabic and Urdu. F2 LEs for CV syllables containing voiced bilabial and dental plosives in nine vowel contexts were examined for 6 speakers of Thai (5 F, 1 M – mean age 25.7 years). The Cairene Arabic data were based on 3 male speakers (2 with a mean age of 24.3 years and 1 speaker aged 60). F2 LEs were examined for initial plosives in CVt/CVtt sequences. The initial plosives were all voiced and included labial, dental, pharyngealized dental and velar places of articulation in the context of 8 vowels. The data for Urdu were based on 5 male speakers (mean age 24.8 years), and F2 LEs were examined for voiced initial plosives in CVC(C) sequences representing labial, dental, retroflex and velar places of articulation, and final plosives included [t], [d], [b], [p], [g] and [k]. Figure 12.3 illustrates the mean values of the slopes plotted against the normalized *y*-intercepts for the individual speakers of the three languages reported in Sussman et al. (1993) by place of articulation. What is evident from the higher-order acoustic space in Figure 12.3 is the individual variation in the slope and normalized *y*-intercept values. However, upon further analysis of the data plotted in this higher-order space, a strong linear inverse relationship between slope and normalized *y*-intercept values was observed across the individual speakers of Thai ($R^2 = .983$), Cairene Arabic ($R^2 = .864$) and Urdu ($R^2 = .900$).

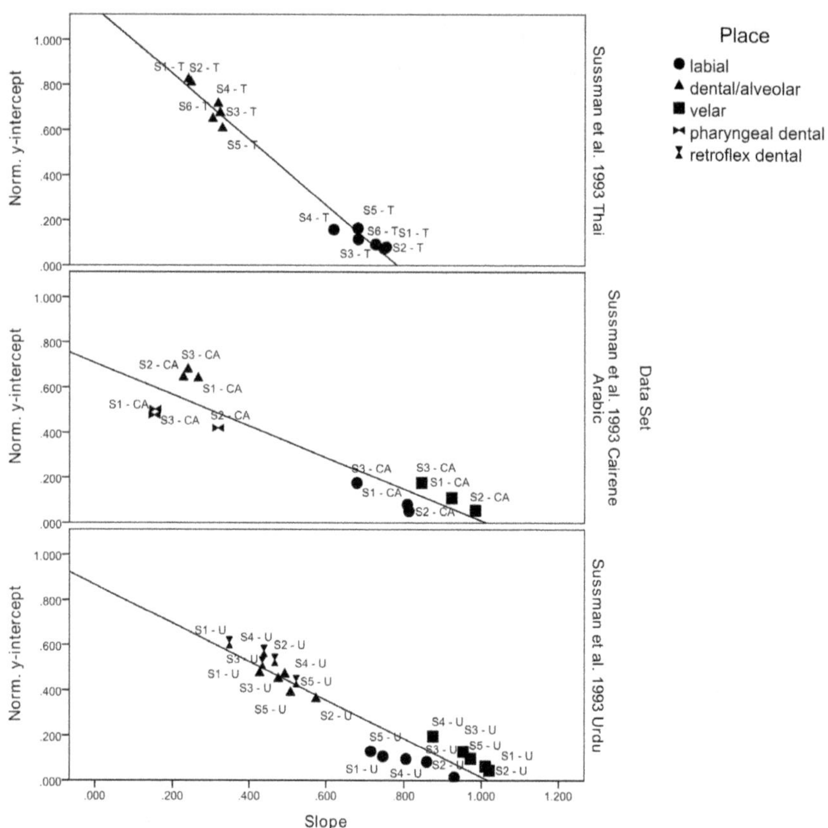

Figure 12.3. Higher-order acoustic space for labial, dental/alveolar, velar, pharyngealized dental and retroflex dental plosives depicting individual differences.

Note: Data for the Thai (6 speakers – panel 1), Cairene Arabic (3 speakers – panel 2) and Urdu (5 speakers – panel 3) participants reported in Sussman et al. (1993): Thai – table 1, p. 1258; Cairene Arabic – table 2, p. 1259; Urdu –table 4, p. 1261.
The slope and normalized *y*-intercept values are inversely related, and display high levels of linearity in the functions for all three data sets (Thai: R^2 = .983; Cairene Arabic: R^2 = .864; Urdu: R^2 = .900).

The mean slope and normalized *y*-intercept values representing the range of plosives for all speakers for the three languages reported in Sussman et al. (1993) are illustrated in Figure 12.4 in a derived higher-order acoustic space alongside data from a Spanish (Martínez-Celdrán & Villalba 1995) and an English (Sussman et al. 1991) study. The slope values for Spanish, Cairene Arabic and Urdu display the same order of magnitude (velar > labial > dental/alveolar). This is in contrast to the English data where the order: labial > velar > dental/alveolar is observed. All five languages displayed higher slopes for labial versus the dental/alveolar plosives. The cross-linguistic data highlight the coarticulation resistance and degree of coarticulation patterns which are both common and different across the five languages. All five languages have lower slope values for the dental/alveolar plosives compared to the labials. This suggests higher levels of coarticulation resistance (and lower levels of coarticulation) for this group of plosives. However, the range in the slope values for the dental

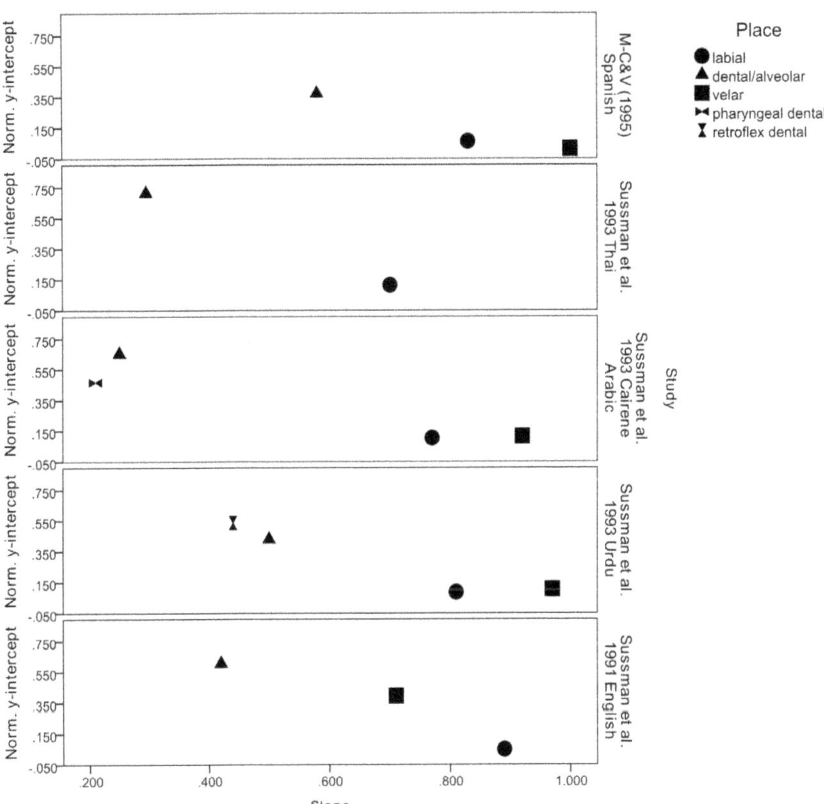

Figure 12.4. Higher-order acoustic space for labial, dental/alveolar, velar, pharyngealized dental and retroflex dental plosives as a function of language and study.

Note: Spanish – Martínez-Celdrán & Villalba 1995, table 1, p. 31 – panel 1; Thai – Sussman et al. 1993: 1258, table 1 – panel 2; Cairene Arabic – Sussman et al. 1993: 1259, table 2 – panel 3; Urdu – Sussman et al. 1993: 1261, table 4 – panel 4; English – Sussman et al. 1991: p. 1315 – panel 5.

and alveolar plosives across the five languages suggests that the degree of coarticulation resistance varies by language. Spanish and Urdu display the steepest slopes for the dental/alveolar plosives. In contrast, those for Thai and Cairene Arabic are the shallowest. These differences could be explained in terms of the alveolar versus dental place of articulation for the voiced plosives (e.g. Martínez-Celdrán & Villalba 1995). The steepest slopes observed for the velar plosives were observed for Spanish, Cairene Arabic and Urdu. This contrasts with the lower slope value for the English velar data (.71) which when examined further as a function of vowel context, was found to reveal a clear allophonic split between the slopes for the palatal [g] (.34) and velar [g] (.87) plosives in front and back vowel contexts, respectively (Sussman et al. 1991: 1315–17). The allophonic split in the F2 LE slope patterns of the velar plosives for the English data reported in Sussman et al. (1991) reflects the more fronted or more backed velar constrictions operating as function of vowel context in English. This merits further investigation in the Thai, Cairene Arabic and Urdu data in Sussman et al. (1993), and the Spanish data reported by Martínez-Celdrán & Villalba (1995). What also needs to be acknowledged at this point, are the potential perseverative effects of coarticulation resistance which might be operating within different CVC(C) sequences. This too merits further investigation.

The data depicted in Figure 12.4 reveal additional patterns of coarticulation resistance and coarticulation, which can be explained in terms of articulatory dynamics. The data for Cairene Arabic displayed a shallower (but non-significant) slope value for the voiced pharyngeal dental plosive, compared to its non-pharyngeal cognate, and suggests a higher level of coarticulation resistance and lower levels of coarticulation with the ensuing vowels in the CVt/CVtt sequences. This lower degree of coarticulation reflects the more complex articulatory gestures and constrictions required in the production of the voiced pharyngeal dental plosive; the execution of a dental obstruction in conjunction with a pharyngeal constriction. In addition, the pharyngeal constriction results in a more posterior lingual gesture which explains the lower normalized *y*-intercept value for F2 compared to the non-pharyngeal cognate in Figure 12.4. The role and significance of F2 LEs in the characterization of pharyngeal consonants in Arabic and Arabic dialects is discussed in more detail below (Section 12.3.2).

Further suggestions of coarticulation resistance are revealed in the slope values for the retroflex dental for the Urdu speakers (see Figure 12.3 – panel 3, and Figure 12.4 – panel 4), which were shallower than for its dental cognate. This reflects a higher level of coarticulation resistance and reduced level of coarticulation for the retroflex variant. However, it is worth noting at this point that this difference was not significant (Sussman et al. 1993).

12.3.2 F2 LEs as a Function of Dialect and Regional Differences in Arabic

Following the report by Sussman et al. (1993) on F2 LEs in Cairene Arabic, further studies of Arabic have been conducted using F2 LEs. These studies have examined F2 LEs in a wide range of phonetic contexts (e.g. Yeou 1997), and their role in the characterization of dialects of Arabic (Embarki et al. 2007). This section considers and discusses the salient points reported in these studies.

Yeou (1997) investigated coarticulation using locus equations in 9 adult male Moroccan speakers of Modern Standard Arabic (MSA) with a mean age of 29 years. A range of consonants and vowels were analyzed, including speech tokens with non-pharyngealized and pharyngealized consonants in the initial CV portion of CVCVC(VC) sequences. F2-onsets were measured at the start of voicing, and vowel targets were measured at maxima/minima points or at the midpoint of the vowel's steady state. The results of the study found steep F2 LE slopes for the voiceless labiodental fricative /f/ (.92) which corresponds to the steeper slope values found for bilabial stops reported in other studies (e.g. Sussman et al. 1991; Fowler 1994; McLeod et al. 2001). In addition, the flatter slope for the voiceless alveolar fricative /s/ (mean .56) agrees with, or approximates slope values reported for alveolar fricatives in other studies (e.g. Tabain 2000, 2002). The slope for the voiceless palatoalveolar fricative (.62) also corresponds to some data reported in Tabain (2002: 27). Data representing the voiceless uvular fricative displayed steep slopes (mean .90), which were similar to those reported for the voiceless labiodental fricative (/f/ – mean .92). Yeou (1997) discusses the role of articulatory dynamics in shaping these results which were previously proposed by Fowler (1994). If we interpret the data in terms of coarticulation resistance and the degree of articulation, these higher slope values suggest higher degrees of coarticulation (and lower levels of coarticulation resistance) between the voiceless uvular fricative and the voiceless labiodental fricative and ensuing vowels in the CV sequences.

If we examine the other consonant data reported by Yeou (1997), the importance of pharyngealized consonants and his assertion of their role as a "Distinct Class" of consonants in Arabic is highlighted and supported. The mean slope value reported for the voiceless pharyngeal fricative (.68) suggests higher levels of coarticulation resistance, and a lower degree of coarticulation for this pharyngealized consonant. Furthermore, the pattern of increased coarticulation and lower degrees of coarticulation of pharyngealized consonants is replicated across four sets of pharyngealized and non-pharyngealized cognates; shallower slopes were found for the pharyngealized consonants relative to their non-pharyngealized cognates (voiced dental fricative – .46 versus pharyngealized voiced dental fricative – .22; voiced alveolar plosive – .48 versus pharyngealized voiced alveolar plosive – .31; voiceless alveolar fricative – .56 versus pharyngealized voiceless alveolar fricative – .35; voiceless alveolar plosive – .66 versus pharyngealized voiceless alveolar plosive – .37). Figure 12.5 illustrates the slope values for the four sets of pharyngealized and non-pharyngealized consonants plotted against normalized *y*-intercept values in a higher-order acoustic space. Also represented in Figure 12.5, for comparison, are the data for the pharyngealizedvoiced dental/alveolar plosive and its non-pharyngealized cognate for the Cairene Arabic data discussed above (Sussman et al. 1993), together with a sample of data for MSA speakers from Morocco, Jordan, Kuwait and Yemen reported in a later study (Embarki et al. 2007). What the data in Figure 12.5 confirm are the lower slopes for all pharyngealized consonants across all data sets when compared to their non-pharyngealized cognates; this supports the distinct nature of this class of consonants (Yeou 1997). However, also evident from the data in Figure 12.5, are the non-uniform differences between the pharyngealized and non-pharyngealized consonant pairs across the different data sets. These patterns may be indicative of both dialect and speaker differences. For example, the Cairene Arabic data (Figure 12.5 – panel 1) display the lowest slopes for /d/ (.25 – Sussman et al. 1993: 1259) and its pharyngealized cognate (.21 – Sussman et al. 1993: 1259) across all the data sets. The individual differences in the slope values for the pharyngealized voiced dental/alveolar plosive across the three Cairene Arabic speakers, which are displayed in Figure 12.3 (see panel 2) are also worth noting, and suggest varying degrees of coarticulation across the speakers; speakers 1 and 3 display similar and shallower slopes (.153 and .155, respectively) compared to speaker 2 (.319). This suggests individual differences even among speakers representing the same dialect, which might be related to other factors. In addition, the relatively small slope difference between the pair (pharyngealized and non-pharyngealized voiced dental/alveolar plosives) for the Cairene Arabic sample (.04) is most similar to that for the MSA speakers from Morocco reported by Embarki et al. (2007) (see Figure 12.5 – panel 5; a value of .039 was calculated from the data in Embarki et al. 2007: 145, table 3); the other data sets display more marked differences between the pharyngealized and non-pharyngealized cognates.

The lowest mean slope value observed for the pharyngealized voiced dental/alveolar plosive in the Cairene Arabic speakers (Figure 12.5 – panel 1) and the lower slope values for the MSA speakers from Morocco reported

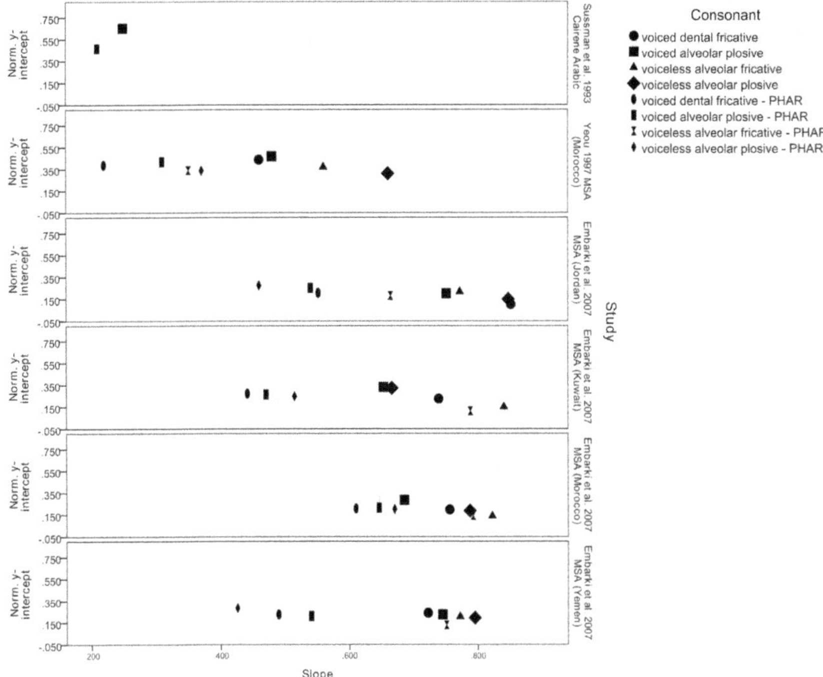

Figure 12.5. Higher-order acoustic space for non-pharyngealized and pharyngealized sounds as a function of Arabic dialect, region and study.

Note: Cairene Arabic – Sussman et al., 1993: 1259, table 2 – panel 1; Modern Standard Arabic (MSA) Morocco – Yeou 1997: 190, table 1 – panel 2; MSA Jordan – Embarki et al. 2007: 145, table 3 – panel 3; MSA Kuwait –Embarki et al. 2007: 145, table 3 – panel 4; MSA Morocco – Embarki et al. 2007: 145, table 3 – panel 5; MSA Yemen – Embarki et al. 2007: 145, table 3 – panel 6.

in Yeou (1997) (Figure 12.5 – panel 2) relative to other MSA speakers, including other MSA speakers from Morocco in a later study (Embarki et al. 2007) (Figure 12.5 – panels 3 to 6), suggest lower degrees of coarticulation and higher levels of coarticulation resistance for the pharyngealized consonants in these two data sets. The lower slope values in the data depicted in Figure 12.5 might be indicative of the adoption of a more extreme pharyngealized constriction in the production of these consonants by the speakers of Cairene Arabic (see Figure 12.5 – panel 1) and the MSA speakers from Morocco in the earlier study by Yeou (1997) (see Figure 12.5 – panel 2). Moreover, the shift in the F2 LE slope values and patterns for MSA speakers from Morocco which are reported a decade later by Embarki et al. (2007) offers a longitudinal perspective, and the possibility of a changing dialect which, over time, has become characterized by lower levels of pharyngealization (see Figure 12.5 – panel 2 versus panel 5).

It is evident from the discussion above that pharyngealization provides an effective index of dialect differences in Arabic (Embarki et al. 2007). Furthermore, if we examine the coarticulation patterns and F2 LE data reported by Embarki et al. (2007) as a function of pharyngealization in MSA representing four regions (Yemen, Kuwait, Jordan and Morocco), this becomes even more clear. When the slope values of the pharyngealized consonants and their non-pharyngealized cognates were analyzed as a function of geographical origin, results revealed geographical differences; flatter slopes were observed in MSA speakers from Eastern areas of Yemen, Jordan and Kuwait compared to those from Morocco. The slope values for the pharyngealized data in MSA therefore provided an effective means of separating the speakers by geographical region. This pattern was replicated in the data representing the four local dialects. In contrast, the slopes for the non-pharyngealized consonants did not display clear geographical distinctions for either the MSA or dialectal Arabic data.

Locus equations therefore appear to be an efficient index of separating pharyngealized consonants from their non-pharyngealized cognates. In addition, they appear to also be able to index the extent of pharyngealization across different varieties of Arabic as a function of geographical region. Figure 12.6 illustrates the slopes and normalized *y*-intercept values for the pharyngealized consonants representing the MSA speakers from Morocco, Jordan, Kuwait and Yemen. The Western variety of Moroccan (Figure 12.6 – panel 1) displays the steepest slopes for all the pharyngealized consonants when compared to the Eastern areas of Jordan (Figure 12.6 – panel 2), Kuwait (Figure 12.6 – panel 3) and Yemen (Figure 12.6 – panel 4). The pharyngealized voiceless alveolar fricative is the only pharyngealized consonant where this difference appears to be less consistent across the MSA regions. Compared to the mean slope value for the Moroccan speakers of MSA (slope = .792 – panel 1), a more marked difference was observed for the MSA speakers from Jordan (slope = .664 – panel 2) for the pharyngealized voiceless alveolar fricative. In contrast, the values observed for the MSA speakers from Kuwait (slope = .788 – panel 3) and Yemen (slope = .751 – panel 4) were marginally lower for the pharyngealized voiceless alveolar fricative.

In summary, the examination of the F2 LE data from a cross-linguistic perspective has highlighted the patterns of coarticulation resistance and degrees of coarticulation which are both common and different across languages, even if we acknowledge the individual differences therein (see Figure 12.3). For example, the relatively steep slopes of labial consonants

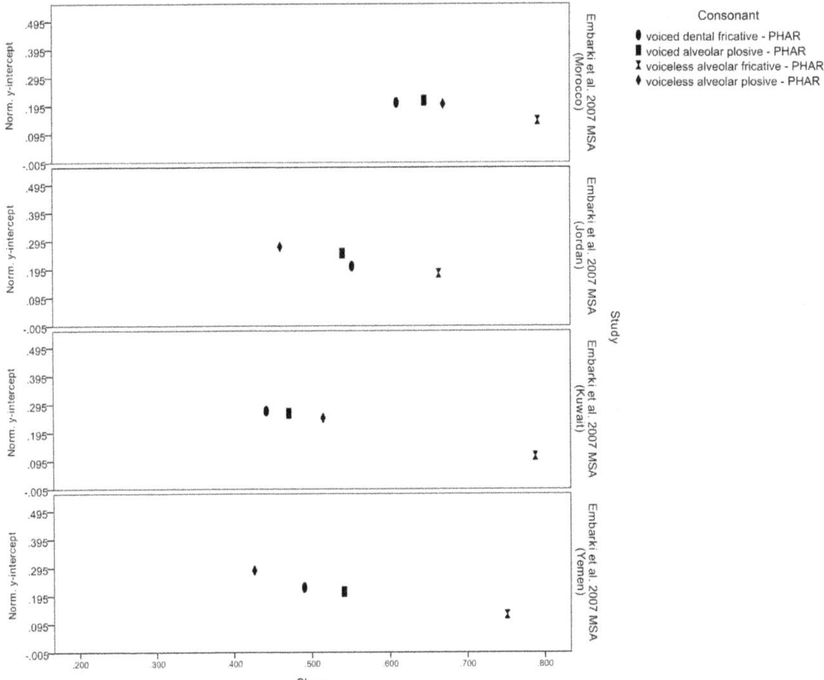

Figure 12.6. Higher-order acoustic space for pharyngealized sounds only (pharyngealized voiced dental fricative, pharyngealized voiced alveolar plosive, pharyngealized voiceless alveolar fricative and pharyngealized voiceless alveolar plosive) as a function of Arabic dialect and region.

Note: Panel 1 – Modern Standard Arabic (MSA) Morocco; panel 2 – MSA Jordan; panel 3 – MSA Kuwait; panel 4 – MSA Yemen (based on data in Embarki et al. 2007: 145, table 3).

across a number of different languages highlight that the articulatory dynamics which underpin labial-vowel sequences lend themselves to low levels of coarticulation resistance, and a greater capacity for coarticulation (e.g. Sussman et al. 1993; Yeou 1997; Tabain 2002). In contrast, consonants which involve both complex and secondary articulation such as the pharyngealized consonants representing different varieties of Arabic display flatter slopes compared to their non-pharyngealized counterparts (e.g. Sussman et al. 1993; Yeou 1997; Embarki et al. 2007). These are indicative of higher levels of coarticulation resistance, and therefore lower levels of coarticulation for this class of sounds. What is also evident from the data reported by Embarki et al. (2007) is the effective use of F2 LEs in indexing the degree of coarticulation for this class of consonants as a function of region and dialect. In addition, the examination of F2 LE slope data representing the pharyngealized consonants of MSA from the same region (Morocco) across a significant time span (a decade) provided some insights into the shifts which might have occurred in this feature of MSA; steeper slopes in the most recent study (Embarki et al. 2007) suggest less extreme pharyngealization.

12.4 Differences in F2 LEs as a Function of Speech Style, Speech Rate and Speaker Adaptation

12.4.1 F2 LEs and Spontaneous versus Citation Forms and Other Linguistic Variables

Here we present three studies which investigated F2 LEs as a function of speech style(citation versus spontaneous speech): Krull 1989 (Swedish); Duez 1992 (French) and Sussman 1998a (American English). The study by Duez (1992) also included analyses of coarticulation as a function of prominence and novelty in an utterance; these results are also reviewed.

Krull (1989) examined F2 LEs in CV syllables in a group of 5 adult Swedish male speakers (aged 40 to 45 years). The initial consonants included bilabial (/b, m/) and dental (/d, n, l/) consonants in a range of vowel contexts. Her data showed that the speakers displayed steeper F2 LE slopes for CV syllables in word samples produced in spontaneous speech samples compared to those in isolated words (reference samples). However, no statistical comparisons were reported for the two conditions.

Krull also found higher levels of dispersion for the spontaneous speech samples compared to the reference samples. The study suggests two possible sources for the different patterns of dispersion between the two sets of speech samples. The first relates to repeated instances of words within the spontaneous samples which carry different levels of emphasis; and the second, to differences in the phonetic context of sounds preceding CV syllables. Krull also reports steeper slopes for /lV/ syllables which carried lexical stress.

If we examine the data in Krull (1989), there are individual differences across the 5 adult males. Different speakers displayed varying degrees of coarticulation across both the bilabial and dental consonants, and the differences in the slopes of the F2 LEs between the spontaneous and reference samples also varied across speakers. This ranged from one speaker showing low levels of coarticulation for both the spontaneous and reference samples to another who displayed steep slopes across both conditions. Figure 12.7 depicts the higher-order acoustic space representing the mean slopes and normalized *y*-intercept values for the labial (/b, m/) and dental (/d, n, l/) consonants derived from the data for the 5 speakers reported in Krull (1989: 100–1). It shows the pattern of variation across the speakers as a function of the two speech conditions and the five consonants. One speaker (S1 – panel 1) displays shallower slopes across all consonants, including the labials, and does not display marked increases in the slope values for the spontaneous speech samples. In contrast, another speaker (S2 – panel 2) displays more notable increases in the slope values for the consonants /n, l/ for the spontaneous speech data, but a smaller increase for /d/. Speaker 3 (S3 – panel 3) shows increases in the slope values across

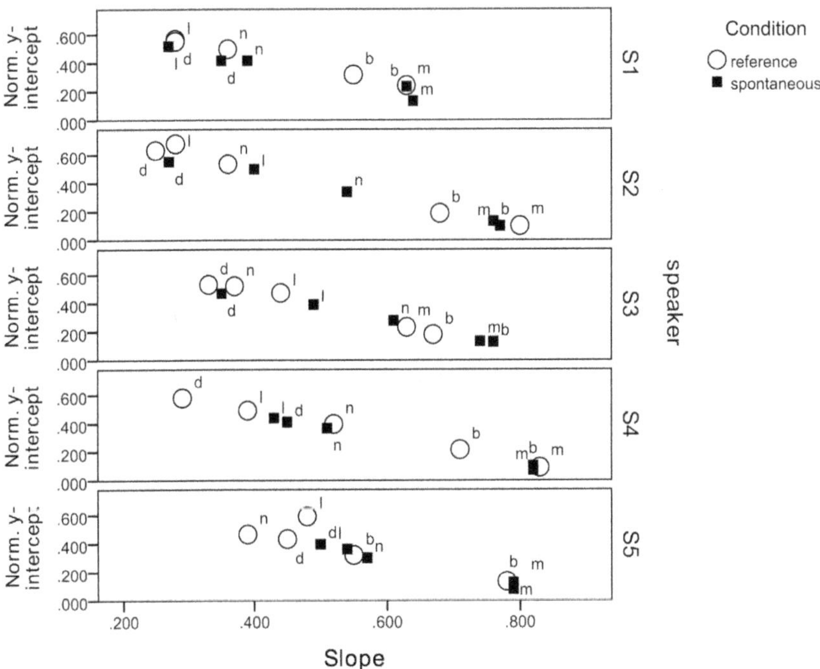

Figure 12.7. Higher-order acoustic space as a function of speaking condition (reference and spontaneous) for the individual speaker values.

Note: Speakers 1 to 5 – panels 1 to 5, respectively (reported in Krull 1989: 100–1, appendix I).

all the consonants for the spontaneous samples, with the largest increases being observed for /n/. Speaker 4 (S4 – panel 4) on the other hand displays a marginal decrease in the slope for /n/, and increased slope values for /d/ and /b/ for the spontaneous condition. Speaker 5 (S5 – panel 5) displays increased slope values across all five consonants for the spontaneous samples with the largest increases being observed for /b/ and /n/.

In a later study of 5 adult male speakers of Standard French aged 20 to 25 years, Duez (1992) also analyzed F2 LE patterns in spontaneous and reference words. Spontaneous speech samples were collected using an informal interview, and reference words were derived from the content of the spontaneous speech samples. These reference samples were collected at a later point via a reading task where participants read the reference words using a slow speech rate. As was the case for the Krull (1989) study, bilabial (/b, m/) and dental consonants (/l, n, d/) were also the focus of the analysis. The "locus" was measured at the first glottal cycle of the vowel and the "nucleus" was measured either at the maxima/minima points within the vowel or at the midpoint of steady state of the vowel. Vowel durations were also measured. Results replicated the patterns reported in Krull (1989), and reported significantly steeper slopes for the spontaneous speech samples across both the bilabial and dental consonants. Spontaneous speech samples also displayed significantly lower *y*-intercept values for the dental place of articulation. Significantly shorter vowel durations in the spontaneous speech samples for both places of articulation are also reported (Duez 1992). In addition, like Krull (1989), Duez (1992) found individual differences across speakers. Figure 12.8 depicts the higher-order acoustic space representing the mean slopes and normalized *y*-intercept values for all 5 speakers derived from the data reported by Duez (1992: 421, table 1). The data in Figure 12.8 represent the labial and dental data for both the reference and spontaneous speech conditions; the Euclidean distances between labial and dental places of articulation for each speech task were also calculated. All 5 speakers in Figure 12.8 appear to display increases in the slope values for the spontaneous speech samples in respect of the labial consonants. However, this increase is marginal for one speaker (S5: .01 – panel 5), but more extensive for two of the other speakers (S1 & S3: .1 in both cases – panels 1 and 3). All 5 speakers also display an increase in the slope values for the dental consonants. However, there are individual differences in the degree of slope increase where S3 (panel 3) and S4 (panel 4) display the largest increases (.2 and .21, respectively). The Euclidean distances between the labial and dental consonants as a function of speech condition indicate larger distances for the reference samples compared to spontaneous samples (see Figure 12.8 for all Euclidean distance values).

This suggests more marked contrasts between the slopes and *y*-intercepts for the labial and dental places of articulation in the reference samples. However, there is also evidence for individual differences in the Euclidean distances between the consonant categories across the two speech conditions; speaker 1 (panel 1) displays the smallest Euclidean distance for the reference samples, whereas speaker 5 (panel 5) displays the largest. In the

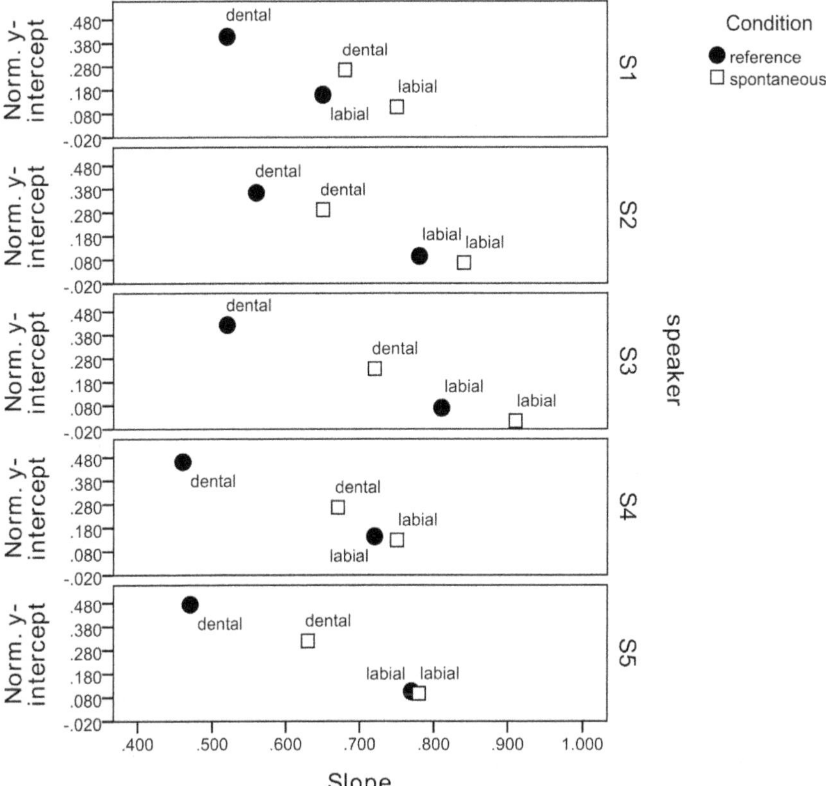

Figure 12.8. Higher-order acoustic space for 5 individual speakers as a function of speech task (reference and spontaneous).

Note: Speakers S1 to S5 – panels 1 to 5, respectively, derived from the data reported in Duez (1992: 421, table 1).
The Euclidean distances between the labial-dental categories for the reference condition for speakers S1, S2, S3, S4 and S5 are .280007143, .348281495, .457233256, .409986585 and .475951941, respectively; the Euclidean distances between the labial-dental categories for the spontaneous condition are .171898226, .294491086, .292585458, .159944522 and .268754535, respectively; the differences between the Euclidean distances for the reference and spontaneous speech samples (reference minus spontaneous) are .108108917, .053790409, .164647798, .250042064 and .207197406, respectively.

case of the spontaneous speech samples, the smallest and largest distances are displayed by speaker 4 (panel 4) and speaker 2 (panel 2), respectively. With regard to the differences in the Euclidean distances between the labial-dental categories for the two speech conditions, speaker 4 displays the largest value, whereas speaker 2 displays the smallest. This suggests that the levels of contrast between the labial and dental consonants between the two speech conditions are fairly stable for speaker 2. In contrast, Speaker 4 shows a marked decrease in the phonetic contrast between the labial and dental consonants in the spontaneous condition (see Figure 12.8 for all the data).

Duez (1992) also analyzed CV syllables as a function of syntactic prominence in non-prominent and prominent syllables using dental consonants (/d, n, l/) and a variety of vowel contexts (/i, e, a, o, u/) in read sentences. The same method of analysis was used for this part of her experiment. Results showed steeper slopes for non-prominent syllables, and non-prominent syllables were also shorter than their prominent counterparts. In addition, Duez (1992) analyzed the F2 LE patterns of CV syllables in novel and second repetition samples in read sentences in a smaller sample of data. Novel words displayed shallower slopes, and therefore greater F2 distances between the consonant and vowel.

In Duez (1992), vowel length appears, in the main, to be related to the degree of coarticulation where shorter vowels are related to a higher degree of coarticulation. This is borne out if we examine the correlation between the total vowel duration for the labial and dental consonants (calculated from vowel duration data in Duez 1992: 421, table 1), and the Euclidean distances between the labial and dental consonants as a function of speech condition across all speakers which were provided in Figure 12.8. This correlation is significant ($n = 10$, $r = .813$, $p = .004$) and is depicted in a scattergraph in Figure 12.9. However, as we can also see in Figure 12.9 there are individual differences in the extent to which vowel duration is related to the Euclidean distances as a function of speech condition.

There is also evidence in Duez (1992) for shorter segments displaying less articulatory reduction, and for longer vowel durations displaying undershoot in vowel targets. Furthermore, the pilot data in her study show that for some speech samples (novel words), the degree of F2 excursion between the onset and vowel target was not related to the significantly longer vowels for this data set.

In a later, and larger-scale study, Sussman et al. (1998a) investigated F2 LEs in the citation and spontaneous speech samples of 22 speakers aged 21 to 55 years (11 M, mean age 33.6 years; 11 F, mean age 35.2 years). Bilabial (/b/), alveolar (/d/) and velar (/g/) plosives in a range of 10 different vowel

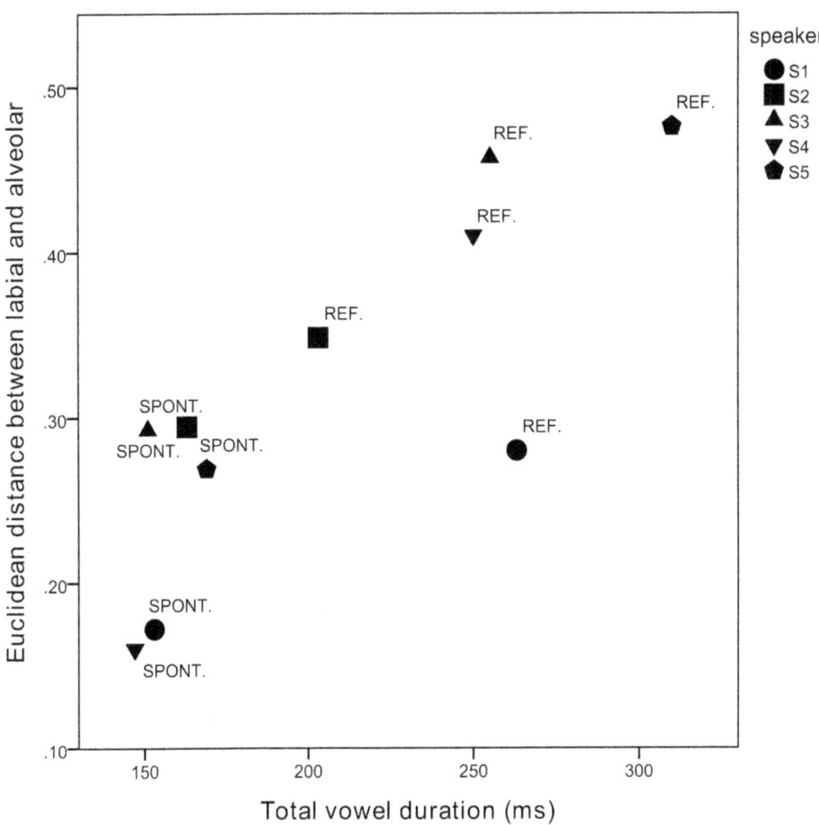

Figure 12.9. A scattergraph of the total vowel duration for S1–S5 for both speech conditions (reference and spontaneous) plotted as a function of the Euclidean distances reported in Figure 12.8.

Note: The total vowel durations (labial + dental context vowel durations for reference samples; labial + dental context vowel durations for spontaneous samples) were calculated using the values reported in Duez (1992: 421, table 1).
A significant correlation was found between the total vowel duration and the Euclidean distance between the labial and alveolar places of articulation across both speech conditions using a Pearson's Product Moment correlation test (n = 10, r = .813, p = .004, two-tailed).

contexts in CVt syllables represented the citation samples, which were read by the participants. The spontaneous speech samples were made up of bV, dV and gV sequences within a read passage, where participants were required to read the passage using a comfortable fast pace. Samples for this set of data were included for analysis when they were judged to be representative of a spontaneous speech style. Results indicated that significantly steeper slopes were observed for the spontaneous speech samples compared to the citation forms only in some cases: the alveolar plosive /d/, and the velar-palatal allophone of /g/ (i.e., [g] in the context of front vowels). The slopes for /b/ and the velar allophone of /g/ ([g] in back vowel contexts) were not significantly different across the two speech styles. Sussman et al. (1998a) suggest that because /d/ and [g]-palatal are characterized by relatively shallow slopes, they have more capacity for increased levels of coarticulation during spontaneous speech. This contrasts with the already steep slopes for the /b/ and [g]-velar plosives which have less scope for an increase in this dimension.

Like Krull (1989) and Duez (1992), Sussman et al. (1998a) found individual differences across speakers. For example, when the data for the /d/ and [g]-palatal contexts were examined, it was found that most, but not all, speakers displayed steeper slopes for the spontaneous speech samples for both contexts (19 out of 22, and 18 out of 22 for the /d/ and [g]-palatal contexts, respectively).

Sussman et al. (1998a) also examined the R^2 values and standard errors of estimate (SE) values as a function of speech style. The citation data displayed a higher mean R^2 value (.76) compared to the spontaneous speech samples (.70). When the R^2 values were compared for each plosive context by speech style, significant differences were found for /b/ and /d/. No significant differences were found for either of the allophones representing /g/. In addition, mean SE values were lower across all stops for the citation condition (85 Hz) compared to the spontaneous speech samples (110 Hz). When SE values were analyzed across both speech styles for the different plosives, all comparisons were statistically significant; citation samples displayed significantly smaller SE values.

When Sussman et al. (1998a) examined the Euclidean distances within the higher-order acoustic spaces of the plosives representing the citation and spontaneous speech samples, the results indicated that although there were individual differences, the pattern across all speakers indicated that the citation samples covered a larger area in the higher-order acoustic space, and when the total degree of separation between /b/-/d/, /d/-/g/ and /g/-/b/ was examined within the higher-order acoustic space, the total distance for the spontaneous samples (1.163251) was significantly diminished compared to the citation data (1.358912). The data also showed that although the distances between all the phonetic categories including the velar allophones were largely preserved across the two speaking conditions, the [g] palatal plosive displayed the greatest reduction in the higher-order acoustic space in the spontaneous speech samples. The bilabial and

[g] velar plosives displayed the smallest change across the two conditions, and the alveolar plosive displayed intermediate patterns of change.

In summary, the three studies reviewed here suggest that individual speakers across different languages make varying levels of adjustment across different speech styles and different phonetic contexts (see Figures 12.7 and 12.8). Different speakers also appear to display varying degrees of change in coarticulation expressed in the higher-order acoustic space as a function of vowel duration (see Figure 12.9). However, despite the individual differences, the overall pattern of results indicates higher levels of coarticulation, and therefore evidence for hypoarticulated speech in spontaneous speech samples as indexed by steeper slopes compared to citation forms. In addition, in spite of the patterns of articulatory reduction observed in spontaneous speech samples, speakers still appear to maintain the contrast between different phonetic categories (Sussman et al. 1998a).

Given the methods of elicitation for spontaneous speech samples (e.g. the comfortable fast rate described by Sussman et al. 1998a), coupled with the results reported by Duez (1992) (see also Figure 12.9), there is evidence to suggest that vowel duration, and therefore speech rate, is an underlying factor determining the coarticulation differences between citation and spontaneous speech samples.

12.4.2 F2 LEs as a Function of Speech Rate

In a study of 4 Croation speakers (2 M, 2 F), Bakran & Mildner (1995) investigated F2 LEs and closure duration as a function of speech rate in /dV/ accented and unaccented syllables. Their results showed increased slopes for "fast" speech samples compared to those in the "slow" category. Their results also showed, however, individual differences in the slope differences between the two speech rates; speakers DH, BB, BL and SM displayed slope differences of .254, .129, .162 and .088, respectively between the two speech rates (based on data in Bakran & Mildner 1995: 28, table 1). In addition, longer closure duration values were found for the "slow" samples. As with the slope values, individual differences were also found; speakers DH, BB, BL and SM displayed duration differences of 29 ms, 44 ms, 65 ms and 46 ms, respectively between the slow and fast rates (based on data in Bakran & Mildner 1995: 28, table 1). What these individual differences suggest is the lack of linearity between rate of speech and levels of coarticulation. The speaker (DH) who displayed the largest increases in coarticulation for the fast samples, displayed the smallest change in closure duration. In contrast, another speaker (SM) displayed evidence of hyperarticulation across both speech rates, and showed the smallest increase in slope for the fast samples, but an appreciable decrease in closure duration.

A later study by Agwuele et al. (2008) included an investigation of F2 LEs as a function of speech rate. Six speakers of American English aged 23 to 35 years participated in the study (2 F; 4 M). V.CV sequences embedded within sentences were elicited via a reading task using three different speech rates ("normal," "fast" and "fastest"). The initial vowel in the sequences included three vowels which were followed by one of three intervocalic consonants /b, d, g/. The second vowel in the sequences included one of 10 vowels representing a range of vowel qualities. This gave a total of 30 different V.CV sequences for each speaker per speech rate (90 samples in total per speaker). Duration and formant measurements were made to establish the effects of speech rate on CV coarticulation and included speech parameters such as duration, F1/F2 vowel space, and F2 LEs. As this review focuses on F2 LEs, the results of this part of their study are discussed here. The mean slope values for the F2 LEs increased from the normal to the fast rate, and from the fast rate to the fastest rate. This pattern was replicated across all three places of articulation (bilabial slopes: .77, .81, .84; alveolar slopes: .58, .70, .78; velar slopes: .85, .96, .99), and suggests that across all places of articulation, the degree of coarticulation increases with speech rate. However, when Agwuele et al. (2008) examined the changes in the slope values of /g/ as a function of the palatal-velar allophonic split, a mixed pattern of results emerged; the set of data representing the velar allophone showed that some speakers displayed increased slopes with speech rate, while others displayed decreases. This was in contrast to the velar-palatal allophone where most speakers (5 out of 6) displayed higher slopes with increasing speech tempo. These results replicate the individual differences for citation and spontaneous speech reported by Sussman et al. (1998a), which were discussed above.

Figure 12.10 depicts the higher-order acoustic space representing the mean slopes and normalized *y*-intercept values derived from the data reported by Agwuele et al. (2008: 202, table 2). When the total degrees of separation between /b/-/d/, /d/-/g/ and /g/-/b/ are examined within the higher-order acoustic space across all speakers using the mean values reported by Agwuele et al. (2008: 202, table 2), the total distance for the normal speech rate samples is larger (.802863907 – panel 1), compared to both the fast (.68476348 – panel 2), and the fastest speech rates (.543979885 – panel 3) (see Figure 12.10 for all Euclidean distance values).

When the Euclidean distances are examined within the higher-order acoustic spaces of the three plosives representing the three different speech rates by individual speaker reported in Agwuele et al. (2008: 202, table 2),

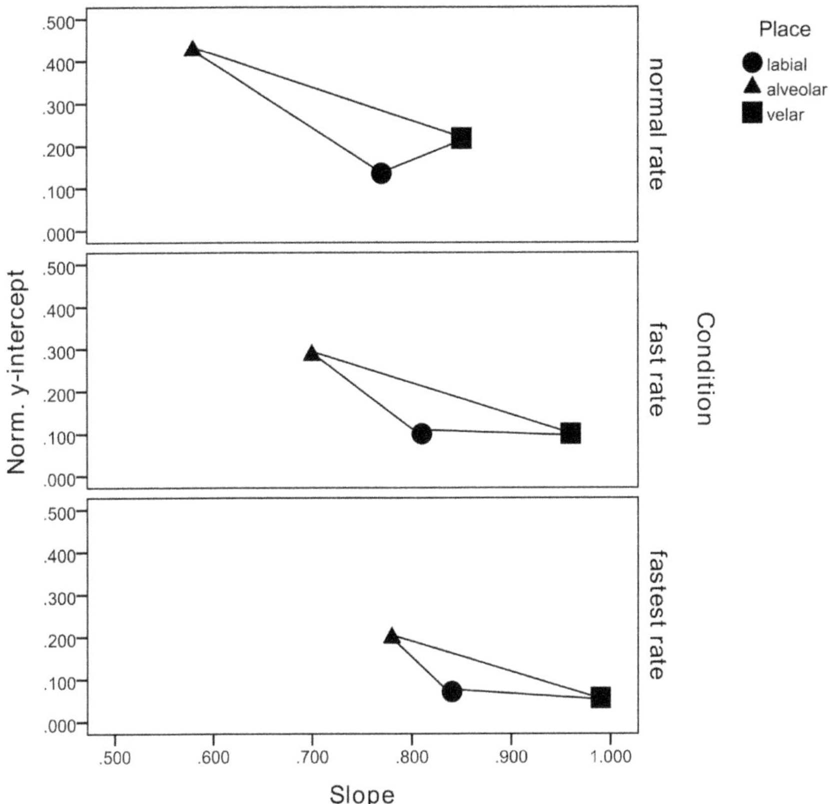

Figure 12.10. Higher-order acoustic space as a function of speech rate.

Note: Derived from the data reported in Agwuele et al. (2008: 202, table 2).
The Euclidean distances between the labial-alveolar categories for the normal (panel 1), fast (panel 2) and fastest (panel 3) rates are .347117055, .21566235 and .140008035, respectively; the Euclidean distances between the alveolar-velar categories are .340828403, .31910030 and .253223715, respectively; the Euclidean distances between the labial-velar categories are .114918449, .15000083 and .150748134, respectively; the total Euclidean distances for the perimeter of the triangles representing all three phonetic category contrasts are .802863907, .68476348 and .543979885, respectively.

the results highlight the individual differences in the slope changes across the three speech rates. More specifically, the patterns of individual variation appear to be most notable for the alveolar and velar contexts, and are illustrated in Figure 12.11. What is evident for the velar context in Figure 12.11 is the marked increase in slope for speaker AP from the slow rate to the fast and fastest rates. In contrast, speaker AJ displays little change for this context. For the alveolar context, all speakers display increased slope values across all three conditions, but the speaker with the most marked increase is speaker AJ (slope values of .49 to .69 to .86). Speaker AP on the other hand displays a smaller but steadier and even increase across the three speech rates (slope values of .53 to .59 to .65).

In summary, the two studies reviewed here suggest that different individuals display varying degrees of change in coarticulation as a function of speech rate and phonetic context (e.g. see Figure 12.11). However, the overall pattern of results indicates increases in slope values and higher levels of coarticulation in the "fast" (Bakran & Mildner 1995; Agwuele et al. 2008) and "fastest" (Agwuele et al. 2008) speech samples. These results are indicative of hypoarticulation in speech samples which are produced with increased tempo.

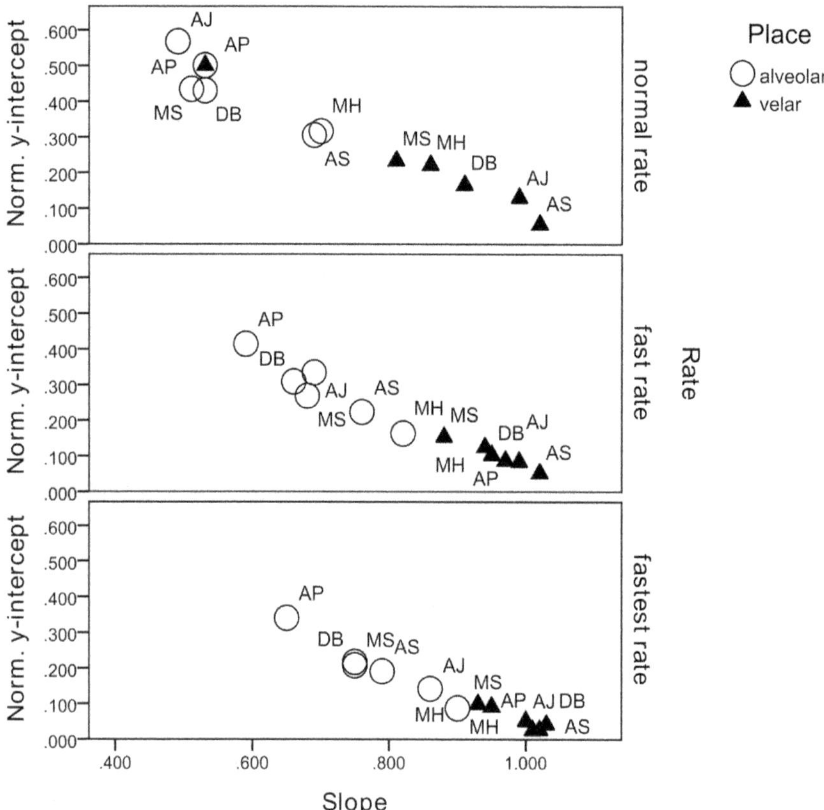

Figure 12.11. Higher-order acoustic space as a function of speech rate and speaker for the alveolar and velar contexts.

Note: Derived from the data reported in Agwuele et al. (2008: 202, table 2).

12.4.3 F2 LEs and Compensatory Strategies Used by Speakers in Different Speech Tasks

The role of F2 LEs in auditory processing and the perception of speech has been discussed and advocated (Sussman et al. 1998b; Sussman 1999, 2002), and there is some empirical evidence to support this view. The perceptual relevance of the relationship between vowel onsets and vowels targets of F2 expressed by F2 LEs has been investigated using synthesized speech and it has been found that listeners are able to use F2 onset and F2 target values when asked to identify stop consonants from synthesized speech samples (Fruchter & Sussman 1997). Further evidence to support the perceptual relevance of F2 LEs comes from empirical data which show that speakers are able to adapt to different speaking conditions and display similar F2 LE patterns to those observed for control conditions. In this section we review two studies which have examined F2 LEs in speech samples elicited under different conditions which require some degree of articulatory compensation and adaptation. The first study is that of Sussman et al. (1995) who investigated F2 LEs in /CVt/ syllables elicited under bite block and normal (control) conditions. The second study is related to speaker adaptation to multiple channels of simultaneous communication; Baillargeon et al. (2002) investigated F2 LEs in CV sequences in CVC words produced during multimodal simultaneous communication (speech and signing), and compared them with those which were a product of the single modality of speech alone.

Sussman et al. (1995) found that the speakers in their study as a group displayed very similar F2 LE functions for speech produced both with and without biteblocks. Furthermore, the adaptation to the bite block condition was largely achieved in the first trial. The highly similar F2 LE functions for these two conditions suggested that in the bite block condition, compensatory articulatory gestures were operating to maintain the acoustic relationship (and therefore acoustic perceptual cues), between the onset and target values of the vowels in CV(C) syllables. Figure 12.12 displays the higher-order acoustic space for all six speakers and the three repetitions for both the bite block (panel 1) and normal (panel 2) speaking conditions, which have been derived from the mean slope and *y*-intercept values for /b, d, g/ presented in Sussman et al. (1995: 3114, table 1). Euclidean distances were also calculated to assess the degree of separation between phonetic categories for the two experimental conditions. The data in Figure 12.12 indicate a marginally smaller acoustic space for the bite block condition. However, the phonetic distinctions and distance between the plosive pairs are largely preserved across both speaking conditions and repetitions. This is supported by the lack of significant differences between the two speaking conditions for the slope and *y*-intercept values across all speakers (Sussman et al. 1995: 3115). The lack of significant differences between the two speaking conditions for the SE values suggests similar levels of dispersion across the two conditions (see Sussman et al. 1995: 3118, table 3, for SE values). These results collectively, suggest that the speakers as a group

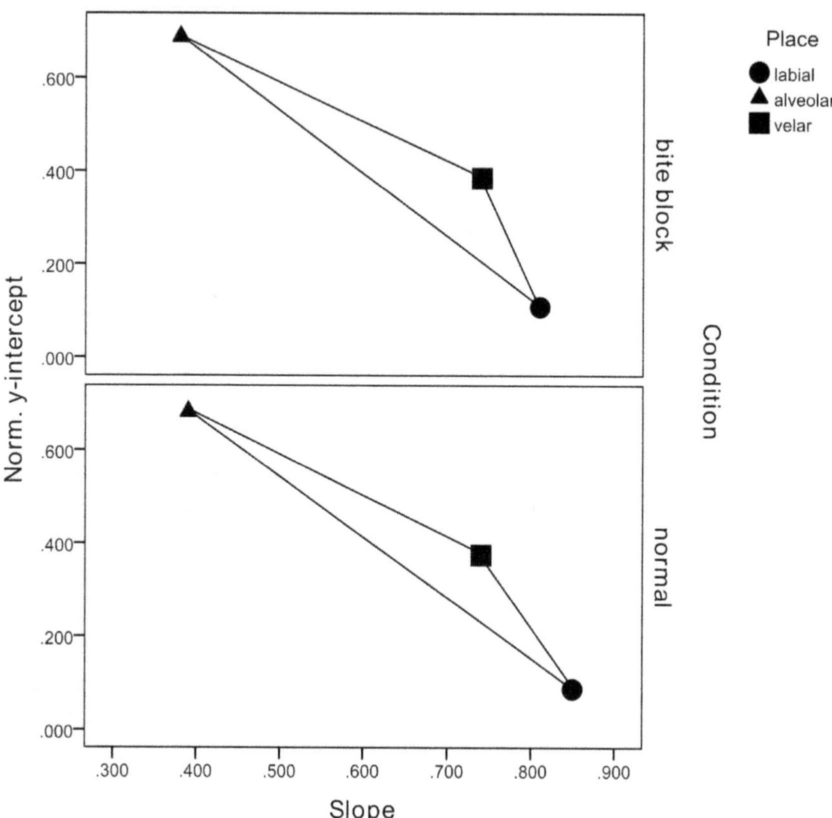

Figure 12.12. Higher-order acoustic space as a function of speaking condition –bite block (panel 1) versus normal (panel 2).

Note: Derived from the mean values reported in Sussman et al. (1995: 3114, table 1). The Euclidean distances between the labial-alveolar categories for the bite block and normal conditions are .721609486 and .751684941, respectively; the Euclidean distances between the alveolar-velar categories are .470541178 and .4655631, respectively; the Euclidean distances between the labial-velar categories are .285223158 and .307825031, respectively; the total Euclidean distances for the perimeters of the triangles representing all three phonetic category contrasts are 1.477373822 and 1.525073072, respectively.

were able to adapt to the bite block condition and achieve articulatory gestures similar to those in the normal speaking condition.

However, what is worth noting at this point, is the evidence of individual differences in the data which are presented in Sussman et al. (1995: 3114, table 2). For example, one male speaker (M3 – panel 3) displayed a greater reduction in the slope values for the bite block condition for all places of articulation (bilabial: .10, alveolar: .06, velar: .07), whereas two other speakers (F1 and F2 – panels 4 and 5, respectively) displayed minimal and similar patterns of change for the three plosives across the two conditions (F1: bilabial: .01, alveolar: .03, velar: .02; F2: bilabial: 02, alveolar: .03, velar: .01). This suggests that F1 and F2 both display higher levels of adaptation to the bite block condition compared to speaker M3 who displays higher slope values, and therefore increased levels of coarticulation, and therefore a reduced articulatory space for the bite block condition. However, despite this increase in coarticulation, speaker M3 maintains the phonetic distinction between the labial, alveolar and velar plosives. Figure 12.13 depicts the data for all the six speakers reported in Sussman et al. (1995) and highlights the range of individual differences within the higher-order acoustic space as a function of speaking condition, including those highlighted for F1, F2 and M3 above.

Like Sussman et al. (1995), Baillargeon et al. (2002) also found that the 12 speakers in their study (6 F, 6 M) were able to compensate and adapt their speech production under different conditions. They also report similar F2 LE functions when producing the CVC target words under the two different modes of speech delivery – speech produced as a single mode of communication (speech only – SA), and speech produced during simultaneous communication (SC) where speech was combined with manual finger spelling (Baillargeon et al. 2002). Furthermore, although significantly longer sentence durations were found for the SC samples compared to the SA samples, no significant differences were found between the two modes of speech delivery for either F2 LE slopes or F2 LE *y*-intercepts. This therefore suggests that the articulatory gestures between the consonants and vowels were largely preserved during simultaneous communication. Even though speech was produced at a slower pace, the participants were able to successfully integrate the bimodal production of speech and finger spelling manual gestures at the same time. Figure 12.14 displays the higher-order acoustic spaces derived from the LE data given in Baillargeon et al. (2002: 56, fig. 1). It is evident from Figure 12.14 that the slope values for the labial and alveolar plosives are slightly higher for the SC samples (panel 2) compared to those for the SA condition (panel 1) (/b/: .854 versus .830; /d/: .550 versus .515), whereas those for the velar plosive are notably higher

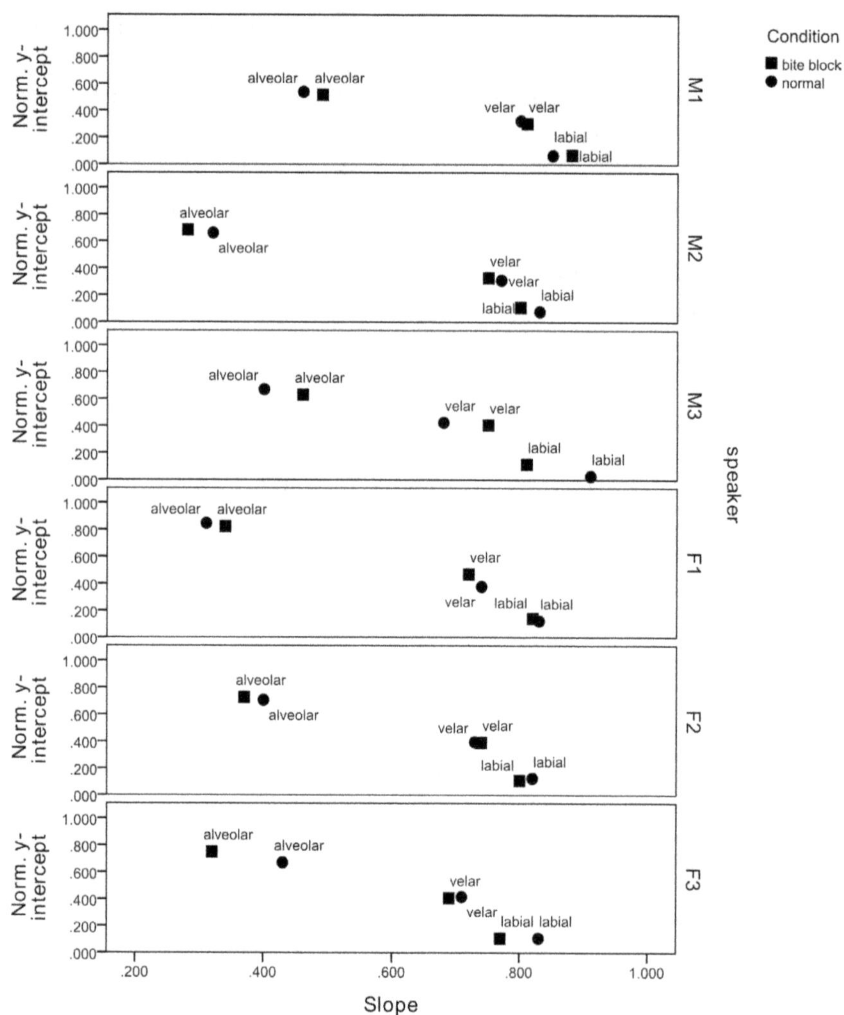

Figure 12.13. Higher-order acoustic space as a function of speaking condition (bite block and normal) and place of articulation derived for the individual speaker values.

Note: As reported in Sussman et al. (1995: 3114, table 1).
Data for speakers M1 to M3 are presented in panels 1 to 3, and data for speakers F1 to F3 are given in panels 4 to 6.

(/g/: .904 versus .841). However, as was noted above, there were no significant differences between the slopes as a function of condition. Furthermore, what is clear from Figure 12.14 is that the distances between the phonetic categories (/b/-/d/, /d/-/g/ and /b/-/g/) are maintained across the two speaking conditions (see Figure 12.14 for all the Euclidean distance values).

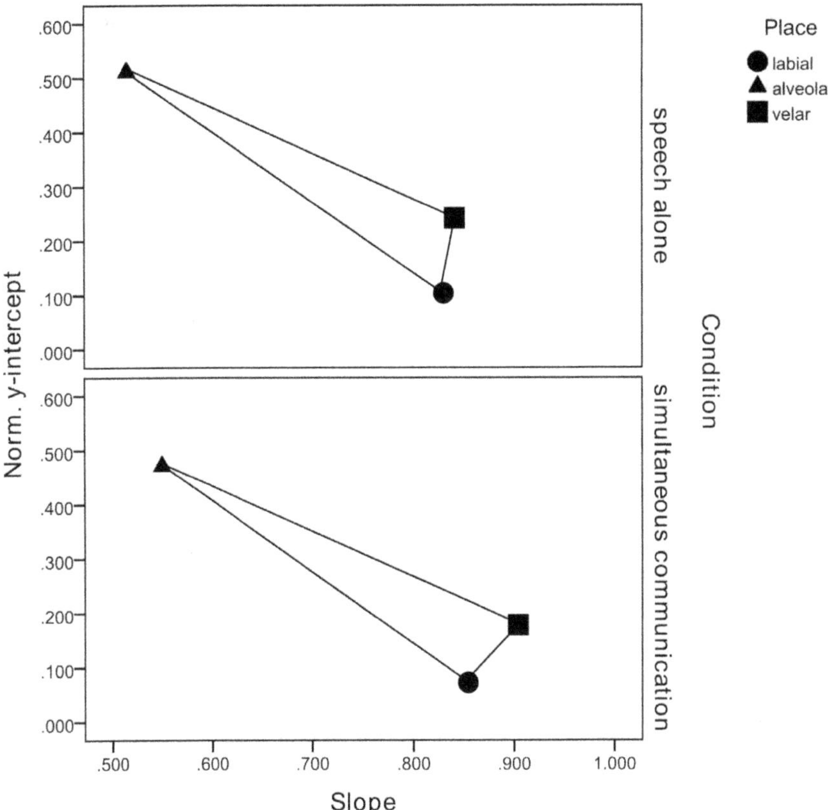

Figure 12.14. Higher-order acoustic space as a function of speaking condition: speech alone (SA) – panel 1 and simultaneous communication (SC) – panel 2.

Note: Derived from the mean values reported in Baillargeon et al. (2002: 56, fig. 1). The Euclidean distances between the labial-alveolar categories for the SA and SC conditions are .514863165 and .501752014, respectively; the Euclidean distances between the alveolar-velar categories are .423129572and .459694029, respectively; the Euclidean distances between the labial-velar categories are .137951758 and .117120194, respectively; the total Euclidean distances for the perimeters of the triangles representing all three phonetic category contrasts are 1.075944495 and 1.078566238, respectively.

12.5 The Role of F2 LEs in Speech and Language Pathology

F2 LE patterns have been used to assess anticipatory coarticulation in adolescents with profound hearing loss (McCaffrey Morrison 2008), and in adults who stutter (Sussman et al. 2011). The former study revealed individual differences, but for the most part, speakers displayed reduced levels of anticipatory coarticulation. The latter study, however, found no evidence of this for either fluent or disfluent speech samples. This section reviews three other speech pathology studies which have investigated F2 LE data in speakers with developmental apraxia of speech (Sussman et al. 1998b, 2000) and acquired apraxia of speech (Whiteside et al. 2010).

12.5.1 F2 LEs and Developmental Apraxia of Speech

Developmental apraxia of speech (DAS) is a motor speech disorder which is characterized by articulatory errors in vowels and consonants, dysprosody, low intelligibility and variable speech patterns (Marquardt et al. 2004). There is evidence from longitudinal data, however, to suggest that variability in speech production decreases with age in children with DAS aged 4 years 6 months to 7 years 7 months (Marquardt et al. 2004). However, it is not clear whether this finding can be explained purely by maturational processes which occur during development, or whether the speech therapy intervention these children received during the course of the study also played a role in achieving the increased levels of stability in speech production and accuracy (Marquardt et al. 2004). However, what this longitudinal study also reported, which is pertinent to this discussion, were the individual differences in variability which were observed in the three participants. This pattern of individual variation in development was also observed in the F2 LE data for the healthy children reviewed above (see Section 12.2). Evidence for individual differences in the variability of speech patterns of children with DAS captured by F2 LE functions are also presented elsewhere (Sussman et al. 1998b, 2000), and are reviewed here.

First, SE and R^2 values as indices of dispersion and linearity between the F2-midvowel and F2-onset values in CV sequences are examined, where higher SE values and low R^2 would be indicative of higher levels of variability and instability. Second, slopes and *y*-intercepts are examined in a higher-order acoustic space, where low slope values and high *y*-intercept values would be indicative of high levels of coarticulation resistance and low levels of coarticulation. The F2 LE data for the children with DAS are compared with healthy age-matched controls from earlier studies (e.g. Sussman et al. 1992), and individual differences are highlighted and discussed.

In their seminal paper on F2 LEs, Sussman et al. (1998b: 253, fig. 11) presented F2 LE functions for /bVt/ (bilabial place), /dVt/ (alveolar place) and /gVt/ (velar place) syllables which were elicited via a repetition task from two children with DAS: DL (DAS1), a 5-year-old; and MG (DAS2), a 4½-year-old. Compared to the SE values reported by Sussman et al. (1992) for both 4-year-olds (mean SE across all places of articulation = 163 Hz) and 5-year-olds (mean SE across all places of articulation = 158 Hz), the SE values for both DL and MG for all three places of articulation were relatively high, and displayed high levels of dispersion in the F2 LE functions (DL – /b/: 271 Hz, /d/: 314 Hz, /g/: 340 Hz; MG – /b/: 322 Hz, /d/: 448 Hz, /g/: 424 Hz [see Sussman et al. 1998b: 253, fig. 11]). However, what the data for these two children with DAS also highlight are the individual differences in their SE values. MG displayed higher SE values than DL, which is indicative of higher levels of variability in the coarticulation patterns for MG in the CVt syllables across all three places of articulation compared to DL. The R^2 values for DL and MG were lower than those reported for the 4- and 5-year-olds in Sussman et al. (1992) across all three places of articulation. The R^2 values for DL (/b/: .597, /d/: .702, /g/: .379) in Sussman et al. (1998b: 253) were markedly lower than those for the 5-year-olds (/b/: .99, /d/: .94, /g/: .918) in Sussman et al. (1992: 775). In addition the R^2 values for MG (/b/: .513, /d/: .253, /g/: .438) were also much lower than those for the 4-year-olds (/b/: .996, /d/: .829, /g/: .934) in Sussman et al. (1992: 774). The higher SE values and lower R^2 values for MG and DL collectively, are indicative of higher levels of variability and therefore lower levels of articulatory stability in the coarticulation patterns of the children with DAS compared to healthy age-matched controls. However, the differences between MG and DL in the SE and R^2 values also suggest varying levels of articulatory stability in two children of similar ages with the same clinical diagnosis.

In a later paper, Sussman et al. (2000) published F2 LE data for five older male children with DAS aged 5 years 9 months to 6 years 8 months. Their results also indicated higher SE and lower R^2 values for all the five children with DAS compared to three age-matched controls. This suggests that higher levels of variability are still present in the coarticulation patterns of older children with DAS when they are compared to healthy age-matched controls. Their results also revealed individual differences in both the SE and lower R^2 values across the five speakers with DAS. For example, speaker DAS5 displayed the highest R^2 and lowest SE values (Sussman et al. 2000: 311, figs. 6 and 7), which might indicate that DAS5 has a higher level of stability in his coarticulation patterns compared to the other four children with DAS in the sample.

When the slope and *y*-intercept values for the DAS speakers are examined across the two studies (Sussman et al. 1998b, 2000), it is possible to observe features in the data which are characteristic of speech development, pathology and individual differences. Figure 12.15 depicts the slope and normalized *y*-intercept values for MG and DL (taken from Sussman et al. 1998b: 253, fig. 11) in a higher-order acoustic space alongside values for healthy children of a similar age (age 4 and 5 years – Sussman et al. 1992) and adults (Sussman et al. 1991: 1315). MG (DAS2 – panel 3) displays a very shallow slope for the labials (.533) which is markedly different to the higher values for both groups of healthy children (panels 2 and 4), DL (DAS1 – panel 1) and the adult group (panel 5). This suggests a high level of coarticulation resistance, and a low level of coarticulation for MG which is atypical for this place of articulation at this stage of development; it approximates the mean slope value (.536) for the 21-month-old infants in Sussman et al. (1996) (see discussion in 12.2 and Figure 12.1). This suggests a level of immaturity in the speech production of MG's labial-vowel sequences. In contrast, however, MG (panel 3) displays a mean slope value for the alveolar place of articulation which is comparable to data for the healthy 4-year-old children (panel 4) and the adults (panel 5), and a mean slope value for the velar place of articulation which is comparable to that for the adults (panel 5). These variable patterns of coarticulation appear to be characteristic of DAS (e.g. Nijland 2003). If we further explore the slope values for speaker DL in Figure 12.15 (panel 1), a notably steeper slope value for the alveolar place of articulation is observed. This suggests a higher level of coarticulation compared to the speakers in the other data sets. Furthermore, when the scattergraph representing the data source for the slope value in Figure 12.15 is examined (see Sussman et al. 1998b: 253, fig. 11), there is evidence of very high F2-midvowel and F2-onset values. This suggests the production of vowels with a more fronted quality in the /dVt/ syllables, and poorly differentiated gestures between the alveolar plosives and ensuing vowels; a pattern which is similar to the data representing the babbling phase in Sussman et al. (1999) (see discussion in 12.2 and Figure 12.1 – panel 1).

The five older children with DAS reported in Sussman et al. (2000) also display variable patterns in slope values. These do not appear to be linked to chronological age and highlight the variable patterns of coarticulation in the children's speech samples. Figure 12.16 illustrates the slopes and normalized *y*-intercept values for the five children with DAS (panels 1 to 5) and three healthy age-matched controls (panels 6 to 8). Speaker DAS1 (panel 1) displays a shallow labial slope (.579), but steeper alveolar (.78) and velar (.837) slopes. The high slope for the alveolar place is similar to that observed for DL in Sussman et al. (1998b), and might be indicative of poorly differentiated articulatory gestures between the plosive and ensuing vowel as discussed above for DL . Speaker DAS2 (panel 2) displays shallow

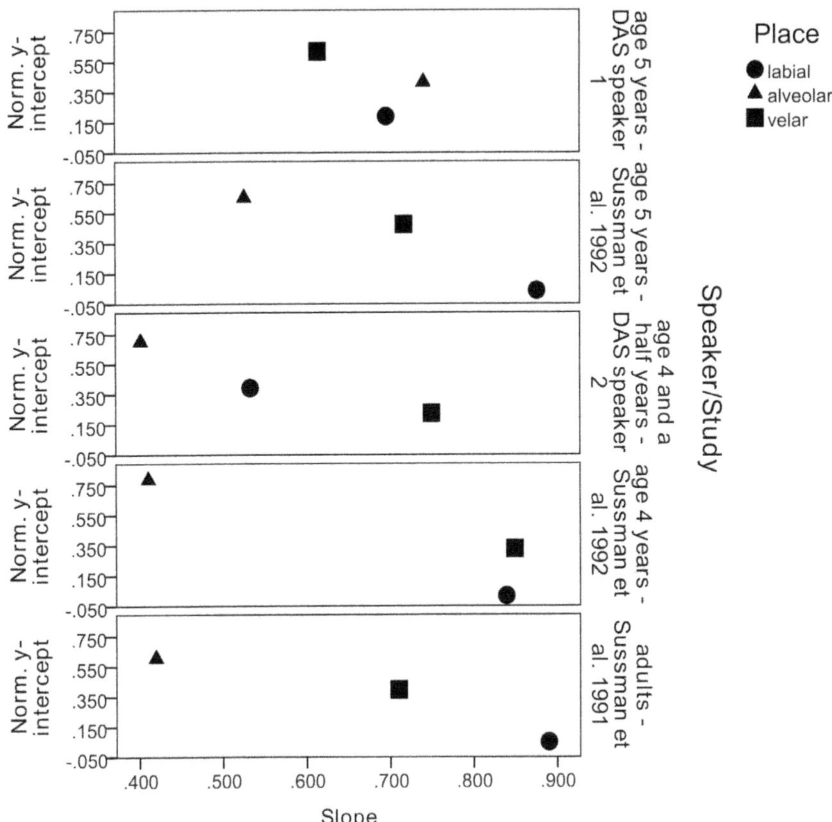

Figure 12.15. Higher-order acoustic space for labial, alveolar and velar plosives for two children with developmental apraxia of speech (DAS).

Note: Data for speaker 1 with DAS aged 5 years (DL – panel 1), and speaker 2 with DAS aged 4½ years (MG – panel 3) are based on the values in Sussman et al.(1998b: 253, fig. 11).
The graph also depicts data for healthy children of a similar age (age 4 – panel 4, and 5 years – panel 2). Data for the 4- and 5-year-olds are based on values in Sussman et al. (1992: 774–5, figs. 1b and 1c). Adult data (panel 5 – based on data in Sussman et al., 1991: 1315) are provided for comparison.

slopes for both the labial (.525) and alveolar (.559) places compared to the velar (.738). The relatively low slope value for the labial (.525) is comparable to the slope values for MG (.533) (Sussman et al. 1998b) and the 21-month-old infants (.536) (Sussman et al. 1996) who were discussed above, and might also be the result of poorly developed speech skills in the production of the labial-vowel sequences. DAS3 (panel 3) displays the steepest slope values for the labial place (.651) compared to values of .583 and .528 for the alveolar and velar places respectively. The most notable pattern for DAS3 is the shallow slope for the velar place of articulation (.528). This is the lowest slope across all speakers, and appears to be an atypical coarticulation pattern for this place of articulation. DAS4 (panel 4) displays slope values of .645, .729 and .75 for the labial, alveolar and velar places, respectively. Of particular note here is the steeper slope for the alveolar plosive, which is similar to DAS1 – this was discussed above. Finally, DAS5 (panel 5) displays high slope values across all places of articulation– labial:

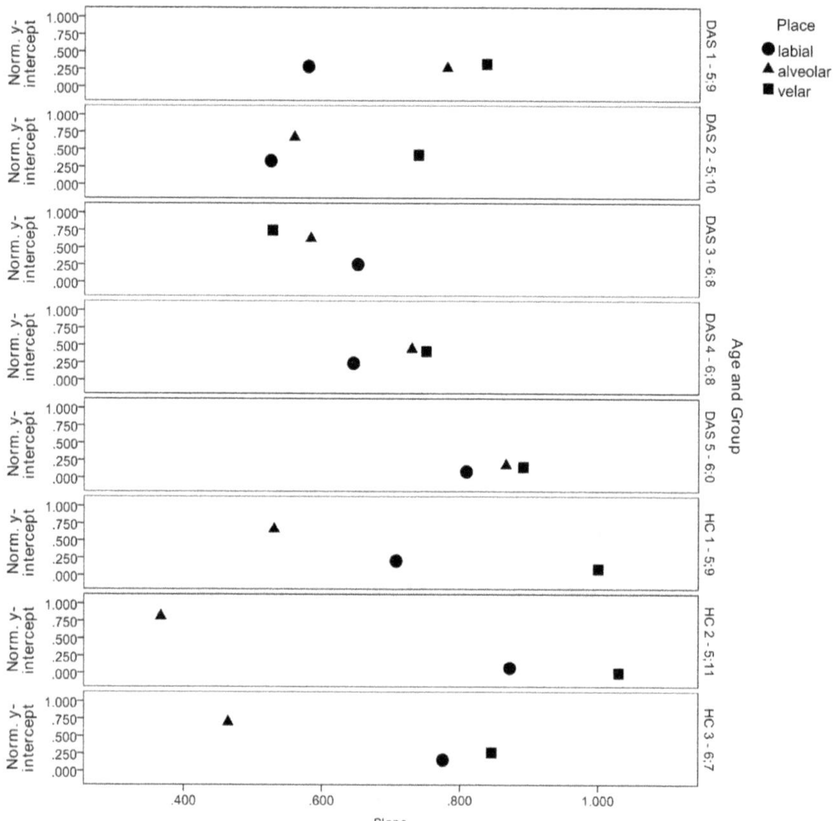

Figure 12.16. Higher-order acoustic space for labial, alveolar and velar plosives for five children with developmental apraxia of speech.

Note: DAS1 to 5 (panels 1 to 5) derived from slope and *y*-intercept data in Sussman et al. (2000: 309, table 2).
The graph also depicts data for three healthy age-matched control speakers, HC1 to 3 (panels 6 to 8) from Sussman et al. (2000: 309, table 2) for comparison.

.809; alveolar: .866; velar: .891. Although the high labial and velar slopes are comparable to the data for a slightly older healthy child (HC 3 – panel 8), the alveolar slope is the highest across all 8 speakers (see Figure 12.16). An explanation similar to that proposed for DAS1 (and DAS4) may also apply here.

In summary, the F2 LE data in both studies by Sussman et al. (1998b, 2000) highlight a number of characteristics of DAS as well as the individual differences of individuals with the same clinical diagnosis. However, in spite of the evidence for individual differences it is possible to characterize the speech patterns displayed by the children with DAS. The high SE and R^2 values for the children with DAS are indicative of highly variable speech patterns relative to healthy age-matched controls. In addition, the more typical and the atypical slope values which were observed for the different speakers across different places of articulation reflect the high levels of heterogeneity in the coarticulation patterns of these speakers. The coarticulation patterns also highlight the articulatory challenges and motor control difficulties faced by children with DAS, and help to explain the poor levels of speech intelligibility observed in this speech disorder (also see Nijland 2003).

12.5.2 F2 LEs and Acquired Apraxia of Speech

Acquired apraxia of speech (AOS) is an acquired motor speech disorder which is characterized by a range of features. Speakers with AOS display struggle and articulatory groping when attempting to initiate speech. They also display a slowed speech rate (e.g. Kent & Rosenbek 1983; Wambaugh et al. 2006), prolonged speech patterns (e.g. Kent & Rosenbek 1983; Wambaugh et al. 2006), voicing errors (e.g. Freeman et al. 1978; Whiteside et al. 2012; Ziegler & von Cramon 1986a), dysprosody (Kent & Rosenbek 1982; Wambaugh et al. 2006), variable and inconsistent articulatory gestures (Itoh et al. 1979; Whiteside et al. 2010) and reduced coarticulation (e.g. Southwood et al. 1997; Whiteside et al. 2010; Ziegler & von Cramon 1986b). The speech characteristics of speakers with AOS are due to disruptions in the motor programs for speech which result in variable, distorted and poorly coordinated articulatory gestures.

Vowel production and coarticulation patterns were investigated in a severe case of acquired apraxia of speech as a function of linguistic complexity (Whiteside et al. 2010). Vowel spaces were used to assess vowel production, and F2 LEs were used to investigate coarticulation patterns. A 77-year-old woman with severe AOS and a healthy age-matched control

(83 years old) participated in the study. /hVd/ syllables which were real words were elicited in three linguistic contexts: isolated word (e.g. "heed"); statement ("I said__."); and question ("Did I say__?"). The /hVd/ syllables were chosen to minimize the articulatory constraints between the initial voiceless glottal fricative and ensuing vowel. In terms of linguistic complexity, the isolated form was viewed as the simplest in terms of linguistic frame and motoric complexity. In contrast, the question was the most complex. The utterance length for the question was longer and the motoric execution of questions required an increase in pitch which placed additional motoric demands on both laryngeal and supralaryngeal systems (e.g., elevation of the larynx, constriction of the pharynx, elevation of the soft palate and constriction of the velopharyngeal port [Yanagisawa et al. 1991]).

The results of the study revealed an increasingly varied and disrupted vowel space for the speaker with AOS, as the linguistic complexity of the task increased (Whiteside et al. 2010). In the case of the question condition, there was both a marked reduction and collapse in the vowel space to a more posterior/backed quality with no clear differentiation between the vowels. This suggested that the increased linguistic and motoric complexity placed additional demands on the execution of the articulatory gestures which became more distorted. This was not observed in the vowel spaces of the healthy matched control speaker.

If we turn our attention to the coarticulation patterns which were captured by the F2 LEs in the data of the speaker with AOS (S1) and the healthy age-matched control speaker (S2) (see Whiteside et al. 2010: 155, table 3), a number of observations are possible. The mean slopes and *y*-intercepts for S1 across the three conditions were – isolated word: .822/204.768; statement: .757/329.089; question: .683/410.953. The slope and *y*-intercept values for S2 were as follows – isolated word: .926/144.897; statement: .934/161.623; question: .896/260.136. If we examine the slope and *y*-intercept data across the two speakers, they are inversely related ($n = 6$, $r = -.916$, $p = .01$). The fact that the slope values for S2 were found to be significantly steeper than those for S1 across all three conditions suggested higher levels of coarticulation resistance and lower patterns of coarticulation for S1. In addition, the steep slopes for S2 did not change markedly across the three conditions, and it was confirmed that there were no significant differences between all slope comparisons (Whiteside et al. 2010: 157, table 4). Speaker S2 was therefore able to maintain the same level of coarticulation resistance and the high levels of coarticulation across the three conditions for the /hV/ articulatory sequences. In contrast, S1 displayed a gradual decrease in the slope values across the three conditions, with a significant difference being observed between the slope values of the isolated word and question conditions. The significantly lower slope value for the question condition suggests a significant increase in the coarticulation resistance and therefore lower levels of coarticulation. S1's speech appeared effortful and her voice quality was characterized by a high pitch and a heightened and tense laryngeal setting (Whiteside et al. 2010). These observations together with the posterior vowel patterns observed for the question condition are congruent with a more pharyngealized and highly constricted voice quality (e.g. Story 2008), and provide a possible explanation for the flatter slopes observed in the question condition. As discussed previously (see Section 12.3), pharyngealization in Arabic is characterized by lower/flatter slopes (e.g. Sussman et al., 1993; Yeou, 1997; Embarki et al., 2007). Given that the slope value for S1 for the question condition (.683) is highly similar to that reported for the voiceless pharyngeal fricative (/ħ/: .68) in Yeou (1997), it seems reasonable to suggest that the pharyngealized setting observed for S1 in the question condition may be contributing to increased levels of coarticulation resistance, which are limiting the extent of gestural overlap between /h/ and the ensuing vowels. Lower levels of coarticulation resistance, and higher levels of coarticulation would normally be expected for this articulatory sequence (Whiteside & Rixon 2003), which is the pattern observed for the age-matched control speaker (S2) in the question condition.

In summary, both the vowel spaces, and the coarticulation patterns expressed by the F2 LEs in Whiteside et al. (2010) were able to capture changes in the speech patterns of an elderly woman with severe AOS (S1) as a function of linguistic complexity. In addition, given the previous body of work on articulatory systems (Story 2008; Yanagisawa et al. 1991), coarticulation and F2 LEs (e.g. Sussman et al. 1991,1998b; Yeou 1997; Embarki et al. 2007), it was possible to offer an explanation for the distortions in both her vowel production and the coarticulation patterns observed in her speech.

12.6 Summary and Concluding Remarks

This review has served to highlight a portion of the large number of studies which have employed F2 LEs as an analytic tool to further our understanding of speech production. F2 LEs not only measure the degree of coarticulation resistance and levels of coarticulation in speech, but are also useful phonetic expressions which measure "tongue body synergy" (Iskarous et al. 2010: 2031). If we accept these views, they help to explain the individual differences and underlying articulatory processes in speech development in both healthy children (Sussman et al. 1992, 1996, 1999 – see Figures 12.1 and 12.2 in this essay), and those with a clinical diagnosis (e.g. Sussman et al. 1998b, 2000 – see Figures 12.15 and 12.16 in this essay). They also help to explain some of the cross-linguistic similarities and differences in coarticulation patterns which have been reported for a range of languages (e.g. Sussman et al. 1993; Yeou 1997; Embarki et al. 2007 – see Figures 12.3 and 12.4 in this essay). Furthermore, through the examination of studies conducted over a period of time, it has been possible to offer plausible explanations for changes in regional dialect characterized by F2 LE functions (e.g. Yeou 1997; Embarki et al. 2007 – see Figures 12.5 and 12.6 in this essay). In addition, the examination of F2 LEs representing pharyngealized consonants in Arabic led to a possible explanation for the coarticulation patterns observed in a speaker with AOS.

This review also revealed individual differences in patterns of coarticulation observed as a function of speech style, rate and speaker adaptation. What emerged was that although speakers generally display higher slopes and higher levels of coarticulation in spontaneous speech samples, this varies across speakers and phonetic context (Krull 1989; Duez 1992 – see Figures 12.7 and 12.8 in this essay). In addition, while there is a link between vowel duration and coarticulation, the adjustments in coarticulation levels between the citation (reference speech) and spontaneous speech samples as a function of vowel duration, are not uniform across speakers (Duez 1992 – see Figure 12.9 in this essay). When coarticulation patterns were examined as function of speech tempo, although higher slopes and higher levels of coarticulation were observed (Bakran & Mildner 1995; Agwuele et al. 2008 – see Figure 12.10 in this essay), both studies revealed patterns of individual variation. There was also evidence of phonetic-specific variation in the data reported in Agwuele et al. (2008), where more notable individual differences were observed for the alveolar and velar places of articulation (see Figure 12.11). Furthermore, while speakers as a whole were able to compensate and adapt to bite blocks during a speech production task (Sussman et al. 1995), it appears that some were able to do this more successfully than others (see Figure 12.13). The ability of speakers to adapt their speech to different communicative settings is further illustrated by the findings of Baillargeon et al. (2002) (see Figure 12.14).

In summary, by drawing together a range of evidence and data from the larger body of work on F2 LEs, it has been possible to draw some conclusions about the speech production patterns in both healthy speakers and those with a clinical diagnosis across the lifespan. What this review also highlights is the value of F2 LEs as an effective research tool for the study of a range of both clinical and non-clinical speech data.

References

Agwuele, A., H.M. Sussman & B. Lindblom. (2008). The effect of speaking rate on consonant vowel coarticulation. *Phonetica,* 65(4), 194–209. http://dx.doi.org/10.1159/000192792

Baillargeon, M., A. McLeod, D.A. Metz, N. Schiavetti & R.L. Whitehead. (2002). Preservation of second formant transitions during simultaneous communication: A locus equation perspective. *Journal of Communication Disorders,* 35(1), 51–62. http://dx.doi.org/10.1016/S0021-9924(01)00066-1

Bakran, J., & V. Mildner. (1995). Effect of speech rate and coarticulation strategies on the locus equation determination. *Proceedings of the XIIIth International Congress of Phonetic Sciences, Stockholm, Sweden,* Vol. 1, pp. 26–9.

Brancazio, L., & C.A. Fowler. (1998). On the relevance of locus equations for production and perception of stop consonants. *Perception & Psychophysics,* 60(1), 24–50. http://dx.doi.org/10.3758/BF03211916

Chennoukh, S., R. Carré & B. Lindblom. (1997). Locus equations in the light of articulatory modeling. *Journal of the Acoustical Society of America,* 102(4), 2380–9.http://dx.doi.org/10.1121/1.419622

Duez, D. (1992). Second formant locus-nucleus patterns: An investigation of spontaneous French speech. *Speech Communication,* 11(4–5), 417–27. http://dx.doi.org/10.1016/0167-6393(92)90047-B

Embarki, M., M. Yeou, C. Guilleminot & S. Maqtari. (2007). An acoustic study of coarticulation in Modern Standard Arabic and Dialectal Arabic: Pharyngealised vs non-pharyngealised articulation. *Proceedings of the XVIth International Congress of Phonetic Sciences,* pp. 141–6.

Fowler, C.A. (1994). Invariants, specifiers, cues: An investigation of locus equations as information for place of articulation. *Perception & Psychophysics,* 55(6), 597–610. http://dx.doi.org/10.3758/BF03211675

Freeman, F.J., E.S. Sands & K.S. Harris. (1978). Temporal coordination of phonation and articulation in a case of verbal apraxia: A voice onset time study. *Brain and Language,* 6(1), 106–11. http://dx.doi.org/10.1016/0093-934X(78)90048-2

Fruchter, D., & H.M. Sussman. (1997). The perceptual relevance of locus equations. *Journal of the Acoustical Society of America,* 102(5), 2997–3008. http://dx.doi.org/10.1121/1.421012

Iskarous, K., C.A. Fowler & D.H. Whalen. (2010). Locus equations are an acoustic expression of articulator synergy. *Journal of the Acoustical Society of America,* 128(4), 2021–32. http://dx.doi.org/10.1121/1.3479538

Itoh, M., S. Sasanuma & T. Ushijima. (1979). Velar movements during speech in a patient with apraxia of speech. *Brain and Language*, 7(2), 227–39. http://dx.doi.org/10.1016/0093-934X(79)90019-1

Kent, R.D., & J.C. Rosenbek. (1982). Prosodic disturbance and neurologic lesion. *Brain and Language*, 15(2), 259–91. http://dx.doi.org/10.1016/0093-934X(82)90060-8

Kent, R.D., & J.C. Rosenbek. (1983). Acoustic patterns of apraxia of speech. *Journal of Speech and Hearing Research*, 26(2), 231–49. http://dx.doi.org/10.1044/jshr.2602.231

Krull, D. (1989). Second formant locus patterns and consonant-vowel coarticulation in spontaneous speech. *Perlius*, X, 87–108.

Lindblom, B. (1963). Spectrographic study of vowel reduction. *Journal of the Acoustical Society of America*, 35(11), 1773–81. http://dx.doi.org/10.1121/1.1918816

Lindblom, B., & H.M. Sussman. (2012). Dissecting coarticulation: How locus equations happen. *Journal of Phonetics*, 40(1), 1–19. http://dx.doi.org/10.1016/j.wocn.2011.09.005

Löfqvist, A. (1999). Interarticulator phasing, locus equations, and degree of coarticulation. *Journal of the Acoustical Society of America*, 106(4), 2022–30. http://dx.doi.org/10.1121/1.427948

Martínez-Celdrán, E., & X. Villalba. (1995). Locus equations as a metric for place of articulation in automatic speech recognition. *Proceedings of the XIIIth International Congress of Phonetic Sciences, Stockholm, Sweden*, Vol. 1, pp. 30–3.

Marquardt, T.P., A. Jacks & B.L. Davis. (2004). Token-to-token variability in developmental apraxia of speech: Three longitudinal case studies. *Clinical Linguistics & Phonetics*, 18(2), 127–44. http://dx.doi.org/10.1080/02699200310001615050

McCaffrey Morrison, H.A. (2008). The locus equation as an index of coarticulation in syllables produced by speakers with profound hearing loss. *Clinical Linguistics & Phonetics*, 22(9), 726–40. http://dx.doi.org/10.1080/02699200802176402

McLeod, A., M. Baillargeon, D.E. Metz, N. Schiavetti & R.L. Whitehead,. (2001). Locus equations as a source of relational invariance for stop place categorization: A direct replication of Sussman, McCaffrey, and Matthews. *Contemporary Issues in Communication Science and Disorders*, 28, 98–103.

Nearey, T.M., & S.E. Shammass. (1987). Formant transitions as partly distinctive invariant properties in the identification of voiced stops. *Canadian Acoustics*, 15, 17–24.

Nijland, L. (2003). Developmental apraxia of speech: Deficits in phonetic planning and motor programming. Doctoral thesis, University of Nijmegen & University of Utrecht, Ponsen & Looijen BV, Wageningen, The Netherlands.

Southwood, M.H., P.A. Dagenais, S.M. Sutphin & J. Mertz Garcia. (1997). Coarticulation in apraxia of speech: A perceptual, acoustic and electropalatographic study. *Clinical Linguistics & Phonetics*, 11(3), 179–203. http://dx.doi.org/10.3109/02699209708985190

Story, B.H. (2008). Comparison of magnetic resonance imaging-based vocal tract area functions obtained from the same speaker in 1994 and 2002. *Journal of the Acoustical Society of America*, 123(1), 327–35. http://dx.doi.org/10.1121/1.2805683

Sussman, H.M. (1994). The phonological reality of locus equations across manner class distinctions: Preliminary observations. *Phonetica*, 51(1–3), 119–31. http://dx.doi.org/10.1159/000261964

Sussman, H.M. (1999). A neural mapping hypothesis to explain why velar stops have an allophonic split. *Brain and Language*, 70(2), 294–304. http://dx.doi.org/10.1006/brln.1999.2182

Sussman, H.M. (2002). Representation of phonological categories: A functional role for auditory columns. *Brain and Language*, 80(1), 1–13. http://dx.doi.org/10.1006/brln.2001.2489

Sussman, H.M., C.T. Byrd & B. Guitar. (2011). The integrity of anticipatory coarticulation in fluent and non-fluent tokens of adults who stutter. *Clinical Linguistics & Phonetics*, 25(3), 169–86.http://dx.doi.org/10.3109/02699206.2010.517896

Sussman, H.M., E. Dalston & S. Gumbert. (1998a). The effect of speaking style on a locus equation characterization of stop place of articulation. *Phonetica*, 55(4), 204–25. http://dx.doi.org/10.1159/000028433

Sussman, H.M., C. Duder, E. Dalston & A. Cacciatore. (1999). An acoustic analysis of the development of CV coarticulation: A case study. *Journal of Speech, Language, and Hearing Research (JSLHR)*, 42(5), 1080–96. http://dx.doi.org/10.1044/jslhr.4205.1080

Sussman, H.M., D. Fruchter & A. Cable. (1995). Locus equations derived from compensatory articulation. *Journal of the Acoustical Society of America*, 97(5), 3112–24. http://dx.doi.org/10.1121/1.411873

Sussman, H.M., D. Fruchter, J. Hilbert & J. Sirosh. (1998b). Linear correlates in the speech signal: The orderly output constraint. *Behavioral and Brain Sciences*, 21(2), 241–99. http://dx.doi.org/10.1017/S0140525X98001174

Sussman, H.M., K.A. Hoemeke & F.S. Ahmed. (1993). A cross-linguistic investigation of locus equations as a phonetic descriptor for place of articulation. *Journal of the Acoustical Society of America*, 94(3), 1256–68. http://dx.doi.org/10.1121/1.408178

Sussman, H.M., K. Hoemeke & H.A. McCaffrey. (1992). Locus equations as an index of coarticulation for place of articulation distinctions in children. *Journal of Speech and Hearing Research*, 35(4), 769–81. http://dx.doi.org/10.1044/jshr.3504.769

Sussman, H.M., T.P. Marquardt & J. Doyle. (2000). An acoustic analysis of phonemic integrity and contrastiveness in developmental apraxia of speech. *Journal of Medical Speech-Language Pathology*, 8, 301–13.

Sussman, H.M., H.A. McCaffrey & S.A. Matthews. (1991). An investigation of locus equations as a source of relational invariance for stop place categorization. *Journal of the Acoustical Society of America*, 90(3), 1309–25. http://dx.doi.org/10.1121/1.401923

Sussman, H.M., F.D. Minifie, E.H. Buder, C. Stoel-Gammon & J. Smith. (1996). Consonant-vowel interdependencies in babbling and early words: Preliminary examination of a locus equation approach. *Journal of Speech and Hearing Research*, 39(2), 424–33.http://dx.doi.org/10.1044/jshr.3902.424

Sussman, H.M., & J. Shore. (1996). Locus equations as phonetic descriptors of consonantal place of articulation. *Perception & Psychophysics*, 58(6), 936–46.http://dx.doi.org/10.3758/BF03205495

Tabain, M. (2000). Coarticulation in CV syllables: A comparison of locus equation and EPG data. *Journal of Phonetics*, 28(2), 137–59.http://dx.doi.org/10.1006/jpho.2000.0110

Tabain, M. (2002). Voiceless consonants and locus equations: A comparison with electropalatographic data on coarticulation. *Phonetica*, 59(1), 20–37. http://dx.doi.org/10.1159/000056203

Wambaugh, J.L., J.R. Duffy, M.R. McNeil, D.A. Robin & M.A. Rogers. (2006). Treatment guidelines for acquired apraxia of speech: A synthesis and evaluation of the evidence. *Journal of Medical Speech-Language Pathology*, 14, xv–xxxiii.

Whiteside, S.P., S. Grobler, F. Windsor & R. Varley. (2010). An acoustic study of vowels and coarticulation as a function of utterance type: A case of acquired apraxia of speech. *Journal of Neurolinguistics*, 23(2), 145–61. http://dx.doi.org/10.1016/j.jneuroling.2009.12.002

Whiteside, S.P., H. Robson, F. Windsor & R. Varley. (2012). Stability in voice onset time patterns in a case of acquired apraxia of speech. *Journal of Medical Speech-Language Pathology*, 20, 17–28.

Whiteside, S.P., & E. Rixon. (2003). Speech characteristics of monozygotic twins and a same-sex sibling: An acoustic case study of coarticulation patterns in read speech. *Phonetica*, 60(4), 273–97. http://dx.doi.org/10.1159/000076377

Yanagisawa, E., L. Mambrino, J. Estill & D. Talkin. (1991). Supraglottic contributions to pitch raising: Videoendoscopic study with spectroanalysis. *Annals of Otology, Rhinology, and Laryngology*, 100(1), 19–30. http://dx.doi.org/10.1177/000348949110000104

Yeou, M. (1997). Locus equations and the degree of coarticulation of Arabic consonants. *Phonetica*, 54(3–4), 187–202. http://dx.doi.org/10.1159/000262221

Ziegler, W., & D. von Cramon. (1986a). Timing deficits in apraxia of speech. *European Archives of Psychiatry and Neurological Sciences*, 236(1), 44–9. http://dx.doi.org/10.1007/BF00641058

Ziegler, W., & D. von Cramon. (1986b). Disturbed coarticulation in apraxia of speech: Acoustic evidence. *Brain and Language*, 29(1), 34–47. http://dx.doi.org/10.1016/0093-934X(86)90032-5

13 An Investigation of Locus Equations in Cited versus Spontaneous Speech in Persian

Golnaz Modarresi Ghavami[1]

13.1 Introduction

Various studies have established that plotting onset frequencies of F2 transitions of CV sequences along the y-axis and their corresponding mid vowel frequencies on the x-axis of a scatterplot results in frequency coordinates that are tightly clustered and linearly correlated and fit by a straight regression line of the form F2-onset = $k \times$ F2-vowel + c, where k and c are slope and y-intercept respectively (Lindblom 1963; Neary & Shammass 1987; Krull 1988, 1989; Sussman 1989, 1994; Sussman et al. 1991, 1992, 1993; Sussman & Shore 1996). The frequency scatterplots thus obtained are called "locus equations" after Lindblom (1963).

It has been suggested that the slope of locus equation regression line quantifies stop place of articulation (Sussman 1989, 1991; Sussman et al. 1991, 1992, 1993) as well as the extent of CV coarticulation (Krull 1987, 1988, 1989; Fowler 1994). Figure 13.1 adapted from Krull (1988) shows extremes of CV coarticulation. The steep regression line in this figure shows cases where F2-onset frequency value is exactly the same as F2-vowel midpoint indicating maximum CV coarticulation as observed with bilabials and velars. When F2-onset frequency value remains constant despite changes in F2-vowel frequency (1600 Hz in the example below), the regression line is completely flat, indicating the absence of CV coarticulation, as indicated by alveolars/dentals.

1 Golnaz Modarresi Ghavami is a faculty member in the Department of Linguistics at Allameh Tabataba'i University, Tehran.

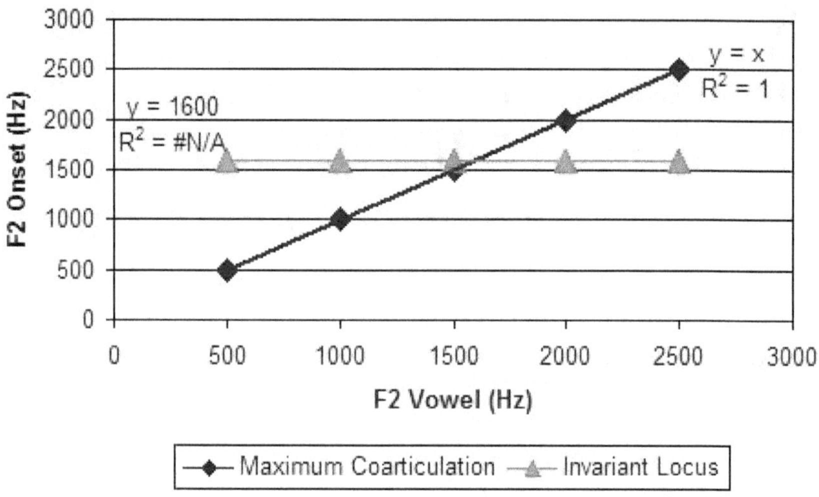

Figure 13.1. Locus equation slopes as indicators of the extent of CV coarticulation. A steep regression line indicates maximum CV coarticulation. A flat regression line indicates a lack of CV coarticulation or the existence of an invariant locus (adapted from Krull 1988).

Further investigation has shown that manipulation of production parameters can increase locus equation slope values for each place of articulation, indicating higher degrees of coarticulation under certain conditions. Krull (1989) was first to compare "laboratory speech" to a more natural, spontaneous speech. Krull's conclusion, based on the analysis of Swedish speakers was that "the slope of the regression line is always steeper for spontaneous speech, which can be interpreted as an indication of stronger coarticulation and/or more formant undershoot" (1989: 92). Krull noted that labials showed a greater slope difference across speaking style relative to coronals.

Duez (1989, 1992) performed a similar analysis on speakers of French and reached a similar conclusion in that locus equation slopes were steeper for CVs produced in spontaneous speech relative to lab speech. However, contrary to the findings of Krull (1989), Duez (1989, 1992) noted that coronals showed greater slope differences across speaking styles relative to labials.

Bakran & Mildner (1995) investigated the stability of locus equation parameters under conditions of altered speaking rates and coarticulation strategies for four Croatian speakers. They observed that slower tempo resulted in lower slopes and consequently less coarticulation compared to faster tempos.

Sussman et al. (1998) analyzed the speech of 22 speakers of American English to test the ability of locus equations to serve as a descriptor of stop place of articulation under conditions of hypo-articulated speech forms found in normal spontaneous speech relative to the citation-style "lab speech." Sussman et al. (1998) observed that locus equation slopes increased in spontaneous speaking style only for alveolars and /g/ in the context of front vowels. Slopes for labials and /g/ in the context of back vowels remained stable across style changes.

The purpose of the present essay is to investigate the effect of speaking style on CV coarticulation in Persian under conditions of hypo-speech found in normal spontaneous speech relative to citation-style "lab speech" characterized by hyper-articulation.

13.2 Method

Subjects. Two male speakers of Persian who were graduate students at the University of Texas at Austin participated in this experiment (mean age = 33). They both spoke English as a second language and one of them was also familiar with Arabic. No attempt was made to achieve dialectal homogeneity. One of the subjects came from Tehran, the capital of Iran, and the second subject originally lived in the southwest of Iran, but had lived in Tehran for approximately 15 years.

Speech material. Initially, subjects produced, with a normal speed, CVr syllables from a list written in Persian orthography within the carrier phrase "calameje Cvr rɑ tecrɑr con" ("Repeat CVr"). Initial consonants in the CVr syllables consisted of the four voiced stops of Persian /b, d, ɟ, ɢ/.[2] The stops were followed by six vowels /i, e, a, u, o, ɑ/. The final consonant was /r/ in order to maximize the number of meaningful tokens in the list. Each CVr token was repeated five times, resulting in a total of 120 utterances per subject (4 stops × 6 vowels × 5 repetitions).

Second, the subjects were asked to read a passage written in Persian orthography which contained real words beginning with bV, dV, ɟV and ɢV,

2 The Persian voiced palatal stop /ɟ/ has a front allophone and a back allophone before front and back vowels respectively as in English. But contrary to English in which the voiced velar stop has a back allophone post-vocalically, Persian has a front allophone irrespective of the preceding vowel.

where V = /i, e, a, u, o, ɑ/. The text was devised in such a way as to be as close to the conversational style as possible and the subjects were asked to read the text with a normal conversational speed. The text contained 150 words with initial voice stops. Each speaker read the text twice, resulting in 300 tokens per subject.

Measurements. The utterances read by the subjects were recorded in a soundproof room using a professional cassette recorder (Superscope 6-CD330) and a high-quality microphone (S12 Hypercardiod Neodymium). The recorded signals were digitized on a Macintosh 7100/80 at 16 bits with a 22,500 (Hz) sampling rate. F2-onset measurements were obtained from cursor readouts placed on wide-band spectrographic display. F2-vowel values were mean frequencies obtained from three sources: (i) directly from the cursor frequency readouts via mouse position placed on the wide-band spectrographic display; (ii) linear predictive coding (LPC) spectra; and (iii) fast Fourier transform (FFT) narrow-band displays. LPC spectra were calculated with 1024 points. Spectrograms were generated with 184 Hz filter setting, a frame advance of 0.1 ms, and 1024 FFT points.

Data sample points. F2-onsets (Hz) for the voiced /b, d, g, ɢ/ were measured at the first glottal pulse of the vowel after the release of the stop. F2-vowel was taken as the "target" frequency most closely corresponding to the mid-vowel nucleus location.

13.3 Results

13.3.1 Citation Style

Four scatterplots were generated for each of the four stops /b, d, ɟ, ɢ/. Each scatterplot included 60 <*x*, *y*> coordinates spanning six vowel contexts repeated five times each for each subject. Figure 13.2 shows locus equation regression functions for the four stops.

As the results indicate, the slopes for the four stop places of articulation were distinct in citation style. The palatal stop /ɟ/ had the steepest slope (mean of 1.05) followed by the uvular and bilabial stops (means of .90 and .89 respectively). The dental stop /d/ had the flattest slope (mean of .44). Thus, the slopes for the four stop place categories of bilabial, dental, palatal and uvular were distinct and varied with place of articulation, although mean slope values for the uvular stop almost overlapped with the slope for /b/. Results indicate CV coarticulation from highest to lowest along the following pattern: ɟ > ɢ, b > d.

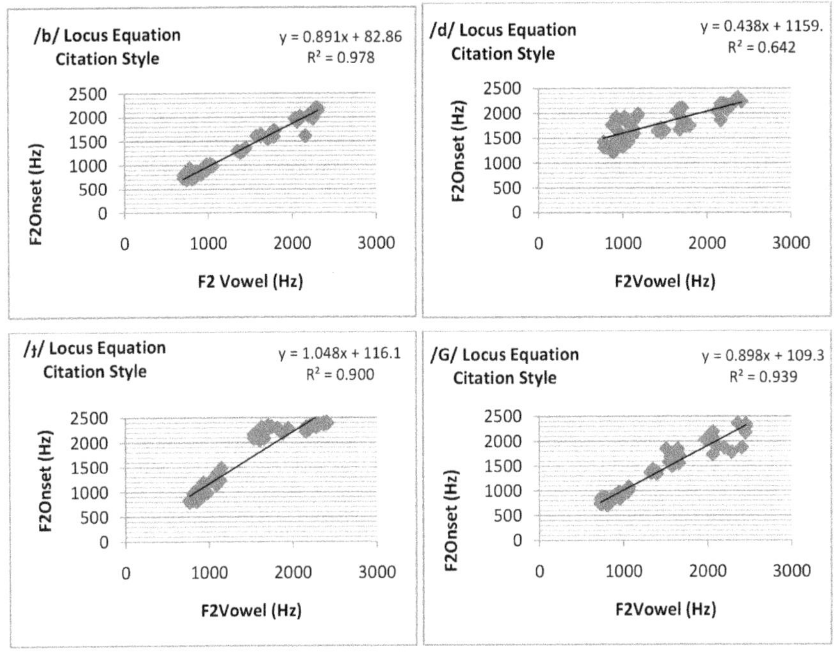

Figure 13.2. Locus equation scatterplots for voiced stop places of articulation: citation style.

Comparing the slope values for /b/, /d/ and /ɟ/ in Persian with the slope values of /b/, /d/ and /g/ in Sussman et al. (1991) and Fowler (1994) for English, it is observed that the general tendency for bilabials to have steeper slopes than dentals is replicated. Sussman et al. (1991) and Fowler (1994) observed that in English labials have the steepest slope and dentals have the flattest slope, with velars being intermediate. Data obtained from Persian voiced stops indicate that dorsals (palatals and uvulars in this case) have the steepest slopes and labials are intermediate between dorsals and coronals, replicating the results obtained for Cairene Arabic and Urdu in Sussman et al. (1993) and for Swedish in Lindblom (1963). This general observation is consistent with Sussman et al. (1993) noting that velars (i.e., dorsals) and labials have language-specific slope values.

13.3.2 Spontaneous Speaking Style

Four scatterplots were generated for each of the four stops /b, d, ɟ, ɢ/ per subject. Each scatterplot included 45–133 <*x*, *y*> coordinates spanning two

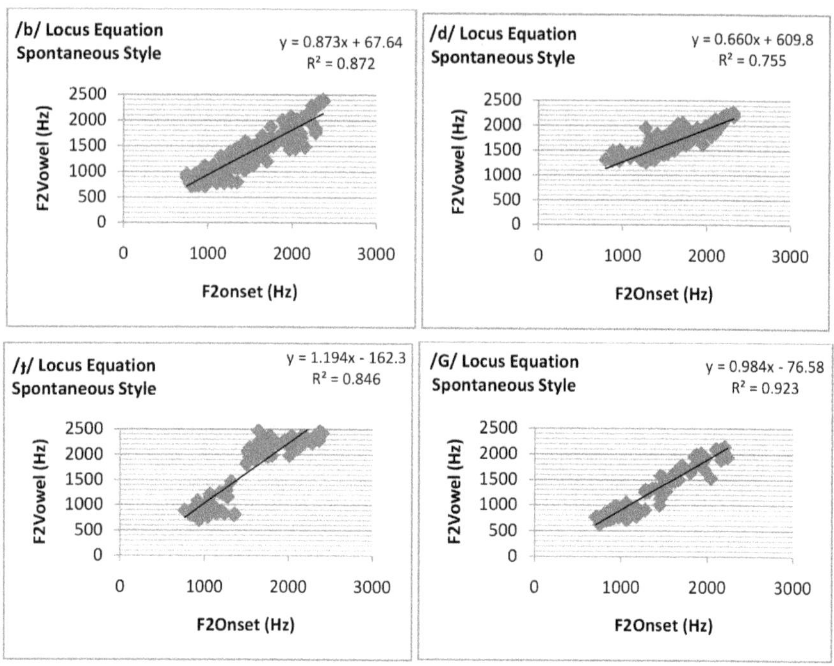

Figure 13.3. Locus equation scatterplots for voiced stop places of articulation: spontaneous style.

repetitions of the text and a different number of stop-initial tokens per text. Figure 13.3 shows locus equation regression functions for the four stops for the two subjects. It is observed that the scatterplots for the two subjects are again highly linear and that the data points in all of the scatterplots tightly cluster along the regression line.

As the above data indicate, the slope values for the four stop places are distinct. Again, the palatal stop /ɟ/ had the steepest slope (mean of 1.19) followed by the uvular stop /ɢ/ (mean of .98). The dental stop /d/ had the flattest slope (mean of .66), and the bilabial stop /b/ was intermediate between uvulars and dentals (mean of .87). Again, results indicate CV coarticulation from highest to lowest along the following pattern: ɟ > ɢ > b > d.

13.3.3 Citation versus Spontaneous Speaking Style

Figure 13.4 compares the slope values for each of the four stops for citation and spontaneous speaking style.

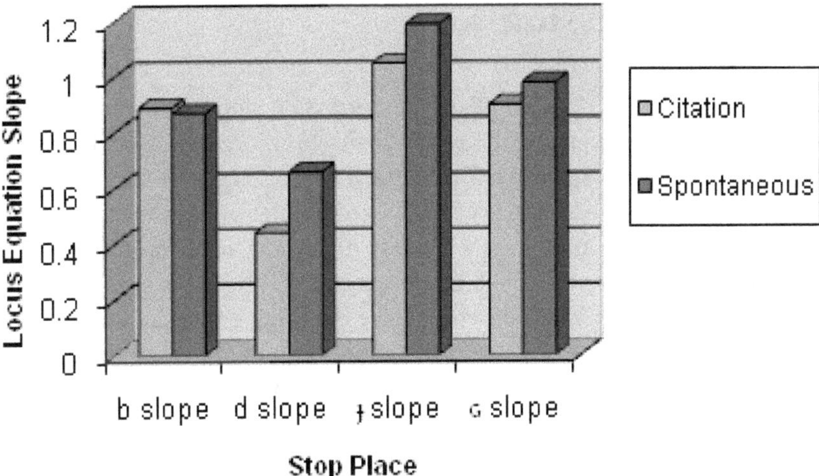

Figure 13.4. Comparison of locus equation slope values for voiced stop places of articulation in citation versus spontaneous style.

The voiced stops, /d/, /ɟ/ and /ɢ/, showed a steeper slope in spontaneous speech compared to citation style. Thus, the general tendency that the slopes of the regression lines are steeper for spontaneous speech (Krull 1989; Duez 1989, 1992; Bakran & Mildner 1995) was replicated. The observation made by Duez (1989, 1992) was also replicated in that coronals showed greater slope differences across speaking styles relative to other places of articulation.

The slope for /b/ remained stable across style changes. This pattern is consistent with the findings in Sussman et al. (1998) in which the slope for /b/ remained stable across style changes. There the postulation was that "...when there is 'room' for increased coarticulatory overlap, spontaneous speech elicits such changes. When coarticulatory overlap is already at near maximum levels – labials and [g] velars – no slope changes occur" (1998: 10). Contrary to this statement, coarticulatory overlap in Persian increased more for dorsals in spontaneous style versus citation style, indicating a greater degree of coarticulation under conditions of hypo-articulation for this place of articulation.

13.4 Discussion

According to Krull (1988, 1989), flatter regression slopes indicate relatively more invariant consonantal locus, as F2-onset is more stable and less influenced by the following vowel. This pattern is observed with dentals/alveolars. Steeper slopes indicate greater CV coarticulation, as the consonantal locus varies directly and linearly with the upcoming vowel target, a pattern observed with velars and bilabials. Fowler (1994) explains these patterns by stating that since labials do not involve the tongue body as a main articulator; the tongue is free to coarticulate with the vowel. For dentals, the tongue is the main articulator for both the consonant and the vowel; thus, the consonant can resist vowel-induced coarticulation. Fowler's explanation for the steep slope of /g/ in English is that, since English does not have a velar/uvular contrast, /g/ can permit more vowel coarticulation, although it is articulated with the tongue. Considering Fowler's argument, we would expect /ɟ/ and /ɢ/, in a language such as Persian that has a palatal/uvular contrast, to permit less vowel coarticulation and consequently to have relatively flatter slopes for these places of articulation. Contrary to this expectation, /ɟ/ and /ɢ/ showed the steepest slopes in both citation and spontaneous speaking styles.

Since in all of the studies conducted so far on locus equations, dentals/alveolars have shown the flattest slopes, it seems that the involvement of the "tongue tip/blade" rather than the "tongue body" in the production of a consonant may have to do with their lower degree of coarticulation with a following vowel. This is consistent with the explanation provided by Iskarous et al. (2010). There, the contention is that the tip of the tongue cannot move without the help or *synergy* of other organs. The tongue body has to move forward and upwards to make the dental/alveolar contact possible and this causes a delay in the vowel initiation, resulting in lower degrees of coarticulation. However, when the "tongue body" is the shared articulator of stop consonants and vowels, as with dorsal consonants, CV coarticulation is at its highest and increases even more in hypo-articulated speech.

References

Bakran, J., & V. Mildner. (1995). Effect of speech and coarticulation strategies on the locus equation determination. *Proceedings of the XIIIth International Congress of Phonetic Sciences, Stockholm*, Vol. I, pp. 26–9.

Duez, D. (1989). Second formant locus-nucleus patterns in spontaneous speech: Some preliminary results on French. *Phonetic Experimental Research at the Institute of Linguistics, University of Stockholm (PERILUS)*, X, 109–14.

Duez, D. (1992). Second-formant locus-nucleus patterns: An investigation of spontaneous French speech. *Speech Communication*, 11(4–5), 417–27. http://dx.doi.org/10.1016/0167-6393(92)90047-B

Fowler, C.A. (1994). Invariants, specifiers, cues: An investigation of locus equations as information for place of articulation. *Perception & Psychophysics*, 55(6), 597–610. http://dx.doi.org/10.3758/BF03211675

Iskarous, K., C.A. Fowler & D.H. Whalen. (2010). Locus equations are an acoustic expression of articulator synergy. *Journal of the Acoustical Society of America*, 128(4), 2021–32. http://dx.doi.org/10.1121/1.3479538

Krull, D. (1987). Second formant locus patterns as a measure of consonant-vowel coarticulation. *Phonetic Experimental Research at the Institute of Linguistics, University of Stockholm (PERILUS)*, V, 43–61.

Krull, D. (1988). Acoustic properties as predictors of perceptual responses: A study of Swedish voiced stops. *Phonetic Experimental Research at the Institute of Linguistics, University of Stockholm (PERILUS)*, VII, 66–70.

Krull, D. (1989). Second formant locus patterns and consonant-vowel coarticulation in spontaneous speech. *Phonetic Experimental Research at the Institute of Linguistics, University of Stockholm (PERILUS)*, X, 87–108.

Lindblom, B. (1963). On vowel reduction. In *Report #29, The Royal Institute Of Technology*. Stockholm: Speech Transmission Laboratory.

Neary, T.M., & S.E. Shammass. (1987). Formant transitions as partly distinctive invariant properties in the identification of voiced stops. *Canadian Acoustics*, 15, 17–24.

Sussman, H.M. (1989). Neural coding of relational invariance in speech: Human language analogs to the barn owl. *Psychological Review*, 96(4), 631–42. http://dx.doi.org/10.1037/0033-295X.96.4.631

Sussman, H.M. (1991). The representation of stop consonants in three dimensional acoustic space. *Phonetica*, 48(1), 18–31. http://dx.doi.org/10.1159/000261869

Sussman, H.M. (1994). The phonological reality of locus equations across manner class distinctions: Preliminary observations. *Phonetica*, 51(1–3), 119–31. http://dx.doi.org/10.1159/000261964

Sussman, H.M., E. Dalston & S. Gumbert. (1998). The effect of speaking style on a locus equation characterization of stop place of articulation. *Phonetica*, 55(4), 204–25. http://dx.doi.org/10.1159/000028433

Sussman, H.M., K. Hoemeke & F. Ahmed. (1993). A cross-linguistic investigation of locus equations as a phonetic descriptor for place of articulation.

Journal of the Acoustical Society of America, 94(3), 1256–68. http://dx.doi.org/10.1121/1.408178

Sussman, H.M., K. Hoemeke & H.A. McCaffrey. (1992). Locus equations as an index of coarticulation for place of articulation distinction in children. *Journal of Speech and Hearing Research*, 35(4), 769–81. http://dx.doi.org/10.1044/jshr.3504.769

Sussman, H.M., H.A. McCaffrey & S.A. Matthews. (1991). An investigation of locus equations as a source of relational invariance for stop place categorization. *Journal of the Acoustical Society of America*, 90(3), 1309–25. http://dx.doi.org/10.1121/1.401923

Sussman, H.M., & J. Shore. (1996). Locus equations as phonetic descriptor of consonantal place of articulation. *Perception & Psychophysics*, 58(6), 936–46. http://dx.doi.org/10.3758/BF03205495

14
A Functional Role for Coarticulation: A Locus Equation Perspective

Harvey M. Sussman[1]

14.1 Introduction

Coarticulation is an inherent characteristic of speech production. Different articulators take care of their specific kinematic responsibilities concurrently, and these independently motivated gestures often induce interactive biomechanical effects. Contextual influences on coproduced speech gestures have been studied from both directions (left-to-right or carryover and right-to-left or anticipatory) and across all major articulators (Hardcastle & Hewlett 1999). The functional role of coarticulation, however, remains controversial. From a motor gestural perspective, coarticulation has historically been viewed as the causal source of the "mapping problem," and the underlying culprit responsible for the "non-invariance" dilemma, two unresolved theoretical issues that continue to plague speech research. The former refers to how (or if) a continuous speech waveform can be mapped onto a series of discrete abstract/symbolic mental representations; the latter relates to the fact that perception of a stop consonant is invariant despite acoustic variability of the signal when the stop is produced with different vowel contexts. Thus, from the very outset, coarticulation was viewed as a disruptive process. For example, it was responsible, in a well known speech analogy, for smashing uniquely decorated and serially ordered Easter eggs, each representing a context-free and hence invariant neural unit of production, into a gooey mess of broken bits of

1 Harvey M. Sussman is a professor in the Department of Linguistics and the Department of Communication Sciences and Disorders at the University of Texas at Austin.

shells, oozing yolks and amorphous albumen (Hockett 1955). The message in this metaphor was that invariance seekers faced a daunting task in trying to recover the supposedly invariant units of production from a hopelessly obfuscated speech output signal. Coarticulation scrambled those context-free eggs. The neural "eggs" remain elusive, and many theorists have abandoned the very concept and the experimental need to even search for them (e.g., Studdert-Kennedy 2005).

14.2 Motor Theory Account of Coarticulation

Perhaps the first explanation for the very existence of coarticulation came from the authors of the motor theory of speech perception:

> ... the motor theory begins with the assumption that coarticulation, and the resulting overlap of phonetic information in the acoustic pattern, is a consequence of the efficient processes by which discrete phonetic gestures are realized in the behavior of more or less independent articulators. (Liberman & Mattingly 1985: 14)

The "economy of transmission" view persisted:

> ... the overlapping of articulatory gestures in speech makes possible parallel, hence rapid, transmission of information. (Mattingly 1998: 276)

Thus, according to this perspective, signal transparency was sacrificed to overcome the temporal resolving limitations of the human ear. To achieve the rapid rate of segments/sec that fast intelligible speech requires, the acoustic signal must somehow encode multiple phonetic segments onto a single portion of a sound. Not a bad trade – two phonetic segments, a stop consonant plus a vowel, encoded in parallel, riding on the same acoustic pattern, the highly variable F2 transition. The only thing lost was the isomorphism between the physical signal and the abstract notion of the segment.

The goal of this article is to argue for a more meaningful functional role for coarticulation in the production and eventual perception of stop consonants. Succinctly stated, that role is maximization of the acoustic contrastiveness of stop place categories. The irony (and importance) of this claim is that the very phonetic segments (stop consonants) that put context-induced variability on the phonetic map, and by so doing, spawned the motor theory/direct realist/gesturalist frameworks, can actually provide a compelling case for an acoustic-based path to speech perception, and in so doing, provide a more meaningful functional role for coarticulation in the production of stop consonants.

A core concept shared by all offshoots of motor theory-based views is that since vowel context-induced coarticulation in stop + vowel utterances shapes the direction and extent of F2 transitions, the resulting signal variability *precludes* an acoustic-based account of phonetic categorization, and hence perception. Schematics of two-formant pattern playback stimuli revealing opposite directions of the F2 transitions signaling [di] versus [du] have long been the "poster tokens" negating a direct auditory path to perception:

> Putting together all the generalizations about the multiplicity and variety of acoustic cues, we should conclude that there is simply no way to define a phonetic category in purely acoustic terms. For if phonetic categories were acoustic patterns, and if, accordingly, phonetic perceptions were properly auditory, one should be able to describe quite straight-forwardly the acoustic basis for the phonetic category and its associated percept. (Liberman & Mattingly 1985: 12)

The arguments to be presented below will attempt to show that coarticulation actually *provides* the articulatory means to generate the auditory path to perception, rather than the contrary argument that it *obscures* and thus negates this path.

14.3 Characteristics of Coarticulation across Articulators

There are several basic issues that first need to be discussed. First, anticipatory coarticulation varies as a function of the specific articulatory system under analysis, as different kinematic properties apply across articulators. Some articulators operate as a valve (e.g., the velum), with basically a binary "closed-open" movement path; some are more sphincter-like in their actions (e.g., the lips), encompassing a protrusion-to-spread movement range. Coarticulatory studies of these two articulators make up much of the coarticulation literature (Hardcastle & Hewlett 1999). The velum and lips operate independently of the tongue, are easier to transduce and capture the acoustic results of their actions – the presence of nasal resonances and lowering of vowel formant frequencies due to lip rounding.

In addition to the primarily binary (as opposed to graded) nature of their movements, the dependent variable indexing velar lowering for upcoming nasals and lip rounding for rounded vowels is the *temporal extent of the "look ahead" anticipatory interval, not the degree of coarticulation per se.* For example, the anticipatory extent of lip rounding in producing the word [*shoe*] is quite short (10s of milliseconds) relative to the across word boundary interval of lip rounding in the French phrase [*une sinister structure*] (100s of milliseconds). In these instances, lip rounding is initiated and maintained over different time spans, but the extent of actual protrusion of the lips in distance is no different in either case. Similarly, anticipatory coarticulation of nasality is dependent on contextual parameters that will either allow (e.g., vowels) or preclude (e.g., fricatives) lowering of the velum prior to an /m, n/ segment. In sum, the coarticulating velum and lips do not adopt intermediate positions along a finely graded spatial continuum.

Stop consonants present an entirely different coarticulation scenario. A stop occlusion at the lips, at the alveolar ridge or along the hard palate, and subsequent release/movement toward a vowel target position, provides uniquely different biomechanical constraints for the tongue tip, blade/dorsum and root. These interactive biomechanical constraints between functionally distinct parts of the tongue create coarticulatory dynamics varying in the *extent of overlap* between tongue contours for the stop relative to the upcoming vowel. In lingual-based coarticulation the CV unit is produced as one gesture, thus the dependent variable is based on indexing articulatory overlap, not time-based events.

By virtue of operating along a graded, rather than binary, continuum, subtle differences in tongue configurational overlap between stop and vowel gestures generate sufficient variation across stop place categories to create contrastively distinctive acoustic signals. Thus, with stop consonants, the appropriate level of phonetic structure to best observe categorical orderliness in the speech signal is not to be found at the level of the single CV token, but rather higher up, in the stop place categories. These phonetic equivalence classes, by virtue of acoustic-based commonalities, shaped by differing degrees of coarticulation, effectively "absorb" the acoustic variability characterizing their allophonic members (Sussman et al. 1998; Sussman 2002).

14.4 Locus Equations

The paradigm that is best suited to quantitatively index the degree of coarticulation, hence overlap, underlying the production of labial, alveolar and velar stops across a varied vowel inventory is locus equations (LEs). Experimental results of LE studies over the past several decades collectively suggest that coarticulation is actually serving in the best interests of perception, or at minimum, to enhance an orderly and lawful category-based structure to allow neural mapping of stop place categories.

The next section will describe how LEs are derived and how they index the coarticulatory differences underlying stop consonant + vowel production. LEs were originally derived by Lindblom (1963). They are linear regressions of the frequency of the F2 transition sampled at its onset, on the frequency of F2 when measured in the vowel nucleus. These frequency values are plotted for a single consonant produced with a wide range of following vowels. F2-onsets are plotted along the *y*-axis and F2-midpoints along the *x*-axis. For a given stop place category, e.g. [dV] as in "*deet, dit, debt, date, dat, dot, dut, doot, daught, dote*," data coordinates have been consistently shown to tightly cluster along a positively correlated distribution. This scatterplot is fit with a linear regression line, the "locus equation," of the form F2-onset = $k \times$ F2-vowel + c, where k and c are constants, slope and *y*-intercept.

Lindblom derived LEs for one Swedish speaker producing words with syllable initial voiced stops preceding seven Swedish vowels. Slope coefficients were .69, .28 and .95 for /b/, /d/ and /g/ respectively. This was the first recognition that LE slopes vary as a function of stop place of articulation. Lindblom's work only appeared in an in-house Stockholm University publication, and the linear scatterplots were regarded as an unusual but intriguing "unidentified phonetic object." They were then ignored by phoneticians for over two decades.

Nearey and Shammass (1987), unaware of Lindblom's earlier work, independently derived LEs, using $<x, y>$ coordinates defined by F2-onsets measured at the first glottal pulse, and a vowel frequency measured at a fixed 60 ms post-release. Ten speakers were analyzed producing /CVd/ syllables, where C = /b, d, g/ preceding 11 medial vowels. Describing the resulting regression lines, the authors concluded: "the slopes and intercepts for the three consonants are distinct and thus represent partly distinctive invariant properties" (p. 17).

The locus equation paradigm has been investigated and expanded in scope by Sussman and colleagues over the past two decades (Sussman

1989, 2002; Sussman et al. 1991, 1993, 1995, 1997, 1998, 1999; Fruchter & Sussman 1997; Lindblom & Sussman 2012). Figure 14.1 illustrates a representative LE scatterplot for 10 [dVt] productions. This plot will be used to summarize the important characteristics of LEs.

The slope of this [dVt] plot is .39, the *y*-intercept is 1217 Hz, and the percentage of total variance accounted for is 92 per cent. The data coordinates can be seen to tightly cluster around the regression line. Interestingly, the five data coordinates plotting *di* productions and five *du* productions (deet and doot), popularized by motor theorists to illustrate the hopelessness of decoding the speech signal via the acoustic waveform, now appear as two distinct data clusters located in acoustic space on the same linear path as all [d] + vowel tokens.

To further drive home the "absorption of variability" phenomenon that is automatically incorporated in a LE scatterplot, schematics illustrating vowel-specific F2 transitions are shown alongside the scatterplot. Steeply rising F2 transitions are placed near front vowel productions (e.g., /i/), and steeply falling F2 transitions are near low back vowels (e.g., /a/). Despite

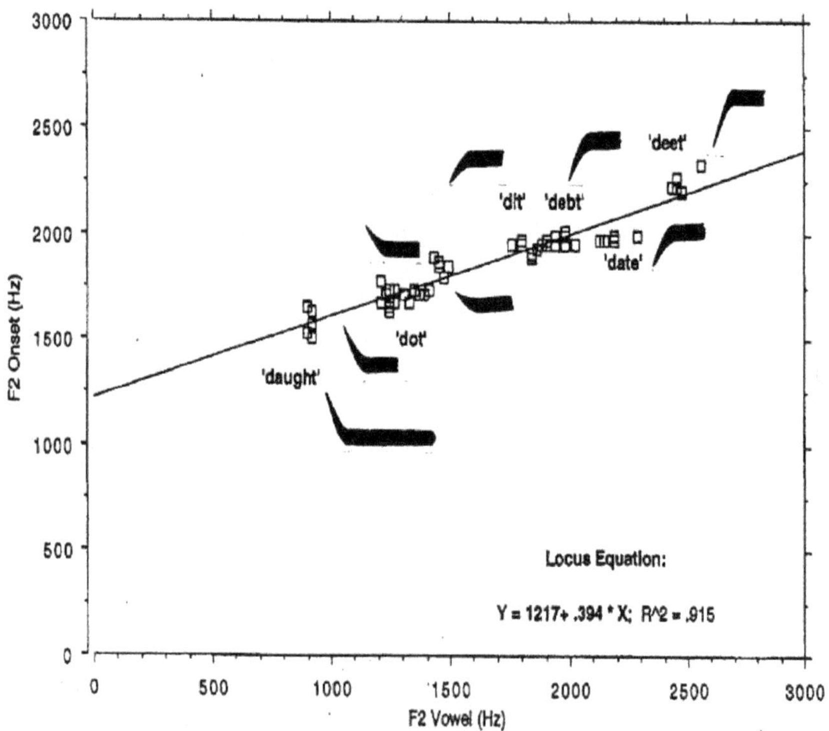

Figure 14.1. Representative LE scatterplot for 10 [dVt] productions.

being characterized by 10 uniquely different F2 transitions, when plotted as a LE, the 10 vowels align themselves in an orderly and lawful linear distribution through F2 transition acoustic space. In more formal terminology, the locus equation scatterplot reveals a self-organizing normalization of the vowel-context induced variability of the F2 transition. The ubiquitous variability of the F2 transition due to vowel contexts has somehow disappeared.

At the higher level of the phonetic category, the <*x*, *y*> coordinates indexing the onset and offset of the varied F2 transitions have now become extremely orderly, and surprisingly, extremely linear. No post hoc normalization algorithm was applied to the speech signal, but rather this is how the allophonic variants of stop + vowel sequences pattern themselves when spoken – it comes for free when we speak. The linearity and contrastive slope values of LEs as a function of stop place have been replicated in every language studied and thus represent a true linguistic universal (Sussman et al. 1993).

There are two options for interpreting LEs – they are either viewed as an intriguing, but unexplainable, phonetic epiphenomenon, or they represent a category-level equivalence class, strongly suggestive of a purposeful coding algorithm. The remainder of the article will attempt to support arguments for the latter option.

14.5 The Locus Equation Slope as an Index of Coarticulation

An important issue to resolve in support of the claim that coarticulation plays a functionally significant role in the contrastive decoding of stop place distinctions is to understand how LE slopes are shaped by coarticulation. If the role of coarticulation was to simply resolve a temporal processing limitation, as claimed by motor theorists, then LE slopes need not change across stop place. The "two-for-one" trade-off (two segments riding on one acoustic cue) is still maintained across stop place, irrespective of what stop consonant is being produced. So, the question becomes: why does coarticulation change in its extent as a function of stop place, and what would happen if it didn't?

Krull (1988), a Swedish colleague of Lindblom, was the first to illustrate how the LE slope numerically captured the extent to which the upcoming vowel affected the frequency onset of the stop/F2 transition. The LE slope hypothetically varies between the extreme values of $k = 0$ and $k = 1.0$. When LE data coordinates exhibit a flat scatterplot, with low slope values (.10, .20, .30), the vowel contexts are not exerting a strong overlapping influence on the position of the stop occlusion/release, and hence F2-onsets vary only to a small extent across vowel contexts, resulting in low slope values. Steeper slopes indicate increasing extents of anticipatory coarticulation as vowel contexts strongly influence stop occlusion placements (think of tongue closure positions for "*geese*" vs "*goose*"). Hypothetically, maximum coarticulation is when $k = 1.0$, as the vowel context directly determines F2-onsets, and the LE plot appears as a 45 degree diagonal.

The validity of the claim that LE slopes serve as an index of anticipatory CV coarticulation has been questioned by researchers who failed in their experimental attempts to correlate specific kinematic movements, illustrating various degrees of coarticulation, with resultant LE slope values (Löfqvist 1999; Tabian 2000, 2002). Strongly supportive results were reported in a variety of studies using computer simulations modeling degree of anticipatory coarticulation (Chennoukh et al. 1997; Lindblom 1998). Most recently, Lindblom and Sussman (2012), using a Principal Component Analysis of tongue movement contours obtained from X-ray films, were able to model different extents of overlap of vowel-shaped tongue contours onto derived stop target tongue contours at the moment of stop release. Subsequent synthesizing of the resultant speech signals and the derivation of LEs with six vowel contexts, produced realistic LE slope values for each stop place category. As the overlap extent systematically increased from 25 to 50 to 75 per cent, the LE slopes similarly increased.

Thus, when the experimental playing fields are equated, a variety of area function models, that simulate different degrees of coarticulatory CV overlap, have all successfully shown that LE slopes accurately capture changes in degree of vowel overlap onto stop consonantal target shapes at release. The validity of the claim that LE slopes index degree of coarticulation is no longer in dispute.

14.6 Higher-Order Locus Equation Space

Figure 14.2 shows the LE slopes/*y*-intercepts for the 20 speakers (10 male, 10 female) analyzed in Sussman et al. (1991). Three distinct clusters are evident, representing labial (diamonds), alveolar (squares) and velar (triangles) stop place categories. While there is considerable across-speaker variability in slope/*y*-intercepts within each stop place cluster, the three stops occupy non-overlapping locations in this higher-order and derived acoustic space. Discriminant analysis procedures, using slope and *y*-intercepts as predictor variables, have revealed 100 per cent correct classification rates of stop place categories. Celdran & Villalba (1995) replicated the discriminant analysis results of Sussman et al. (1991) for Spanish speakers, and also obtained 100 per cent correct classification of stop place categories for both voiced and voiceless stops.

The take-home messages from these LE studies are multiple: (1) the LE slope, which indexes degree of CV coarticulation, is a statistically powerful phonetic marker of stop place categories; (2) acoustic-based orderliness across [bV, dV, gV] utterances first emerges when their collective F2 transition onsets/offsets are displayed at the level of the category; (3) the contrastive equivalence classes must possess an articulatory/acoustic commonality across the allophonic variants comprising each category. Ironically, this long-sought commonality within stop place categories might very well be the lawful acoustic shaping of F2 transitions as produced by "tweaking" CV

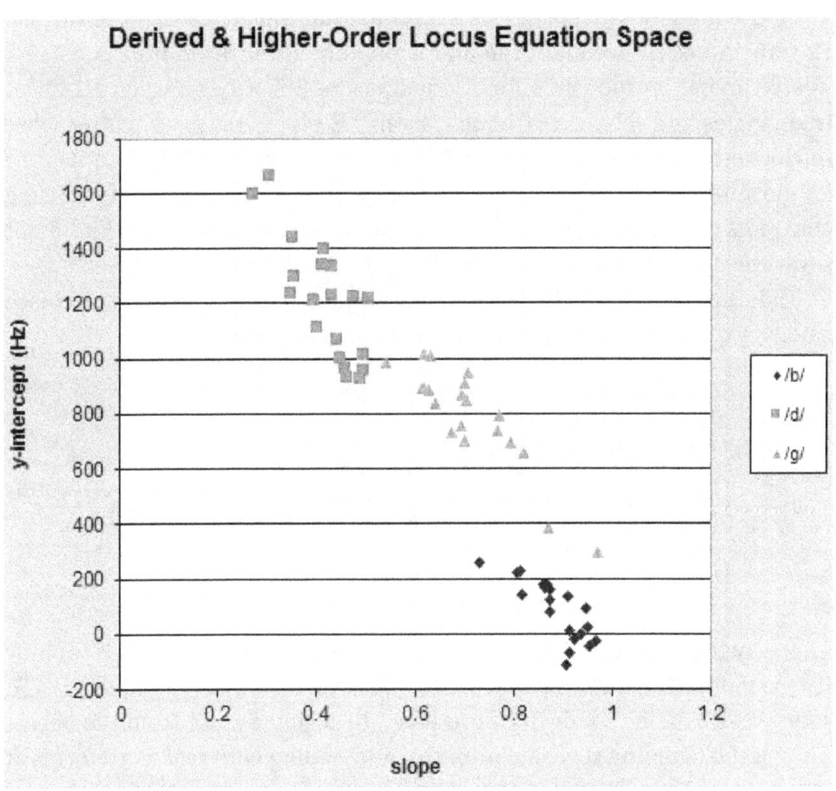

Figure 14.2. LE slopes/*y*-intercepts for the 20 speakers.

coarticulatory extents as a function of stop place category. There appears to be a prescribed range of anticipatory coarticulation per stop place category, with well established tolerance limits for speaker-specific variations within each category.

14.7 Accounting for the Linearity of LEs

One key issue to resolve was uncovering the source of why LE scatterplots were so linear. The articulatory-to-acoustic transform has always been considered a non-linear function (Stevens 1972). Iskarous et al. (2010), working with kinematic-based data (electromagnetic midsagittal articulography), reported high degrees of correlation between the horizontal position of the tongue body at consonant release in relation to tongue body position at mid-vowel time points. Their linear regression plots suggested lingual-based articulatory synergy as underlying the linearity of LEs.

Lindblom & Sussman (2012), examining the time course of the various F2 transitions, showed that the uniformity of F2 transition time constants was ultimately responsible for producing the linearity between F2-onset frequencies and F2-vowel frequencies in LE plots. Thus, no matter what the locus-to-target distance, the F2 transition reaches a fixed percentage of its movement path in the same amount of time. When non-uniform time constants were simulated to form F2 trajectories, the simulated LEs did not show the characteristic linearity of normally produced LEs.

The next section will show how degree of coarticulation and stop place category distinctions longitudinally develop in a young child.

14.8 The Development of CV Coarticulation: Babbling to First Words

One way to assess the functional role of coarticulation is to ascertain how it develops with language acquisition. Sussman et al. (1999) analyzed CV sequences, where C = /b-d-g/, produced by a single child from the beginning of the babbling stage at 7 months, and ending with real word forms at 40 months. The objective was to provide an empirically based account of the developmental progression of CV coarticulation from infancy to first words. From 7 to 16 months the child's babbling and spoken output was recorded in weekly 1-hour sessions; after 16 months recordings were made monthly, ending at 3 years of age.

Initially, three experienced transcribers located all CV utterances that could be broadly transcribed as having an initial obstruent sounding like a [b], [d] or [g], followed by a vocalic-like sound. Following this initial screening, two investigators then located each transcribed CV and displayed the waveform and its spectrogram. To be included in the analysis both investigators had to agree on the identification of the stop as either /b/, /d/ or /g/ as originally transcribed. Lack of agreement led to the removal of the token from the data corpus. The total number of CV sequences analyzed as babbles, spanning 7–19 months, were 2578 (1248 transcribed as /bV/, 819 as /dV/ and 511 as /gV/). The total number of first words analyzed, transcribed as beginning with stop-like sounds (spanning 11–40 months) was 5310. Of these, 1855 were initial /bV/, 2417 were /dV/ and 1038 were /gV/ sequences. Speech samples were considered to be words if they reasonably matched an adult model and were stable over repeated attempts (Vihman 1993). LE scatterplots were separately derived for each stop place from samples measured each month. LE slopes derived from babbling utterances and early first words overlapped for a period of 5–6 months.

14.9 Labials

LE slopes for labial + vowel utterances revealed an interesting developmental pattern. As a benchmark, consider normal adult labial slopes to vary between .73 and .97, with a mean = .90 (from Sussman et al. 1991). There is a high degree of CV anticipatory coarticulation for labial productions as the tongue is already in vocalic position during the labial occlusion. Interestingly, the initial four months of babbling (7–10 months) revealed slope values that were considerably below adult norms – .45, .41, .34 and .30. These slopes derived from pre-linguistic babbling utterances are in the range of adult *alveolar* CV productions, and far lower than typical labial values. Obviously the infant is producing random gestures by simply opening and closing her mouth with her tongue at rest in a "neutral" position. Interesting changes occurred by 13, 14 and 16 months as LE slopes approached .80. Similarly, LE slopes derived from early first words started out at a slope of .60 at 12 months and fluctuated between .65 and .85 from 16 months to 40 months, now close to adult norms. Thus, the child began production of labial + vowel sequences with minimal anticipatory tongue positioning for the upcoming vowel. This is not surprising for pre-linguistic babbling utterances. It is interesting that later babbling (13–16 months) was closer to labial slopes derived from early first words, and beginning with the end of year two, slope values remained fairly steady and close to adult norms. Thus, the child "learned" that while her lips were together for the occlusion phase of the /b/, her tongue could be more nearly positioned for the upcoming vowel. Once the motoric independence between closure of the lips for /b/ and positioning of the tongue for the vowel was established, that coarticulatory interaction remained stable, and relatively high LE slopes, comparable to adult values, were seen throughout the remaining analysis period.

14.10 Alveolars

The mean adult LE slope for [dV] sequences in Sussman et al. (1991) was .41, with a range of .27 to .50. Babbling tokens transcribed as [dV] sequences had a LE slope of .86 in months 7–8. Slope values started to decrease thereafter – .72, .62, .61, .48, .40 – and steadily declined to closely approach adult norms by 12 months. Interestingly, for much of the second and third years, her alveolar slopes were actually lower than the adult norm and fluctuated primarily between .20 and .35.

Thus, in the case of alveolars the child learned how to achieve a degree of articulatory differentiation between the tongue tip/blade position for the occlusion phase, and the tongue body configuration for the vocalic portion. By the end of the first year, alveolar productions were already yielding the lowest slopes and the least degree of CV coarticulation across the three stop places. Comparing labials to alveolars, it can be seen that in the former the child learned how to "tweak up" the degree of CV anticipatory coarticulation, and for the latter learned how to "tweak down" coarticulation.

14.11 Velars

The mean adult LE slope for [gV] sequences in Sussman et al. (1991) was .75, with a range of .54 to .97. Velar slopes in phonologically mature speakers show two allophonic clusters – [g] preceding front vowels (e.g., "geese") and [g] preceding back vowels (e.g., "goose"). In our infant analyses a single line was fit through all data points, as no allophonic clustering was observed in her spoken output. Velar slopes were highly variable during the babbling stage, and typically exceeded the adult norm. Word productions with initial [gV], however, starting at 11 months, yielded LE slopes only slightly exceeding normal adult values and remained stable at these values throughout the sampling period up to 40 months. Since the C and V are both produced by the body of the tongue in velars, their realization can be characterized as the upcoming vowel "dragging" the tongue to various closure positions either forward or backward. Thus, phonological maturity for velars was very dependent on establishing a varied front-back vowel space.

By empirically observing well-patterned divergences among stop place locus equation slopes over the first three years of babbling/speech productions in a single child, it seems reasonable to conclude that changes in degree of coarticulation paralleled the attainment of phonological maturity in acquiring the three stop place categories. Together with the divergences of LE slopes as a function of stop place categories, there was also a notable progression of increasing "tightness" and linearity to all the /b-d-g/ scatterplots. Standard error of estimates steadily lowered from early babbling CV utterances to second and third year first words containing initial CV sequences.

14.12 Locus Equations in Children with Developmental Apraxia of Speech

Developmental apraxia of speech (DAS) is an enigmatic speech/language disorder with suspected rather than documented neurological causes. It is commonly described as an inability to carry out coordinative movements of speech articulators in the absence of impaired neuromuscular function. This definition, however, obscures the fact that deficits have been uncovered in input, organizational and output processes underlying speech/language behavior (Shriberg et al. 1997).

Sussman et al. (2000) employed LEs to assess the acoustic integrity of stop + vowel utterances in children diagnosed with DAS ($N = 5$) relative to age-matched typically developing children ($N = 5$). Figure 14.3 presents representative examples of LE plots for imitated [bV, dV, gV] productions. Speech output from a typically developing child is shown in the left column relative to a child diagnosed with DAS in the right column. The typically developing child produced LEs with relatively tight linear clustering of data

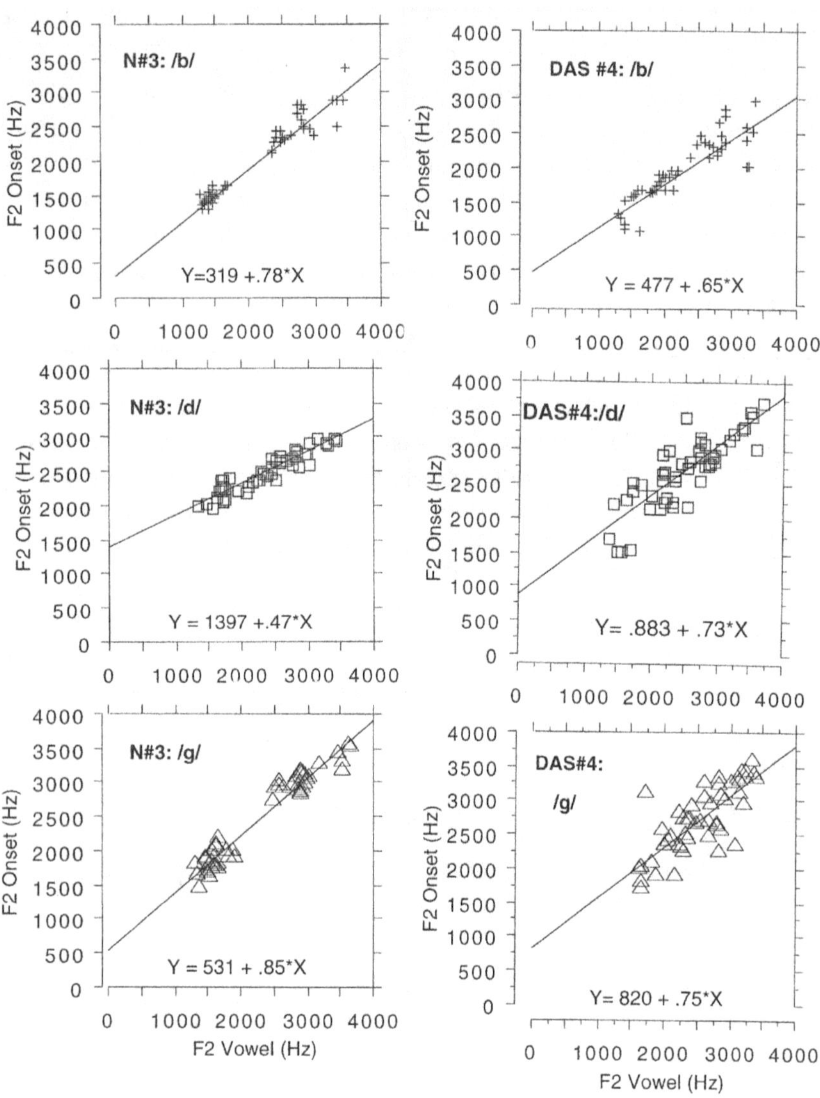

Figure 14.3. Representative examples of LE plots for imitated [bV, dV, gV] productions.

points for all three stops and contrastive slopes/y-intercepts. The mean *R*-squared value across the five normal speakers was .913. Compare these scatterplots to those of the DAS child. Standard error of estimates exceeded 250 Hz for the alveolar and velar plots in the DAS child, as the benchmark linear clustering is clearly absent. In addition, and more importantly, slope values for the three stop places are not divergent, but rather closely approximate each other.

To illustrate the contrastive distances in stop productions in LE space for the two groups, Euclidean distance plots were derived from the slope × (normalized) *y*-intercept values of each set of LE plots, and group means are shown in Figure 14.4. Euclidean distance lines were calculated between each stop pair and each leg of the triangle was added to yield a summary perimeter distance. For the typically developing group the [b-d-g] Euclidean distance was 1.63499. This distribution of stop place coordinates is very

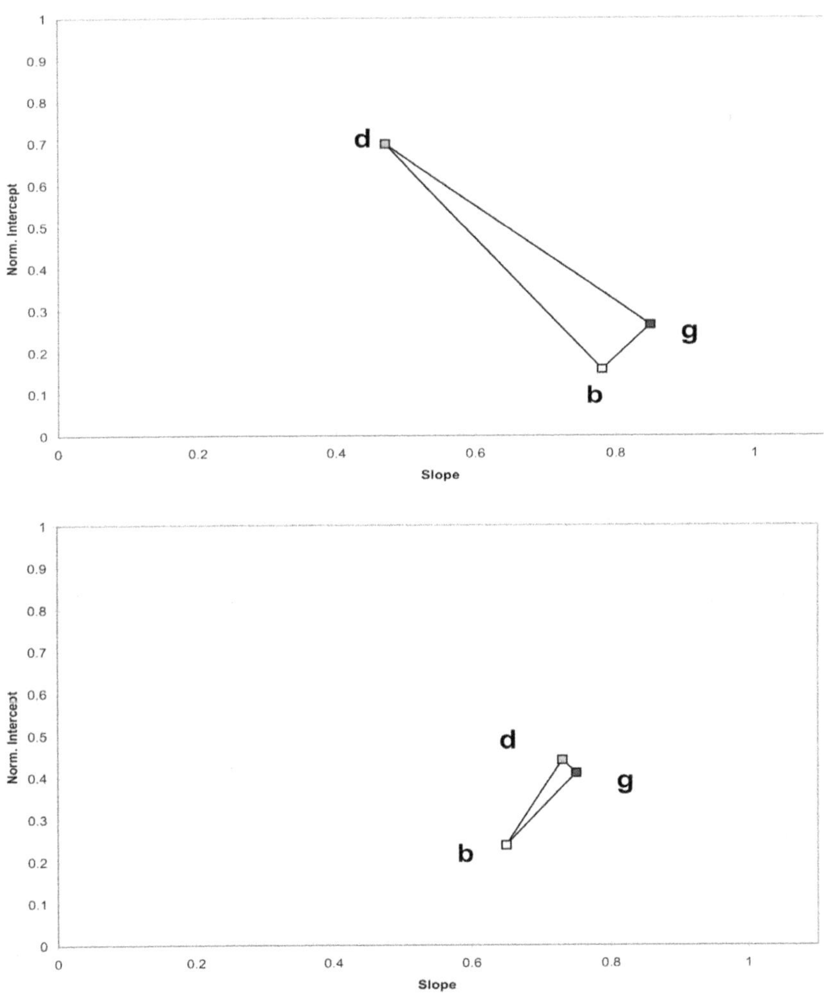

Figure 14.4. Euclidean distance.

similar to those seen in adult speakers. In contrast, the LE scatterplots for the DAS group all show close proximity of [bV, dV, gV] slope × *y*-intercept means, with a total perimeter Euclidean distance of only 0.46461. The close proximity of alveolar and velar stops in LE acoustic space highly correlates with the low intelligibility ratings of these two stop place categories in the speech of children with DAS.

The take home message from this study is very obvious – the lack of contrastiveness in stop place LE slopes can be directly attributed to the inability of the DAS children to differentially control the degree of CV coarticulation in producing the three stop place categories. The near similarity of slope values across the three stop places indicates a failure to properly contrast these classes of CV sound sequences. The only thing that accomplishes a contrastive distinction among stops is to vary the extent of CV anticipatory coarticulation. Apparently, normal neurological development is needed for such an articulatory motor skill to effectively develop.

14.13 Neural Representations of Phonetic Categories

The instantiation of phonemic-based entities in neural tissue has long been sought. Other than the psychological reality of phonemes based on data from speech errors (e.g., *guinea pig cage – guinea kig page*), it has been extremely difficult to demonstrate their existence using imaging techniques such as fMRI. Recently, however, Chang et al. (2010) provided strong experimental support for the existence of phoneme-category based entities in the left posterior superior temporal gyrus (pSTG). Four subjects undergoing a craniotomy for brain surgery had a customized high-density 64-electrode microarray placed on the cortical surface of the posterior temporal cortex, caudal to the point where the central sulcus intersects the Sylvian fissure. Subjects listened to a randomized sequence of CV tokens comprising a stop place continuum varying from /ba/ to /da/ to /ga/ in 14 equal steps. F2 starting frequencies ranged from 800 to 2100 Hz. Following traditional categorical perception procedures, both identification and discrimination functions were derived from each subject. Clear perceptual category boundaries were demonstrated between /ba/ (tokens 1–4), /da/ (tokens 6–9) and /ga/ tokens (10–14). In a subsequent two-step ABX discrimination task, clear discrimination peaks were found only for stimulus pairs spanning the phoneme boundaries. The obtained evoked potentials for each stimulus presentation peaked at

110 ms after stimulus onset. Using this time window they next attempted to relate the spatially distributed neural responses to the spectrotemporal changes underlying the psychometric identification and discrimination functions. They used an information-based strategy to determine how neural activity patterns encode speech, specifically the degree to which a multivariate pattern classifier was able to distinguish single-trial response patterns of the evoked cortical potentials. In the time frame surrounding 110 ms, multidimensional scaling and confusion matrices showed a clear clustering of the 14 stimuli into *only three clusters*: stimuli 1–4, stimuli 5–9 and stimuli 10–14. The pSTG neurons did not show 14 different evoked response patterns, one for each acoustic CV stimulus, but rather only three category-related responses emerged.

Discrete differences in cortical activations (< 4 mm) were observed to underlie the phonemic discriminations. The authors state:

> the pSTG implements rapid categorical phonetic analysis, integrating spectro-temporal features to create invariant higher order linguistic structure. (p. 4)

And

> Our results provide direct evidence for acoustic-to-higher order phonetic level encoding of speech sounds in human language receptive cortex. (p. 1)

Of particular interest to locus equation theorists, the first multidimensional scaling dimension (MDS) correlated linearly with F2-onset frequency, and the second MDS dimension correlated with the size of the F2 transition, defined as the absolute value of the difference between the onset F2 Hz and the vowel F2 Hz. The clustering patterns observed were also noted to be due to the specific *combination* of the two different, phonetically relevant, feature dimensions: F2-onset frequency and the F2 transition. The issue of whether or not phonemes exist as distinct neural entities, as opposed to linguistic abstractions derived from lexical contrasts, has now achieved brain-based support. A current research project underway, using a multivariate pattern analysis (MVPA) technique, with fMRI imaging, is attempting to expand Chang et al.'s results by using bV, dV and gV tokens presented with three vowel contexts. Additional support for the neural relevance of locus equation plots would be obtained if voxel patterns were contrastively sensitive to the three groups: */bi, ba, bu/* versus */di, da, du/* versus */gi, ga, gu/*. Such an outcome would go a long way to establish a neural connection to what a LE scatterplot functionally signifies.

References

Celdran, E.M., & X. Villalba. (1995). Locus equations as a metric for place of articulation in automatic speech recognition. *Proceedings of the XIIth International Congress of Phonetic Sciences* [Sweden], 1, 30–3.

Chang, E.F., J.W. Rieger, K. Johnson, M.S. Berger, N.M. Barbaro & R.T. Knight. (2010). Categorical speech representation in human superior temporal gyrus. *Nature Neuroscience*, 13(11), 1428–32. http://dx.doi.org/10.1038/nn.2641

Chennoukh, S., R. Carré & B. Lindblom. (1997). Locus equations in the light of articulatory modeling. *Journal of the Acoustical Society of America*, 102(4), 2380–. http://dx.doi.org/10.1121/1.419622

Fruchter, D., & H.M. Sussman. (1997). The perceptual relevance of locus equations. *Journal of the Acoustical Society of America*, 102(5), 2997–3008. http://dx.doi.org/10.1121/1.421012

Hardcastle, W.J., & N. Hewlett. (1999) (eds.). *Coarticulation: Theory, Data, and Techniques*. Cambridge: Cambridge University Press.

Hockett, C. (1955). *A Manual of Phonology*. Baltimore, MD: Waverly Press.

Iskarous, I., C.A. Fowler & D.H. Whalen. (2010). Locus equations are an acoustic expression of articulator synergy. *Journal of the Acoustical Society of America*, 128(4), 2021–32. http://dx.doi.org/10.1121/1.3479538

Krull, D. (1988). Acoustic properties as predictors of perceptual responses: A study of Swedish voiced stops. *Phonetic Experimental Research at the Institute of Phonetics University of Stockholm (PERILUS)*, VII, 66–70.

Liberman, A.M., & I. Mattingly. (1985). The motor theory of speech perception revised. *Cognition*, 21(1), 1–36. http://dx.doi.org/10.1016/0010-0277(85)90021-6

Lindblom, B. (1963). On vowel reduction. Report No. 29, Speech Transmission Laboratory, The Royal Institute of Technology, Sweden.

Lindblom, B. (1998). An articulatory perspective on the locus equation (Open Peer Commentary), *Behavioral and Brain Sciences*, 21(2), 274–5.

Lindblom, B., & H.M. Sussman. (2012). Dissecting coarticulation: How locus equations happen. *Journal of Phonetics*, 40(1), 1–19. http://dx.doi.org/10.1016/j.wocn.2011.09.005

Löfqvist, A. (1999). Interarticulator phasing, locus equations, and degree of coarticulation. *Journal of the Acoustical Society of America*, 106(4), 2022–30. http://dx.doi.org/10.1121/1.427948

Mattingly, I.G. (1998). Why did coarticulation evolve? (Open Peer Commentary). *Behavioral and Brain Sciences*, 21(2), 275–6.

Nearey, T.M., & S.E. Shammass. (1987). Formant transitions as partly distinctive invariant properties in the identification of voiced stops. *Canadian Acoustics*, 15, 17–24.

Shriberg, L., D. Aram & J. Kwiatkowski. (1997). Developmental apraxia of speech I: Descriptive and theoretical perspectives. *Journal of Speech, Language, and Hearing Research (JSLHR)*, 40(2), 273–85. http://dx.doi.org/10.1044/jslhr.4002.273

Stevens, K.N. (1972). The quantal nature of speech: Evidence from articulatory-acoustic data. In E.E. David & P.B. Denes (eds.), *Human Communication: A Unified View*. New York: McGraw Hill.

Studdert-Kennedy, M. (2005). How did language go discrete? In M. Tallerman (ed.), *Language Origins: Perspectives on Language* (pp. 48–67). Oxford: Oxford University Press.

Sussman, H.M. (1989). Neural coding of relational invariance in speech: Human language analogs to the barn owl. *Psychological Review*, 96(4), 631–642. http://dx.doi.org/10.1037/0033-295X.96.4.631

Sussman, H.M. (2002). Representation of phonological categories: A functional role for auditory columns. *Brain and Language*, 80(1), 1–13. http://dx.doi.org/10.1006/brln.2001.2489

Sussman, H.M., N. Bessell, E. Dalston & T. Majors, T. (1997). An investigation of stop place of articulation as a function of syllable position: A locus equation perspective. *Journal of the Acoustical Society of America*, 101(5), 2826–38. http://dx.doi.org/10.1121/1.418567

Sussman, H.M., C. Duder, E. Dalston & A. Cacciatore. (1999). An acoustic analysis of the development of CV coarticulation: A case study. *Journal of Speech, Language, and Hearing Research (JSLHR)*, 42(5), 1080–96. http://dx.doi.org/10.1044/jslhr.4205.1080

Sussman, H.M., D. Fruchter & A. Cable. (1995). Locus equations derived from compensatory articulation. *Journal of the Acoustical Society of America*, 97(5), 3112–24. http://dx.doi.org/10.1121/1.411873

Sussman, H.M., D. Fruchter, J. Hilbert & J. Sirosh. (1998). Linear correlates in the speech signal: The orderly output constraint. *Behavioral and Brain Sciences*, 21(2), 241–99. http://dx.doi.org/10.1017/S0140525X98001174

Sussman, H.M., K.A. Hoemeke & F.S. Ahmed. (1993). A cross-linguistic investigation of locus equations as a phonetic descriptor for place of articulation. *Journal of the Acoustical Society of America*, 94(3), 1256–68. http://dx.doi.org/10.1121/1.408178

Sussman, H.M., T.P. Marquardt & J. Doyle. (2000). An acoustic analysis of phonemic integrity and contrastiveness in developmental apraxia of speech. *Journal of Medical Speech-Language Pathology*, 8, 301–13.

Sussman, H.M., H.A. McCaffrey & S.A. Matthews. (1991). An investigation of locus equations as a source of relational invariance for stop place categorization. *Journal of the Acoustical Society of America*, 90(3), 1309–25. http://dx.doi.org/10.1121/1.401923

Tabian, M. (2000). Coarticulation in CV syllables: A comparison of locus equation and EPG data. *Journal of Phonetics*, 28(2), 137–59. http://dx.doi.org/10.1006/jpho.2000.0110

Tabian, M. (2002). Voiceless consonants and locus equations: A comparison with electropalatographic data on coarticulation. *Phonetica*, 59(1), 20–37. http://dx.doi.org/10.1159/000056203

Vihman, M.N. (1993). Early phonological development. In J. Bernthal & N. Bankson (eds.), *Articulation and Phonological Development* (3rd ed., pp. 78–124). Englewood Cliffs, NJ: Prentice-Hall.

15
Interaction of Yoruba Tones with VCV Segments: A Research Note

Augustine Agwuele[1]

15.1 Introduction

This research concerns some acoustic properties of Yoruba syllables with focus on the interaction of stop consonants + vowels, associated F0 and formants. The aspect reported here is extracted from a larger experimental study of segmentals and suprasegmentals of Yoruba speech sounds, the goal of which is to establish the nature of Yoruba tone by exploring the possibility of separately quantifying and teasing apart inherent contextual changes from "imposed prosodic conditions" following the procedures established by Lindblom et al. (2007).

Coarticulation is not only the nature of speech production, it "is a conceptualization of speech behavior that implies discrete and invariant units serving as input to the system of motor control, and an eventual obscuration of the boundaries between units at the articulatory or acoustic level" (Kent & Minifie 1977: 115). Thus a traditional abstractionist conceptualization of the phonetic and phonological structure views the input signal to be an invariant signal that is altered by the production process (Liberman & Mattingly 1985; Hockett 1955). Surrounding this approach is not only the question of how listeners recover this invariant signal, there is also the problem of "mapping" which reflects the perennial issue pertaining to the nature of the primitives of phonology (Luce & McLennan 2005). The search for invariance for the most part dwells on the place of articulation in stop consonant + vowel utterances "as they typify the coarticulated nature of speech" (Sussman et al. 1991). Studies of overlay to this constellation (i.e., prosody) across CV, phrasal and sentential units have provided rich information on the nature of their effects on vowel quality, and on the reciprocal

1 Augustine Agwuele is an Associate Professor of Linguistics in the Department of Anthropology at Texas State University, San Marcos.

influences between adjacent segments (Lindblom 1963; Van Bergem 1993; Lindblom et al. 2007; Agwuele 2003).

Although there is a growing range of formal linguistic studies of Yoruba speech sounds, the majority of these experimental studies have focused heavily on their phonological and assimilation processes with the intent of articulating the rules that constrain their occurrences. For instance, there is the phenomenon of downstep/downdrift or raising: a systematic decrease or increase in pitch values for successive tones that has attracted a lot of scholarly attention. Works on these themes include Laniran & Clements (2003), Connell & Ladd (1990), Oyetade (1988) and Courtenay (1971) among others. Acoustic analyses of downdrift in La Velle (1974) showed that F0 lowering for low tone occurs at phrase final position and when the first low tone is immediately preceded by a contrastively higher tone. However the study did not find final phrase lowering for mid and high tones. Akinlabi (1985) studied Yoruba tone in its phonological usages, suggesting that the mid tone of Yoruba has no independent existence (see Akinlabi & Liberman 2001). Related to studies on the occurrences, restrictions and representations of tones are those interested in patterns of intonation in tonal languages such as Fajobi (2005) which is an acoustic analysis of sentence pattern of Yoruba tone in declarative and interrogative utterances, and Hombert (1977), an acoustic study of Yoruba segments and tones. Hombert examined voiced and voiceless consonants, perturbation of pitch and vowel heights, with focus on the intrinsic fundamental frequency of vowels and distribution of tone. The work showed for instance that F0 difference between high and low vowels is more pronounced between high tones than with low tones. Van Niekerk & Barnard (2012) made statistical analyses of Yoruba tones realized in continuous speech in different contexts. They noted the canonical values in a contour form for each of the tones, documented individual differences in tone realization and observed anticipatory coarticulatory effects.

Collectively, these studies could be described as affirming Abraham's (1958: xvii) view that "there are certain classes of words which are temperamentally inclined and whose tones fluctuate under the influence of their environment, some succumbing to the influence of words preceding them, while others are affected by what follows." A modern way to rephrase this utterance would be to say that each (Yoruba) tone evinces robust fundamental frequency when uttered in citation forms; however, under the influence of coarticulation, i.e., contextual effects, the F0 patterns become modified. Thus rephrased, the issue pertains to the intractable problem of contextually conditioned variability that is incongruence with linearity and invariance, an issue that has seen significant scholarly contributions, e.g.,

Joos (1948), Liberman et al. (1952), Sussman et al. (1991), and Iskarous et al. (2010). The present study notes spectrographically analyzed speech waveforms of Yoruba in order to observe F0 patterns in VCV segments under contextual coarticulatory interactions.

15.2 Methodology

15.2.1 Speech Sample and Elicitation of Data

Yoruba has 7 oral vowels [i, e, ɛ, a, ɔ, o, u] 5 nasal vowels [i, ɛ, a, ɔ, u] that occur following oral consonants, 18 consonants, 4 of which are voiced stops: labial, alveolar, velar and labiovelar, i.e., [b, d, g, and gb], and 3 tones, low, mid and high (Akinlabi 2005; Ward 1952). Finally, Yoruba operates open syllables mostly of CV nature. Closed syllables are absent except for instances of nasalized vowels, and there are no consonant geminates.

The test material consisted of V1CV2 sequences paired against V1CV2 sequences. In all cases V1 and V2 were symmetrical, 6 vowels [i, e, ɛ, a, ɔ, o] were chosen to maximally exploit the Yoruba acoustic space. The medial consonants were /b, d, g, gb/. To obtain the VCV test sequences required careful selection of words without minding syllable boundaries. While nonsense words are often used in experimental studies, natural, meaningful words would seem closer to reality since they would not shock the native speaker's sensibilities neither would they require practice in order to produce them naturally. Thus for this study, meaningful Yoruba nouns in VCV sequences were examined. Examples of the tokens are:

(a) ab[**ebe**]lúbe versus ab[**èbè**]lùbé
(b) [**ada**]ha versus [**àdà**]bà, (b2) od[**odo**] versus [**odo**]do
(c) g[**ege**]le versus g[**ègè**]é
(d) **egbé** versus **egbè**

The items in brackets were the focus of investigation. In some cases, it was not immediately possible to obtain VCV segments from the same position in the sequence, for example b2, or to have similar consonants follow the collocation as in (b).

A group of 30 females and 30 males participated in the original study. However, the report focuses on the first 10 subjects for which there were acoustic measurements. These consist of 6 males and 4 females. The list of words was randomized and the subjects read the words from the list. Each subject produced a total of 144 tokens [6V × 4C × 3 repetitions × 2 tones]. Additional sets of data were collected. This involved reading out loud each Yoruba vowel in a carrier phrase of the type "*mope* [test word] *le meta*," = (I said [test word] 3 times). Each subject produced a total number of 108 tokens (6V × 3C × 2 tones × 3 repetitions). Only 2 of the 10 subjects, 1 male and 1 female, produced carrier sentences, thus the observations pertaining to sentence are limited to these 2 subjects. All the subjects were recorded in the afternoon to avoid F0 variation as noted by Garrett & Healey (1987).

15.2.2 Recording and Measurement Procedures

The subjects were recorded in natural conditions, e.g., open rooms (lab and offices) using a unidirectional microphone (RCA RP3503) directly into a Dell laptop using Praat. The recorded signals were sampled at 22 kHz, digitized and filtered using Praat (Boersma & Weenink 2004), which was also used for all acoustic measurements. Acoustic measurements were made from wide band spectrograms. F2 and F1 values were obtained for V1- and V2-mid, V1-offset and V2-onset following already established procedures (Sussman et al. 1991). Instances of tokens with wrongly realized tones were removed. For instance, some speakers produced flower (*ododo*) instead of truth (*ododo*). Finally, F0 tracks were obtained using Prosody Pro (Xu 2013).

15.3 Results and Observations

15.3.1 Yoruba Tone Citation Form

In Table 15.1 is a summary of F0 Hz obtained from the midpoint and offset of V1; onset and midpoint of V2 for mid and low tone /b, d, g/ and for/ gb/ mid-high and mid-low tone condition. The values for each test vowel for the reported measurement points were obtained by averaging across the 10 subjects separately for each stop place consonant. Following the result is a summary statistical result that examines the relationship between the measurement points within and across speech conditions. Overall, the table and the statistical comparisons provide results that do not always support existing information on inter- and intra-vowel F0 differences as a function of tone condition and stop place category.

Table 15.1. Summary measurements for pitch (F0) at V1-mid (m), V1-offset (f), V2-onset (o), V2-mid (m) for mid-tone and low-tone conditions.

	Mid-tone				**Low-tone**			
VCV	**V1-m**	**V1-f**	**V2-o**	**V2-m**	**V1-m**	**V1-f**	**V2-o**	**V2-m**
ibi	188	183	178	184	163	159	155	156
Idi	176	177	173	178	157	158	155	156
Igi	176	175	172	179	160	152	148	149
Mean	180	178	174	180	160	157	153	154
ebe	178	177	177	178	164	158	157	157
ede	176	174	173	174	158	152	150	159
ege	174	172	170	173	157	150	147	149
Mean	176	175	173	175	160	154	152	152
ɛbɛ	181	178	178	177	158	153	153	152
ɛdɛ	173	173	172	173	151	147	147	145
ɛgɛ	181	181	180	180	154	148	148	147
Mean	178	177	177	177	154	149	149	148
aba	172	177	178	175	147	158	163	159
ada	168	173	173	17	157	163	166	169
aga	156	164	169	173	143	145	149	154
Mean	166	171	173	173	149	155	159	161
obo	186	185	183	188	158	15	151	152
odo	181	177	177	177	157	153	152	152
ogo	172	169	168	171	158	153	151	153
Mean	180	177	176	179	158	153	151	152
ɔbc	178	173	172	175	159	154	153	152
ɔdc	173	181	183	185	160	155	155	156
ɔgc	176	176	175	178	161	153	153	152
Mean	176	176	177	179	160	154	154	153

A Univariate ANOVA tested the effects of tone on vowels and consonants. Results indicated a significant main effect for tone, $F(2, 1180) = 145$, $p < 0.000$. There was also a significant main effect for vowel, $F(5, 1180) = 3$, $p < .030$. But there was no main significant effect for consonants; also, the interaction of the two main effects, tone and vowel, was not significant, thus indicating that the effect of tones on both were similar across conditions. Paired samples *t*-tests were used to make post-hoc comparison between F0 values for V1CV2 *within* and *between* tone conditions:

(a) Mid-tone condition: Paired samples *t*-test between F0 values for V1 relative to V2 was not significant. This result suggests that the tone of a vowel of a mid-tone condition remained stable across intervening stops.
(b) Low-tone condition: A paired samples *t*-test between V1-mid (M = 157.23, SD = 30.17, N = 466) and V2-mid (M = 153.85, SD = 30.17, N = 466) values was significant, with a *t*-statistic of 3.35 and *p*-value of 0.00. While these results suggest that V1-mid is different from V2-mid produced with low-tone, the difference of 4 Hz may not be perceptually significant; as such this might be an example of the automatic downstep phenomenon, whereby the pitch of sequences of like tones reduce without any conditioning tone (Hombert 1974: 169; Connell & Ladd 1990: 2; Laniran 1992; Laniran & Clements 2003).
(c) The Pearson correlation coefficient was used to measure the extent to which F0-V1-final and F0-V2-onset varied together. There was a positive correlation (0.94) between F0 at the offset of V1 and at the onset of V2. Thus, the course of the tone preceding an intervocalic consonant and following it are correlated.

Between tone comparisons. Using paired *t*-tests, F0 of V2-mid of mid-tone (M = 178) condition was compared to that of V2-mid in low-tone condition (M = 153). They were significantly different at $p < 0.000$. V1-mid mid-tone (M = 177) values were significantly higher than V1-mid low-tone (M = 157). These results were expected.

Unlike /b, d, g/ where V1 and V2 were consistently either mid-tone or low-tone, for /V1gbV2/ sequences, V1 was mid-tone while V2 varied between low and high-tone. Within mid-low tone condition, a paired samples *t*-test found F0 of V1 (M = 178) to be significantly different from preceding V2 (M = 156); the *t*-statistic was 0.000. Similarly, with a *p*-value of less than 0.000 and *t*-statistic of −19, the difference between F0 of V1 and V2 of mid-high tone was significant.

The different patterning of results obtained for /gb/ and /b, d, g/ underscores the influence of anticipating the upcoming tone height on the preceding one. In both tone conditions, ML and MH, F0-final and F0-onset were positively correlated.

Summary observations for tone

- In V1CV2; F0 (tone) remains stable across the intervocalic consonant.
- For V1CV2 (low-tone) sequences, V1 and V2 were found to be significantly different. V2 was significantly lower than V1, perhaps due

to noted automatic downstep (Laniran 1992) or final lowering (La Velle 1974; Pierrehumbert & Beckman 1988).

- Between tone conditions: F0 of mid-tone were consistently higher than F0 of low tone.
- V1gbV2: mid to low vs mid to high: F0 of high was significantly higher than F0 of mid, but
- F0 of mid before low was significantly lower than F0 that preceded high-tone condition.
- There is a positive correlation between the course of tone preceding and following intervocalic consonants. Thus, there was an anticipatory (Farnetani 1997) influence of the upcoming (post-consonant) tonal condition on the pre-consonant tonal condition.

Intrinsic F0. Ladefoged (1964: 41) hypothesized that "we should expect each linguistically significant tone to be slightly higher in syllables containing the vowels /i, u/," and found that in Itsekiri (a Niger-Congo language in Nigeria), stems containing these vowels were 5 Hz higher. The results presented in Tables 15.1 and 15.2 did not show any correlation of F0 with vowel height. Yoruba does not appear to support the notion of intrinsic vowel F0. An analogous finding was made by Van Nierkerk and Barnard (2012).

Given the range of F0 in /gb/ for the 6 vowels presented in Table 15.2 for /gb/, there was no support found for Hombert (1977) which claimed that F0 difference between high and low vowels is more pronounced between high tones than with low tones.

Using the raw data whence Tables 15.1 and 15.2, the summary comparisons of the course of F0 for each stop place consonant is generated in Figure 15.1 as a function of tone condition.

Table 15.2. Summary measurements for pitch (F0) at V1-mid, V1-offset, V2-onset, and V2-mid for mid-high tone and mid-low tone conditions.

	Mid-high tone				**Mid-low tone**			
VCV	**V1-m**	**V1-f**	**V2-o**	**V2-m**	**V1-m**	**V1-f**	**V2-o**	**V2-m**
Igbi	192	193	198	221	184	177	167	160
egbe	185	192	201	216	182	174	165	152
ɛgbɛ	183	187	191	200	181	174	169	155
agba	173	186	195	205	165	162	161	158
ogbo	188	194	202	218	178	168	158	150
ɔgbɔ	183	191	199	212	179	174	166	162

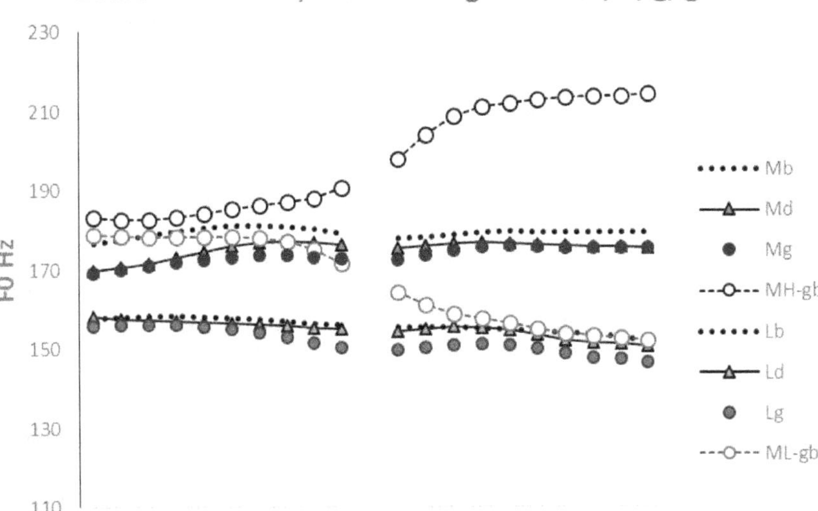

Figure 15.1. Summary comparisons of the time-plot of three tones in their citation form for /b, d, g/ (mid and low tone) and for /gb/ (high and low tone).

Figure 15.1 is a summary comparison of the three tones in their citation form. The plots were obtained by summarizing over the 10 subjects and collapsing over the 6 vowels separately for each intervening stop consonant. The tone pattern of the vowels as a function of stops appears in the order of /b, d, g/ taken from V1 final point, and (b, gb, d, g) from the final point of V2. A statistical test using one-way ANOVA did not find any significance for the difference between stop consonants in each tone condition. Nevertheless, the slight deviations and patterning are suggestive of the different influences exerted by the intervening consonants. We know that there are no two speakers that are alike, but in spite of inter-speaker variations, there is uniformity in the tonal tendencies of each speaker within their own range. In general, high tones tend toward the higher region of the speaker's acoustic range, low tones are in the lower region and mid tones are between. Each tone is distinct, there is no overlap between the mean values of each tone. Furthermore, each tone level in absolute pitch is distinct from the other; thus, high tone is absolutely higher than mid-tone which in turn is higher than low tone (cf. Ladd 1990: 4). Both low-tone and mid-tone conditions exhibit lowering across the tone contour. For mid tone there was a lowering of F0 for /b, d, g/ at the offset of V1 but not at V2 offset. For low-tone condition, final lowering was observed at both V1 and V2 offsets (cf. La Velle 1974).

15.3.2 Yoruba Tone Citation Form and Carrier Sentence

Although this report was based on data from 10 subjects, only 2 of the subjects (a male and a female) produced the same test words in carrier sentences. Thus, the observations can only be temporary in nature.

Presented in Table 15.3 is the summary of F0 values obtained for tokens from citation form (C) compared with tokens produced in carrier sentence (S). The result for the male subject is in the upper half of the table that is further divided into two parts, showing values for mid-tone condition to the left and for low-tone condition to the right. From the top of table downward are each stop consonant, e.g., the first line in the table for the male subject reads \b\-C, that is bilabial stop tokens of citation form, while \b\-S stands for bilabial tokens of carrier sentence.

Table 15.3 contains the average of F0 summed over vowels for each of the stop place categories /b, d, g/ for carrier sentence (S) and citation (C). Because of the extraction procedure for F0 across V1CV2, it was easy to consistently extract values for the six measurement points, more so because the midpoints and offset points have been implicated in determining levels and targets of the tones. Presented are values from measurement points: F0-V1-onset, V1-mid, V1-offset, V2-onset, V2-mid and V2-offset. They are presented separately for the male and female, underscoring the differences between them. For the male, citation values from the measurement points are higher than the values for sentence conditions. The opposite pattern obtains for the female subject where the sentence forms have F0 values that are larger than analogous values in the citation form. This anomalous patterning for the female subject might be idiosyncratic since only one subject is involved. In order to further access differences between speech styles (citation and sentence), statistical tests were conducted for the measurement points. Immediately apparent was the difference between male and female subjects. To do this, both male and female values were combined.

Table 15.3. Summary of F0 of Yoruba vowels as a function of tone in citation form and carrier sentence, for two subjects.

	Mid						**Low**					
Male	**V1-o**	**V1-m**	**V1-f**	**V2-o**	**V2-m**	**V2-f**	**V1-o**	**V1-m**	**V1-f**	**V2-o**	**V2-m**	**V2-f**
\b\-C	159	161	162	162	165	166	143	142	142	175	175	171
\b\-S	113	111	108	106	104	104	127	126	125	126	127	127
\d\-C	152	156	157	157	157	157	144	141	141	172	170	166
\d\-S	121	121	121	122	124	124	107	106	105	106	106	106
\g\-S	153	156	156	156	160	160	145	142	138	173	173	168
\g\-S	123	122	122	123	124	124	115	111	109	108	108	107
Female												
\b\-C	200	206	204	201	205	205	182	182	177	175	175	171
\b\-S	243	241	239	239	240	241	204	196	192	191	191	191
\d\-C	198	205	202	202	204	203	175	177	172	172	170	166
\d\-S	222	223	219	217	220	222	191	187	184	183	184	185
\g\-S	198	203	201	200	203	202	178	180	174	173	173	168
\g\-S	229	228	226	226	228	230	199	194	190	188	189	189

Within tone and speech conditions. Pair samples t-tests were conducted to gauge the difference between F0-V1-mid and F0-V2-mid for *mid-tone condition for citation form* produced by both subjects. The result was not significant. However, for *low-tone condition for citation form,* the difference between F0-V2-mid (M = 161) of the first vowel, and F0-V2-mid (M = 173) of the second vowel, accessed using paired samples t-test, was significant: $t(41) = -3.990, p = 0.000$.

For *mid-tone condition carrier sentence,* paired t-test found no difference between F0-V1-mid and F0-V2-mid values. However the result for *low-tone condition carrier sentence* showed F0-V1-mid to be significantly different from its counterpart F0-V2-mid; $t(40) = 3.856, p = 0.000$.

Between speech styles. Focusing mainly on V2, a paired samples t-test was conducted to compare F0-pitch in V2-mid values of mid-tone produced in citation style and V2-mid values of mid-tone produced in carrier sentence. No significant difference obtained. Contrarily, a paired samples t-test was significant for the difference between F0-V2-mid in low-tone of citation form (M = 173) and its counterpart, F0-V2-mid in low-tone of carrier sentence (M = 152): $t(40) = 3.459, p = 0.001$.

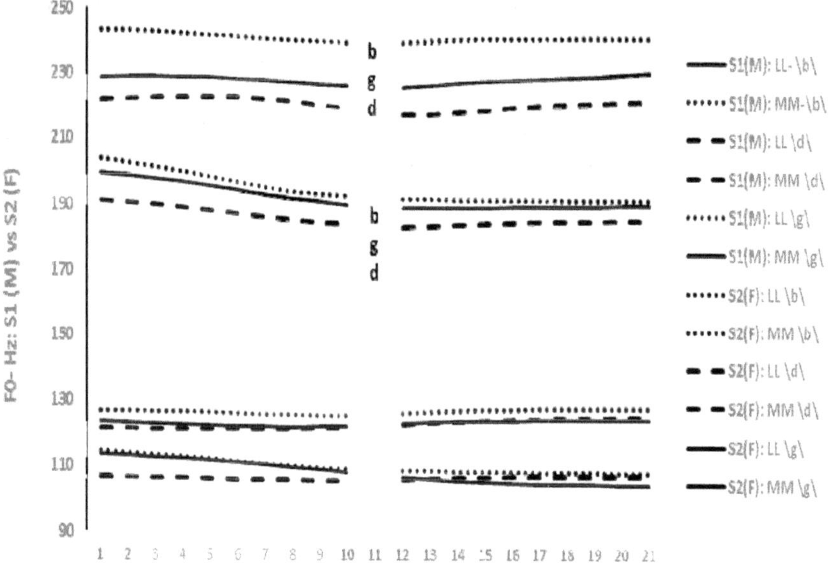

Figure 15.2. Summary comparisons mid vs low tones in carrier sentence for S1 (male subject) and S2 (female subject).

Observation. According to these results, there was no significant difference between F0 values of V1 relative to V2 for mid-tone conditions regardless of speech style. But not so for low-tone conditions, where for both speech styles, V1 was significantly different from their corresponding V2. Similar comparisons across speech styles produced comparable significant findings.

Plotted in Figure 15.2 are the F0 transitions for the sequence V1CV2, comparing mid-tone and low-tone produced by one male and one female subject. There are pairs of two distinct groupings: the top group starting from around 190 Hz upwards to 240 Hz are the mid-tone trajectory for the female (topmost 3 lines) and male subject. The topmost row with the dotted line for instance shows the traces for /b/, female subject, the solid line is the trajectory for /g/ and the spaced line is the trace for /d/. The same is done for the male subject between 190 and 240 Hz. A closer look at the each of the subjects shows differences in the internal relationships between the measurement points as a function of tone condition.

15.3.3 Tone and Formants

A well established and proven tool to acoustically analyze the interaction of stop + vowel segments is the locus equation (Lindblom 1963; Sussman et al. 1991) The locus equation provides categorical orderliness to phonetic structure that is not found on the level of single CV tokens (Sussman et al. 1991; Sussman & Shore 1996). The slope parameter of the locus equation is considered an index of the degree of coarticulation (Neary & Shammass 1987; Krull 1988), and a quantification of the extent of CV coarticulation (Mrayati et al. 1988). Locus equation (LE) parameters slope and intercept also uncover and quantify prosodic overlay separately from context induced variability (Lindblom et al. 2007; Agwuele et al. 2008). Duez (1992) found that LE slopes for accented syllables were greater than those for unaccented syllables, and similar observations were made by Cole et al. (2004). Consequently, Lindblom et al. (2007) proposed modified LEs that showed sensitivity to prosodic factors, with LE parameter successfully dissociating prosodic overlay from context induced variability and quantifying each. Agwuele et al. (2008) implemented this modified LE approach to capture the effect of speech rate separately from contextual effect. The present study applies the traditional LE to examine the subtle interactions between Yoruba stop + tone bearing vowels. First, a description of the formants for the Yoruba vowels is presented in the form of vowel chart in Figure 15.3.

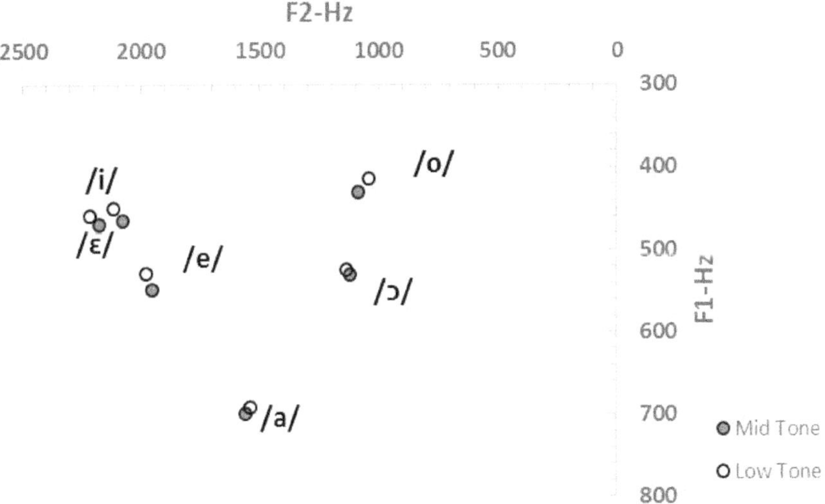

Figure 15.3. Yoruba vowel chart as a function of low and mid tone.

Figure 15.3 shows the 6 test vowels within their acoustic space as a function of tone. Ladefoged & Maddieson (1996: 297) noted that the Yoruba /e, o/ are closer to /i, u/ than are /ɛ/ and /ɔ/. However, this observation is not borne out by the data shown in Figure 15.3: /ɛ/ overlaps with /i/, while /o/ (with lower F1 and higher F2) differs from Ladefoged & Maddieson's.

Because of the basic descriptive nature of this report on the interaction of tone bearing units with associated consonants across mid and low tone, F1 and F2 formants values were statistically tested.

Mid-tone condition. Paired samples *t*-tests were conducted to assess the significance of the difference between the F1 of V1 and V2 for each vowel. The results were mixed: there was a significant difference found for two of the vowel pairs /a, e/ at $p < 0.000$, but not for /o, ɛ, i, ɔ/. Similarly, F2 of V1 was significantly different at $p < 0.000$ for both /a, e/ but not for the other four.

Low-tone condition: Again, paired *t*-tests were conducted to examine the difference between F1 values of V1 and V2. Different from mid-tone condition, significant differences were observed for four of the six vowels at $p < 0.001$, the exceptions being /ɛ/ and /o/. Similar *t*-tests were conducted to gauge the difference between F2 of V1 relative to V2. The same four vowels were found to be significantly different also at $p < 0.001$.

Finally, F2-V2 of each vowel in mid-tone condition was compared to its equivalent in the low-tone condition. Significant difference obtained for /a, e, o/, but not for /ɛ, i, ɔ/.

Summary observations

- In mid-tone condition: F1 and F2 of the symmetrical V1 and V2 were overall the same (4 out of 6 vowels)
- In low-tone condition: some F1 and F2 of the symmetrical V1 and V2 were significantly different (4 out of 6 vowels)
- Between mid- and low-tone conditions: F2 for V1 was significantly different from F2 for V2 of /a, e, ɛ/ but not for/ i, o, ɔ/.

Locus equations were used to further explore the interaction of CV as a function of stop place category.

15.3.4 Locus Equations

Locus equation (LE) regressions were obtained for each stop place consonant by regressing the frequency of the F2 transition sampled at its onset on the frequency of F2 when measured in the vowel nucleus. Because the regression lines for the plots were not visible under the raw-data points, they are summarily presented without their corresponding data points for each stop place category in Figure 15.4. In Figure 15.5, the slopes for /g/ are presented separately for front and back vowels.

The LE plots showed strong overlap between the data points of mid-tone and low-tone conditions. Nevertheless, LEs remain viable in providing a categorical normalization of vowels according to stop place categories. The stops were carefully separated and distinguished without any overlap, they appear in the order of /g, gb, d, b/.

Visual inspection of the slopes did not suggest any significant difference between low- and mid-tone conditions as captured by the LEs. If different tones yielded different patterns of coarticulation as a function of tone, then based on the slope values (summarized in Table 15.4), it would seem that the correlation of F2-onset with F2-mid cannot be the primary factor implicated in such differing patterns of coarticulation for CV-segments in tonal Yoruba language; at best, it will be one of the complex factors that act in concert with, e.g., tone.

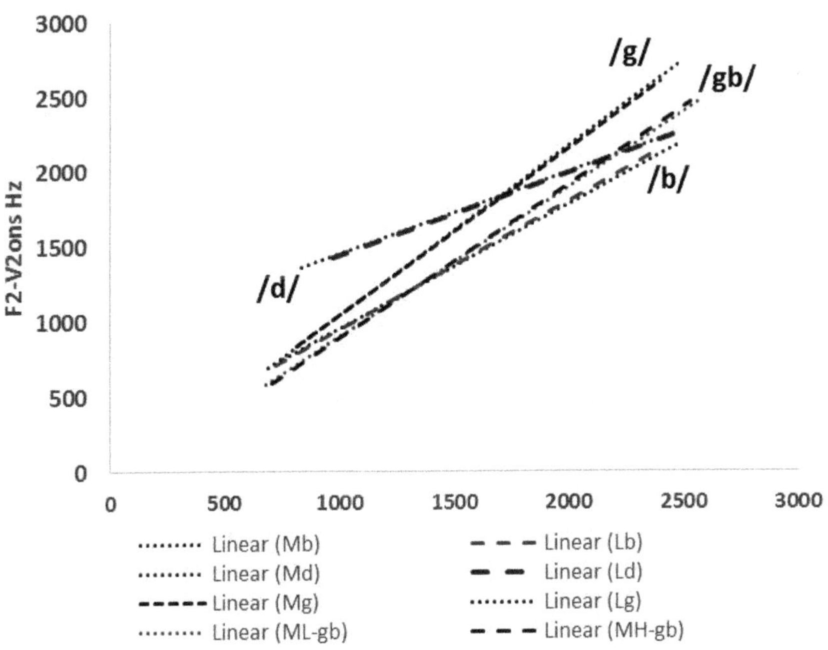

Figure 15.4. Locus equation slopes for /b, d, g, gb/ as a function of mid- and low-tone conditions.

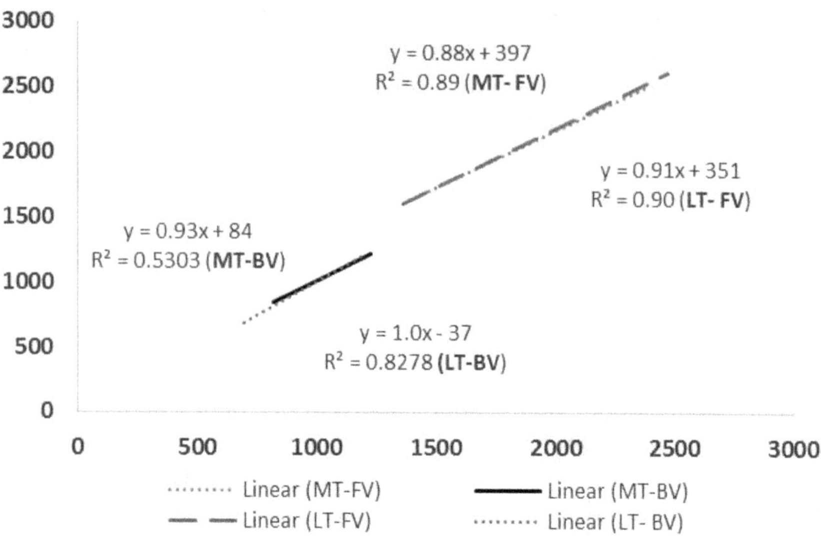

Figure 15.5. Locus equation slopes for /g/ showing front and back vowels as a function of mid- and low-tone conditions.

Table 15.4. Summary of LE parameters of slope, intercept and R^2 for 10 subjects as a function of tone.

Cons.	y-int.	Slope	R^2	y-int.	Slope	R^2
	Mid			**Low**		
/b/	0.83	120	0.95	0.86	88	0.96
/d/	0.55	900	0.83	0.55	891	0.82
/g/	1.11	–72	0.97	1.13	–89	0.97
	High			**Low**		
/gb/	0.99	–95	0.92	1.03	–148	0.89

Table 15.4 is a summary of the LE parameters of slope, intercept and R^2 for each stop place category /b, d, g/ and for /gb/. The lack of any appreciable difference in the R^2 values as a function of tone is an indication that there is equal amount of variance between F2-onset and F2-mid. The R^2 ranges from 0.08 to 0.96, thus there is a strong correlation between the dependent and independent variables. The data points from each of the tonal conditions lie closely to the line of best fit.

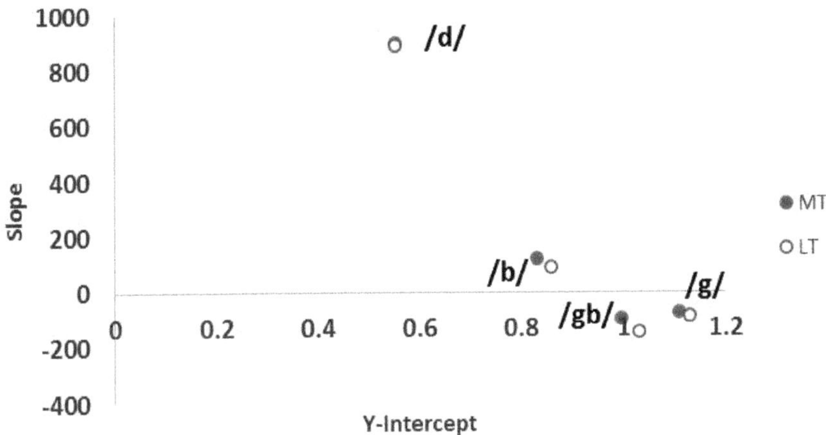

Figure 15.6. Second-order locus equation slope and intercept computed for /b, d, g, gb/ and for mid- and low-tone conditions.

The implementation of LEs has always included the second-order locus plot of slope and intercept. In Figure 15.6 is the second-order LE slope and intercept computed based on F2-onset = $k \times$ (V2-mid) + c for all subjects, for /g, gb, d, b/ and for mid- and low-tone conditions. Figure 15.6 shows the second-order LEs. Filled round points are tokens of mid tones while unfilled round points are analogous low tones.

Figure 15.6 shows that the slope and intercept parameters define a higher-order derived acoustic space that distinguishes stop place categories and tonal conditions. Bilabial and labial-velar stops show non-overlapping clustering across tone level, velar showed a slight overlap, while /d/ is overlapped. By combining slopes and intercepts, second-order LEs discriminated low-tone conditions across the stops, this is different from the LE scatterplots of direct F2 measures, where no appreciable difference was observed as a function of tone.

Notes on /gb/. Discussing West African languages in general, Ladefoged & Maddieson (1996: 334) indicate that the transition from a preceding vowel into the /gb/ is velar whereas the transition into the following vowel is more labial-like. If their observation is right, then it would mean that the F2-offset at the boundary of VC would be /g/-like, hence there is expected to be a transition that will influence locus equations parameters. In order to determine if the transition into /g/ has /g/ flare and if the transition out to V2 reflects /b/ features, V2-offset was plotted against V2-mid and V2-onset was plotted against V2-mid. The results, in Figure 15.7, show some noticeable differences between them.

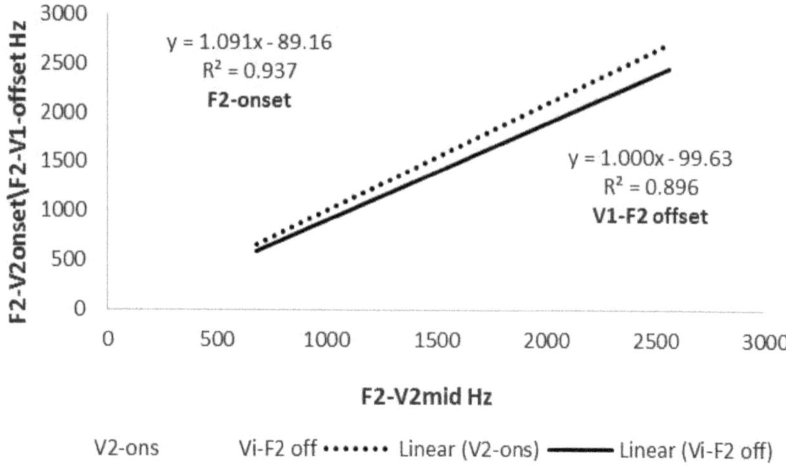

Figure 15.7. Plot of F2-V1-offset and V2-mid versus F2-V2-onset and V2-mid.

The patterning in Figure 15.6, combined with the results in Table 15.4, show that /gb/ is independent of /g/ and of /b/ but closer to /b/ within the LEs' acoustic space. However, since /g/ flare means "a velar pinch" at the VC boundary F3-offset, F3 would be needed to accurately explore Ladefoged & Maddieson's observation. It must also be noted that measurements for locus equations analyses were obtained from the first glottal pulse of V2 rather than from the bursts, as such most of the transitions were lost, thus much of the coarticulation bearing information were missing.

Discriminant analysis for token classification was conducted following Sussman et al. (1991). The goal was to use F2-onset and F2-V2-mid values to quantify stop place categorization across vowel context. The analysis reported 33 per cent classification of F2 coordinates. Table 15.5 is a summary of the results.

Table 15.5. Results of discriminant analysis showing per cent classification of place of articulation for all subjects (N = 10) across all vowel contexts (the predictor variables were F2-onset and F2-mid frequencies).

	Predicted group membership			
	/b/	**/d/**	**/g/**	**/gb/**
/b/	65	4	3	29
/d/	4	22	50	29
/g/	11	49	21	19
/gb/	54	24	3	19
				X = 32

Sussman et al. (1991) obtained on the average 83 per cent classification for /b/, 80 per cent for /d/ and 68 per cent for /g/ – in essence a perfect separation of stops; however, in addition to /b, d, g/ Yoruba also has a labial-velar place. The discriminant analysis a la Sussman did not separate that category as smoothly. For instance, it produced a 65 per cent classification of bilabial. Labio-velar /gb/ was mostly classified as a bilabial (54 per cent), alveolar /d/ was classified as velar (50 per cent), and velar was classified as alveolar (49 per cent). It might be that some places are not well handled by discriminant analysis, in which case there must be some other aspects that make /gb/ a perceptually robust segment.

15.3.5 Multiple Regression Analyses

Multiple regression analyses was used to further explore the influence of the three predictor variables – F2-V1-mid, F2-V2-onset and F0-V2-mid – on F2-V2-mid. The analysis was conducted with the data collapsed over tone conditions. The multiple regression model with all three predictors produced an overall significant result: $R^2 = 0.81$, $F(3, 633) = 869.17$, $p < 0.000$. Based on this result, 81 per cent of the variations in F2-mid are explained by the three variables. With respect to each of the three predictor variables, the effect of F2-V2-onset was significant (coefficient = 1.03, SE = 0.03, $p < 0.000$), so also was the effect of F2-V1-mid (coefficient = −0.323, SE = 0.02, $p = 0.000$]. The effect of (tone) F0-V2-mid was just barely not significant (coefficient = 0.478, SE = 0.256, $p = 0.063$). The result showed that the V2-mid target value is closely determined and influenced by the preceding V1 and by the CV interface and less so by tone (F0) of V2. This observation would seem consistent with the LE perspective that stop place category is a function of the transition of F2 starting from the CV boundary to the middle of the vowel.

Comparable analyses were conducted for /gb/ sequences. The overall result for the model was significant: $R^2 = 0.91$, $F(3, 292) = 994.56$, $p < 0.000$. The regression model also yielded significant results for its predictors. The variables, F2-V1-mid (coefficient = 0.288, SE = 0.075, $p = 0.000$) and F2-V2-onset (coefficient = 0.906, SE = 0.017, $p = 0.000$) exerted positive and significant influences; however, the effect of F0-V2-mid was not significant (coefficient = −0.097, SE = 0.206, $p = 0.638$).

As has been shown, V1 and V2 exerted influence on the onset of V2, however, V2 remains dominant in closely influencing V2 at the CV2 interface. Although the effect of tone was statistically not significant, there appears to be an appreciable influence of tone as revealed by a three-dimensional

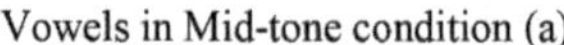

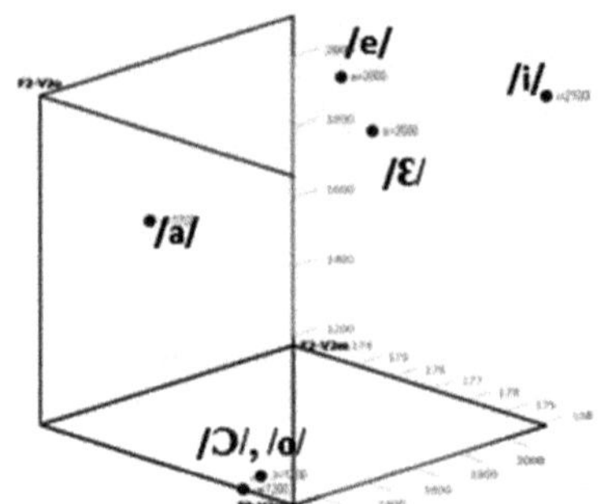

Vowels in Low-tone condition (b)

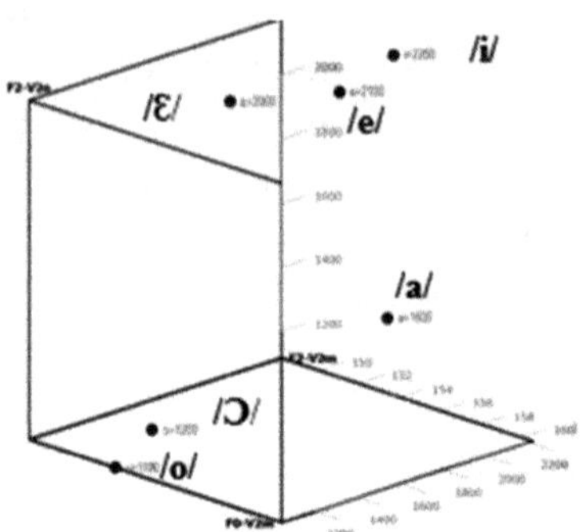

Vowels in High-tone condition (c)

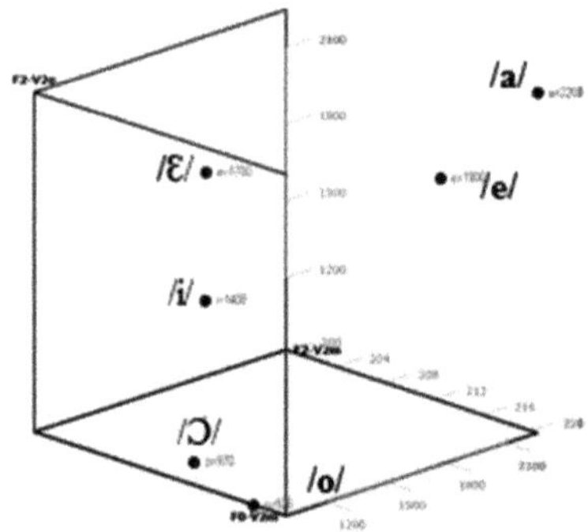

Figure 15.8. 3-D plots of six vowels for (a) mid-tone, (b) low-tone and (c) /gb/ high-tone conditions.

plot of F0-mid, F2-onset and F2-mid of V2. The results presented in Figure 15.8 show that the "acoustic space" of Yoruba vowels is closely influenced by tone.

In Figure 15.8 are plotted on the *x*-axis, F2-V2-mid; on the *y*-axis, F2-V2-onset; and on the *z*-axis, F0-mid. The plots compare the positioning of the vowels as a function of their tones. If according to Akinlabi & Liberman (2000), the Yoruba mid tone is underspecified or is neutral as often described, then the plot of Figure 15.8(a) could be considered the norm, unmarked, and the displacements of the vowel points in Figure 15.8 (b) and (c) reflect the effects of low and high tone respectively.

15.4 Conclusion

This research note has mainly focused on the acoustic properties of tone in interactions within VCV segments. The observations affirm some existing findings in the literature and confound some others. For instance, Laniran (1992) in a phonetic study of Yoruba reported downdrift for sequences of low tones, which was confirmed by our research. Unlike La Velle (1974) that reported utterance final lowering for Yoruba low tones, but not for mid or high tones, in our study lowering was found for mid tone at V1-offset but not V2-offset. For low-tone conditions, F0 lowering was observed at both V1- and V2-offsets. The data also showed a difference for F0 of vowels between the mid and low tones in the citation form measurements but less so in the carrier phrase. Of all the cues implicated in the perception of tone such as amplitude (Whalen & Xu 1992) and duration (Fu et al. 1998), overall F0 contour is considered the most dominant (Xu 1997). Native speakers are said to be more sensitive to it than to pitch height (Gandour 1978; Massaro et al. 1985). The data of this research revealed some effect of place of articulation on the F0 values as summarized in Table 15.1, but also on the overall contour of F0. The four stop consonants were shown to exert differing influences on the height of the tones as revealed by LE plots and second-order LE plots. For this study, there is relative stability for each tone within its sphere. Although Hombert (1977) found small variations in F0 that correlated with Yoruba vowel heights, and Whalen & Levitt (1995) suggested that each vowel has an intrinsic value, there was not found any correlation between F0 and vowel heights; thus Yoruba, similar to Mambila, a tonal language in Nigeria (Connell 2002), does not support the universality of intrinsic vowel F0. The differences between the F0 for the vowels were not significant. Finally, Yoruba vowels were shown to be susceptible to tonal perturbations as shown by the 3-D plot and as reported for prosody in several other studies of non-tonal languages (Lindblom et al. 2009; De Jong 1995; Agwuele 2004; Agwuele et al. 2008).

References

Abraham, R.C. (1958). *Dictionary of Modern Yoruba*. London: University of London Press.

Agwuele, A. (2003). The effect of stress on consonantal loci. In *Proceedings of the 15th ICPhS*, Vol. 1 (pp. 787–90).

Agwuele, A. (2004). Effect of stress on coarticulation. In *Conference Proceedings, From Sound to Sense.*Cambridge, MA: MIT.

Agwuele, A.H.S., H.M. Sussman & B. Lindblom. (2008). The effect of speaking rate on consonant vowel coarticulation.*Phonetica*, 65(4), 194–209.

Akinlabi, A. (1985). Underspecification of tones in Yoruba. PhD dissertation, University of Ibadan.

Akinlabi, A. (2005), The sound system of Yoruba. In Nike S. Lawal, Mathew N.O. Sadiku & Ade Dopamu (eds.),*Understanding Yoruba Life and Culture*. Trenton, NJ: Africa World Press.

Akinlabi, A. & M. Liberman. (2001). Tonal complexes and tonal alignment. In M. Kim & U. Strauss (eds.), *Proceedings of the North East Linguistics Society* 31 (pp. 1–20). Amherst, MA: Graduate Linguistic Student Association.

Akinlabi, A., & M. Liberman. (2000). The tonal phonology of Yoruba clitics. In B. Gerlach & J. Grizjenhout (eds.), *Clitics in Phonology, Morphology and Syntax* (pp. 31– 62). Amsterdam: Benjamins.

Boersma, P., & D. Weenink. (2004). Praat [Version 4.2]: Doing phonetics by computer. http://www.praat.org.

Cole, J., H. Choi & H. Kim. (2004). Acoustic evidence for the effect of accent on CV coarticulation in radio news speech. In Augustine Agwuele, Willis Warren & Sang-Hoon Park (eds.), *Proceedings of the 2003 Texas Linguistics Society Conference: Coarticulation in Speech Production and Perception* (pp. 62–72). Somerville, MA: Cascadilla Proceedings Project

Connell, B., & D.R. Ladd. (1990). Aspects of pitch realization in Yoruba. *Phonology*, 7(1), 1–29. http://dx.doi.org/10.1017/S095267570000110X

Connell, B. (2002). Tone languages and the universality of intrinsic F0: Evidence from Africa. *Journal of Phonetics*, 30(1), 101–29. http://dx.doi.org/10.1006/jpho.2001.0156

Courtenay, K. (1971). Yoruba: A "terraced-level" language with three tonemes. *Studies in African Linguistics*, 2 (3): 239–55.

De Jong, K. (1995). The supraglottal articulation of prominence in English: Linguistic stress as localized hyperarticulation. *Journal of the Acoustical Society of America*, 97(1), 491–504. http://dx.doi.org/10.1121/1.412275

Duez, D. (1992). Second formant locus-nucleus patterns: An investigation of spontaneous French speech. *Speech Communication*, 11(4–5), 417–27. http://dx.doi.org/10.1016/0167-6393(92)90047-B

Fajobi, E. (2005). The nature of Yoruba intonation: A new experimental study. In T. Falola & Ann Genova (eds.), *Yoruba Creativity: Fiction, Language, Life and Songs* (pp. 183–222). Trenton, NJ: Africa World Press.

Farnetani, E. (1997). Coarticulation and connected speech processes. In W.J. Hardcastle & J. Laver (eds.), *The Handbook of Phonetic Sciences* (pp. 371–404). Oxford: Blackwell.

Fu, Q., F. Zeng, R.V. Shannon & S.D. Soli. (1998). Importance of tonal envelope cues in Chinese speech recognition. *Journal of theAcoustical Society of America*, 104(1), 505–10. http://dx.doi.org/10.1121/1.423251

Gandour, J.T. (1978). The perception of tone. In V.A. Fromkin (ed.), *Tone: A Linguistics Survey* (pp. 1–76). New York: Academic Press. http://dx.doi.org/10.1016/B978-0-12-267350-4.50007-8

Garrett, K.L., & E.C. Healey. (1987). An acoustic analysis of fluctuations in the voices of normal adult speakers across three times of day. *Journal of the Acoustical Society of America*, 82(1), 58–62. http://dx.doi.org/10.1121/1.395437

Hockett, C.D. (1955). *Manual of Phonology*. Indiana University Publications in Anthropology and Linguistics (No. 11), Bloomington, IN.

Hombert, J.M. (1974). Universals of downdrift: Their phonetic basis and significance for a theory of tone. *Studies in African Linguistics*, Supplement 5, 169–83.

Hombert, J.M. (1977). Consonant types, vowel height and tone in Yoruba. *Studies in African Linguistics*, 8(2), 173–90.

Iskarous, I., C.A. Fowler & D.H. Whalen. (2010). Locus equations are an acoustic expression of articulator synergy. *Journal of the Acoustical Society of America*, 128(4), 2021–32. http://dx.doi.org/10.1121/1.3479538

Joos, M.A. (1948). Acoustic phonetics. *Language*, 24(2), 5–136. http://dx.doi.org/10.2307/522229

Kent, R.D., & F.D. Minifie. (1977). Coarticulation in recent speech production models. *Journal of Phonetics*, 5, 115–33.

Krull, D. (1988). Acoustic properties as predictors of perceptual responses: A study of Swedish voiced stops. *Phonetic Experimental Research at the Institute of Linguistics, University of Stockholm (PERILUS)*, VII, 66–70.

Ladd, D.R. (1990). Metrical representation of pitch register. In J. Kingston & M. Beckman (eds.), *Papers in Laboratory Phonology 1: Between the Grammar and the Physics of Speech* (pp. 35–57). Cambridge: Cambridge University Press.

Ladefoged, P. (1964). *A Phonetic Study of West African Languages*. Cambridge: Cambridge University Press.

Ladefoged, P. and Ian Maddieson. (1996). *The Sounds of the World's Languages*. Oxford: Blackwell Publishers.

Laniran, Y.O. (1992). Intonation in tone languages: The phonetic implementation of tones in Yoruba. PhD dissertation, Cornell University.

Laniran, Y.O., & G.N. Clements (2003). Downstep and high raising: Interacting factors in Yoruba tone production. *Journal of Phonetics*, 31(2), 203–50. http://dx.doi.org/10.1016/S0095-4470(02)00098-0

La Velle, C. (1974). An experimental study of Yoruba tone. *Studies in African Linguistics*, Supplement, 185.

Liberman, A.M., P.C. Delattre & F.S. Cooper. (1952). The role of selected stimulus: Variables in the perception of the unvoiced stop consonants. *American Journal of Psychology*, 65(4), 497–516. http://dx.doi.org/10.2307/1418032

Liberman, A.M., & I. Mattingly. (1985). The motor theory of speech perception revisited. *Cognition*, 21(1), 1–36. http://dx.doi.org/10.1016/0010-0277(85)90021-6

Lindblom, B. (1963). On vowel reduction. Report No. 29, Speech Transmission Laboratory, The Royal Institute of Technology, Sweden.

Lindblom, B., A. Agwuele, H.M. Sussman & E.E. Cortes. (2007). The effect of emphatic stress on consonant vowel coarticulation. *Journal of the Acoustical Society of America*, 121(6), 3802–13. http://dx.doi.org/10.1121/1.2730622

Lindblom, B., H.M. Sussman & A. Agwuele. (2009). A duration-dependent account of coarticulation for hyper-and hypoarticulation. *Phonetica*, 66(3), 188–95. http://dx.doi.org/10.1159/000235660

Luce, P.A., & C.T. McLennan. (2005). Spoken word recognition: The challenge of variation. In D.B. Pisoni & R.E. Remez (eds.), *The Handbook of Speech Perception* (pp. 591–609). Oxford: Blackwell Publishing Ltd.

Massaro, D.W., M.M. Cohne & C.C. Tseng. (1985). The evaluation and integration of pitch height and pitch contour in lexical tone perception in Mandarin Chinese. *Journal of Chinese Linguistics*, 1, 267–89.

Mrayati, M., R. Carré & B. Guérin. (1988). Distinctive region and modes: A new theory of speech production. *Speech Communication*, 3(7), 257–86. http://dx.doi.org/10.1016/0167-6393(88)90073-8

Neary, T.M., & S.E. Shammass. (1987). Formant transitions as partly distinctive invariant properties in the identification of voiced stops. *Journal of the Acoustical Society of America*, 15(4), 17–24.

Oyetade, B.A. (1988). Issues in the analysis of Yoruba tone. PhD dissertation, SOAS, University of London.

Pierrehumbert, J., & M. Beckman. (1988). The phonology of American English intonation. PhD dissertation, MIT, Cambridge, MA.

Sussman, H.M., H.A. McCaffrey & S.A. Matthews. (1991). An investigation of locus equations as a source of relational invariance for stop place categorization. *Journal of the Acoustical Society of America*, 90(3), 1309–25. http://dx.doi.org/10.1121/1.401923

Sussman, H.M., & J. Shore. (1996). Locus equations as phonetic descriptors of consonantal place of articulation. *Perception & Psychophysics*, 58(6), 936–46. http://dx.doi.org/10.3758/BF03205495

Van Bergem, D.R. (1993). Acoustic vowel reduction as a function of sentence accent, word stress, and word class. *Speech Communication*, 12(1), 1–23. http://dx.doi.org/10.1016/0167-6393(93)90015-D

Van Niekerk, D.R., & E. Barnard. (2012). Tone realisation in a Yorùbá speech recognition corpus. In: *The Third International Workshop on Spoken Language Technologies for Under-resourced Languages, Cape Town, South Africa* (pp. 54–9).

Ward, I.C. (1952). *An Introduction to the Yoruba Language*. Cambridge: Heffer.

Whalen, D.H., & A.G. Levitt. (1995).The universality of intrinsic F0 of vowels. *Journal of Phonetics*, 23(3), 349–66. http://dx.doi.org/10.1016/S0095-4470(95)80165-0

Whalen, D.H., & Y. Xu. (1992). Information for Mandarin tones in the amplitude contour and in brief segments. *Phonetica*, 49(1), 25–47. http://dx.doi.org/10.1159/000261901

Xu, Y. (1997). Contextual tone variations in Mandarin. *Journal of Phonetics*, 25(1), 61–83. http://dx.doi.org/10.1006/jpho.1996.0034

Xu, Y. (2013). ProsodyPro: A tool for large-scale systematic prosody analysis. In *Proceedings of Tools and Resources for the Analysis of Speech Prosody (TRASP 2013)* (pp. 7–10). Aix-en-Provence, France.

16
Harvey Sussman's Scientific Contributions: A Brief Summary and Assessment

Randy L. Diehl[1]

During his career, Harvey Sussman has been an extraordinarily productive researcher, publishing over 100 articles, mostly in peer-reviewed journals, that address central issues in articulatory and acoustic phonetics, speech perception and neurolinguistics. What follows is a brief summary and assessment of some of Harvey's most important contributions.

16.1 Speech Articulation: Measurements and Theoretical Description

Harvey's scientific reputation in the earlier years of his career rested on a series of innovative studies of articulatory dynamics and electrophysiology, as well as on his development of an important theoretical model of articulatory control. As a graduate student, Harvey understood the need for accurate articulatory measurements, and to that end he designed and implemented several novel transducers to track jaw and lip movements (Sussman & Smith 1970a, b). Later, working with Peter MacNeilage and Robert Hanson at the University of Texas at Austin, Harvey carried out one of the first detailed studies of lip and jaw movements during the production of VCV syllables, incorporating measurements of articulatory displacement and velocity along with corresponding measurements of electromyographic activity. Although the findings were preliminary, they

1 Randy Diehl is a professor in the Department of Psychology, Dean of the College of Liberal Arts and David Bruton, Jr. Regents Chair in Liberal Arts at the University of Texas at Austin.

yielded important insights, for example, into the tradeoffs between aerodynamic and neuromuscular forces in the realization of articulatory movements (Sussman et al. 1973).

In an effort to study the basic building blocks of articulatory control, Harvey and his colleagues began conducting experiments on the activity of single motor units in the speech musculature. This work posed serious methodological challenges, but they managed to obtain clean and interpretable results that enhanced our understanding of speech motor control (Sussman et al. 1973; Sussman 1977).

Perhaps owing to his graduate training in the Behavioral Cybernetics Lab at Wisconsin, Harvey gave a lot of thought to how servomechanisms might provide apt models for understanding articulatory control. In a classic paper, "What the tongue tells the brain" (1972), Harvey offered an elegant argument for the role of a closed-loop feedback system in regulating tongue movements. On recently rereading this paper, I was struck by the strength of the evidence that Harvey adduced to support this model.

16.2 Hemispheric Specialization for Language

In the mid-1970s, Harvey (with Peter MacNeilage and Jack Lumbley) carried out a series of studies on hemispherical specialization using a novel pursuit auditory tracking paradigm (Sussman et al. 1974, 1975). In a typical experiment, listeners matched a continuously varying tone presented to one ear with a second tone presented to the other ear by moving some part of their body. Matching performance turned out to be reliably better when the tone frequency controlled by either tongue or jaw movements was presented to the right ear rather than the left ear, indicating left hemisphere dominance for this task. However, a right ear advantage (REA) was not observed when the tone frequency was controlled by hand movements. These studies are important in showing that left hemisphere dominance occurs not only for standard dichotic listening tasks but also for tasks involving speech motor control.

In follow-up experiments (Sussman & MacNeilage 1975a), Harvey reported that the above-described REA associated with speech movements also occurs for patients who have had either right or left anterior temporal lobectomies. However, a similar speech-movement-related REA was not observed for stutterers, although the latter do demonstrate the typical REA for standard dichotic listening tasks (Sussman & MacNeilage 1975b, c). The pursuit auditory tracking task that Harvey pioneered was thus found to be useful in studying language lateralization in a variety of clinical and nonclinical populations.

16.3 The Representation of Phonological Categories in the Human Brain

As a graduate student at the University of Minnesota, I found myself struggling to find a suitable dissertation topic, when someone passed along a copy of "Neurophysiological feature detectors and speech perception" (Abbs & Sussman 1971), which was based on a conference paper that Harvey had presented in 1969 while still a graduate student. The feature detector notion had been discussed earlier by vision scientists, but I believe Harvey was the first to apply it to the domain of speech perception. Eimas & Corbit (1973) and a host of other investigators (myself included) went on to test the hypothesis that phonetic/phonological features (e.g., [+voice]) are recognized by the human auditory system by means of neural structures that are specifically tuned to such features. The preferred methodology for testing the feature detector hypothesis was a selective adaptation procedure (borrowed from vision studies) whereby a particular feature was presented repeatedly to a listener so as to fatigue the relevant feature detector and hence alter speech identification performance in predictable ways. During the decade of the 1970s and beyond, a great many selective adaptation studies were published by speech researchers, and variations on the feature detector hypothesis came to dominate theoretical discussions concerning the mechanisms of speech perception. Although Harvey did not participate directly in the selective adaptation boom, there is no question that his papers served as an important stimulus to this work.

In recent years, Harvey has built on the early work on feature detectors for speech by appealing to animal models of auditory perception. In particular, he has cited neuroethological work on combination-sensitive neurons in avian and mammalian species that are tuned to certain information-bearing elements of acoustic signals (Sussman 1989; Sussman et al. 1998). It is worth quoting Harvey directly:

> Auditory maps in the mustached bat and the barn owl represent the best-known examples of how auditory substrates organize, represent, and signal information. In both cases, there are 2D maps of bivariate acoustic

> space in which there are linear functions that represent categories (or equivalence classes). In the bat, these linear functions are "isovelocity" contours. In the barn owl, they are "iso-ITD" [interaural time differences] functions. The organizational principles underlying the auditory decoding systems of the mustached bat and the barn owl can offer valuable clues for models of human speech perception (Sussman et al. 1998).

Consider the case of the barn owl. Konishi's group has described neurons sensitive to particular combinations of frequency and phase that form linear functions within the 2D frequency × phase space such that every point within a given function corresponds to the same ITD (Sullivan & Konishi 1986; Wagner et al. 1987). Thus, the iso-ITD linear functions are "emergent properties" derived from the more basic acoustic parameters of frequency and phase.

Harvey's fundamental claim is that evolution tends to be conservative and, therefore, it is reasonable to suppose that mechanisms that subserve audition in avians and non-human mammals may also be exploited for use in human audition. Specifically, he proposes that combination-sensitive neurons may serve as feature detectors for phonetic categories, and that the linearity observed in the 2D neural sensitivity maps of bats and barn owls may also be an important design feature of those phonetic categories and their neural representation. This brings us to an extraordinary body of empirical work that has helped to define Harvey's research career over the last several decades.

16.4 Locus Equations

It has been known since the 1950s that the slope and direction of the second formant (F2) transition is an important cue for place of articulation in stop consonants (Delattre et al. 1955). Klatt (1979, 1987) was perhaps the first investigator to note that for a given place category (e.g., /b/ or /d/ or /g/) in various vowel contexts, a plot of F2-onset frequency of the consonant-vowel (CV) transition against F2 of the following vowel midpoint yields an approximately linear scatterplot. Harvey confirmed this basic result, noting the analog between the linearity of neural maps in the bat and barn owl and that of locus equations in humans (Sussman 1989). He went on to conduct a lengthy series of experiments on locus equations that shed light on several classic problems in experimental phonetics and speech perception.

Consider some key findings. First, locus equations are robust with respect to variations in speaker gender (Sussman et al. 1991), age (Sussman et al. 1991, 1992, 1993) and language (Sussman et al. 1993). They are also quite stable with respect to differences in voicing and manner classes, for example, voiced stops vs voiceless stops vs fricatives vs nasals (Sussman 1994). Locus equations are also relatively unaffected by the presence or absence of a bite block requiring compensatory tongue movements to achieve consonant and vowel targets (Sussman et al. 1995).

An issue arises whether the linearity of locus equations falls out automatically from the underlying physics of speech production or whether it is instead under talker control. To help address this issue, Harvey studied the form of locus equations in infant babbling (Sussman et al. 1996) and also in the utterances of children with developmental apraxia of speech (Sussman et al. 1992). In both cases the scatterplots were noisy and nonlinear, suggesting that the linearity typically observed may not be physically automatic. However, simulation experiments carried out by Björn Lindblom and reported in Sussman et al. (1998) using an articulatory model derived from the acoustics of tubes did suggest that the human vocal tract may be configured to yield linear locus equations.

It remains an interesting question whether the linear output "might be accidental, part of some non-speech-related adaptation having nothing to do with perception, or part of a speech production system coadaptation to speech perception" (Sussman et al. 1998: 253). In the later paper, Harvey and his colleagues opted for a perceptual explanation, which they call the "orderly output constraint." They conjecture that the human speech production apparatus is constrained to produce outputs that are "mappable" in the auditory system (cf., the discussion of findings for the mustached bat and the barn owl). The claim is that the linearity and low noisiness of locus equations enhances the mappability.

Two other aspects of Harvey's work on locus equations are worth emphasizing. First, for several decades, researchers at Haskins Laboratories had claimed that acoustic cues for place of articulation demonstrated a lack of invariance, especially across different vowel contexts (Liberman et al. 1967; Liberman & Mattingly 1985). While this may be true at a lower level of description (e.g., the slope and direction of the F2 transition), Harvey has noted that locus equations provide a higher-level, or derived, form of relational invariance for place of articulation cues. Second, again as noted by Harvey (Sussman et al. 1991) following work by Krull (1988), the slope of the locus equations yields a direct measure of the degree of coarticulation between a consonant and the following vowel. This is an interesting point because although coarticulation is fundamental to theories of speech production, the notion has remained rather ill-defined and qualitative. Locus equations are thus a more precise, quantitative metric for describing coarticulation.

16.5 Recent Modeling of Coarticulation

Harvey's seminal work on locus equations has led in recent years to the development of new models of coarticulation. With collaborators Augustine Agwuele and Björn Lindblom, Harvey has developed a principled and quantitative account of the effect of speaking rate and presence or absence of emphasis on coarticulation (Agwuele et al. 2008; Lindblom et al. 2009). Building on this work, Lindblom & Sussman (2012) produced a paper – "Dissecting coarticulation: How locus equations happen" – that is arguably one of the most important articles to appear in phonetics during the last decade or so. This study is notable for its use of multiple methodologies, including articulatory synthesis, cineradiography, principal component analysis and estimation of time constants for F2 transitions, and for its comprehensive and rigorous treatment of theoretical issues. The authors first derived quantitatively the notion of consonant and vowel "targets" and then, by positing a simple form of interpolation between successive targets, were able to show a close match between theoretically predicted and observed formant frequencies as expressed in the form of locus equations. Significantly, the linearity of locus equations was shown to be a byproduct of the observed uniformity of F2 transition time constants. Thus, the articulatory model did an excellent job of simulating normal coarticulation and, in particular, of explaining the detailed character of locus equations.

16.6 Concluding Remarks

This brief review does not begin to do justice to the broad scope of Harvey's empirical and theoretical investigations. I have generally omitted discussion, for example, of his many studies of speech production and perception in clinical populations such stutterers, aphasics and apraxics. Nevertheless, I hope I have demonstrated that Harvey's research has always been characterized by both methodological innovation and theoretical rigor and that he has been unfailingly committed to tackling and resolving the most fundamental problems in phonetics and language studies.

References

Abbs, J.H., & H.M. Sussman. (1971). Neurophysiological feature detectors and speech perception: A discussion of theoretical implications. *Journal of Speech and Hearing Research*, 14(1), 23–36. http://dx.doi.org/10.1044/jshr.1401.23

Agwuele, A., H.M. Sussman & B. Lindblom. (2008). The effect of speaking rate on consonant vowel coarticulation. *Phonetica*, 65(4), 194–209. http://dx.doi.org/10.1159/000192792

Delattre, P.C., A.M. Liberman & F.S. Cooper. (1955). Acoustic loci and transitional cues for consonants. *Journal of the Acoustical Society of America*, 27(4), 769–73. http://dx.doi.org/10.1121/1.1908024

Eimas, P.D., & J.D. Corbit. (1973). Selective adaptation of linguistic feature detectors. *Cognitive Psychology*, 4(1), 99–109. http://dx.doi.org/10.1016/0010-0285(73)90006-6

Klatt, D.H. (1979). Synthesis by rule of consonant-vowel syllables. Speech Communication Group Working Papers No. 3 (pp. 93–104). Cambridge, MA: MIT Press.

Klatt, D.H. (1987). Review of text-to-speech conversion for English. *Journal of the Acoustical Society of America*, 82(3), 737–93. http://dx.doi.org/10.1121/1.395275

Krull, D. (1988). Acoustic properties as predictors of perceptual responses: A study of Swedish voiced stops. *Phonetic Experimental Research at the Institute of Linguistics Stockholm University (PERILUS)*, 10, 87–101.

Liberman, A.M., F.S. Cooper, D.P. Shankweiler & M. Studdert-Kennedy. (1967). Perception of the speech code. *Psychological Review*, 74(6), 431–61. http://dx.doi.org/10.1037/h0020279

Liberman, A.M., & I. Mattingly. (1985). The motor theory of speech perception: Revised. *Cognition*, 21(1), 1–36. http://dx.doi.org/10.1016/0010-0277(85)90021-6

Lindblom, B., & H.M. Sussman. (2012). Dissecting coarticulation: How locus equations happen. *Journal of Phonetics*, 40(1), 1–19. http://dx.doi.org/10.1016/j.wocn.2011.09.005

Lindblom, B., H.M. Sussman & A. Agwuele. (2009). A duration-dependent account of coarticulation for hyper- and hypoarticulation. *Phonetica*, 66(3), 188–95. http://dx.doi.org/10.1159/000235660

Sullivan, W.E., & M. Konishi. (1986). Neural map of interaural phase difference in the owl's brainstem. *Proceedings of the National Academy of Sciences of the United States of America*, 83(21), 8400–4. http://dx.doi.org/10.1073/pnas.83.21.8400

Sussman, H.M. (1972). What the tongue tells the brain. *Psychological Bulletin*, 77(4), 262–72. http://dx.doi.org/10.1037/h0032374

Sussman, H.M. (1977). Recruitment and discharge patterns of single motor units during speech production. *Journal of Speech and Hearing Research*, 21, 127–44.

Sussman, H.M. (1989). The neural coding of relational invariance in speech: Human language analogs to the barn owl. *Psychological Review*, 96(4), 631–42. http://dx.doi.org/10.1037/0033-295X.96.4.631
Sussman, H.M. (1994). The phonological reality of locus equations across manner class distinctions: Preliminary observations. *Phonetica*, 51(1–3), 119–31. http://dx.doi.org/10.1159/000261964
Sussman, H.M., D. Fruchter & A. Cable. (1995). Locus equations derived from compensatory articulation. *Journal of the Acoustical Society of America*, 97(5), 3112–24. http://dx.doi.org/10.1121/1.411873
Sussman, H.M., D. Fruchter, J. Hilbert & J. Sirosh. (1998). Linear correlates in the speech signal: The orderly output constraint. *Behavioral and Brain Sciences*, 21(2), 241–99. http://dx.doi.org/10.1017/S0140525X98001174
Sussman, H.M., K. Hoemeke & F. Ahmed. (1993). A cross-linguistic investigation of locus equations as a phonetic descriptor for place of articulation. *Journal of the Acoustical Society of America*, 94(3), 1256–68. http://dx.doi.org/10.1121/1.408178
Sussman, H.M., K. Hoemeke & H.A. McCaffrey. (1992). Locus equations as an index of coarticulation for place of articulation distinctions in children. *Journal of Speech and Hearing Research*, 35(4), 769–81. http://dx.doi.org/10.1044/jshr.3504.769
Sussman, H.M., & P.F. MacNeilage. (1975a). Dichotic pursuit auditory tracking after anterior temporal lobectomy. *Archives of Otolaryngology (Chicago, Ill.)*, 101(6), 389–91. http://dx.doi.org/10.1001/archotol.1975.00780350053014
Sussman, H.M., & P.F. MacNeilage. (1975b). Studies of hemispheric specialization for speech production. *Brain and Language*, 2, 131–51. http://dx.doi.org/10.1016/S0093-934X(75)80060-5
Sussman, H.M., & P.F. MacNeilage. (1975c). Hemispheric specialization for speech production and perception in stuttering. *Neuropsychologia*, 13(1), 19–26. http://dx.doi.org/10.1016/0028-3932(75)90043-3
Sussman, H.M., P.F. MacNeilage & R.J. Hanson. (1973). Labial and mandibular dynamics during the production of bilabial consonants: Preliminary observations. *Journal of Speech and Hearing Research*, 16(3), 397–420. http://dx.doi.org/10.1044/jshr.1603.397
Sussman, H.M., P.F. MacNeilage & J. Lumbley. (1974). Sensorimotor dominance and the right-ear advantage in mandibular-auditory tracking. *Journal of the Acoustical Society of America*, 56(1), 214–16. http://dx.doi.org/10.1121/1.1903258
Sussman, H.M., P.F. MacNeilage & J. Lumbley. (1975). Pursuit auditory tracking of dichotically presented tonal amplitudes. *Journal of Speech and Hearing Research*, 18(1), 74–81. http://dx.doi.org/10.1044/jshr.1801.74
Sussman, H.M., H.A. McCaffrey & S.A. Matthews. (1991). An investigation of locus equations as a source of relational invariance for stop place categorization. *Journal of the Acoustical Society of America*, 90(3), 1309–25. http://dx.doi.org/10.1121/1.401923

Sussman, H.M., F.D. Minifie, E.H. Buder, C. Stoel-Gammon & J. Smith. (1996). Consonant-vowel interdependencies in babbling and early words: Preliminary examination of a locus equation approach. *Journal of Speech, Language, and Hearing Research (JSLHR)*, 39(2), 424–33. http://dx.doi.org/10.1044/jshr.3902.424

Sussman, H.M., & K.U. Smith. (1970a). Transducer for measuring mandibular movements. *Journal of the Acoustical Society of America*, 48(4A), 857–8. http://dx.doi.org/10.1121/1.1912215

Sussman, H.M., & K.U. Smith. (1970b). Transducer for measuring lip movements during speech. *Journal of the Acoustical Society of America*, 48(4A), 858–60. http://dx.doi.org/10.1121/1.1912216

Wagner, H., T. Takahashi & M. Konishi. (1987). Representation of interaural time difference in the central nucleus of the barn owl's inferior colliculus. *Journal of Neuroscience*, 7, 3105–16.

Harvey M. Sussman.

To My Friend Harvey Sussman

Neuro-Phonetician and Master of One-Liners

The fact that we speak
is totally unique and
something that you study
- with me as your buddy.

You use Visible Speech,
extend its reach,
take a closer look.
What's on the hook?

A new paradigm!
- simple but sublime -
providing a view otherwise hard to attain
of the making of movements by the brain:
A coarticulatory mosaic
- a pattern that is anything but prosaic.

So when other folks see speech signals as a "mess,"
you simply could not care less.
They say: "Awful!"
You say: "Lawful!"

Few are the relations
that are built around Locus Equations.
Ours is one,
equal to none.

Harvey, my man
Let's charge ahead!
Many more Eureka moments to come!

Happy Birthday
and warmest wishes from

Björn[1]
(euro-phonetician)

1 Bjorn Lindblom is Professor Emeritus in the Department of Linguistics at the University of Texas at Austin and in the Department of Linguistics at Stockholm University, Sweden.

Index

www.ingramcontent.com/pod-product-compliance
Lightning Source LLC
LaVergne TN
LVHW021127110826
R19582500001B/R195825PG844660LVX00014B/25

* 9 7 8 1 7 8 1 7 9 1 8 2 0 *